AN AMERICAN LIBRARY
HISTORY READER

CONTRIBUTIONS TO LIBRARY LITERATURE
John David Marshall, Editor

BOOKS, LIBRARIES, LIBRARIANS, Selected by
John David Marshall (with Wayne Shirley and Louis
Shores), 1955. #1

OF, BY, AND FOR LIBRARIANS, Selected by
John David Marshall, 1960. #2

AN AMERICAN LIBRARY HISTORY READER,
Selected by John David Marshall, 1961. #3

In preparation:

BETTER LIBRARIES MAKE BETTER SCHOOLS,
Selected by Charles L. Trinkner. #4

AN AMERICAN LIBRARY HISTORY READER

Contributions to Library Literature

Selected by

JOHN DAVID MARSHALL

With a Foreword by
Wayne Shirley and Louis Shores

THE SHOE STRING PRESS, INC.
HAMDEN, CONNECTICUT
1961

For My Parents

ACKNOWLEDGMENTS

The final responsibility for the content of this collection of essays in American library history rests with the editor — a responsibility I am happy to assume. Indeed, I welcome it. Every anthology is also the work of a number of people; and it need hardly be noted that a book of readings is, by definition, a collective effort.

The assembling of other people's writing presents a number of knotty though always interesting editorial problems, and certainly such an enterprise entails no little time, planning, and effort. My life as a week-end anthologist has been thoroughly enjoyable and pleasant because of the assistance and encouragement which a number of people have given me. I should like to record here my debt to those who in one way or another have helped in the making of this book.

I gratefully note here and specifically acknowledge elsewhere the right to reprint the essays included in this book. The authors and original publishers without exception have been more than generous in granting permission to reprint. A special note of thanks must go to the editor and the publisher of the Wilson Library Bulletin for granting permission to reprint so many essays which first appeared there.

Wayne Shirley, Librarian of Finch College in New York City, and Louis Shores, Dean of the Florida State University Library School in Tallahassee, Florida, have served with great distinction the cause of American library history as co-founders and as Chairman and Secretary respectively of the American Library History Round Table. The enthusiasm with which they greeted my proposal that I compile for publication a collection of essays in American library history places me heavily in their debt. For the help and encouragement they have so freely given me during the preparation of this volume and for the generous foreword which they have written for it, I am more grateful than either can ever know.

For editorial advice, counsel, and never-failing interest, I am grateful to John H. Ottemiller, Associate Librarian of Yale University and President of The Shoe String Press, Inc. My debt is equally great to Frances Ottemiller for many courtesies.

Their contributions to this book are too large to properly acknowledge here.

Harold J. Mason, Assistant Manager of Kraus Periodicals, Inc., New York, New York, obtained for me copies of a number of the periodicals in which the essays contained in this book first appeared. I should like to record my very warm appreciation of his courtesy and my debt to this periodicals-librarian turned periodicals-dealer.

A number of individuals have shown a friendly interest in my adventures in anthology. For their interest and encouragement I wish to acknowledge the following:

W. Porter Kellam and Evelyn M. Fritz, Director and Associate Director of Libraries respectively, University of Georgia, Athens, Georgia;

David Marshall Stewart, Chief Librarian, Nashville (Tennessee) Public Library;

John B. Howell, Jr., Librarian, Mississippi College, Clinton, Mississippi;

Lawrence Clark Powell, Dean, and Andrew H. Horn, Assistant Dean, School of Library Service, University of California at Los Angeles; and

Cornelia Ayer Graham, Librarian Emerita, Clemson College, Clemson, South Carolina.

Merne M. Hinds, friend and co-worker in the Acquisitions Division of the University of Georgia Libraries, very generously agreed to assist with proofreading. For this help I am truly appreciative.

For never complaining of the noises my Smith-Corona Portable made as I pounded on it late into the evenings and on weekends go my thanks again to Mrs. Henry West of Athens, Georgia. Every anthologist requires a patient and understanding landlady: I have one.

The dedication of this book to my parents is small expression indeed of my thanks to them for so much for which there can never be words.

JDM

CONTENTS

TABLE OF CONTENTS

PART THREE — BIOGRAPHICAL ESSAYS

x

TABLE OF CONTENTS

FOREWORD

The American Library History Round Table was approved
by Council in December, 1946, and it met first at the San
Francisco Conference of the American Library Association in
June, 1947. In those days, getting a Round Table established
was a simple matter. A vote of the ALA Council was sufficient
authority; and the writers remember their feelings of uncertain-
ty about whether or not the vote would be favourable. Perhaps
because it was made about 6:00 P.M., when matters go through
quickly, the motion was passed without debate.

The Round Table took a leaf from its parent organization by
interesting a distinguished historian at the outset. Just as the
American Library Association had succeeded in 1876 in inducing
Justin Winsor to serve as first president, the ALHRT was successful in obtaining an early essay from Dr. Stanley Pargellis
of the Newberry Library.

The Round Table exists to provide a forum for library history. There are only two officers. Meetings include no business
or organization procedure; they are devoted exclusively to program. The two or three papers are usually followed by spontaneous reminiscences and augmentation by the audience. Because
no tape recorder has been available, many of these comments
have been lost.

Several notable presentations were spoken rather than read
from manuscript. Memorable was Carl B. Roden's recollections
of William Frederick Poole when the latter was chief librarian
and the former a page in the Chicago Public Library. Keyes
Metcalf recounted first-hand experience of life with E. H.
Anderson at the New York Public Library. Save for a few such
unwritten talks most of the ALHRT papers are included in this
volume. To these papers have been added several library history essays which were not given before the Round Table.

The American Library History Round Table is grateful to
the library periodicals that have published so many of its
papers, particularly the Wilson Library Bulletin which almost
from the beginning offered to publish most of the essays.
Special acknowledgment is due John David Marshall who has
devoted week-ends and spare time in a professional labour of

FOREWORD

love assembling these scattered papers for publication into a book. We give our warmest endorsement to this AMERICAN LIBRARY HISTORY READER which represents the first fruits in book form from the meetings of the American Library History Round Table. We hope it will stimulate the writing and publication of many more essays in American library history.

WAYNE SHIRLEY, Chairman ALHRT

LOUIS SHORES, Secretary ALHRT

BY WAY OF INTRODUCTION

American library history is a subject which more librarians might well pursue with vigour and profit. There is a great deal in our history that is at once interesting and perhaps even inspiring. There is too in our history much from which we can learn. From the perspective which our history can provide, it may be possible to find a few directions for at least a partial solution to some of the problems about which we hear and read so much. For these reasons alone the pursuit of library history merits our attention and should occupy at least some of our time.

That some librarians have turned their attention — if for only a moment or two — from more immediately practical matters to the study of library history is fortunate. It is also well that there exists within the American Library Association a small but active group known as the American Library History Round Table. For more than a dozen years now this informal organization has provided at conferences of the American Library Association a forum for American library history.

Many of the papers originally given before the Round Table have been published in various professional journals. These papers make informative and interesting reading, for they provide accounts and recollections of some of the men and women and events that have left their mark upon librarianship in the Western Hemisphere.

A number of these studies in American library history and biography are included in this volume. To these papers I have added certain other essays which, while not prepared for presentation before the ALHRT, fall within the scope of this AN AMERICAN LIBRARY HISTORY READER. The present collection brings together a selection of some thirty contributions to the literature of American library history.

The anthologist, as I have noted elsewhere, always becomes vulnerable to a slightly unfair kind of criticism: criticism for what he left out as well as for what he put in. Such criticism is one of the hazards of the anthologist's art and craft. His introductions, which are often defensive, frequently disintegrate into lengthy explanations as to why certain items were chosen and others not. The anthologist who follows this course too quickly becomes an apologist.

There are, of course, gaps in this collection. The very nature of any anthology makes such gaps inevitable. It is my hope, however, that these may not be too conspicuous or too great in number. The selection of essays for this volume — like that found in BOOKS, LIBRARIES, LIBRARIANS and OF, BY, AND FOR LIBRARIANS — is a personal one; the arrangement, of necessity, arbitrary. I can only say that I like these essays in American library history and that I think they merit the preservation a book — and only a book — can give them. Like Montaigne, "I have gathered a posie of other men's flowers and nothing but the thread that binds them is my own." I very much hope that those who read this volume will like the selections and the thread that binds them together.

That the American librarian's heritage is a goodly one will, I believe, be evident from a reading of the pages that follow. It is a heritage that all librarians may well be proud of. If these essays should give the beginning and the veteran librarian alike a sense of his professional history and some idea and appreciation of the heritage to which he is heir and to which each in his time is a contributor, the aim of AN AMERICAN LIBRARY HISTORY READER will have been achieved.

I wish you, my fellow librarians, pleasant and fruitful reading.

— JOHN DAVID MARSHALL

University of Georgia
Athens, Georgia
March 5, 1961

PART ONE — INTRODUCTORY ESSAYS

THE IMPORTANCE OF LIBRARY HISTORY

Louis Shores

Louis Shores is Dean of the Florida State University
Library School and Editor-in-Chief of Collier's Encyclopedia. The essay here published for the first time is a
paper read before the first meeting of the American
Library History Round Table at the June, 1947, conference
of the American Library Association in San Francisco.

After three score years and ten, our national professional
association on petition by fifty of its members, has activated
a round table for the study of library history.

That the American Library Association should have waited
so long may be considered surprising or not, depending upon
the individual's professional priorities. True, the first president of the A.L.A., Justin Winsor, was himself a distinguished
historian. True, also, is the fact that during the last seventy
years many scholars of history have served with distinction
as librarians. Officially, too, our association has cooperated
with the American Historical Association in efforts of mutual
interest, not the least of which has been the GUIDE TO HISTORI-
CAL LITERATURE. [1] And such basic history reference works as
Larned, [2] (also a librarian), Ploetz' EPITOME, CHRONICLES
OF AMERICA, PAGEANT OF AMERICA, and the Cambridge
histories, to cite only a few, have through the years had enthusiastic library support.

Despite this natural affinity between historians and librarians the first seven decades of our professional organization's
existence have not produced much library history. An evidence
of the paucity of library history research can be found in Lawrence S. Thompson's "Translator's Preface" to Albert Predeek,
A HISTORY OF LIBRARIES IN GREAT BRITAIN AND NORTH
AMERICA. [3]

"The first and only study of British and American

Grateful acknowledgment is here made to the author for providing
the compiler with a copy of this essay and for granting permission
to include it in this volume.

libraries from the Renaissance to the beginning of
World War II has been contributed . . . by Dr. Albert
Predeek, director of the library of the Technische
Hochschule, in Berlin-Charlottenburg, which was
bombed and burned in November 1943."[3]

Predeek himself writes, "There is no general description and
history of British librarianship," in his "Notes" to GREAT
BRITAIN FROM 1500 TO THE PRESENT, [4] and he adds in his
notes on the United States of America, "In spite of extraordinarily large number of monographic studies there are very
few comprehensive works."[5]

These observations are supported by the 460 items of bibliography which reveal many studies, essays, surveys, and
other pieces on phases of administration, technical processes,
selection, finance, statistics, but relatively few that can be
described as library history, per se.

Justification for this neglect can be found in the parallel
of our nation's history. Driven to pragmatism by the severities
of fashioning a living out of a wilderness, our forefathers struggled with economics long before they undertook esthetics. Likewise, spurred by the desire to extend library service to all of
the people, our library pioneers devoted themselves to the
bread and butter problems of finance and buildings, circulation
and technical processes, organization and administration.
There was simply no time for the luxury of history.

This necessity can be understood. But when the bug of research bit the profession in the early thirties the continued
neglect of history was more difficult to understand. James
Westfall Thompson, a historian, did considerable with medi-
eval libraries. But even the Graduate Library School at the
University of Chicago in its early days considered library
history with apology as an area of research. As I wrote in my
own doctoral dissertation, ". . . libraries so careful in the
preservation of all other materials only too frequently have
failed to organize and preserve their own records."[6]

The tragedy of this neglect and apology for library history
is emphasized in any consideration of the meaning of history
itself. If we accept both the broad definition of history as the
story of man's past and the specific charge to preserve the
records of civilization, then the negligence of librarianship

THE IMPORTANCE OF LIBRARY HISTORY

approaches a professional misdemeanor. How can we assume responsibility for the dissemination of these records and at the same time suppress through procrastination an important segment of them? If institutions constitute a significant phase of historical study, then which single institutional type can have greater importance to the story of man's past than the repositories of the record?

Imbued with the conviction of the importance of library history, Dean Wayne Shirley of the Pratt Institute Library School and the writer began at the very first post-war A.L.A. in Buffalo to plan for a unit in our professional association. We were encouraged by Carl Milam, Executive Secretary, Orwin Rush, first Executive Secretary of the Association of College and Reference Libraries, Stanley L. Pargellis of the Newberry Library, and many other librarians with an interest in the history of their profession.

This first meeting of the American Library History Round Table is, therefore, in itself of historical importance. It begins what I hope will be an official recognition by the A.L.A. of the importance of library history. It inaugurates, also, what I believe will be systematic attention hereafter to the chronicling of our professional achievement as manifested in the ever increasing dissemination of good ideas through libraries. As a result of these meetings we should guarantee the publication of at least two or three solid historical essays each year.

It is difficult to predict what special interests will develop as a result of these Round Table meetings. The opportunities are almost without limit. Perhaps as good a place to begin is with our own libraries. If no systematic collecting of memorabilia has been undertaken in the past, it would be well to go back to our own shops and begin now gathering and organizing.

You know better than I what resources are available. Legal documents for most libraries' origins exist. The charter, if there is one, provides a starting point. Annual reports of the librarian and public library board or college library faculty committee minutes are rich in primary materials. Nor should the library's records be overlooked. The accession book, before it is offered sacrificially to the Great God Efficiency, should be exploited creatively for the story of a library's book selection. Mines of information are often hidden in circulation statistics pre-empted for budget promotion. Among the borrowers' cards, if they have been retained for any time, are the elements for mixing and compounding materials into chronicles of unexpected portent. For I daresay that much innovation today is a repetition of yesterday's costly professional mistakes. Hidden in the books, themselves, are often forgotten inscriptions and dedications to the library, to say nothing of annotations vandalizing public property. In short, the true library historian will overlook nothing in the library or the community that might even remotely contribute to the story of an institution of historical significance.

After our own library, there are our associations, local, state, and regional, principally. How many city and county library associations have chronicled their story? Not many, I fear. Even more astonishing is how few state library association histories are noted in our bibliographies. Can it be that our library schools have considered the subject beneath master essay, leave alone doctoral dissertation? Then there are the regional organizations. We in the South have two. The Southeastern is a confederation of the libraries of nine states, and the Southwestern of six. Both the Pacific Northwest and New England have distinguished regional library associations. If their histories have been published, I confess I have discovered no entry in the bibliographies I have consulted.

I look at our great national association and wonder at the neglected opportunities. The Association of College and Reference Libraries and its predecessor, the College and Reference Division, have a history almost as old as that of the A.L.A. itself. Without listing them here, there are other units of the A.L.A. so rich in incident as revealed by the Proceedings that I marvel the officers have not established historical projects before this. There are, in addition, other national library associations like S.L.A. and associated organizations like the school library groups in education associations, and bibliographical and publishing agencies with library implications that would fill a section of good research studies. And I haven't even touched on government bureaus, federal and state, concerned with libraries.

What about the librarians? Biography is no inconsiderable auxiliary of history. It requires no oracular powers to foresee revival after revival of interest in American library pioneers. The spectacular notables like Melvil Dewey, Charles Amni

THE IMPORTANCE OF LIBRARY HISTORY

Cutter, John Cotton Dana, William Frederick Poole, and others will hardly escape repeated attention here. It is even probable that their private lives exposed in these meetings will result in "standing room only" signs, after a while. But much more important is the possibility that library history will discover the unsung greats among our predecessors and contemporaries, too, the tip-toeingest whisperers among our colleagues whose talents are sometimes overlooked by nominating committees. Library history can thus restore perspective and grant some token of belated recognition to those who deserved more in their professional lifetime.

The importance of history to civilization has been recognized philosophically, scientifically, spiritually for lo these many centuries. It is inconceivable that librarianship concerned with the records of civilization can continue to relegate its own chronicle to insignificance. The birth of the American Library History Round Table attests to the growing importance of library history.

NOTES:

1 Ed. by George Matthew Dutcher, et al; prepared by the Committee of Bibliography of the American Historical Association in cooperation with the American Library Association, 1931.

2 HISTORY FOR READY REFERENCE, Springfield, Mass. 12v.

3 Chicago, American Library Association, 1947. p. v.

4 Ibid., p. 132.

5 Ibid., p. 149.

6 Shores, Louis. ORIGINS OF THE AMERICAN COLLEGE LIBRARY. New York, Barnes & Noble, 1935. p. ix.

LONG LIFE TO THE LIBRARY HISTORY ROUND TABLE

Stanley Pargellis

Stanley Pargellis is Librarian of the Newberry Library in
Chicago, Illinois. The essay here reprinted is a paper
read before the American Library History Round Table
at the Midwinter meeting of the American Library Association in Chicago in 1948.

Mr. Shirley [1] has asked me to talk about things which the
Library History Round Table might do. The assignment is one
I welcome, in so far as any man ever relishes an assignment
to write a talk, for I have been going about telling various un-
historically-minded groups what the advantages and uses of
history are. Librarians in general are another unhistorically-
minded group; their thinking rests more upon the intellectual
framework and assumptions of the social scientists; they tend
to be systematizers, blueprint-makers, counters, planners,
worshippers of the mimeograph, discoverers of laws governing the actions of men in groups, standardizers, fillers-out
of forms, fomenters of vast projects, disregarders of men
and women as individuals, and interested only in mankind —
and books — in the mass. Since I believe in none of those things
by themselves, but only when thoroughly leavened with large
doses of history and philosophy and poetry, I stand before you
as something of a heretic in this year and age, who nevertheless considers these librarians of the schemer variety to be
the real heretics in the long timespan of human affairs.

The setting-up of the Round Table, therefore, from my
point of view, can turn out to be one of the most salutary innovations in modern library history. Infant though the Round
Table is, I hope it will prove to be another Athena, sprung in
full panoply of knowledge and understanding from the head of
all-wise Jove himself. Here it has emerged into a library
world where almost no one talks about past experience, past
practices, or past policies. Mr. Roden and his reminiscences

Reprinted from Wilson Library Bulletin, 22:601-603+, April, 1948,
by permission of the author and the publisher.

of W. F. Poole are the rare exception. [2] For the most part
the library world busily discusses its often trivial agenda in
terms of the fleeting present only, occasionally with a pious
hope for the future, but seldom with any sense of the past from
which both present and future spring. Creatures of a day we
deliberately allow ourselves to be, like those butterflies whose
whole span of existence is compressed into the hours between
sunup and sunset. We act in paradoxical contrast to the very
nature of our trade itself. For of all trades in the world, that
of librarian, by virtue of the stuff with which it deals, ought
to emancipate us, as far as men are capable of being emanci-
pated, from an evanescent kind of existence.

This Round Table, as I see it, can concern itself with several things. It can occasionally, as today, listen to descriptions
of men like Poole, whose mark upon Chicago libraries can
never be eradicated, nor indeed his mark upon the practice of
librarianship. Even after sixty years or more, his INDEX is
unreplaced, and remains in some ways more useful, because
its coverage of periodicals is wider, than the recent index to
the periodicals of the 1890's.

There are seventy-four librarians listed in the DICTIONARY
OF AMERICAN BIOGRAPHY. [3] Some of them we all know,
like John Shaw Billings, creator of both the Surgeon General's
Library and of the New York Public Library in its present
form, or Justin Winsor of Harvard. Others, like Herrick of
Yale, who brought to library administration the same accuracy
and thoroughness he put in on the Hessian Fly; or that other
entomologist, Harris of Harvard, whose book on injurious insects in New England is still used; or Samuel Swett Green, who
made the Worcester Free Library internationally known, are
not even names to most librarians today. One of the attractive
characteristics of scientists and medical men is the scrupulous
care they take in assigning precise credit to their living colleagues for some scientific discovery, and a few medical men,
like the late Harvey Cushing and our own Chicago Ernest E.
Irons, realize that the advances which medicine makes could
be much greater than they are if more attention were paid to
past medical investigations. No young doctor, reading the lives
of the great doctors who are gone, but can take inspiration
from the quality of their devotion, and the play of their imagina-
tions. In the same way librarians can take inspiration from the

lives and achievements of the great librarians of the past and from their concepts of the purposes of libraries. We talk wistfully of librarianship as a profession. Any profession must have a kind of code of its own, and I am not speaking here of the systematic corpus of knowledge which a professional man must acquire—but rather a sense of the significance of the profession which does not change as it is handed down from generation to generation, an ethic, if you care to call it that. I'd like to see the Library History Round Table try to isolate such an ethic for librarians, not the sort of thing that a committee might draw up in a couple of meetings or so, its expenses paid at the Edgewater Beach, but drawn out of the lives of great librarians since the Renaissance, when modern libraries began.

The interplay of men and institutions provides also a field for the Round Table. It is an old conflict: in the political field—government by laws or government by men—any professional man, I imagine, would resolve the conflict by saying that of course men govern, but they govern best within the framework and the spirit of the institutions which they serve. Every librarian should know the history of his library. However much of an innovator he tries to be, he is most successful when he fits his innovations into the pattern he has inherited.

Every library, like every individual, is unique; there is no other in the world exactly like it. The task of the librarian, and I mean everyone who works in a library, is to preserve that uniqueness, and not to lose it as the institution adapts itself to the necessities and changes of a constantly changing environment. Dean Roscoe Pound of the Harvard Law School used to say the same thing every year to freshman classes—that they were entering upon a great tradition, and that the utmost any of them could hope for, and the greatest thing they should strive for, was to lay another stone in the great temple of the common law. Personally I prefer Pound's view of men and institutions to the modern concept of law as merely another one of the social sciences, one of the agencies to be manipulated and used for creating some particular variety of social and economic structure. Every librarian ought to fit, if he can, another stone into his own institution, another book. To do that intelligently he should know the policies which his library has followed in the past, where it is strong, what it has

been collecting, what its previous relations have been with
university or city or state administrations, where, in short,
in the life of an institution he himself fits.

The Round Table might well take a leaf from the program
practices of the Newcomen Society, which, made up largely
of businessmen, listens annually to one of its members talk
about the history of his business.

The heads of American libraries might be invited to recount the salient facts in the growth of each of their institutions,
the steps which made it unusual and the men who played a part
in its growth. Such talks, it is unnecessary perhaps to add,
should be really historical, carefully based on the sources, on
the minutes of trustees, the reports of previous librarians,
on correspondence, on every kind of material which a good
historian, professional or otherwise, would use.

So much then for men and institutions. This Round Table
could take up another related question. How has the development of any particular library fitted into the development of
the community of which it is a part? This question might be
treated, and advantageously, in terms of comparative statistics, or extensions of services. But I would be more interested
myself in seeing it treated as a part of intellectual history.
Intellectual history is a comparatively recent development in
the historical field. Its methodology has not yet been clarified.
Lovejoy, in his GREAT CHAIN OF BEING, and in other works,
has isolated as a fruitful field of study not the ideas of great
thinkers but the assumptions upon which a great number of
much smaller men think and act. The great chain of being,
for instance, references to which fill the social, educational,
and political literature as well as the belles-lettres of the
eighteenth century, was the belief that God, in the single in-
stantaneous act of creation, linked together every living organism in one vast related chain, from the lowest forms of
life up through man, who stood about the center of the chain,
through all the orders of the hierarchy of angels up to the
throne of God himself. It was the duty of every living thing to
fulfill as completely as he could, in accordance with the law
of God and of Nature, the place to which he was appointed.
That assumption, that explanation of the meaning of existence,
permeated the thinking of most of the vocal eighteenth-century
world, and if a man set up a library, that assumption governed

his concept of the nature and ends for which the library should be used.

In the nineteenth century, in the palmy days of public library building, the assumption was still that men were primarily rational beings who hungered for the opportunity to learn the best that had been thought and said in the world, in order that they might grow into fuller individuals and more competent and selfless citizens. What has happened to that assumption today? Is it still true? How and for what reasons has it been modified? Upon what assumptions do men think and act today? And what is the place of the public library in relation to such assumptions? To some cynics today it would appear that the public library has become a means of providing entertainment for the citizenry at public expense, and that if the library wanted to continue this modern equivalent of "bread and circuses", it would furnish free movies, free dance halls, and free bars. The cynic is wrong—I know enough of the things Mr. Roden has done in Chicago to know how wrong the cynic is—but his function is to probe, and one function of the Round Table is to find sound and scholarly answers to such probing and embarrassing remarks. For the historian, I like to think, serves potentially the wisest and most serene of the great disciplines, without the fussy impatience of the social scientists who have not yet got themselves either a subject matter or a methodology which can qualify as a great discipline, or the unreality into which philosophy loves to lure her devotees, or the impersonal abstractions of the pure scientists.

And that leads me to the last of the things which the Round Table might sponsor, which of course is the writing of library history. If it does, I hope that the history it sponsors is in the old broad tradition. The historical world—I hesitate to confess this—is split asunder today. There are those who believe that history should be written for historians alone, that if fifty people who know what's what read your book, you should be more than satisfied, that the business of history is finding out and proving beyond the shadow of any doubt some series of facts and explanations about the past which make more intelligible the long and vexed career of men organized in human societies that move and change through time. Some historians go even further and discuss, as at Cleveland last month, the extent to which modern doctrines of historical relativism have

limited the quest for certainty. You know as well as I what that
means. And on the other hand, there are those historians who
feel that history must be written to be read, that it is an art
and even a literary art, that whoever writes of great and colorful events without due measure of color in his words fails to
convey the full meaning of those events, that because men are
so fashioned that they must have some kind of history and will
read bad history that is readable if they are not furnished with
sound history that, being readable also, is therefore good, it
is the business of historians to give them good history.

Belonging to the second rather than the first school, I of
course would like to see the Round Table sponsor my definition
of good history, though I believe that there is room enough in
Clio's pastures for every kind of animal, even social scientists'
history. Before anyone starts writing about libraries in the
past, let him read and ponder a few of the essential guides to
good historical writing. Let him read Allan Nevin's GATEWAY
TO HISTORY for a broad and liberal view of what history can
be; and let him study and study again such manuals as Sherman
Kent's ON WRITING HISTORY, or Allen Johnson's THE HIS-
TORIAN AND HISTORICAL EVIDENCE, or that great stand-by
of historiography courses, Langlois and Seignobos' INTRO-
DUCTION TO THE STUDY OF HISTORY. Otherwise he may
fall into the wretched habit of beginning his history of the
Public Library of Chicago, say, as Mr. Roden will not, with
the invention of writing, or the geological configurations of the
Great Lakes region, or the social mores of Americans since
the Puritan era. And he may misinterpret his evidence and
read into the facts what is not there – or worse still, choose
facts that fit his own predetermined conclusions. Or he may
write too narrowly, contenting himself with the mere recital
of developments in some library's past, without ever tying it
to the intellectual and social and economic world of which it
must be part.

I welcome this fledgling institution of the Round Table, let
me repeat. The effects it may have, if humbly managed, are
incalculable. I would like to see all libraries, as far as possible, assume in their communities something of that serenity
of the far-visioned and the wise which is lacking in the modern
world. Our institutions cannot appear serene unless their servants have some measure of serenity also. And serenity, while

PARGELLIS

it may come from other sources than the study of history, can
also come from viewing the broad horizons which history, and
not least the history of libraries, holds out before all those who
take the trouble to do a little climbing. May long life and success attend this Round Table.

NOTES:

[1] Wayne Shirley, Chairman of the American Library History Round
Table – JDM

[2] C. B. Roden spoke on William F. Poole before Dr. Pargellis gave
his paper; Mr. Roden's presentation was spoken rather than read
from manuscript, and there is no record of its publication in Library Literature. S. H. Kessler's essay on Poole (Wilson Library
Bulletin, 28:788-790, May, 1954) is included in this volume – JDM

[3] These 74 librarians in DAB are Samuel A. Allibone, William Beer,
John S. Billings, Carl H. A. Bjerregaard, William H. Brett, James
H. Canfield, James R. Chadwick, John V. Cheney, William H. Cobb,
Joseph G. Cogswell, Frederick M. Crunden, Charles A. Cutter,
John C. Dana, Raymond C. Davis, Lyman C. Draper, Daniel S. Dur-
rie, John Edmonds, William R. Eastman, Mary S. C. Fairchild,
Daniel W. Fiske, Weston Flint, Charles Folsom, Sam W. Foss,
Samuel A. Green, Samuel S. Green, Appleton P. C. Griffin, Reuben
A. Guild, Thaddeus W. Harris, Edward C. Herrick, Edward S. Hol-
den, Henry A. Homes, James K. Hosmer, Mary F. Isom, Charles
C. Jewett, John W. Jordan, Margaret C. Klingelsmith, Andrew J.
Lamoureux, Josephus N. Larned, Henry E. Legler, George H.
Moore, Nathaniel F. Moore, Charles A. Nelson, Theodore S. Par-
vin, George W. Peckham, Frederic B. Perkins, Mary W. Plum-
mer, Fitch Poole, William F. Poole, Herman Rosenthal, Frede-
rick Saunders, John C. Schwab, Katharine L. Sharp, William S.
Shaw, John L. Sibley, Charles R. Skinner, John J. Smith, Lloyd
P. Smith, Oscar G. T. Sonneck, Ainsworth R. Spofford, Bernard
C. Steiner, Lewis H. Steiner, Alfred B. Street, Reuben G. Thwaites,
Philip R. Uhler, John C. Van Dyke, Addison Van Name, Frederic
Vinton, James W. Ward, George Watterson, James L. Whitney,
John F. Williams, Justin Winsor, James Winthrop, Mary E. Wood.

– JDM

PART TWO – HISTORICAL ESSAYS

FRANKLIN AND HIS FRIENDS CHOOSE THEIR BOOKS

Edwin Wolf 2nd

Edwin Wolf 2nd – author with John F. Fleming of ROSEN-
BACH: A BIOGRAPHY (1960) – is Librarian of The Library
Company of Philadelphia. The essay here reprinted is a
longer version of a paper read before the June, 1955,
meeting of the American Library History Round Table
at the Philadelphia conference of the American Library
Association.

The books chosen by the directors of the Library Company
of Philadelphia in the first decade of its existence represent a
unique selection for colonial America. It was unique because it
was made by and for a group of merchants, tradesmen, and ar-
tisans struggling to gain wealth and position.[1] Benjamin Franklin, pragmatical and intellectually curious, was their leader and
prototype. The books these men decided to order for their com-
munal use reveal more clearly than any other evidence their cultural interests, and, in a way, their aspirations.

Other libraries of a different nature had preceded the Library
Company on the American scene. Three colleges – Harvard in
1638, William and Mary in 1693, and Yale possibly in 1701 – had
already established collections of books.[2] These institutions had
been founded by clerics primarily to educate young men for the
ministry, although this purpose was not adhered to as strictly by
the Virginia institution as by those of New England. Consequently, their libraries, largely formed by the gifts of interested individuals in England and the colonies, were strongly theological
in character. The selection of books was essentially determined
by what the colleges or the donors thought the professors and
students ought to read, rather than by what the readers wanted
for themselves. To be sure, these could have been at times one
and the same, but the underlying philosophy of the choice was
didactic. In this respect, the choice of books by members of the
Library Company differed; their choice was autodidactic. The

Reprinted from Pennsylvania Magazine of History and Biography, 80:
11-36, January, 1956, by permission of the author and the publisher.

desire for the book stemmed from the reader.

In addition to the college libraries, there were in the colonies a number of private collections – probably more than has been generally supposed – the most famous and largest of which were those of William Byrd of Westover, of the Winthrops, the Mathers, and Thomas Prince of Boston, and of James Logan of Philadelphia.[3] The books in these private hands ranged in selection from an overwhelming predominance of theological writings to a cultured English gentleman's choice, typical in the case of Byrd, refined and intellectualized in the case of Logan. Louis B. Wright has noted that in dwelling upon the appetite of the Puritans for works of divinity we sometimes forget the taste of Virginians for religious literature.[4] In the private Virginia libraries of the seventeenth and very early eighteenth centuries which he surveyed, Wright noted a heavy weighting of theology and law. However, all these collections reflected the interests of an individual rather than a group, and are representative of the highest level of colonial culture, a level where the company was few.

We know much less about the third type of library which existed in the British colonies before the Library Company was organized.[5] In documents there are records of "a publick library of Boston" as early as 1674, possibly one provided for by Captain Robert Keayne in his will in 1653, but no lists or books survived the fires of 1711 and 1747 which destroyed it. What type of library it was and how it operated are unknown, but Samuel Eliot Morison does not believe it amounted to more than "a small collection of theology".[6] More information is extant of the various collections which the Reverend Thomas Bray sent to many towns through the Society for the Propagation of the Gospel in Foreign Parts. Between 1680 and 1730 the Society established thirty-eight libraries in America, but the books sent were chiefly intended as parochial libraries for the use of missionaries, and hence were almost entirely theological.

Most of these collections were established in churches, but the books sent to Annapolis in 1697 were housed in the State House, and became in fact a public library. In 1698 another Bray collection went to King's Chapel at Boston, and the same year one to Trinity Parish in New York. Others were established at Christ Church in Philadelphia, Charleston, and elsewhere. The plan was widened in 1700 to provide for "lending laymen's libraries", but these collections never grew and never became

a significant factor in the cultural life of any community. One
more public library should be mentioned, that founded by the
Reverend John Sharp of New York in 1700. He left his own collection of books to a public library, which was organized by the
Corporation of the City, but allowed to remain moribund until
1754 when it became the nucleus of the New York Society Library,
a subscription library following the pattern of the Library Company of Philadelphia.

It was because there was available in Philadelphia no library
of a general nature which would give its readers not only borrowing privileges, but also a choice of books attuned to their
wants, that the Library Company was founded, the first of many
subscription libraries which were thereafter established to meet
the same needs in other localities. Its history is well known.[7] It
was founded in 1731 by Benjamin Franklin and his associates of
the Junto to turn their limited financial resources into the greatest variety of books for their common use. The Company ordered its first books from London at the end of March, 1732, and
received its first shipment in October of that year. Thereafter,
the library was steadily enlarged, chiefly by purchase, partly
by gift, until it became the library of Philadelphia, a significant
and permanent part of the city's intellectual resources.[8]

An account of the books included in the first shipment in 1732
and of the early printed catalogues of the library was published
recently.[9] Although broadsheet lists of the works available to its
members were printed by Franklin in 1733 and 1735, no copies
of either have survived. The earliest extant printed record of
the books in the collection is the fifty-six-page octavo catalogue
of 1741, which lists by size and in no other order, three hundred
and seventy-five titles.[10]

These titles are the subject of the present study. That they
represent a popular, democratic choice is apparent from the minutes of the Company, which contain such entries as those of July
15, 1734, "a list of Books was drawn out & made Choice of, from
Lists brought by several of the Committee",[11] and of April 10,
1738, when it was ordered "that an Advertisement be put up in
the Library Room to acquaint the Subscribers that the Directors
would be willingly assisted in the Choice of the next Parcel of
Books which they are to send for".[12] The standard procedure for
getting books was for a list to be made out and sent off to Peter
Collinson, the scientist friend of Bartram and Franklin, who had

agreed to act as the Company's volunteer London agent. Sometimes a few of the books specified could not be obtained or were too expensive; sometimes Collinson or a member of the company who happened to be on the spot made other suggestions. By and large, however, the collection consisted of specific orders which originated from the group in Philadelphia, augmented, of course, by gifts from members and friends.

In selecting the titles for the first order, the Company asked the advice of James Logan, "the best Judge of Books in these Parts"[13] and the owner of a private library which was probably the best selected of any collection then in America. There is no doubt that his experience and erudition were factors in the Company's choice. In an unpublished history of the Library Company, Miss Dorothy F. Grimm has pointed out that many of the books included were also to be found in a list printed in John Clarke's AN ESSAY UPON STUDY (1731),[14] a copy of which was acquired by the library as early as 1735.[15] Other suggestions by other writers including John Locke[16] may also have been used, but basically the selection was that of the directors. One fact of that selection becomes apparent from a comparison of the Library Company list with those of other libraries of the period, including its succeeding sister subscription libraries throughout the country.[17] A great many of the works must have been recognized as standard texts and indispensable for any collection. A very high proportion of them were to be found in Logan's library, in the collections of both Yale and Harvard, and to an even greater degree in such a later, similar institution as the New York Society Library. The books of the Library Company differed not in individual titles, but rather in the predominance of certain fields of learning to the virtual exclusion of others. In fact, they were essentially the "best sellers" of the first half of the eighteenth century.

The 375 titles listed in the 1741 catalogue[18] can be roughly divided into subjects as follows: history, 114; literature, 69; science, 65; theology, 38; philosophy, 33; social sciences, 28; arts, 13; linguistics, 10; and general, 5. These are, of course, general categories, and a single work could belong in one or another category. For instance, ecclesiastical history could be theological or historical; I have placed such titles where I think they fit best.

It is of more than passing interest that of the 375 titles, eighty-four were gifts, which, subtracted from the main classes,

would leave as works actually ordered: history, 91; literature,
55; science, 51; theology, 25; philosophy, 28; and social sciences, 21. It should also be noted that, as in all of the later subscription libraries, almost all the books were in English. There
were only thirteen works in foreign languages in the Library
Company collection, of which ten were gifts. The only ones apparently ordered were Grotius' DE JURE BELLI in Latin, DON
QUIXOTE in the original Spanish, and Pascal's LETTRES PRO-
VINCIALES in the original French, and in each case the Company also owned an English translation.

It is immediately obvious that the readers of Philadelphia,
the self-educated citizens, who wanted books for their own general edification, were interested chiefly in history, literature,
and science. These subjects accounted for almost two hundred
of the two hundred and ninety-one works which they bought. It is
also obvious that they ordered theology with an extremely light
hand. By comparison, the 1723 catalogue of the library of Harvard College, with its supplements to 1735, shows that approximately two thirds of its books were theological.[19] Yale's collection in 1743 was not so heavy; about one half of the library
consisted of theological books.

By way of explanation of the very few theological works in
the Company's library, it should be noted that of the three hundred and twenty-three imprints listed by Hildeburn as printed in
Pennsylvania during the eleven years 1731-1741,[20] only fifty-
three were not theological tracts, laws and official papers, almanacs, or periodicals. Hence, it may be assumed that the
Philadelphians who wanted a regular fare of sermons and religious polemics found them easily and cheaply available at every
bookstore. They sent abroad for more expensive works not printed here and only occasionally to be bought at home.

Breaking down the largest class – history – we find, as one
would expect, that English history forms the largest subgroup.
The most comprehensive work was Rapin-Thoyras' HISTORY
OF ENGLAND, a standard Whig text, which was to be found in
most libraries in America, both institutional and private. It is
interesting that this history, written for the instruction of foreigners by a Frenchman who came to England with William of
Orange, remained the best and most popular general history of
England until the publication of Hume's. Other standard works
were Camden's BRITANNIA, Buchanan's HISTORY OF SCOT-

LAND, Burnet's sturdily Whig HISTORY OF HIS OWN TIME,
Clarendon's HISTORY OF THE REBELLION, and Sir William
Temple's WORKS. The lesser books, including a biography of
Oliver Cromwell, who became somewhat of a hero in the colonies, were miscellaneous in character, dealing chiefly with the
period from the Commonwealth to the reign of Queen Anne.
    European history was fairly well represented. Here the rec-
ognized classic of the times seems to have been Pufendorf's
INTRODUCTION TO THE HISTORY OF THE PRINCIPAL KING-
DOMS AND STATES OF EUROPE. But the most sensational,
and probably most read, work was the spicy, semifictional survey of European diplomacy, manners, and intrigue, published
anonymously by Marana as LETTERS WRITTEN BY A TURK-
ISH SPY. Yale catalogued this title under "Books of Diversion".
For a more accurate picture of cities and life on the Continent,
the Philadelphians chose Bishop Burnet's objective eyes and
pen, his travel LETTERS, as their guide. Indicative of the vast
curiosity of these men, as well as the search for more esoteric
works, is the large number of histories and accounts of various
countries all over the world. There was no isolationist feeling
in the colonial city whose prosperity was built on trade. Including the books added as gifts, the lands covered were Africa,
Denmark, Holland, France, Hungary, Italy, Persia, Poland,
Portugal, Russia, Spain, Sweden, Switzerland, and Turkey,
as well, of course, as classical Greece and Rome. In addition,
there were a few accounts of voyages of discovery and exploration in all quarters of the globe
    Of all these, the histories of the Abbé Vertot seem of par-
ticular significance. His name is virtually unknown today, and
yet in the first half of the eighteenth century his chronicles of
the "revolutions" in Rome, Brittany, Spain, Sweden, and Portugal were best sellers. Technically superficial and romantic,
these works expressed a liberal view of history which found a
sympathetic audience in an era when the rights of kings were
being increasingly questioned. In America, where a search after rights and liberties had been responsible for the settlement
of most of the colonies, Vertot's works were ubiquitous. There
was hardly a library which did not contain them, and it is interesting to conjecture upon their influence on the revolution in
America. The Abbé de Mably, one of the most radical of the
mid-eighteenth-century philosophers, said of Vertot, "Je le

regarde comme celui de tous nos écrivains qui a été le plus capable d'écrire l'histoire".[21]

Along the same lines, the inclusion of Midon's THE HISTORY OF THE RISE AND FALL OF MASANIELLO, the Neapolitan fisherman who provoked a popular revolt, Molesworth's ACCOUNT OF DENMARK, THE HISTORY OF THE REVOLUTIONS IN THE EMPIRE OF MOROCCO, and Krusinski's HISTORY OF THE REVOLUTIONS IN PERSIA shows that there was available to colonial Americans a diversified historical background dealing with uprisings and the mutability of kings and states. These works, treating of the subversion of established monarchies, seem to have been in most American libraries, public and private, indicating that the precedent for revolution existed in the most esteemed historical texts. To be sure, they also bought more general and less exciting works: Raleigh's HISTORY OF THE WORLD and Helwich's CHRONOLOGY, both one-volume compendiums of all recorded history, Bentivoglio's HISTORY OF THE WARS OF FLANDERS, and other books on the Dutch Republic, Comines' MEMOIRS OF FRANCE in the late Middle Ages, Davila's HISTORY OF THE CIVIL WAR OF FRANCE, Maimbourg's HISTORY OF THE LEAGUE, several works on Naples but nothing general on Italy, Mariana's GENERAL HISTORY OF SPAIN, Stevens' HISTORY OF PERSIA, and Kantemir's HISTORY OF THE GROWTH AND DECAY OF THE OTHMAN EMPIRE, all of which, judging from other library lists, enjoyed great popularity.

Actually, about one eighth of all the histories, which include geographies and books of travel, were of some American interest, a high proportion acquired by gift. The large quarto ATLAS GEOGRAPHICUS in five volumes, Heylyn's COSMOGRAPHY, still current with additions and emendations a century after it first appeared, and an otherwise undescribed "Collection of Maps" provided general coverage. Garcilasso de la Vega's COMMENTARIES OF PERU, a gift from James Logan, and Solis' HISTORY OF THE CONQUEST OF MEXICO were the best accounts of the early history of Spanish America they could have secured.

Since the members of the Library Company were in the process of making the history of British America, or were ambitious to do so, they could not look upon the comparatively few major works on the subject as of extreme importance. As a matter of fact, when Franklin later urged Collinson to secure for the library old tracts dealing with the early settlements, the directors soon brought a halt to these—to them pointless—acquisitions.[22] In view of Franklin's efforts, the inclusion of Bishop White Kennett's BIBLIOTHECAE AMERICANAE PRIMORDIA among the miscellaneous books of reference is noteworthy. Kennett here compiled the first important bibliography of Americana per se, impelled by his conviction that such a collection of books as his would be valuable for many people concerned in or with the colonies, "especially the Governours and other Administrators of Justice in her Majesty's Plantations" who would learn from them "what Good Names and sufficient Estates have been gotten by Justice and Moderation, what Examples of Ruin and Infamy to Tyrants and Oppressors, what Credit and Comfort in Governing always and everywhere ACCORDING TO LAW".[23] Unfortunately, the directors of the Company did not take to heart the Bishop's wisdom. However, Benjamin Eastburn, the surveyor, gave them A SHORT ACCOUNT OF THE FIRST SETTLEMENT OF THE PROVINCES OF VIRGINIA, MARYLAND, NEW-YORK, NEW-JERSEY AND PENNSYLVANIA, and David Bush donated to the common use Beverley's HISTORY OF VIRGINIA. And, in addition, the Company did buy Lahontan's and Hennepin's accounts of New France, Esquemeling's exciting stories of pirates in the West Indies, Martyn's REASONS FOR ESTABLISHING THE COLONY OF GEORGIA, and Neal's sober HISTORY OF NEW ENGLAND.

By almost any standard of the day, the Library Company's coverage of the field of ancient history was inadequate, although English editions of Thucydides, Polybius, Caesar, Tacitus—widely read for its translator Gordon's prefatory discourses proclaiming straight Whig doctrine, which, Tolles notes,[24] was as much a party document as his political writings—Sallust, and Plutarch were to be found. Another Tacitus in Latin and a Livy in Dutch, both gifts, were probably little used. The only comprehensive, modern work on the subject was Echard's ROMAN HISTORY, a five-volume set. The Library Company members, most of them, had little Latin and less Greek, and apparently no consuming desire to do much about it.

The same, almost purposeful, avoidance of Greek and Latin classics, which in other libraries, both academic and private, played so large a role, is obvious also in the next largest field—literature. It was overwhelmingly English in character. With the exception of an Ovid and a Plautus, again both gifts, the ancient

classics which they possessed were in English translations —
Pope's Homer, Croxall's Aesop, Creech's Horace and Lucretius,
Dryden's Juvenal and Virgil, Rowe's Lucan, and a few others.
The gentlemen and scholars who formed other contemporary collections were proud of their familiarity with the ancient tongues.
On the other hand, Franklin in all his suggestions for the curriculum of the Academy of Philadelphia, later the University of
Pennsylvania, urged an emphasis on the use and teaching of English instead of, as was customary, on Latin and Greek.[25] There
was not one book in Greek in the whole library until a good many
years later. By comparison, it should be noted that approximately one half of the books in Harvard College Library at this same
period were in foreign languages, chiefly Latin, the scholar's
lingua franca, and that in James Logan's personal collection the
percentage was even higher.

When it came to belles lettres in English, the large number
of books of a lighter nature was probably the result of the expansion of the membership of the Company beyond the first small
group of serious philosophic inquirers. The democratic "popular" taste is evident in the choice which seems based on contemporary popularity rather than on appreciation for or seeking after the great works of the past. The giants of England, Chaucer
and Shakespeare, were notably lacking, but they were, of course,
not such giants then. Spenser came as an early gift; a few of the
late Stuart and Restoration literary lights like Cowley, Waller,
and Congreve were present in collected works, as was Milton
with PARADISE LOST and his prose. But it was the Augustans,
then gleaming untarnished, who caught the fancy of the Philadelphians.

It should be noted that there were comparatively few plays included and no chapbook romances. This was before the flowering
of the English novel. Most of the literature consisted of poems
and essays. Dryden was represented only by his FABLES and by
his translations already mentioned, but his successors received
more favorable treatment. Pope's EPISTLES IN VERSE was
bought when it appeared; his DUNCIAD came in an augmented edition; both his MISCELLANIES alone and the series issued with
Swift found ready readers, as did Pope's LETTERS. The full flavor of the eighteenth-century selection is in the choice of works —
not always among the most important — of other members of the
dominant factor in English letters, the Scriblerus Club. Swift

was represented fittingly enough by his bookish TALE OF A TUB, but GULLIVER'S TRAVELS found no place on the shelves until 1743. Arbuthnot, Pope's doctor friend and the host of the club, was represented as a scientist rather than a poet, but both Gay and Parnell's poetry found favor.

Most of the rest of the list of poets reads like – and is, in fact – a roll call of yesteryear's best sellers: Glover's LEONIDAS, raised to fleeting popularity by the critical war which raged about it, Garth's DISPENSARY, a dated but amusing satire of medical interest, Blackmore's CREATION and ELIZA, Philips' PASTO-RALS, Pomfret's POEMS, Needler's WORKS, and that perennial eighteenth-century favorite, Thomson's SEASONS. Except for Butler's HUDIBRAS, which seems to have enjoyed a greater popularity among the colonial Virginians than any other poem, Prior's POEMS ON SEVERAL OCCASIONS, and Watts's HORAE LYRICAE, the authors and the works in this field are distinguished only by their mediocrity in present-day eyes. As Louis B. Wright observed succinctly, "In general, the most commonly found literary works were not books by the greatest authors."26

Special mention must be made, however, of the inclusion of the three major collections of periodical essays, the Tatler, the Spectator, and the Guardian. Franklin wrote in his autobiography that he had consciously modeled his style upon that of the Spectator,27 but it was more than clarity of writing and catholicity of content which would have appealed to the Philadelphians. The essays represented the kind of middle-class English thinking, the intelligent but quizzical attitude to life and manners, and the common-sensical virtues that were almost identical with those of Franklin and his friends. In addition, Addison and Steele were both ardent Whigs whose political thinking would have found a receptive audience among their American readers. How popular these books were with the members of the Library Company is shown by the fact that the original copies, probably read to tatters, soon had to be replaced with other sets, and even these show the physical signs of much use.

In foreign literature, the members were but little interested. They bought Boileau's WORKS, the TALES AND FABLES and the classic, political novel, TELEMACHUS, of Fénelon, DON QUIX-OTE, and Gracian's HERO, all in English translations. To this meager group of continental writers, Franklin added by gift two of a three-volume set of Montaigne's ESSAYS. It is interesting that John Clarke in his ESSAY UPON STUDY, after damning light literature, wrote, "I know but two Romances I can heartily recommend, THE HISTORY OF DON QUIXOT, and the Adventures of Telemachus", calling the former "the finest Piece of Invention in the Ludicrous Merry Way, and withal the most innocent, that ever was penned by any Author whatever, I believe, whether Antient or Modern".[28] That must have represented the opinion of most, for the only foreign work of literature bought in its original language was a Spanish edition of DON QUIXOTE. But more in line with the general radical tone of the whole collection was the inclusion of TELEMACHUS, in its day a brave novel, prophetic of the eighteenth century, which had as its moral that kings exist for the sake of their subjects, not subjects for the sake of kings. Professor Howard M. Jones, writing of the second half of the century, found that among Philadelphians of that period, Fénelon was the most popular French author and TELEMACHUS consistently one of the most popular works.[29]

If the small number of theological books was one of the distinctive features of the library, the high percentage of scientific ones was equally so. The collection was begun at the very time when the flowering of the age of scientific inquiry initiated by Descartes had reached so advanced a stage in England that for the first time a scientist–Newton–was being widely hailed as one of the British immortals. The Royal Society, a loosely knit group of amateurs in the seventeenth century, had become a major influence in English life fifty years later. The struggles of the theologians against the natural philosophers were becoming more academic, and although scientists still nodded politely toward religion, they were prepared to carry on their experiments wherever they might lead. In America this spirit of inquiry took root quickly, and its basic principle, knowledge through experience, was Americanized in the much later popular expression, "I'm from Missouri".

The underlying discipline of the physical sciences was, of course, mathematics. The two works chosen for the members of the Library Company, who, like William Parsons, a shoemaker who became surveyor general of the province, were desirous of teaching themselves fundamentals, were John Ward's YOUNG MATHEMATICIAN'S GUIDE and Ozanam's CURSUS MATHEMATICUS, translated into English by Desaguliers. To these were added De Chales' edition of Euclid. But for the more advanced, those who may have gotten their grounding in the remarkable scientific collection of James Logan, there were Ozanam's challenging and popular MATHEMATICAL RECREATIONS, L'Hôpital's standard work on solid geometry, AN ANALYTICK TREATISE ON CONICK SECTIONS, and Motte's translation of Newton's PRINCIPIA. This last work, the first appearance of Newton's magnum opus in English, was supplanted as an authority on the Newtonian theory by Dr. Henry Pemberton's VIEW OF SIR ISAAC NEWTON'S PHILOSOPHY, which was one of the two books that Peter Collinson sent as a gift with the first shipment in 1732.[30]

The Philadelphians were from the beginning ardent Newtonians. Among them, Thomas Godfrey, the self-taught inventor of the quadrant, had a particular bent for astronomy, and it may be assumed that he was delighted to have available Keill's INTRODUCTION, which consisted of his astronomical lectures delivered at Oxford, and Gregory's ELEMENTS OF ASTRONOMY, which was donated by the surveyor Benjamin Eastburn. Both Keill and Gregory were followers of Newton, and carried on experiments to advance his theories; their works were the best handbooks of the science available at the time. Gifts of the old-fashioned works of Moxon on globes, Holder on the calendar, and Serle on dials came from David Bush. More useful would have been Leybourn's still valued work on dialing, and THE CELESTIAL WORLDS DISCOVERED by the great Dutch horologist Huygens. A willingness to listen to the religio-scientific school was shown by the inclusion of Cotton Mather's THE CHRISTIAN PHILOSOPHER, a gift, and Derham's exposition of final causes in his ASTRO-THEOLOGY, subtitled A DEMONSTRATION OF THE BEING AND ATTRIBUTES OF GOD FROM A SURVEY OF THE HEAVENS, which had reached a sixth edition by 1731.

In an allied field the Library Company bought also Derham's companion volume, PHYSICO-THEOLOGY, but their most comprehensive work on physics was Desagulier's SYSTEM OF EXPERIMENTAL PHILOSOPHY, which, with its rich mine of "curious Experiments", may have stimulated and guided the scientific inquiry which had been made possible by Thomas Penn's gift of an air pump in 1738. With some of the essential books and, as time went on, scientific equipment as well, the Library Company became in fact the first scientific society in Philadelphia. In its rooms the native natural philosophers proved by experiment what they had read about, and in the field of electricity, particularly, began to make new tests to learn what was still unknown about that phenomenon. Hauksbee's PHYSICO-MECHANICAL EXPERI- MENTS would have helped them, for he first described the rub- bing of glass with various substances to produce an electrical glow.[31] It is frequently forgotten that the "several of us", re- ferred to by Franklin as making electrical experiments in his first letter on electricity to Collinson in 1747, were specifically identified in a footnote: "i. e. of the Library-Company, an insti- tution of the Author's, founded 1730".[32] Clare's work on the MO- TION OF FLUIDS completed their handful of specialized books on physics.

Of course, they did have a group of books which treated of sci- ence generally, the most important of which was a set of the stan- dard abridgment of THE PHILOSOPHICAL TRANSACTIONS OF THE ROYAL SOCIETY. The Royal Society represented for the Americans the kind of organization that they wished for them- selves, and when, two years after the Library Company catalogue was printed, Franklin issued his call to form the American Philo- sophical Society, he had in mind the success and influence of the English body. Franklin had met its venerable president in London, when the nineteen-year-old printer had been there in 1727, and contributions to the Society's TRANSACTIONS from Americans increased as colonial scientists discovered new natural phenom- ena in the vastness of their land and as they further developed ideas transmitted from the old world or originated new ones of their own. After all, in 1734 the account of the invention of the quadrant by the Library Company member, Thomas Godfrey, had appeared in the TRANSACTIONS. There was both pride and de- sire for knowledge in the choice of this set. As a complement, the collection was augmented by a gift of Sprat's standard history of the Royal Society.

Recognition of and respect for Francis Bacon's position as a pioneer in the development of science was widespread in America. His writings were to be found in most of the libraries in the colo- nies, and he was represented in the Library Company by the three- volume quarto edition of THE PHILOSOPHICAL WORKS, edited by Dr. Peter Shaw, which was bought after Francis Richardson had donated a separate printing of the SYLVA SYLVARUM. The pro- gress of the post-Baconian century was evidenced and became available to the members through the collected works of the late seventeenth-century giant of the physical sciences, Robert Boyle, in an edition also edited by Shaw.

To help them with their own written reports of new discoveries, the Philadelphians had a most important attempt to standardize scientific terminology, AN ESSAY TOWARDS A REAL CHARACTER AND A PHILOSOPHICAL LANGUAGE, written by John Wilkins, the first secretary of the Royal Society, with the help of Ray, Willughby, and others. A more popular work was the PHILOSOPHICAL GRAMMAR of Benjamin Martin, instrument maker and ardent Newtonian, who gathered together in simple form an epitome of the theories and findings of the day in the field of the physical and mathematical sciences. However, even Martin's compilation seems to have been too difficult for many of the readers, for two copies were bought of the French naturalist Pluche's SPECTACLE DE LA NATURE; OR, NATURE DISPLAYED, which consisted of discourses, chiefly on the less erudite phases of natural history, "thought most proper to excite the Curiosity, and form the Minds of Youth". It was diffusely written, did not reflect the tremendous advances of the first part of the eighteenth century, and yet was the single most popular, general work on natural history at that time.

It was not, however, the kind of book which would have proved very useful to a member like Joseph Breintnall, who was an enthusiastic amateur botanist. He needed and found on the shelves such a solid work as Salmon's ENGLISH HERBAL, which the Library accepted as the best book of its kind then available, although they chose as well the much earlier flower book, PARADISUS TERRESTRIS of the herbalist Parkinson. Apparently, James Logan, whose pioneer work on the fertilization of corn had appeared at Leyden in 1731, and John Bartram, who was a friend of many of the members but did not himself become a shareholder until a few years later, exerted little influence on the selection, for most of the works were more practical than theoretical. It was another botanist, Collinson, who sent as a gift with the first shipment in 1732 Philip Miller's GARDENER'S DICTIONARY, a massive work which kept its currency throughout the century and which Franklin kept in his room "between the Clock and our Bedchamber".[33] If Collinson had not so kindly sent it, the valuable compendium would certainly have been bought, for it seems to have been a <u>sine qua non</u> in its day. Patrick Blair's BOTANICK ESSAYS was the only technical study in the field of botany which the library contained.

The larger number of agricultural works reflected far more the day-to-day interests of the members, and the modernity of the works showed that in farming at least, the Americans were concerned with the latest practical improvements. In England, Richard Bradley's ignorance of the classical languages caused some eyebrows to be raised when he foisted himself into the chair of botany at Cambridge, but he was a well-received, prolific, and enthusiastic writer, and the Americans asked Collinson to buy as many of his writings as he could. Apparently, all that was obtainable was Bradley's NEW IMPROVEMENTS OF PLANTING AND GARDENING, which reached seven editions between 1717 and 1739. One wonders why Hopkinson and Collinson in 1732 sent to Philadelphia in the place of ordered titles which could not be secured so recondite a work as Switzer's DISSERTATION ON THE TRUE CYTHISUS OF THE ANCIENTS, unless it was because it happened to be bound with the same author's far more down-to-earth COMPENDIOUS METHOD for raising foreign vegetables like broccoli and celery in a kitchen garden. There was also one vade mecum or country gentleman and farmer's handbook to farming, cooking, home medicine, and so forth— THE COMPLETE FAMILY-PIECE.

The up-to-date character of the library's interests is best shown by the purchase of the works of two of the most important agricultural innovators of the day, Jethro Tull and William Ellis, almost as soon as their books appeared. Tull's HORSE-HOING HUSBANDRY, in which the use of the seed drill in combination with the horse hoe was first recommended, was by far the most influential contribution to better farming that had been written perhaps for centuries. The GENTLEMEN'S MAGAZINE stated what many must have felt, that Tull had "done more towards establishing a rational and practical method of husbandry than all the writers who have gone before him".[34] The new methods and theories were immediately picked up and elaborated on by Ellis, and the library bought two of his latest works, THE PRACTICAL FARMER and CHILTERN AND VALE-FARMING. It would have been difficult then to have selected better books in the field.

Connecting the areas of husbandry and medicine was a single veterinary text, FARRIERY IMPROVED, by Henry Bracken. Medical works formed the largest single specialized group within the general field of science. The only separate chemical work was almost within this field, for it was written by the great Leyden physician Boerhaave. Certainly, in this category the influence of the Philadelphia doctors Thomas Bond and Thomas Cadwalader, both early members of the library, was strongly felt. The former, just about the time the Library Company was organized, gave his first anatomical demonstrations to a group of local physicians "who had not been abroad". Drake's NEW SYSTEM OF ANATOMY became available on the library's shelves shortly thereafter. For the professionals, as well as the self-practitioners, Quincy's NEW MEDICINAL DICTIONARY and particularly his COMPLETE ENGLISH DISPENSATORY and Pomet's COMPLEAT HISTORY OF DRUGGS, with their wealth of prescriptions, were essential tools. That old faithful of English medicine, Thomas Sydenham, was represented by a collected edition of his works, and the newer school by Shaw's NEW PRACTICE OF PHYSICK and THE ART OF SURGERY by Daniel Turner, the recipient from Yale of the first medical degree—an honorary one—granted by an American college.

Old opinions on medicine were presented with the new in Allen's SYNOPSIS MEDICINAE, where they were collected and briefed under the heads of the various diseases. Recognition of the validity of some older theories was evidenced by the choice of MEDICINA STATICA, containing the aphorisms of Sanctorius—an early edition of which was received by gift—with the recent essays by Keill and Quincy. Another old favorite was Cornaro's SURE AND CERTAIN METHODS OF ATTAINING A LONG AND HEALTHFUL LIFE, a standard work on geriatrics, which was supplemented by the gift of Cheyne's ESSAY OF HEALTH AND LONG LIFE, which recommended temperance and vegetarianism. An indication of the desire to provide general texts rather than specialized ones is the fact that the only two works dealing with a single phase of medicine were the literary Dr. Arbuthnot's essays UPON AIR and UPON ALIMENT.

The theological works in the library can be skimmed over quickly, for they show a peripheral interest in the subject, more from a historical point of view than from a sectarian one. Bibles were books for the home, and not for lending, so it is not surprising that the three Bibles, all of antiquarian interest, among them a copy of the Great Bible of 1541, were gifts. The purchase of a verse translation of the Psalms by Blackmore was probably made for literary rather than liturgical reasons.

FRANKLIN AND HIS FRIENDS CHOOSE THEIR BOOKS

In spite of the Quaker predominance in Philadelphia – or possibly because individual Quakers owned books on their sect in their personal libraries[35] – the only works dealing with that group were the two-volume edition of the collected works of William Penn, which, of course, contained much of a political nature, Sewell's standard HISTORY OF THE QUAKERS in the edition a section of which was Franklin's first printing on his own, and the DISCOURSES of Logan's good friend and correspondent, Thomas Story. Such apparently indispensable sets as Fox's ACTS AND MONUMENTS, a gift from Robert Grace, and Burnet's HISTORY OF THE REFORMATION OF THE CHURCH OF ENGLAND gave the members as much coverage as they wanted for the history of the Anglican Church. And the works of Richard Hooker and Archbishop Tillotson, both considered excellent reading, provided them with representative theological thinking as background.

It was perhaps inevitable that the members of the Library Company, more freethinking than orthodox, should have chosen much of their little controversial theology on the subject of the argument between the proponents of natural and revealed religion. The DISCOURSE CONCERNING THE BEING AND ATTRIBUTES OF GOD by Samuel Clark, the translator of Newton's OPTICS and the founder of the "intellectual" school which deduced the moral law from logical necessity, found nothing in science to controvert religion, and Wollaston in his RELIGION OF NATURE DELINEATED strongly upheld that theory. The scientist Ray's WISDOM OF GOD, the demand for which had sent it into edition after edition, attempted to conciliate the two schools. And Bishop Berkeley's ALCIPHRON, written while he was in America, may be said, in view of his strong attack on freethinkers, to represent the old-fashioned school.

The Philadelphians were broad-minded, perhaps at an earlier period than a similar group in New England or the South would have been; their interest was intellectual and not blindly partisan, although they shared the general English suspicion of popery politically tied to Stuart tyranny. They did not hesitate to buy such varied works as two of the mystic William Law's most widely read treatises, Trapp's bitterly anti-Catholic PRESERVATIVE AGAINST POPERY, and Pascal's MYSTERY OF JESUITISM, the English translation of his famous LETTRES PROVINCIALES. To these were added standard histories of older forms of religion: Josephus, Prideaux, and Godwin for Judaism and the Jews, a HISTORY OF THE HEATHEN GODS for Greek and Roman mythology, Boulainvilliers for Mohammedanism, Cracanthorp's account of the old Greek Church, Platina's LIVES OF THE POPES (given by James Logan), two editions of Sarpi's history of the Council of Trent, criticizing papal power, and Limborch's HISTORY OF THE INQUISITION, condemning persecution. Without any attempt to secure all the voluminous tomes with which every theological student was expected to be familiar, the members were able to get a Protestant-slanted picture of what many different peoples at many different times had believed.

Less sectarian philosophy was more to their taste. Stanley's HISTORY OF PHILOSOPHY was their one-volume guide to the various classical schools. Xenophon's MEMORABLE THINGS OF SOCRATES, which so charmed the boy Franklin that he "dropt my abrupt contradiction and positive argumentation, and put on the humble inquirer and doubter",[36] Plato's WORKS, translated from the Dacier edition, an old edition of Plutarch's MORALS, "Englished" by Philemon Holland and donated by Breintnall in 1733, and the then fashionable MORALS of Epictetus, translated by Dean Stanhope, were their legacies from Greece. However, Rome's wisdom was considered plumbed with Cicero, whose DE FINIBUS, TUSCULANAE DISPUTATIONES, and DE NATURA DEORUM, all in translation, were the only works they owned of the later age.

In the more modern era lay two thirds of the library's strength, and, one would assume, most of the members' interest. With the exception of a handful of minor works and two books on logic – one by the Dutch philosopher Burgersdijck and the other by the Port-Royalist Nicole[37]–and two titles by Locke, all given by Franklin in 1733, all the other titles represented the readers' own choice. To balance the Port-Royalist, the members selected, perhaps because of Clarke's repeated high recommendations,[38] De Crousaz's NEW TREATISE OF THE ART OF THINKING. These were the times when logic, as a system of proper rules and directions for the conduct of understanding in its inquiries after truth, was hailed as the invention by which "have the Moderns been chiefly able to outstrip the Antients in Knowledge, so prodigiously as they have done".[39] Crousaz's system of logic and Locke's substance in his ESSAY UPON HUMAN UNDERSTANDING were paramount in the field. It is interesting to note that

the only editorial comment in the whole printed catalogue of
1741 follows the entry of the latter work – "Esteemed the best
Book of Logick in the World".

It was Locke who apparently dominated the speculative thinking of the Philadelphia group as he did that of all England in the
first half of the eighteenth century. Except for Pope and Abbé
Vertot, the library contained more titles by Locke than by any
other author. Besides the ESSAY, there were the massive three-
volume edition of his WORKS, A COLLECTION OF SEVERAL
PIECES, and TWO TREATISES ON GOVERNMENT. Locke's
economic and humanitarian interests and his liberal views, his
thoughts on education, toleration in a broad sense, the constitution of Carolina, currency reform, and state responsibility
for the poor, approached from the viewpoint of scientific psychology, were a major influence on the thinking and government of
the British colonies, and later of the independent nation which
evolved from them. In 1776, when Jefferson was first concerned
with what later became his famous Bill for Religious Freedom,
he copied out pages of notes from Locke and Shaftesbury to but-
tress his own thinking on the subject.[40]

A train of followers – the revolutionaries in America, the Encyclopedists in France, and the political economists in England –
borrowed from Locke, but others, stimulated by him, opposed
his ideas. The Library Company included some of their works
too. A COLLECTION OF PAPERS WHICH PASSED BETWEEN
THE LATE LEARNED MR. LEIBNITZ AND DR. CLARK was
one of the results of the intellectual ferment which Locke created; Leibnitz supported his theories, Clark opposed them. The
Earl of Shaftesbury, whose tutor Locke had been, later criticized
him, yet his work was strongly colored by the spirit of his preceptor. Shaftesbury's CHARACTERISTICS, as the first work to
elaborate on the doctrine of "moral sense", found a sympathetic
audience in the city whose founding and development had been a
groping attempt on the part of William Penn to build a community
which would function morally. That Shaftesbury was a deist would
not have bothered most of the Philadelphians, and they were more
in sympathy with his supporters than his attackers, Hobbes and
Mandeville. No work by either of these men was purchased before 1741, but Hutcheson's major contribution in defense of
Shaftesbury, AN ENQUIRY INTO THE ORIGINAL OF OUR IDEAS
OF BEAUTY AND VIRTUE, and his ESSAY ON THE CONDUCT

OF THE PASSIONS were secured. Hutcheson's phrase "the
greatest happiness of the greatest number" can almost be said
to have inspired the Declaration of Independence.

Perhaps it was symptomatic of the members' position in society—not yet in the higher ranks, but determined to rise—that
they chose a comparatively large number of books on behavior
and manners. Halifax's MISCELLANIES, with political as well
as personal commentary, La Bruyere's WORKS, and Nicole's
MORAL ESSAYS treated of the proper way of life on a high moral and philosophical level. THE MANNERS OF THE AGE, written "to expose the vicious and irregular Conduct of both Sexes",
was on a somewhat earthier plane, and THE LADIES LIBRARY
and THE GENTLEMAN'S LIBRARY contained specific suggestions for polite deportment.

However, there was as serious an interest in the government
of states as in that of individuals. There is no doubt that many
of the colonials expected something to develop in the American
governments closer to utopian ideals than had been possible in
England, and the two great English works, More's UTOPIA and
Harrington's OCEANA, were to be found in most of the early
libraries of this country. As Michael Kraus wrote, "Onto America was projected the blueprint of a society far removed from
the European reality."[41] More and Harrington were the chief
architects of the blueprint as far as the Philadelphians were
concerned, and the former was a favorite among the Quakers
on account of its advocacy of the principle of religious toleration.[42]

In contrast, they also bought the WORKS of the realist Ma-
chiavelli, and found a model for political reasoning in Acherley's
BRITANNIC CONSTITUTION, which set forth a justification of
the accession of William III and the Hanoverian succession. The
absolutism of the Stuarts was unpopular in America, and the
fact that Algernon Sidney's DISCOURSES ON GOVERNMENT
was as highly esteemed as it seems to have been was possibly
due as much to his position as one of the martyrs of Stuart tyranny as to the profound liberal views of his work. To a great
degree Sidney's advocacy of republicanism was reflected in the
thinking of the leaders of the Revolution, and his firm belief in
political freedom was widely quoted. Toward the end of his life
Benjamin Rush, writing to John Adams, recalled that he had
read "Sidney upon Government" when a young man, and cited
his opinion against slavery.[43] In much the same vein, although

more polemical in style, John Trenchard and Thomas Gordon's CATO'S LETTERS, another thoroughgoing Whig work which popularized the philosophy of representative government, was read eagerly throughout British America, and was ordered by the Library Company in 1732.

When it came to the wider plane of the principles of nations and international law, the members bought the two works of unchallenged primacy in the field, Grotius' THE RIGHTS OF WAR AND PEACE, both in English and in Latin, and Pufendorf's LAW OF NATURE AND NATIONS, through which, as Locke noted, they might be "instructed in the natural Rights of Men, and the Original and Foundations of Society, and the Duties resulting from thence".[44] They seemed less interested in the philosophy of English common law, which was a part of their daily lives, and they bought basic, general works which would serve as reference books rather than texts for reading: Jacob's NEW LAW DICTIONARY, Molloy's DE JURE MARITIMO & NAVALI, a practical handbook for the Philadelphia merchants "such as trade and have any Dealings at Sea", Godolphin's ORPHAN'S LEGACY, a guide to the intricacies of wills and estates, Wood's standard INSTITUTES OF THE LAWS OF ENGLAND, Duncomb's TRIAL PER PAIS on juries, A COMPLETE COLLECTION OF STATE TRIALS, and a few others.

More valuable in our eyes are two American legal items. The first was a manuscript collection of the three fundamental documents of Pennsylvania—Charles II's Charter to Penn, Penn's Charter of Liberties for Pennsylvania, and Penn's Charter of the City of Philadelphia. It is interesting to note that they were first gathered together in print by Franklin the year before the Library Company catalogue was printed. The second, a gift from Henry Pratt, was A BRIEF NARRATIVE OF THE CASE AND TRYAL OF JOHN PETER ZENGER. The account of the Zenger trial, at which the principle of freedom of the press was established for the American colonies, was the only work on the contemporary American scene in the library at this early date. In 1741 the Philadelphia lawyer Andrew Hamilton, who had conducted the brilliant and successful defense of Zenger, was admitted to membership in the Library Company.

The willingness of the members to buy books for study and serious reading did not exclude the purchase of books on the useful arts to meet more immediate needs. They were, after all, not scholars, but merely ambitious men who wanted to use their leisure to improve themselves. No more complete mirror of their philosophy could be found than Defoe's COMPLETE ENG-LISH TRADESMAN, a didactic book of advice which glorified the small tradesman's life and offered moral – yet very practical – guideposts to the way to wealth, which Franklin made his own when he wrote as the sage Poor Richard. Since the thrifty eight-eenth-century tradesman was a jack-of-all-trades in his shop or home, the members felt that Price's BRITISH CARPENTER and THE BUILDER'S DICTIONARY would be useful "do-it-your-self" books.

They matched this utilitarian concern with an interest in architecture as such, for Philadelphia was, as men like these succeeded in life, becoming a city of fine homes. They bought Palladio's ARCHITECTURE, the single work which had the great-est influence on English style during that period, and Campbell's VITRUVIUS BRITANNICUS, which also reflected the neoclassical Palladian tone of Christopher Wren's London. The Philadelphians did not, however, have a leisured gentleman's interest in art from a collector's point of view, and they added nothing in this field except a few books on classical antiquities, including Mont-faucon's seven-volume ANTIQUITY EXPLAINED. But again, they supplemented these few books on a down-to-earth level with Du-breuil's PRACTICE OF PERSPECTIVE, an introduction to draw-ing and draftsmanship. Closely allied and possibly bought at the request of the professional scriveners Breintnall and Brockden was Bickham's PENMANSHIP, the most popular of all the writ-ing books of the period when the round cursive English hand, used by men like Franklin and Washington and the model for Spencerian forms, was supplanting the earlier seventeenth-cen-tury script.

Three works on useful arts seem rather specialized for the group, but two of them were gifts, and the other may have been suggested by Franklin. This last was the typographically hand-some A GENERAL HISTORY OF PRINTING by Samuel Palmer, the London printer under whom Franklin worked in 1725. The others were Sutherland's SHIP-BUILDING UNVEILED, given by Godfrey whose interest in navigation made him famous, and Gau-ger's FIRES IMPROVED, given by Robert Grace. The latter dealt with the construction of fireplaces and chimneys, and it is significant that, when Franklin invented his improved Pennsyl-

vania stove, Grace manufactured the product.[45] One wonders if
this volume did not provide the two men with the information
necessary to design and build their stove.

One more basic discipline was covered by the collection – linguistics. English grammar was the members' primary concern,
as it had been that of young Franklin, who mentions having used
Greenwood's ENGLISH GRAMMAR to improve his mastery of the
language.[46] In addition to this widely used text, the Library Company secured Brightland's similar work. Their dictionary was
the best of the period, Bailey's UNIVERSAL ENGLISH DICTION-
ARY, upon which Dr. Johnson based his later massive work.
These were the essential tools for a thorough reading and writing knowledge of good English, an asset highly esteemed by the
ambitious tradesman.

There was probably no other library of the same size in the
colonies which, like the Library Company, included only one
Latin grammar. They did buy A RATIONAL GRAMMAR by the
dramatist James Shirley, modernized by Phillips, but showed
the same lack of interest in classical studies that had been shown
in their other choices by not bothering about anything more advanced than this beginner's text. Franklin said he was able to
pick up Latin through his study of the romance languages. He
noted that in 1733 he began studying languages with French,
which he easily mastered.[47] Perhaps, because he had already
bought himself French textbooks which he was willing to lend,
the Library Company at first did not buy any. However, they did
get Veneroni's ITALIAN MASTER and Altieri's Italian dictionary, together with Stevens' Spanish grammar and dictionary, so
that Franklin and others might progress to other tongues. Of
more utility to most of the members, living as they did in a heavily German-settled region, would have been Beiller's German
grammar and Ludwig's dictionary.

Finally, the collection contained a few works of general reference, the most significant of which was Clarke's ESSAY UPON
STUDY. It was a reflection of the universal acceptance of the
texts which Clarke recommended that so large a proportion of
those on his list of the best books in various fields of learning
were chosen by the members. It is not surprising to find that in
1751, when Franklin wrote his IDEA OF THE ENGLISH SCHOOL[48]
for the trustees of the Academy of Philadelphia, almost all the
books that he mentioned were among those praised by Clarke and

already owned by the Library Company. Two other purchase guides which the members had available, in addition to booksellers' trade catalogues, were the Historia Litteraria, a periodical list with critical comments of "the most Valuable Books Published in the Several Parts of Europe", and the London Magazine, which had only begun publication in April, 1732, with its essays, news, and valuable book reviews, both of which were subscribed to and received as issued.

Literally the weightiest set, and the most expensive purchase the members made, was Bayle's six-volume folio HISTORICAL AND CRITICAL DICTIONARY, the most scholarly encyclopedia of the age, which to the anger of some clerical critics was written from a tolerant, rational point of view, preparing the way for Diderot and the Encyclopedists. To complete its reference material, the library bought Chamber's UNIVERSAL DICTIONARY OF ARTS AND SCIENCES, a more practical omne gatherum, which remained a current authority until later in the century when Rees expanded Chamber's work into his once highly regarded CYCLO-PAEDIA.

Here then was the collection which the members of the Library Company gathered for their own use in the first ten years of their co-operative venture. While the number of books grew from 375 titles in 1741 to 2,033 in 1770, the general character of the collection remained as it had been. An interest in history remained predominant, but more and more contemporary American political pamphlets were purchased as they came out, reflecting the members' rise in status from onlookers to participants in the government of the province. In literature, the policy of buying the most popular current books continued, and Fielding, Richardson, Smollett, Gray, and Johnson made their due appearance in the library. In science, new books, including that of Franklin himself on electricity, were added to keep the Philadelphians abreast of new discoveries, men like Linnaeus, Musschenbroeck, Haller, and Pringle replacing their predecessors as authorities. However, as strictly scientific institutions like the Pennsylvania Hospital and the American Philosophical Society began to function and form their own libraries, the proportion of scientific books does not seem to have been necessary, and was not maintained. Yet, the three major, distinctive features of the earliest choice were constant: comparatively few theological works were added, almost no books in a language other than English were bought, and the radical, Whig tone of selection was continued.

As the years went by, other subscription libraries, modeled on the Library Company, were organized throughout the colonies. The same kind of clientele apparently demanded the same kind of books, and it is more than coincidence to find that existing printed lists of the other early libraries include a high proportion of the identical works which the Philadelphia library chose. The choice reflects the basic character of American colonial middle-class culture. As the 1789 cornerstone of the new Fifth Street building of the Library Company stated, that institution founded "by the Philadelphian Youth (Then chiefly Artificers) . . . which tho' small at first, is become highly valuable And extensively useful".

NOTES:

1 Francis R. Packard, CHARTER MEMBERS OF THE LIBRARY COMPANY (Philadelphia, 1942).

2 Hellmut Lehmann-Haupt, Ruth Shephard Granniss, and Lawrence C. Wroth, THE BOOK IN AMERICA (New York, 1939), 355-360.

3 Ibid., 297-304; Carl L. Cannon, AMERICAN BOOK COLLECTORS AND COLLECTING (New York, 1941), 1-37.

4 Louis B. Wright, THE FIRST GENTLEMEN OF VIRGINIA (San Marino, Calif., 1940), 126-127.

5 Lehmann-Haupt, Granniss, and Wroth, 355-358; Samuel Eliot Morison, THE PURITAN PRONAOS (New York, 1936), 141-142.

6 Ibid., 141.

7 George Maurice Abbott, A SHORT HISTORY OF THE LIBRARY COMPANY OF PHILADELPHIA (Philadelphia, 1913); Austin K. Gray, THE FIRST AMERICAN LIBRARY (Philadelphia, 1936).

8 Its place in Philadelphia life is evidenced by the fact that Franklin in his autobiography speaks of it as "the Philadelphia public library", and that other individuals referred to it variously as the "City Library" and the "Philadelphia Library".

9   Edwin Wolf 2nd, "The First Books and Printed Catalogues of the
    Library Company of Philadelphia", The Pennsylvania Magazine
    of History and Biography (PMHB), LXXVIII (1954), 45-55.

10 A CATALOGUE OF BOOKS BELONGING TO THE LIBRARY COM-
    PANY OF PHILADELPHIA (Philadelphia, 1741).

11 Manuscript Minute Book of the Library Company of Philadelphia
    (LCP), I, 43.

12 Ibid., 73.

13 Ibid., 6.

14 Dorothy F. Grimm, A HISTORY OF THE LIBRARY COMPANY
    OF PHILADELPHIA, 1731-1835 (unpublished dissertation, Uni-
    versity of Pennsylvania, 1955), 55.

15 Ordered by the Company, Nov. 13, 1734, and received from Eng-
    land, Apr. 18, 1735. Manuscript Minute Book, I, 46, 51.

16 John Locke, SOME THOUGHTS CONCERNING EDUCATION (Lon-
    don, 1699).

17 A detailed comparison of such catalogues as those of the New
    York Society Library, the Redwood Library of Newport, the Li-
    brary Company of Burlington, the Juliana Library of Lancaster,
    the Union Library Company of Hatborough and others with the
    early Harvard and Yale catalogues would make an interesting
    study. My observations are based upon a superficial reading of
    some of them.

18 In my article cited above, I made an erroneous count of 372.

19 Morison, 143, counts 2,183 theological titles out of a total of
    3,517 in the 1723 catalogue.

20 Charles R. Hildeburn, A CENTURY OF PRINTING: THE ISSUES
    OF THE PRESS IN PENNSYLVANIA, 1685-1784 (Philadelphia,
    1885), I, nos. 417-740.

21 Gabriel Bonnot de Mably, DE LA MANIERE D'ECRIRE L'HIS-
    TOIRE (Paris, 1783), 77. Mably praises all Vertot's writings
    highly, and, after citing his work on the Swedish revolution as a
    model to be followed, gives Voltaire's account of Charles XII as

a history not to be imitated. Ibid., 180. I am grateful to Professor Caroline Robbins of Bryn Mawr for having called my attention to Mably's praise, and for having most graciously read over the whole paper and made other suggestions which I have herein incorporated.

22 Gray, 25-26.

23 White Kennett, BIBLIOTHECAE AMERICANAE PRIMORDIA (London, 1713), vii.

24 Frederick B. Tolles, "A Literary Quaker: John Smith of Burlington and Philadelphia", PMHB, LXV (1941), 319.

25 In his "Observations relative to the Original Founders of the Academy in Philadelphia", written in June, 1789, in protest against the priority then being given to the classics, Franklin recalled, "As in the Scheme of the Library I had provided only for English Books, so in this new Scheme my Ideas went no farther than to procure the means of a Good English Education." Albert Henry Smyth, ed., THE WRITINGS OF BENJAMIN FRANKLIN (New York, 1905-1907), X, 9.

26 Wright, 135.

27 "I thought the writing excellent, and wished, if possible, to imitate it." Smyth, I, 241.

28 John Clarke, AN ESSAY UPON STUDY (London, 1737), 250-251.

29 Howard M. Jones, "The Importation of French Books in Philadelphia, 1750-1800", Modern Philology, XXXII (1934), 160.

30 It is of more than passing interest to note that the nineteen-year-old Franklin met Pemberton in London, and Pemberton promised to give the youth an opportunity of seeing Newton. Unfortunately, the opportunity never arose. Smyth, I, 278.

31 I. Bernard Cohen, BENJAMIN FRANKLIN'S EXPERIMENTS (Cambridge, Mass., 1941), 32-37.

32 Ibid., 169.

33 Smyth, III, 396.

34 G. E. Fussell, MORE OLD ENGLISH FARMING BOOKS FROM TULL TO THE BOARD OF AGRICULTURE (London, 1950), 5.

35 Tolles, 312, states that Smith's own library was "well stocked with the writings of Quaker preachers and controversialists".

36 Smyth, I, 244.

37 Pierre Nicole, LOGIC; OR, THE ART OF THINKING (London, 1717). This book, with Franklin's signature on the title page, is still in the Library Company, and may be the only book that Franklin owned in Boston which has survived. In his autobiography he mentions having read it when he was about sixteen years old. Smyth, I, 243.

38 Clarke, 143, 222.

39 Ibid., 142.

40 Julian P. Boyd, ed., THE PAPERS OF THOMAS JEFFERSON (Princeton, N.J., 1950), I, 544-550.

41 Michael Kraus, THE ATLANTIC CIVILIZATION: EIGHTEENTH CENTURY ORIGINS (Ithaca, N.Y., 1949), 216.

42 Tolles, 319.

43 Lyman H. Butterfield, ed., LETTERS OF BENJAMIN RUSH (Princeton, N.J., 1951), II, 997-998.

44 John Locke, SOME THOUGHTS CONCERNING EDUCATION, 330.

45 Smyth, I, 370.

46 Ibid., 243-244.

47 Ibid., 347.

48 Appended at the end of Richard Peters, A SERMON ON EDUCATION (Philadelphia, 1751).

THE COONSKIN LIBRARY

Vinnie J. Mayer

Vinnie J. Mayer read the essay here reprinted before the
American Library History Round Table during the Cleve-
land, Ohio, conference of the American Library Associa-
tion in 1950. At the time she was Cataloger, Ohio State
Archaeological and Historical Society Library, Columbus.
Mrs. Mayer died in 1953.

The Western Library Association, popularly known as the
Coonskin Library, may well be considered one of the finest examples of civic improvement – a "Madonna of the Trails" – of
things cultural. Its organization was not wholly spontaneous,
but very largely the natural outgrowth of contemporary group
enterprises. Cooperative effort was necessary for the erection
of homes, schools, churches, roads, and civil government.

Men who possessed titles to lands along Federal Creek and
its tributaries had long been waiting at Belpre and Marietta to
settle on their new home sites. Following the Treaty of Greene
Ville in 1795 when the Indians no longer had a legal right to Federal Creek lands, these Revolutionary War veterans moved their
families from New England across the mountains, down the rivers, and up the streams to what are now Ames, Dover, Bern,
Trimble, and York townships of Athens County, Ohio. Seldom
did one family make the journey alone, for there was comradeship, security, and spiritual courage in numbers. Heartache,
disappointment, sickness, and death were more easily overcome
when shared with others.

Most of the twenty-eight original landowners in Ames Township participated in the legendary barn-raisings, quilting bees,
etc., of the frontiersmen. Their school, organized in 1801, was
taught successively by Harvard graduates Moses Everett and
Charles Cutler. By sheltering this little school in a room of his
home, Ephraim Cutler unconsciously took one of the first firm
steps toward the establishment of Ohio's system of public schools.

Reprinted from Wilson Library Bulletin, 26:43-49, September, 1951,
by permission of the publisher.

A few months later this same little room housed one of Ohio's earliest public libraries.

Money or currency was very scarce in this little community which depended upon payment in kind to meet its own individual needs. Early records give underscored evidence of the struggle to raise the $7.50 per capita yearly assessment to pay the school-teacher. Even the twenty children, representing six families, were not unmindful of the importance of the little school. Their famous April 13, 1803 letter of teacher-appreciation was echoed one hundred and thirty-five years later when the state of Ohio paid tribute to this same family as it dedicated Cutler Hall at Ohio University; and re-echoed appreciation when this university rededicated Cutler Hall in 1947.

The crude pathways from house to house and from village to village sufficed to break individual isolation and facilitated the procurement of meagre necessities—salt, shoes, etc. Such roads were, however, wholly inadequate for the marketing of their sur-pluses. New markets were becoming available and the old ones were humming with activity, especially since the Mississippi River had been opened to Ohio River flatboats by the purchase of Louisiana Territory in 1803. The markets had to be reached! Products had to be sold or exchanged for many desirable items— window glass, cloth, shoes, saddles, tea, hinges, men's wear, locks, fishhooks, nails, indigo, soap, nutmeg, linen, lemons, and only through cooperative effort could the pathways be turned into roads. Since the territorial government imposed road-build-ing responsibilities on each male inhabitant upwards of fifteen years of age, it was necessary to have community planning and agreement. A supervisor had to be selected and the Court of Quarter Sessions of each county had to accept and approve each road petition (duly subscribed to by twelve or more petitioners). Each man had to specify how he would pay his road tax—either in money or in labor. Occasionally the road supervisor received extra labor; persons fined for intoxication were often required to serve out the fine in road work.

It is legendary that the plans for the Coonskin Library were made at a road meeting, the dates of which vary from 1801 to 1803. This variance may be due to the fact that it was just a road meeting, and only in later years when its significance be-came apparent did participants reminisce to compute the exact date. However, a present-day tour over the roads in Athens

County through Ames, Chauncey, Millfield, Across the Creek, New Concord, and Sugar Run impresses upon one the problems which must have confronted these men. These men, who had won the Revolution, lost their private fortunes, and now holding titles to vast virgin acres, had a right to the potential wealth stored in the new markets which were developing just over the hill and down the river a ways. A new life was being offered to those who would accept it. It is little wonder that their attention was turned to thoughts of items beyond the range of meager necessities. The little blacksmith shop probably receded far into the background as these men envisioned towns, churches, schools, libraries, mills, well stocked farms, and comfortable homes. In the midst of such planning they launched a new project—that of establishing a library.

It would be vastly interesting to find recorded (I have tried to find evidences of these) the number of meetings preliminary to the final drafting of the by-laws and regulations of the Western Library Association. Who were the committeemen assigned to draft the by-laws and articles of incorporation? When and where did they meet? Why did they choose to elect their first school master, Moses Everett, to write the document for them? Did all the fifty-odd charter members sign the document February 2, 1804 as did Josiah True when he went to a "libery meaten", or was it taken from home to home for signature?

Financing the projected library was the next problem. Characteristically, they turned to opportunities about them for the solution. Money, however earned, was very precious. A few could earn money by serving on the grand jury—twenty cents per day; as a justice of the peace some one could exact small fees; two dollars was paid for carrying the election returns to Marietta; chainmen for surveyors could earn seventy-five cents a day; making out tax duplicates for the year paid six dollars. Yet salt cost three dollars a bushel; shoes, six dollars; and tea was two dollars a pound. Interest, at least, had to be paid on land debts as most owners, whether in Marietta, Belpre, or Ames, had obtained their acreage on credit and were heavily in debt to some one of the original title holders—the Cutlers, Putnams, Browns, and others, and imprisonment for debt was a thing to be constantly feared and avoided.

Even though wolves, panthers, and bears menaced the farmer's livestock as well as the farmer himself, Josiah True saw

47

in them the opportunity for each one to obtain library funds. He proposed that within the year each interested member should bring in five or ten coonskins or turn in the cash equivalent earned, presumably, from the sale of animal scalps to the county or state, or of pelts to the agents of John Jacob Astor. Account books of the period record numerous sales of bear, deer, and otter skins; other records show that raccoon skins continued to bring high prices until about 1842 when the silk hat was preferred to the beaver hat or coonskin hat.

Between the date of this spring meeting of 1803 and February 2, 1804 there must have been a great deal of activity in the preparation for this project. One hunts eagerly for more diaries like that of Josiah True's which records, October 15, [1803] "kill three racoon, panther, 1 cat"; October 16, "kill she bare"; February 25, 1804, "went huntin' 12 bares"; March 15, "kill 3 racoon"; March 17, "kill panther"; March 18, "kill one she [bear] 3 cubs". What a sight it must have been when some fifty-four persons like George Ewing and Josiah True deposited their "accumulated wealth" of five or ten coonskins at the home of Christopher Herrold and there signed the "Laws and Regulations of the Western Library Association".

In the early spring of 1804, Samuel Benjamin Brown who was returning to Boston to move his family to Ames Township, transported the cargo back east—to the old home community. Here there were understanding relatives and friends who knew the needs of the western settlement and appreciated its cleanliness, its progressive spirit—for "its brick chimneys" offered sharp contrast to other Ohio River settlements. What a journey this must have been! Floating down rivers, swimming the streams, hiring horses or wagons, protecting the cargo, and being ever alert to possibilities of robbery must have been a real challenge. Arriving in Boston, he sold the furs to the agents of the John Jacob Astor Company. (I have often speculated on the Bostonians' reaction to Brown and his load of furs from the West.)

Rev. Manasseh Cutler, father of Ephraim Cutler, and Rev. Thaddeus M. Harris, first librarian of Harvard and teacher of Ames's first two schoolteachers, aided Samuel Brown in his selection of 51 book titles, August 8, 1804, for which he paid $68.45-1/2, less a discount of $7.72. The unique cargo was taken back to Ames presumably over the same route and by the same method, even though the trip west would be very trying. Rivers were low, sand bars were numerous, diseases prevalent, and settlements sparse. At length, at the home of Captain Benjamin Brown, in Ames, trials of the trip were quickly forgotten. On December 4, 1804, at the home of Silvanus Ames, the books were turned over to the library association, which was charged an additional amount of $12.12 for carriage and paper. In all, the first 51 books cost the association $73.50. The cost of each volume is carefully recorded in the minute book of the association and for a very practical reason. Each paid-up subscriber of the association could borrow books equivalent to two-thirds of the amount of his stock. The most expensive books were: Morse's GAZETEER, Morse's GEOGRAPHY, Adam's VIEW ON RELIGION, Goldsmith's ANIMATED NATURE, Winchester's LECTURES, and Ramsey's AMERICAN REVOLUTION; however, Winchester's LECTURES did not circulate very well. The first 51 books purchased included books on religion, travel, biography, and history. The short life span occasioned by the prevalence of diseases, danger, or disaster may have been an influential factor in the emphasis on topics religious. Scarcely a family had escaped the hand of death in its first few years of frontier life.

The present day cataloger will be interested in the simple cataloging methods used. As each volume was recorded in the minute book of the association, the same number was written on the first leaf of the book, together with name of the association and the date of its acquisition. Circulation records were equally simple. Following the patron's name, the librarian merely recorded the number of the volume borrowed. When the book was returned, a diagonal line through the book number, cancelled the patron's responsibility for the volume given to his care unless it was necessary to record on the opposite page, fines incurred by the borrower.

By December 17, 1804, when the association had accepted the first 51 volumes, twenty-four persons had paid for their shares ($2.50 per share). This is a fairly good proportion of the community's population of one hundred people. From time to time additional patrons—Samuel Beaumont, Joshua Wyatt, George Ewing, and Zebulon Griffin—purchased shares in the new enterprise. The price of a share was raised to $3.50 in February 1805, later to $4, and finally to $5 in January, 1842. Shares were exchanged, bought and sold, borrowed, given as wedding gifts, and willed to one's descendants. The minutes are mute on the sale of shares from September 16, 1806 until December 1821. Attention during this time is directed toward the election of officials, assessment of annual dues, collection of fines, acceptance of new readers (nonshareholders), and the audit of its reports. Minutes for the years, 1821-1824 are missing.

Prior to 1810 administration of the society was vested in the standing committee of three, elected annually, one of whom was the librarian. His duties were altered as the times changed. The first librarian was Ephraim Cutler, elected in February 1805; the last one was J. W. Glazier who was elected in 1858 and served until 1861. After 1810 the act of incorporation vested administrative powers in a board of directors, three in number; required that the elected librarian be bonded and specified his duties; and required a yearly audit of the books by a justice of the peace. Later the association created the office of treasurer. Occasionally the librarian received compensation for his duties but, apparently, the other officers were not paid.

The board of directors had to be present (absence from these meetings brought penalties) during the day the library was open to examine returned books for damages and to levy fines: 6 1/4 cents per share on each share if books were not returned before the time of the library meeting; in later years this was rescinded. For failure to return books before the end of the current library meeting a fifty-cent fine was levied on the borrower; this was reduced to 25 cents in 1832. Thumb marks, grease spots, burns, dog-eared pages, and torn places demanded fines ranging from 12 1/2 cents to 50 cents. Collection of fines presented problems. In 1804, if a member refused to pay his fines at the annual meeting his privileges as a member ceased until all arrearages were made up, which if not done within one year his share was to be forfeited for the good of the association. By 1813 he was expected to pay up in six months; in 1818 he was required to pay within thirty days; in 1819 he was given three months; and by 1832 all delinquent books were fined 25 cents per volume. Frequently, fines were cancelled, especially when assessed of widows, aged people, and penitent children.

Patronage, at first, was limited to shareholders, who ran the risk of being fined if they loaned a book to nonshareholders. Doubtless, the scarcity of money made this penalty a thing to be avoided. This attitude changed rapidly: a shareholder who would be responsible for the book could loan it to a nonshareholder. (What a volume the record of the reading done by non-shareholders would make!) The cost-value equation of loans gave way to a straight numerical system—two books per share each quarter; later three books per quarter, and finally the library was open the year round, but a patron could not draw more than three books at a time. Finally, reading privileges were extended to any nonshareholder who was willing to pay fifty cents per year. But why pay the fifty cents when one could borrow a volume from a shareholder free?

A chart of the book circulation revealed interesting data. In fact, two charts were made, one for the book circulation from 1825 to the division with Dover in 1830 (circulation records for the years 1805-1824 have not been located). The second chart covers the years 1830-1863. Summarized, the charts reveal definite reading trends: 1, a gradual turning from the stern and austere; 2, interest in national affairs; 3, reading for pleasure; 4, interest in science. Absorption in the RUSSIAN CAMPAIGN and Ramsey's AMERICAN REVOLUTION gave way to a quickened interest in HISTORY OF MEXICO between 1844 and 1850; A PLEA FOR AFRICA circulated rather freely from 1838 onward; Gillis' HISTORY OF GREECE, Frost's HISTORY OF THE UNITED STATES circulated more freely than Rollin's ANCIENT HISTORY or Gibbon's HISTORY OF ROME. The Waverley novels, especially IVANHOE, TALES OF MY LANDLORD, and KENIL-WORTH were widely read. DEERSLAYER, CAMILLA, BEGGAR GIRL, and EVELINA were not overlooked. Biographies of Washington, Cortez, Perry, and Nelson attracted considerable attention; while WORLD DISPLAYED, POLAR REGION, LIVING ANIMAL, and Johnson's CLIMATE constituted the bulk of their books dealing with science. However, with the exception of the Waverly novels, book circulation was meager from 1851 to 1861. Two examples typify the readers' appreciation of the little library. George Ewing found DON QUIXOTE a more rapid cure than medicine for a minor ailment; and in 1875 Mrs. J. K. Mower stated: "When the library was known to the writer, twenty-five years ago, it was not a large but very choice collection of the best English literature, comprising poetry, history, science, and fiction. A nearly complete catalog of it could doubtless be furnished by many, to whose young minds it was a 'nursing mother', and by whom it is held today in the same affectionate reverence as the now gray-haired and venerable 'boys and girls' for whose special benefit it was first instituted."

The acquisitions of the association did not keep pace with publications available, even though one of its members owned a bookstore! Neither did the library keep pace with the changing times, and the number of recorded patrons did not grow proportionately with the increased township population. Did the commercial – coal mining, brick, and tile manufacture – and agricultural developments detract from the interest in reading and thus lessen the demands on the library? Did the increased amount of currency permit the citizenry to purchase their own libraries? Did interest in the development of internal improvements allow the little community too little time to read? Were the officers so absorbed by affairs of the civic world that the library became a pleasant leisure-time hobby? Whatever the cause, waning interest is reflected in all records of the Western Library Association. The list of patrons and the reading habits of each reveal a similar trend.

Diversity of interests among the charter shareholders wrought changes in the destiny of the association. The original Ames settlement was, in 1805, a township of 360 square miles; by 1828 it had been reduced to 6 square miles as the boundaries of Morgan County claimed two townships, Hocking County claimed three more townships; Bern, Dover, Trimble, and York townships were established in Athens County. With the exception of Dover Township, shareholders residing in the outlying townships generally sold their stocks back to the association or to other residents of Ames.

Not so Dover shareholders, however; they wanted books not cash. Travel from the Sunday Creek settlement (Dover) to Federal Creek (Ames) was hazardous and difficult. Mud holes, impaired bridges, limited vehicles were constant obstacles to the Dover shareholders. As always, a practical solution was devised; one director was to be from Dover. He should be permitted to withdraw books equivalent to the stock owned by Dover shareholders. Josiah True was the first director to be chosen to represent Dover. From 1816 to 1829 several directors gave this service to the Dover readers. In that year they were authorized by the Western Library Association to form a separate library association. On April 30, 1830, Dover readers drew from its parent organization a proportionate share of the original assets and $7 in cash. From the minute book of the Western Library

Association we can extract book titles taken by the Dover Library Association which was incorporated December 21, 1830. Patrons whose names disappear from the Western Library Association at this time, may well have been the first readers of the Dover section.

The books of the Dover association were housed in the home of Josiah True and the homes of his descendants, Austin True and Sarah True Sprague, until 1906 when a portion of the books were given either to the Athens County Pioneer Association or directly to Ohio University. The original bookcase still remains in the home of a descendant of the True family—Dr. W. V. Sprague of Chauncey, Ohio. The rest of the Dover books were exhibited at the Philadelphia Centennial, 1876, by J. P. Weethee and Thomas Ewing, and then taken to the home of General Thomas Ewing. A fire destroyed a large number of these; the salvaged ones were kept in the home of Mary Ewing Martin until her entire library was sold in 1943.

The "Library Room", according to the minute book, was the meeting place for the annual, monthly, or quarterly sessions of the shareholders. Apparently the small library was moved yearly from home to home until about 1840. By that time the library had nearly 250 volumes and was kept in the Walker home—a most convenient place for all the patrons since the Walkers operated a mill, a grocery store, and a dock for river craft navigating the Hocking River. Apparently the books were kept in the Walker home until 1862 when the library was sold to A. W. Glazier, E. H. Brawley, and J. H. Glazier.

Possessions of the Western Library Association were meager enough. During its fifty-seven years of existence it owned two bookcases, and a total of 285 accessioned volumes (exclusive of the Dover holdings) although there is evidence that not all books were recorded. To the present writer the Coonskin Library includes all books acquired by the Western Library Association. Locally and "legendarily" only the first purchase of 51 books constitutes the "Original Coonskin Library". Ten of these first 51 books, together with the first case that housed them, are property of the Ohio State Museum. A concentrated effort has been made and is still being carried on to locate the remaining 41 books. Each claim is carefully checked. The museum also owns the second case, purchased in 1853, 215 books which were renumbered after the division with Dover and 140 of the purchases after 1830.

As stated previously, the library was sold in 1861 to J. H. Glazier, E. H. Brawley, and A. W. Glazier for $63, which was apportioned among its shareholders. These three men attempted to conduct a library from the home of E. H. Brawley, but abandoned the effort in 1862 when they sold the collection to William P. Cutler for $73.50. In 1876 it became the property of his daughter Sarah J. Cutler, who in 1917 loaned it to the Ohio State Archaeological and Historical Society and in 1933 willed it to that organization. The books in this collection are kept together as a unit, forming one link in the museum's permanent exhibit pertaining to Ohio history, and may be seen by all visitors.

Just when the term "coonskin" was applied to the library has not been ascertained. It was used by Ephraim Cutler as early as 1846 in a report which he gave before the Washington County School Association; the term also appears in Howe's HISTORICAL COLLECTIONS OF OHIO published in 1847. Interest in the little library has been intermittent through 150 years. S. P. Hildreth requested Ephraim Cutler to write an article on it for his MEMOIRS OF THE EARLY SETTLERS OF OHIO, published in 1854. It is given considerable space in Walker's HISTORY OF ATHENS COUNTY, 1869. It was featured at the Philadelphia Centennial in 1876. It was in 1875 the object of a three-cornered controversy, and in 1880 when the superintendent of education John Eaton appointed a committee to establish the date of the earliest library in Ohio. The committee reported Belpre, 1795, Cincinnati, 1802, and the Coonskin in 1804.

The Athens County Pioneer Association considered in 1882 the establishment of a monument to its memory, but decided only to write a MEMORIAL HISTORY OF THE "WESTERN LIBRARY ASSOCIATION," ORIGINATED IN THE NORTHWEST TERRITORY ANNO DOMINI, 1801. Biographies of Ephraim Cutler and of George Ewing treat it tenderly. The CENTENNIAL HISTORY OF OHIO (1888) mentions it. In 1898 it was accorded recognition in Ames Centennial edition of the Athens Messenger and Herald. In 1905 it was featured in the Farm and Fireside Magazine. The Ohio State Archaeological and Historical Society published in 1917 Sarah J. Cutler's article on the library. On October 21, 1929, the Nabby Lee Ames Chapter of the D. A. R. erected a monument at the site of the first "road-library" meeting in 1803. In 1932 articles appeared in various papers such as the

THE COONSKIN LIBRARY

Millersburgh, Ohio, Home County Farmer and Free Press, October 21; Cleveland Plain Dealer, October 17; Upper Sandusky Union, October 25; and in the first and third volumes of the OHIO REFERENCE LIBRARY (1937). The Flushing, Ohio, Home News Record carried a feature article, January 26,1950. Now, for the benefit of the Ohio State Museum, the citizens of Amesville and Dover (who have cooperated wholeheartedly), and the American Library Association, an effort has been started to collect the vast amount of material pertaining to the Coonskin Library. It is the desire of all, especially of the people of Ames and of Dover to have the library in its entirety preserved.

Perhaps the significance of the Western Library Association cannot be found in its acquisitions, for it certainly failed to avail itself of the new books and periodicals emerging during its life span—its proximity to Cincinnati, "the cultural center of the West", and to Ohio University may have negated the need to do much with the library; or perhaps in its isolation from these centers, it may have been content with what it had; or the very meeting which fostered its birth may have nurtured the cause of its destruction, for the establishment of good roads siphoned many of the ablest citizens away from its very doorsteps. Doubtless, the prominent members of the association—Ephraim Cutler, George Ewing, Thomas Ewing, Bishop Ames, Judge Walker, and many others—had built up their own private libraries to aid them in their professions of law, government, ministry, medicine, agriculture, commerce, bookselling, and teaching, thus leaving the little library to amble its way leisurely to its own termination. Whatever the cause, the two little communities on either side of the ridge were banded together by common interests during the life span of that first generation, and now the remains of those people lie side by side in two little almost forgotten cemeteries—Cutler cemetery near Amesville and New Concord cemetery not far from Chauncey.

The real importance of the Coonskin Library seems to lie in the fact that it is a concrete, tangible evidence of the spirit that has motivated the thoughts of leaders in the local and state government of Ohio to strive for the establishment of opportunities for its citizens. This library is also a tribute to that vast army of followers who support all good things.

Whether one views the project as one unit—the Western Library Association—or as three separate segments—the first purchase of 51 books, the Dover Library Association, and the Western Library Association—it is still a monument to community enterprise; a Madonna of the Trails of things cultural, and it will continue to furnish thoughts for the newspaper, club room, and schoolroom for the rest of time.

OPENING THE PEOPLE'S LIBRARY ON THE LORD'S DAY

Sidney Ditzion

Sidney Ditzion is a member of the history faculty of the City College of the City of New York. The essay here reprinted is a paper read before the American Library History Round Table at the Atlantic City conference of the American Library Association in 1948.

Unlike the professional practice of law and medicine in the United States, librarianship has been quick to respond to the social requirements of its clientele. If one were to seek the essential difference in orientation, he would probably find that the lack of an individual profit motif in library service explains its readiness to adjust to the needs of those it serves. Librarians have always been in group practice.

No sooner had the tax-supported public library begun to replace the old "social" fee-paying institution than practicing librarians began to revise their techniques to suit a new reader group – the entire citizenry of cities and towns. Catalogs were rearranged with a simple subject approach; bookshelves, heretofore jealously guarded by "keepers of books", were thrown open to the prying public; rules and regulations were relaxed; hours of opening were extended. All these adaptations took place quite as if they were ordained in the natural order of events.

When, however, it became clear that public libraries could not perform fully without opening on Sunday, the road ahead was far from smooth. Even here we must recognize that resistance to change was inherent not in the practice of librarianship but in the general social lag. The struggle over this particular adaptation (a struggle violent enough to split the whole number of Bostonians into two warring factions) was fought on secular as well as religious grounds. The cultural anthropologist, seeking to describe patterns of behavior on either side of such a schism, would have found, on the one hand, the conservatives in politics and religion advocating strict observance of the Sab-

Reprinted from School and Society, 70:49-53, July 23, 1949, by permission of the author and the publisher.

bath and, on the other, the progressives in politics and religion advocating loose construction of Sabbatarian laws. These two basic social outlooks always lurked behind the reasons or rationalizations presented in support of opposing points of view.

The idea of opening a library for public use on Sunday was not an invention of the tax-supported, free-public-library era nor was the question argued solely with reference to this type of library. The first decade of the free library's existence did, however, bring forth the earliest vigorous suggestions for using the Sunday library as a counteragent to social evils. These suggestions were largely à propos of the movement to lay low that public enemy number one of city life – drink!

Charles Loring Brace, a social worker and reformer, had tried to attract only the "dangerous classes" into his coffee-and-reading rooms in New York. A long editorial in the liberal New York Daily Tribune, April 18, 1855, proposed this kind of institution for the entire male working class.[1] According to this editorial it was pure naïveté to expect to keep men and women from drinking on Sundays without substituting some other form of recreation. The unpleasant home conditions "of the workingman in New York, especially of the foreigner", forced him to seek the rich and colorful surroundings which the saloon offered: Go to the cellars, damp and sloppy, or to the close dirty attics in Roosevelt and Cherry, and Oliver, and Orange Streets . . . and then go to the brilliant grogshop, with lights and warmth . . . and, above all, the all-forgetting glass, which changed for the moment Poverty to Wealth, and the stings and rubs, and rancor of the poor man's life to jollity and fun – and then wonder, if you can, that the Sunday grogshop is crowded, and that each pure Sabbath sun looks on crimes which make earth hideous.

The solution was obvious. It was to open cheerful rooms, provided with books and papers where men could "chat over a smoking cup of coffee or tea". During the week, so the prescription went, the available books could be informational and entertaining, but Sunday circulation had to take on a moral slant, "such as temperance or anti-gambling tales". Prospective librarians of these institutions were warned, however, not to make the emphasis on morality too strong in the beginning. Only after "drinkers and low people" had come to like the place could they be served with religious fare. The good to be derived from the type of library described by the Tribune was never demon-

strated. The idea attained realization only in the Brace libraries, which, as we know, were established only in the very worst
wards of New York City. The failure of the campaign is not at
all surprising when one considers how very tardily this city got
around to accepting the idea of even a weekday free library.

The question of Sunday opening for the tax-supported free library was first raised in Boston in 1859. On this occasion the
trustees unanimously voted down the proposed extension of hours
because, as the trustees claimed, besides being too costly, Sunday opening was unnecessary. The idea remained dormant until
the fall of 1864. This time the action was vigorously pushed in
the Board of Aldermen and concurred in by the Common Council in spite of a recommendation for postponement by the latter's
own public-library committee. A negative vote by the library
Board of Trustees was also disregarded.[2]

Mayor F. W. Lincoln, faced by the opposition of the trustees
and by pressure from large numbers of influential Bostonians,
found it expedient to veto the measure. His reasons (the reasons
of petitioners against the bill inasmuch as there were no counter-
petitions from the public at large) were presented in detail in
the veto message.[3]

The arguments which had been presented in behalf of Sunday
opening, said Mayor Lincoln, were not sufficiently compelling
to risk upsetting that class of citizens which had "been the most
liberal patrons and the best friends" of the library. If it were
argued that the library would attract non-church-goers on Sunday, one could point out that "unfortunately, the absentees from
public worship are not generally of that class who are much interested in their own intellectual and moral improvement". If,
however, this bit of logic would not hold water, then one could
demonstrate that the limited space accommodations of the library would be so overcrowded on Sunday as to defeat the objectives of those who sought that "quiet and repose which are so
essential to serious reading". Besides, it was a good thing to
enforce the observance of at least the Christian Sabbath, if only
to counteract "the tendency of the crowded population of a large
city to break away from those wholesome restraints which give
dignity and virtue to the community".

This explanation satisfied neither the people nor their representatives. The subject was raised repeatedly in ensuing years
only to meet with defeat. Only after persistent pressure, added

hearings in the Common Council, and a shift in the attitude of
the public press, did the city government and board of trustees
take simultaneous action to open the library on Sunday.[4]

As we view the Boston scene, we find little in the Sunday
opening literature (which included detailed public statements,
editorials, and articles) that went beyond restating the formula
of Sabbatarian adherence. This concern for the library workers
who would supposedly have to work seven days a week was a
transparent cavil. Likewise was the fear that this act would hurt
the laboring class, whom it was specifically intended to help, by
setting the precedent for a longer work week. The appeal to a
Massachusetts law which forbade all but work of charity on Sunday was a resort to friendly tradition in legal garb. One argument, which outdistanced the rest for ingenuity, was that the
city should not knowingly provide a place of holiday rendezvous,
"not always for innocent purposes", for the young men and wom-
en of Boston. Personal advertisements had already appeared
in the press arranging "dates" at the public library, "dates"
having purposes quite other than the use of the library's reading
facilities.

These secular arguments were marshaled to provide a last-
ditch defense for the much weakened Sabbatarian forces. At a
time when the pressing needs of hard-working urban populations
were making inroads upon religious tradition, every possible
breech was being blocked with utmost determination. In and of
itself, the opening of a library on Sunday might not be serious;
but who could tell but that it might be an entering wedge for a
Sunday theatre and other "improper" holy day amusements?
The very dignity and virtue of the community were being attacked.
The wishes of patrons and supporters of the free library were
being overruled. The desires of the deceased Edward Everett
and the opinion of the esteemed Edward Everett Hale were being
overridden. Virtually everybody important was against it.[5]

Friends of the Sunday library were not impressed by any of
these arguments. The mayor's veto message of 1865 was con-
demned as being "unworthy of an independent and intelligent magistrate;[6] it is barren of arguments, and notable only for subser-
viency to a phantastical dogmatism he must himself condemn
upon more careful consideration". Liberal churchmen joined
other public supporters of the movement in roundly lambasting
this antiquated notion of Sabbath observance. Not only did they

not see wherein the Bible or the state law placed an injunction
on public libraries, but they even welcomed such an extension
of service as an apt supplement to the work of churches and
schools.[7]

Besides, was it not a minority of the community which opposed opening on Sunday? Was not this minority composed of
orthodox ministers and their supporters? Had not these ministers always opposed public education? Why was it that they
would agree to opening religious reading rooms on the Sabbath?
And were not those self-righteous lay protectors of the public
morality the same people who owned memberships in the Athenaeum and other private reading clubs which were open on Sundays? The rich were members of these institutions and not a
word is said; the poor ask for a like privilege and a storm of
protest is raised. The majority of the people were working
people. Working people had time to use libraries only on Sunday.
By all the canons of democracy, the library must be kept open
on Sunday.[8]

The workingman himself, if we are to judge from representative statements in the labor press, had strong views on both
sides of the Sunday opening question. In its issue of June 5, 1865,
the Daily Evening Voice, published by the workingmen's assembly of the Boston area, declared for Sunday opening.[9] Its position was based largely on the Horatio Alger formulation of a
social mobility made possible by educational opportunity for poor
boys. Nathaniel Bowditch, Joshua Bates, and Theodore Parker,
outstanding prestige names in the poor-boy-who-achieved-fame
tradition, would have urged Sunday library facilities for those
now at the bottom of the ladder. Thus spoke the Evening Voice.

But the Workingmen's Advocate, representing labor's left
wing, took quite another position. It interpreted Sunday reading
as a capitalist plot to further improve the worker's industrial
skill by educating him on his day of rest. It was, therefore,
opposed.[10]

The strongest case for Sunday opening was that made from
the humanitarian point of view. In answer to the test question in
the state statute, "Is it, or is it not an act of charity?" the reply of the humanitarian was, "It is, definitely!"[11] The library
would keep the "baser classes" out of rum shops and would aid
the cause of morality generally by taking young men and women
from haunts of dissipation and vice. Those of ample means could

read at home, go to the Athenaeum, or take a ride out to the beach. The poor youths who lived in boarding-houses and had no friends or relatives to visit, could resort only to liquor establishments and houses of ill fame. Not everybody attended church on Sunday. Some provision had to be made for those who chose not to.[12]

The most complete statement on the affirmative side of the debate was made by Henry Ward Beecher, minister, lecturer, and editor, in a speech delivered at the request of Henry Demarest Lloyd and several hundred other members of the Mercantile Library in New York.[13] Notwithstanding the suggestion made by one of the Beecher's biographers that the speech was just another of Beecher's bids for public recognition, it must have been a sincere gesture since it risked – and reaped – a whirlwind of disapproval from the orthodox. Beecher was extremely careful not to raise any doubts as to his own strong belief in churchgoing. He pointed out that available church space could not hold the entire population. Beecher explained the meaning of the Sabbath as a day of physical rest and went on to show how badly the hard-worked, poorly housed residents of large cities needed this rest on the Sabbath. With conditions such as they were, one did not have to be explicit about where young people would wander in search of recreation and relaxation on the Lord's day.

Beecher's treatise was complete even to the point of taking into account a serious objection to asking library workers to man their posts on Sunday. This very plausible argument, which seemed incontrovertible to those who used it, did not hold water for long. Where there was a will, there was a way; and the supporters of Sunday opening knew many ways. A system of volunteers would do violence to no one's wishes to observe the Sabbath. Half-day work on Sunday would leave ample time for religious services. Special attendants could be hired for Sundays only. As to the law which would make library workers liable to punishment if they worked on Sundays – ridiculous! Non-Christians were available in sufficient numbers to do the work, and the law could not touch them!

Within the profession of public librarianship itself, opposition was pretty much confined to C. C. Jewett and his colleagues in Boston, and even this opposition wilted in the face of public fire. Jewett did not want his own staff to work on a seventh day and refused to hire inexperienced librarians for Sunday service. If extra pay were offered, jealousy and feelings of discrimination on the part of Sabbath observers would result. If Jewett had opposed Sunday opening only as a means of protecting the rights of his staff, no one could have blamed him. But so consistent and complete was the rationale of his opposition and so flavored with the emotion of religious objection, that he was accused of basing his point of view on his own predilections. Once it was intimated that his position as a churchwarden had much to do with his opposition. Another time someone at a Common Council hearing accused him of not wanting to travel in on Sundays from his home in Braintree.

Virtually no other prominent librarian in the national association spoke disapprovingly of Sunday opening, except with regard to the very special problem which existed in the one-librarian library. Green, Winsor, Poole, Brett, Cutler, and Cole among others made unqualifiedly favorable reports on the project.[14] W. E. A. Axon, one of the most vocal of British librarians at international professional conferences, spoke repeatedly in favor of Sunday opening.[15]

Melvil Dewey explained that he had begun his study of the question with a strong prejudice against it but had been forced in the intervening years to change his opinion. He, too, had a very special consideration in the back of his mind. Inasmuch as "this association has been singularly free from the stigma of being a trades union", he very much regretted the spirit which favored Sunday service with extra pay. Reconciling professional interest with missionary spirit, he prescribed an appeal to the public not to deprive librarians of their Sabbath, but to give added monetary support so that library managements could hire the necessary extra help.[16] Dewey's point of view, while here applied to a specific problem, actually summarized the working philosophy of the entire profession: the realization of self-interest through a show of democratic altruism.

DITZION

NOTES:

1 C. L. Brace, "The dangerous classes of New York and twenty years among them", N.Y., Wynkoop & Hallenbeck, 1872, p. 266-97, New York Daily Tribune, April 18, 1855, p. 4, col. 5-6.

2 "Report on the opening of the Public Library on Sundays", Boston, Mass., City Documents, 1864, no. 80.

3 "Objections of the Mayor to the opening of the Public Library on Sundays", Boston, Mass., City Documents, 1865, no. 49.

4 "Report upon opening the Reading Room of the Public Library on Sundays", Boston, Mass., City Documents, 1867, no. 75: "Mayor's [Wm. Gaxton] message, giving his reasons for not approving the order concerning the opening of the public library on Sunday", Boston, Mass., City Document, 1872, no. 69. Most of the newspaper material used in this treatment of the Sunday question is to be found in a clipping book kept by the Boston Public Library from 1865 to 1873. There are some hundred pages of newspaper clippings in this source which support statements made hereinafter. The author has in his possession a copy of the manuscript for this article in which specific newspaper citations appear in the footnotes to document specific ideas.

5 Edward Everett Hale to Charles C. Jewett, May 11, 1865 (Ms. in Boston Public Library); M. Field Fowler, "Protest or remonstrance of . . . against opening the doors of the Public Library, Boston, on the Lord's Day". Boston, Rockwell and Rollins, 1867; M. Field Fowler, "Essay on the Sunday library and horse car questions", Boston, Alfred Mudge and Son, 1872.

6 For text of veto message, see "Objections of the Mayor to the Opening of the Public Library on Sundays", Boston, Mass., City Docs., 1865, no. 44.

7 Charles K. Whipple, "The origin of our Sabbatical laws", The Radical, III (1867), pp. 110-116; Nathaniel C. Nash, "The Sunday law unconstitutional and unscriptural. An argument presented in Committee of the Whole in Massachusetts Legislature", Boston, Printed for the Author, 1868; "To the people of Boston: for whose use, benefit, and convenience the Public Library was founded", (signed) "Examiner". (Internal evidence connects the author of this broadside with the Parker Fraternity, publishers of The Radical); "The reasons why they keep the library locked

64

up on Sundays", Boston (1872?) p. 8; "Pious Misrepresentations" (Boston, 1872?); Unitarian Review, XXI (1884), pp. 265-67; Harper's Weekly, XXVI (1882), p. 66, col. 3.

8   Charles M. Ellis, (Council for the petitioners) "Argument for opening the reading room of the Public Library of the City of Boston on Sunday afternoons", Boston, A. Williams Co., 1867; "Reasons why they keep the library locked up on Sundays", op. cit., ("The official report of the proceedings of the Board of Aldermen tells us that these conspirators represent . . . four Baptist Churches, two Methodist Churches, four Presbyterian Churches, four Orthodox Congregational Churches"); Boston Public Library, Twenty-third Annual Report, 1875, p. 19.

9   See also resolution passed at the 4th annual convention of the New England Labor Reform League thanking the Boston City Government for opening the public library on Sunday, The Word, I (Apr. 1873), 2; and letter from Wm. B. Wright, ibid., p. 3.

10   Workingman's Advocate, May 8, 1869, p. 2, col. 4. Six days were enough "to satisfy the maw of capital . . . Far distant be the day when the customs of infidel France will be accepted as a model for either the American or British mechanic". The attitude of the workingmen changed considerably by the end of the century. As demonstrated by their activities in behalf of Sunday concerts in the Carnegie Library at Pittsburgh, they were willing and eager to use whatever cultural facilites were offered them on Sundays. (Pittsburgh Leader, Oct. 1, 1896; Pittsburgh Post, Nov. 26, 1896; National Labor Tribune, Dec. 10, 1896, p. 1.) One may also mention, in this connection, the resolution of the Central Labor Union of Fall River to ask the public library trustees of that town to keep the library open from noon until 7 P.M. on Sundays. (Massachusetts Labor Bureau, "Labor and industrial chronology of the Commonwealth of Massachusetts, 1899", Boston, Wright and Potter, 1901, p. 187. The success of this request was reflected in the Union's vote of thanks in the month following the making of the request.)

11   One exception was found in a temperance organ which applauded the New York Sabbath Committee's successes against Sunday libraries along with Sunday street processions, theaters, railroad travel, etc. "The Sabbath Question", National Temperance Advocate, VIII (1873), 138.

12   Manuscript notes (in Boston Public Library) on debates in the

Common Council, date uncertain; Boston, City Document 1867, no. 63, p. 4; Harper's Weekly, XIII (1869), p. 259, col. 3; The Express (Boston), Feb. 26, 1871; "On a Christian use of Sunday", circular, Feb. 10, 1872; Lawrence Mass. Public Library, Fifteenth Annual Report, 1886, p. 15; Allegheny Carnegie Free Library, Annual Report, 1891, p. 12.

13 Paxton, Hibben, "Henry Ward Beecher; An American portrait", N.Y., Geo. H. Doran, 1927, p. 281; Henry Ward Beecher, "Libraries and public reading rooms: Should they be opened on Sunday . . . April 22, 1872". N.Y., J. B. Ford and Co., 1872; also Christian Union, V (1872), pp. 379-81.

14 Library Journal II (1877), pp. 274-75; V (1880), pp. 265-66; X (1885), p. 405; XII (1887), p. 230; XIV (1889), pp. 176-90, conf. no. p. 279; XVII (1892), conf. no. 45-46; XVIII (1893), p. 431, conf. no. pp. 44-46; U.S. Commissioner of Education, Report, 1892-93, pp. 771-94, 941.

15 Library Journal III (1878), pp. 258-9; IV (1879), p. 420. Reuben Guild, representing the college field, was a lone voice when he spoke against Sunday work. His opposition was, more than anything else, a matter of academic strategy. He was interested in keeping the status of the college librarian on a par with that of his colleagues in the faculty.

16 Ibid., XIV (1889), conf. no. 280-81.

NORTHERN LIBRARIES AND THE CONFEDERACY, 1861-1865

George Winston Smith

George Winston Smith is Professor of History at the University of New Mexico in Albuquerque. The essay here reprinted is in part a paper read before the American Library History Round Table in 1955 during the Philadelphia conference of the American Library Association.

Even the casual observer of current modes in fashions, interior decoration, and cuisine can hardly fail to realize that World War II and the occupation of Japan have hastened acculturation of East and West. Sukiyaki dinners prepared with an hibachi, shoji screens, tatami matting, the Japanese "look" in furniture, scrolls, flower arrangements, and cocktail gowns, to say nothing of the loads of souvenirs which homecoming GI's, baseball players, and other visitors to the Orient are bringing home all would seem to indicate that the age-old curiosity for an erstwhile enemy's culture has not abated. So it was also during the War Between the States, when Adams Express and other transportation agencies were burdened with packages of mementoes headed northward. Even during the war many of these reached their final destination in Northern libraries.

The sea shells, minerals, and artifacts which had traditionally filled the exhibit cabinets of libraries in the North were joined there or superseded by the souvenirs from southern battlefields and communities. In the New York Mercantile Library there were on permanent exhibit military buttons and a part of a gunlock from Harpers Ferry arsenal, a banknote from Winchester (Virginia), various military passes, and even seaweed which had fouled the propellers of Northern monitors in Charleston harbor. Confederate envelopes, bonds, mercantile account books, and family Bibles began to appear in the acquisition lists of these libraries. From Clara Barton, then nursing the wounded, the American Antiquarian Society library received a grisly

Reprinted, with minor changes by the author, from The Virginia Librarian, 3:7-8, April, 1956, by permission of the author and the publisher.

reminder of the war's carnage in the form of shot and shell, and a "large torpedo found in Fort Wagner with a hand of a dead soldier attached to the lock".

Such interest in the Confederacy would seem to have indicated a curiosity such as that which William Howard Russell described early in the war when he saw crowds of New Yorkers pausing to gaze at a bloody cap of Confederate origin which was on display in a store window. Even less inspiring was a type of collecting which was undertaken to justify prevailing northern propaganda stereotypes. As an illustration there was the muster and pay-roll of a Confederate company which a Massachusetts captain of volunteers forwarded to a northern library, and which the librarian thought was significant because nearly every member of "the rebel company" had made his mark, "instead of signing his name for the receipt of pay." It was equally significant, however, that much more of the collecting activities were due to Northern interest in the Confederacy, and especially to an awareness of the value which the "fugitive publications" of that era would possess in the future.

Accounts of travel in the Confederacy by European visitors, such as Fremantle's THREE MONTHS IN THE SOUTHERN STATES and the descriptions of Northern observers in the South, for example, Hepworth's WHIP, HOE AND SWORD, OR THE GULF DEPARTMENT IN 1863 could be found on the shelves of most Northern libraries. Moreover, in spite of the prevailing hostility toward the South, Edward A. Pollard's pro-southern THE FIRST YEAR OF THE WAR and his THE SECOND YEAR OF THE WAR were acquisitioned by some libraries, including the new Detroit Public Library. The Providence Athenaeum did not hesitate to announce, in 1863, the addition to its collection of Dr. John H. Van Evrie's NEGROES AND "NEGRO SLAVERY:" THE FIRST AN INFERIOR RACE, THE LATTER ITS NORMAL CONDITION.

Although Southern newspapers disappeared from the reading rooms of Northern libraries early in the war, representative publications of the Northern press and periodicals, both domestic and foreign, which criticized the Lincoln administration and even expressed sympathy for the Southern people were not purged from the lists. Pickering Dodge, who was "connected by marriage with ardent secessionists", resided in Baltimore the first winter of the war, and compiled a large clipping collection from newspapers, many of them Southern, for presentation to the

American Antiquarian Society library, which also acquired
scattered issues of Texas and Louisiana newspapers (the latter
"printed in that State on the blank side of gorgeously colored
and gilded housepaper") presented by a federal soldier who was
wounded at Port Hudson. Moreover, a former employee of the
American Antiquarian Society, Charles Goodwin, sent to the library from the South "various books and articles taken from the
enemy, and papers illustrative of affairs in the rebel States . . . ."
From Captain Charles G. Thornton, who was serving in the Army
of the Mississippi, the same library acquired the provisional
and permanent constitutions of the Confederate States of America,
bearing Richmond imprints of 1861, and the Proceedings of the
Louisiana secession convention.

John Langdon Sibley, the librarian of Harvard College, also
was eager to acquire Southern accessions. Already proud of his
reputation as a "sturdy beggar", Sibley sounded his first appeal
when the war was but a few months old, in his annual report of
July 12, 1861. He then wrote:

> . . . One of the greatest favors to the future historian
> and philosopher would be to collect all the books, pamph-
> lets, maps, files, newspapers, engravings, photographs,
> caricatures, ephemeral publications of every kind, even
> to printed notices, circulars, handbills, posters, letter
> envelopes, and place them beyond the reach of destruction,
> that as a collection they may reflect the sentiments and
> feelings, which otherwise will in a great measure pass
> into oblivion with the occasions which gave them birth. If
> I could, I would appeal to every inhabitant of the continent
> to send me everything which could be obtained in order
> that every phase of mind, in every section of the country,
> North, South, East, West, for the Union and against the
> Union, for secession and against secession, might be
> represented on our shelves, in all the variety of reason-
> ing and imagination, virtue and vice, justice and injustice,
> fiction and fact, freedom and oppression, kindness and
> cruelty, truth and caricature, that can be found. I would
> say, send me collections, if possible; but, if not, send to
> me a single pamphlet, book, or picture, if you have one
> to spare.

Although his report, published in the annual report of the Harvard overseers, had a limited circulation, it was reprinted in a Boston newspaper, and Sibley was able to enlist the services of still more widely distributed publicists' columns. George William Curtis, for example, announced in his Lounger column of Harper's Weekly that the Harvard librarian was inviting the contribution to his library of "every published scrap upon either side relating to the struggle".

Tangible results of such appeals were soon to be found in the Harvard accession lists, as alumni and friends of the college sent in a variety of Southern items. These, to mention only a few, included books, pamphlets, and newspapers presented by the indefatigable friend of libraries in the Boston vicinity, Samuel Abbott Green, who was then a surgeon with the 24th Massachusetts Volunteers. Charles O. Boutelle of the United States Coast Survey, gave the Harvard college library a copy of the first printed edition of the South Carolina secession ordinance. In addition there were several publications procured by Charles Henry Davis, fleet captain of the South Atlantic Blockading Squadron, and "curiosities, pamphlets, and books from Port Royal", collected by Stephen Minot Weld. Among the latter was the official account of the Denmark Vesey uprising, written by the magistrates of the court, Lionel H. Kennedy and Thomas Parker, whose rare pamphlet (AN OFFICIAL REPORT OF THE TRIALS OF SUNDRY NEGROES CHARGED WITH AN ATTEMPT TO RAISE AN INSURRECTION IN THE STATE OF SOUTH CAROLINA, Charleston, 1822) became the principal source for later historical accounts of this slave revolt.

The manner in which these benefactors of Harvard College library acquired their gifts was not indicated in the Harvard college librarian's acknowledgment of their acceptance. At Beaufort, South Carolina, however, there was considerable pillaging of private dwellings, including planters' libraries, at the time of the federal occupation, and the Beaufort Public Library likewise did not enjoy immunity until federal officers ordered it to be protected and boxed for shipment to the North. When this collection arrived in New York City the federal government, acting through customs officials, ordered an auction sale catalogue to be printed (. . . GOVERNMENT SALE. CATALOGUE OF AN IMMENSE COLLECTION OF LIBRARY BOOKS IN ALL DEPARTMENTS OF LITERATURE, ARTS AND SCIENCES . . . TO BE SOLD AT

AUCTION BY ORDER AND UNDER DIRECTION OF HIRAM BAR-
NEY, ESQ., COLLECTOR OF THE PORT OF N.Y., ON MON-
DAY EVENING, NOV. 17TH, 1862, AND THE SUCCEEDING
EVENINGS OF THE WEEK, BY BANGS, MERWIN & CO. . . .
[New York], C. C. Shelley, Printer [1862], 95 pp.) Before the
sale date, however, the Beaufort library had become a cause
celebre among such northern scholars as E. A. Duyckinck, Francis Lieber and others, who urged the Treasury Department to
cancel the sale and prevent the library's dispersion.

By 1864 there were a sufficient number of pamphlets and
other Confederate imprints appearing in the North or in Europe
to permit aggressive librarians, such as Charles Coffin Jewett
of the Boston Public Library, to make, compared to earlier
years, relatively large purchases. Most prominent among these
far-sighted collectors was William Frederick Poole, the great
librarian of the Boston Athenaeum. Poole, as an overseer of
Harvard University at the time when Sibley's call for acquisitions
had gone out in 1861, had been in a position to observe the exe-
cution of Sibley's policy. In the last months of the war he was
equally aware that many of the "fugitive publications" of the Confederacy were not only unavailable but even unidentified in the
North. When, for example, James Kelly brought out THE AMER-
ICAN CATALOGUE OF BOOKS . . . PUBLISHED IN THE UNITED
STATES FROM JAN. 1861 TO JAN. 1866, he thoughtfully included as an appendix "A List of Books Published in the Southern
States During the War". This list, however, contained a mere
forty-two titles. The "peculiar historical interest" of the Confederate publications no doubt was more significant to Poole because of the possibility that they might be lost, destroyed, or
exploited for private gain, but it was the bibliophile in Poole
which was uppermost at the time. The report of the Boston Athenaeum's library committee (probably written by Poole himself)
revealed this motivation when it declared:

> A Poor Richard's Almanac of 1752 is priced in an
> English sale catalogue at five times its weight in gold;
> and one hundred years hence, a rebel almanac, or a
> dingy file of Southern newspapers, may, perhaps, reach
> a corresponding value.

The war had no sooner ended than Poole began to redouble

his efforts to procure Southern publications. Most of the 522
pamphlets purchased by the Boston Athenaeum in 1865 were published in the South during the war years. In addition, Francis
Parkman, the historian, and his friend Dr. Algernon Coolidge
were provided with funds by the Athenaeum when they made a
post-bellum tour of Virginia battlefields. In spite of the fact
that Parkman returned to the North sooner than he had planned
because of ill health, he was able to make "valuable purchases"
for the Athenaeum in Virginia. Among the Boston Athenaeum's
Southern accessions of 1865 were files of the Richmond Examiner
(1861-1865), the Richmond Enquirer, the Richmond Whig, the
Richmond Sentinel, the Augusta (Georgia) Sentinel, the Mobile
Advertiser, and some twenty-five other Southern newspapers.
Poole also obtained holdings of such Confederate periodicals as
the Southern Punch, the Southern Illustrated News, and the Southern Literary Messenger. Beyond these there were accessions of
Southern school books, military manuals, almanacs, railway
guides, novels, manuscripts, and government documents. The
Boston Athenaeum's Civil War library was perhaps of greatest
importance to historical scholars in the decades which immediately followed the war. Ainsworth Spofford, in 1869, declared
that this "collection of books, pamphlets, and newspapers relating to the recent Civil War" was "among the completest known".
Even after the appearance of THE WAR OF THE REBELLION:
THE OFFICIAL RECORDS OF THE UNION AND CONFEDERATE
ARMIES, James Ford Rhodes (in 1917) praised the Athenaeum's
Civil War section for its extraordinary variety, and its latest
catalogue continues to support this opinion.

Whether motivated by avarice or malice, or by the more
laudable motives of the bibliophile or historian, the Civil War
collectors and librarians had, probably without realizing it, begun to travel along "the road to reunion". For although the Southern materials which they gathered together have upon occasion
been subjected to misuse and misinterpretation, they nevertheless have provided the basis for the more accurate understanding
of the true nature of the Confederacy which has begun to emerge
through the painstaking research of scholars in later years.

SOUTHERN UNIVERSITY LIBRARIES DURING THE CIVIL WAR

Benjamin Edward Powell

Benjamin Edward Powell—a former President of the Amer-
ican Library Association—is Librarian of Duke University,
Durham, North Carolina. The essay here reprinted is a
paper read before the American Library History Round
Table during the 1956 conference of the American Library
Association in Miami Beach, Florida.

As the American Library Association comes again to the
South—to the southern extremity of the Old South—we are within
a decade of the centennial of that Irrepressible Conflict. It seems
appropriate, therefore, that someone from the South say something nice about our colleagues and guests from the North. We
shall not be ridiculous and tell you that your forebears are for-
given for the havoc wrought down this way in 1864 and 1865, but
a friendly gesture is permitted. So, I shall give this paper the
subtitle: "Not All Yankee Soldiers Were Scoundrels". If you
think I am being disrespectful of the dead and the aged, just remember that it hasn't been a hundred years yet. Give us a full
century, and maybe another, and the title might be changed to
read "Southern University Libraries During the Civil War; or,
How They and Other Cultural Resources in the South Were Protected by the United States Troops".

But before I become too sentimental, let me explain that my
interest in this particular aspect of the Civil War was stimulated
by an exploration made into the archives of eight southern universities several years ago. For fifty years after Appomattox,
reference to the occupation and plunder by northern forces appeared frequently in these archives. The inference might be
drawn that southern institutions and their libraries suffered ter-
rific damage, in addition to the debilitating effect the presence
of these forces had upon the South generally. The president of
the University of Alabama, to cite one example, in reporting to
his trustees in 1911, said:

Reprinted from Wilson Library Bulletin, 31:250-254+, November,
1956, by permission of the author and the publisher.

> It should be kept in mind that our library was burned in 1865 and as a result the collection of books is far below the average of those of other institutions of like age and rank.

Other references of a similar nature appeared to warrant an examination of the university book collections and their treatment during the war – were they burned, carted off to Yankee libraries, destroyed through neglect, or did they survive to form the nucleii upon which our present collections have been built?

That the Civil War and its aftermath affected the development of education institutions and libraries in the South should be obvious to everyone at all familiar with history. The book resources of the region were not extensive in 1861 but some excellent foundations had been laid and some momentum generated. But that momentum was lost and not regained for thirty years. From 1890 to 1920 life was being breathed again into many of these institutions and ground was being laid for their transformation from colleges into universities, with the necessary professional schools, research laboratories, and libraries. But progress was slow. The southern states had been laid waste in the 1860's by military operations. Property values had been reduced by two billion dollars, population by one-fourth, and livestock by two-thirds; trade had been disrupted and government grossly mismanaged. Moreover, debts ranging as high as fifty million dollars cost some of the states most of their income for several decades. The region was impoverished.

For purposes of comparison I examined the growth records of five middlewest and western libraries which were established in the middle years of the nineteenth century: (Michigan, 1837; Wisconsin, 1848; Minnesota, 1851; California, 1858; Illinois, 1867) and found that in 1860 each of our southern institutions contained an average of twice as many books as held by the western libraries. By 1880 the western libraries were ahead; they were three times larger in 1900; and by 1920 eight times the size of our southern university libraries. In 1880 the western institutions were spending four times as much for books as the southern libraries and in 1920 eight times as much. Their total university expenditures were ten times greater than in southern universities in 1920. But for much of this period each southern university was spending a larger percentage of its total income on libraries than its western neighbors. Apologies for the inadequacy of our libraries should not have been necessary, therefore, before 1900. Reasons were plentiful and obvious. But how many were obliged to build "from the ground" after the war.

In 1860 all of the states included in this report (Alabama, Georgia, Louisiana, Mississippi, North Carolina, South Carolina, Tennessee, and Virginia) had state-supported institutions of higher learning, at least in theory. The youngest, the Louisiana Seminary of Learning and Military Academy, later to become Louisiana State University, was only one year old when Sumter was fired upon. Its president was about the last man you would expect to find in that post – William Tecumseh Sherman, who drew much attention to himself before the war was ended. Georgia was the first state to receive a charter for a university (1785); its neighbor, the University of North Carolina (chartered in 1789) received its first students in 1795, six years before Georgia. But only at South Carolina (1805) and Virginia (1825) did libraries flourish from the beginning. Both institutions had first-rate libraries by 1860, and South Carolina in 1840 had become the first state university to construct a building exclusively for library purposes. In the eight institutions, however, there were only about 88,000 volumes, and two-thirds of them were at Virginia and South Carolina.

The president of the University of Alabama had reason to complain. Most of the university's buildings were destroyed on April 4, 1865. On March 20th General J. H. Wilson instructed General McCook to:

> detach one brigade of your division with orders to pro-
> ceed rapidly, by the most direct route, to Tuscaloosa
> to destroy the bridge, factories, mills, University
> (Military School), and whatever else may be of bene-
> fit to the Rebel Cause.

General John C. Croxton was chosen to carry out the mission, and that he did. His official report said, in part, about his activities in Tuscaloosa:

> On April 4th destroyed the foundry, the factory, two
> niter works, the Military University, a quantity of stores,
> and supplied the command with all the rations we could carry.

It is reported that the commanding officer allowed one book to be removed from the library of between 8,000 and 10,000 volumes before the torch was set. He, or the librarian, according to the story, brought out a copy of the Koran. Since the present collection does contain some books acquired before the war, it is apparent that those out on loan were restored to the library when it was rebuilt. When the university reopened in 1869 the library contained about 1,800 volumes, many of which came as gifts.

The Louisiana Seminary's library of 2,000 volumes, which Sherman had selected, was dispersed and lost at the hands of the Yankees. The man who did much to restore it after the war was the institution's first president. As a matter of fact, Sherman made inquiries about the institution throughout the war and was solicitous of its welfare.

Federal troops occupied the Louisiana buildings briefly in 1863, but inflicted little damage. The Confederate soldiers who followed were less careful tenants, though the small library was still intact when the Federal forces returned in 1864 under the command of General T. K. Smith. Major W. C. B. Gillespie, of Missouri, is one of the principal authorities for the story of what happened to the books and scientific apparatus. General Smith first visited the campus, then ordered Gillespie to take a wagon with a detail of ten men and bring out the instruments and the most valuable books. Major Gillespie had no stomach for such business, but brought in a wagonload. The next day he told his ranking officer he didn't like what was being done and asked the general to send someone else.

Such an attitude was not uncommon among the Federal officers and troops. Major James A. Connolly expressed himself similarly as he watched Sherman's men carry off the books of the state library at Milledgeville, Georgia: "I'd feel ashamed of myself every time I saw one of them in my bookcase at home." He admitted that he did not mind stealing horses or mules, but theft or destruction of libraries sickened him. He said:

> Leave them here to enlarge and increase for the benefit of the loyal generations that are to people this country long after we shall have fought our last battle and gone into our eternal camp. Sherman will someday regret that he permitted this library to be destroyed.

In fairness to the general, one must admit that much property was destroyed without his permission. He was ruthless in his retaliation when hostility was encountered where peaceful and orderly occupation had been assured, but he was generally partial to books. He is reported to have assured South Carolinians he would protect their books because South Carolinians needed them, and implied that if more had been available down there and more had been read, war would have been averted.

Many of the Louisiana books were reported to have been stored in Memphis where they were burned in a warehouse fire late in the war. Gillespie claimed that Smith took what he wanted and sent the remainder to Memphis. We know that about fifty years after the war, the son of General Smith wrote to Dr. Boyd, then president of Louisiana State University, as follows:

> In 1864, when Alexandria was captured by Union troops, my father was in command and he rescued from destruction certain papers belonging to the university which have been preserved and are in my possession. As I believe they will be of special interest as relics, if for no other purpose, I shall send them today by express.

If I remember correctly, these were manuscript records which may be seen today in the LSU archives. All of the books were lost, and the Yankees must bear the onus, regardless of their expressed reasons for moving them.

Only two university libraries, those of Alabama and Louisiana, were actually destroyed or completely dispersed during the war. Their total holdings were fewer than 10,000 volumes.

What of the others? Every university except Virginia was closed at some time during the war and reconstruction: Alabama from the fire in April 1865 to April 1869; Georgia from October 1863 to January 1866; LSU from June 1861 to April 1862 and from April 1863 to October 1865; and Mississippi from April 1861 to April 1865. The University of North Carolina remained open throughout the war but was closed for a brief period in 1868 and from December 1870 to September 1875; South Carolina from June 1862 to January 1866 and again in the late 1870's. Classes were suspended at Tennessee from 1862 to 1866.

Georgia had a library of about 8,000 volumes in 1863 when the university was closed and most of the buildings converted

into hospitals for Confederate troops. It was housed in a new
building constructed in 1861 as a combination library, museum,
and lecture hall. The library occupied the second floor, and reports from the campus in 1863 described the books as in excellent shape: "No mildew on them, no insects in them—the result
of perfect ventilation."

The books were made available to citizens of the town and to
"refugees from their homes", and were fairly heavily used during the war. The chancellor spent six to eight hours daily in the
library for a year or so during the war, giving service to readers. The collection was intact when classes were resumed in
1866.

The University of Mississippi was only thirteen years old
when the war came. The university and all of its equipment came
through the four year conflict without incident. The book collection, then in the stately old Lyceum building, suffered more from
the operations of dirt daubers than from the Union forces; and
there were Union forces all over the town in December 1862
when Grant was making Oxford, the seat of the university, his
headquarters. He had halted there while the railroad from the
Tallahatchie River northward was being repaired. Relations
with the townspeople were friendly. At least two reasons why
no damage was suffered by the university were advanced: that
some of Grant's Illinois friends persuaded him to spare the university; and that Professor F. A. P. Barnard, one time professor at Alabama, and later president of Columbia University, and
other members who had gone back to the north, had influence
and used it to protect the institution. Grant's men were well
disciplined, and did not depend upon the citizens for food until
Van Dorn captured the Federal supply base a few miles away.
Then they foraged over a wide area of the state, but always in
a more businesslike way and with more dignity than one usually
associates with stealing.

When the University of North Carolina was reopened in 1875,
one of the blackboards of a recitation room still carried an observation made back on December 1, 1870, most likely by an
anti-state-administration student, "This old university has bust-
ed and gone to hell today."

UNC was able to continue classes throughout the war, but the
Republicans, then in power in the state, were more than it could
stand. During the five years the campus was deserted everything

deteriorated, including the books, but the university's collection and those of the two society libraries were still on the shelves when classes were resumed and were in fair condition.

Just before Sherman and Johnson met for surrender terms on the outskirts of Durham, North Carolina in April 1865, four thousand Michigan cavalrymen occupied Chapel Hill. As a precautionary measure, the books had been moved from Smith Hall to Old East, and there they remained until after the war. Relatively inaccessible, they were not damaged by the troops. As a matter of fact, the entire damage suffered by the village at the hands of the invaders was estimated at no more than $100. The general in command of the cavalry was accorded much hospitality in Chapel Hill; and particularly at President Swain's house, whose daughter he courted and married before the end of the year. The library building suffered a more ignominious fate than any other building in the town. Chancellor House, the harmonica-playing head of the institution in Chapel Hill, says it became a horse stable. Michigan horses were quartered on its ground floor. While this misuse of the university's facilities was deplored by the community and state, it turned out happily for all, says Mr. House, "because since the war Michigan horses have been noted for their intelligence and University of North Carolina students for their horse sense".

The controversy about Sherman will remain lively as long as the Civil War is studied. That he was an enigma is perhaps one of the most charitable appraisals ever made of him south of the Mason-Dixon line. He hated war, was reluctant to get into it, was sentimental about his school in Louisiana — yet waged relentless and devastating war upon the South. And not all of his northern colleagues understood or appreciated him any more than did his southern foes.

On that devastating "march" Sherman's men were ordered to restrict foraging to parties under commissioned officers, but to forage as liberally as needs demanded. To corps commanders alone was entrusted the authority to destroy mills, cotton gins, etc.; and for them this general principle was to be followed: "Where hostility is encountered, retaliate according to the measure of such hostility."

It is said that Sherman's men were impatient to get to South Carolina, the State they regarded as most responsible for the war, and that dire threats were made as they moved northward.

Sherman's General Order Number 26 should have prevented the Columbia holocaust. It read:

> General Howard will . . . occupy Columbia, destroy the public buildings, railroad property, manufacturing and machine shops; but will spare libraries, asylums, and private dwellings.

What actually happened in Columbia will never be known, but soon after the Federal troops occupied the town on February 17, 1865, fire broke out and before it was brought under control 486 buildings, most of the town of eight thousand people, had been destroyed. Despite Sherman's order and his assurance that the university would be spared, the fire came close and destruction of the buildings appeared inevitable. And when danger from the major fire had passed, a band of drunken cavalry tried to force their way onto the campus, swearing to set fire to the buildings. They were held off by the guard placed there by General Howard until reinforcements could be sent. The library was saved; only 97 volumes were reported to be lost and they were in the homes of professors in town. Sherman contended that the fire was spread from cotton which General Wade Hampton's men had set on fire. He also said later in his MEMOIRS that he had wanted to make Hampton lose face there in South Carolina where he was such a hero. Who started the fire no longer really matters. The library of the University of South Carolina was saved, but thousands of volumes in private collections were destroyed there in Columbia and throughout the state and the South. Among them was the state library of 25,000 volumes in Columbia, the extensive library of Dr. D. R. W. Gibbes, and those of William Gilmore Simms, General D. F. Jamison, and Paul Hamilton Hayne of Charleston.

The attitude of the citizens was aptly expressed in the diary of Emma Florence LeConte, daughter of the South Carolina scientist, who watched the city burn from her home across the street from the university:

> I would rather endure any poverty than live under Yankee rule. I would rather have France or any other country for mistress—anything but live as one nation with Yankees. That word, in my mind, is a synonym for all that is mean, despicable, and abhorrent.

Tennessee was still East Tennessee University. Its library
of 5,000 volumes was somewhat dissipated during the war, but
more from neglect during the four years when classes were suspended than by troops and stragglers. During the war years first
the Confederate and then the Union forces occupied the buildings.
But much of the library was reassembled in 1866 when classes
were resumed.

Virginia, the last, alphabetically, of the universities I shall
mention in these notes, rocked along through the war and reconstruction without once closing its doors. Enrollment, to be sure,
was at times low and was made up of boys too young to fight and
of men who had been disabled in the war. Annual appropriations
to the library were suspended in 1861, and no books were bought
during the war except those urgently needed. A similar condition
with respect to funds existed in every university in the South.
The Virginia faculty ordered one hundred dollars set aside early
in 1861 for the purchase of issues of the important periodicals,
newspapers, and other documents relating to the impending war.
Northern librarians and archivists were more diligent about preserving such materials than southern librarians. Only Virginia
in the South made an organized effort to collect these documents
as they came from the presses. Fisk P. Brewer, the carpet-bag-
ger librarian of the University of North Carolina from 1869 to
1870, sought to assemble such a collection in Chapel Hill, but
this of course was after the war.

Only in March 1865 was the University of Virginia exposed
to Union forces. They immediately threw a guard around it to
protect it from stragglers and plunderers. William Wertembaker,
Virginia's librarian who served in this capacity with a few inter-
ruptions from 1826 to 1881, returned to the rotunda after the
war to find the books had been kept with neatness and care and
were in good condition. The rotunda, too, that fine old building
of Jefferson's, was spared and still serves Virginia usefully,
although it suffered a disastrous fire in 1895.

If any of you have not seen this building which served the Old
Dominion as a library for 112 years, you should do so; and stop
in Columbia, South Carolina, for a visit to the South Caroliniana
Library, that beautiful old building, with Roman-Doric columned
portico, which housed the University of South Carolina libraries
for 101 years; then move on to Chapel Hill and see Smith Hall
at the University of North Carolina, now the famed Playmakers

Theatre, but from 1850 to 1907 the library building of the University of North Carolina.

The South was battle-scarred, hungry, and poor in 1865. The book collections of southern universities were not distinguished at the beginning of the war, but they survived the war remarkably well. An army doesn't live off the land, as Federal forces did for a time in the South, without needless destruction of property and wasteful losses. We know from World War II, when our armies did not have to live off the conquered countries, how difficult it was to make men behave and respect other people's property. Two libraries of educational institutions were destroyed along with at least two state libraries; and countless private collections were burned or dispersed—private collections which conceivably would have come to rest in libraries of southern universities.

Heavy destruction of private libraries, then, and the economic malnutrition of the region, were jointly responsible for having retarded university library development in any form in the South for generations after the Civil War. Other conditions peculiar to the region which have contributed to the slow development of research libraries since the war, and particularly since 1900, are to be found in our system of colleges; separate schools for boys and girls, land grant colleges and state universities on separate campuses, separate schools for whites and Negroes, and, to a greater degree than necessary, separate schools for the denominations. When the tidal wave of students predicted for the next twenty years reaches the campuses, we shall probably for the first time need all the facilities these schools can provide—but that is another story.

THE HISTORY OF THE ALA
INTELLECTUAL FREEDOM COMMITTEE

David K. Berninghausen

> David K. Berninghausen is Director of the Library School,
> University of Minnesota, Minneapolis. The essay here re-
> printed is a paper read before the American Library His-
> tory Round Table during the 1953 Midwinter meeting of the
> American Library Association in Chicago.

From the records of man's unending struggle to learn and
know comes this extract from Thomas Jefferson's letter to Du-
fief in 1814:

> Are we to have a censor whose imprimatur shall say
> what books may be sold, and what we may buy? And who
> is thus to dogmatize religious opinions for our citizens?
> Whose foot is to be the measure to which ours are all
> to be cut or stretched? Is a priest to be our inquisitor,
> or shall a layman, simple as ourselves, set up his
> reason as the rule for what we are to read, and what we
> must believe? It is an insult to our citizens to question
> whether they are rational beings or not, and blasphemy
> against religion to suppose it cannot stand the test of
> truth and reason. If [a book or idea] be false in its
> facts, disprove them; if false in its reasoning, refute
> it. But, for God's sake, let us freely hear both sides.

The American Library Association since 1939 has consciously promoted the concept that man's freedom to seek the truth
where and how he will, without trying to fit his discoveries into
predetermined patterns, is man's most precious and unique gift.

The ALA Library Bill of Rights, first written by Forrest
Spaulding for the Des Moines Public Library, was adopted by
ALA in San Francisco in 1939. It has encouraged librarians to
hold to the principle that the users of free public libraries must

Reprinted from Wilson Library Bulletin, 27:813-817, June, 1953, by
permission of the author and the publisher.

have the opportunity to examine all information on all sides of all issues. In 1941 Mr. Spaulding reported to the Council of ALA that in general the public seemed to understand the aim of preserving opportunities for free reading in libraries.

Ten years later some people may have thought that there was something paradoxical about the strong stand against censorship taken by librarians.

Outside observers are likely to view the keepers of books as by nature rather conservative. And so they are. Since it is the peculiar function of librarians to preserve the records of man's dreams, failures, and achievements, there is nothing remarkable about their respect for old traditions.

But perhaps there seems to be something surprising about the vigorous resistance of librarians to those who attempt to insist that their private prejudices shall control library book selection. Have these conservative keepers of books lost their perspective and become advocates of dangerous ideas?

The pressures for censorship have focused our attention upon the function of libraries as communication agencies in our society. A democratic society has need for all the information it can get. The library is one of the chief sources, if only because it contains both books and periodicals presenting all points of view. It is a very important source of information, but it can be significant only so long as it holds to its principles.

It cannot be overemphasized that the library can do no better than any other institution, if it surrenders its principles to the expediency of the moment. If a church, a labor union, or a monopoly can control—or materially influence—the selection and distribution of library materials, then the library's proper function in a free society cannot be exercised.

Forrest Spaulding recognized this in 1940 and asked the ALA Council to appoint a standing committee to throw the force and influence of the ALA behind any individual librarian or library board confronted with any demands for censorship of books or other material upon a library's shelves. Sterling North and Alfred C. Nielsen joined Mr. Spaulding in this recommendation, and the Council voted unanimously to authorize appointment of a Committee on Intellectual Freedom.

In May 1940 the committee was created by Council, with the title: Committee on Intellectual Freedom to Safeguard the Rights of Library Users to Freedom of Inquiry. The committee was created to recommend such steps as may be necessary to safeguard the rights of library users in accordance with the Bill of Rights of the United States and the Library Bill of Rights as adopted by Council in 1939. The original committee consisted of Forrest Spaulding, chairman; Jens Nyholm; and Hiller C. Wellman.

Apparently not much happened in 1942 and 1943. In 1944 Leon Carnovsky, chairman, strongly urged that ALA adopt a positive plan of action to meet censorship. In 1945 the committee members were: Emily M. Danton, Frederick G. Melcher, Jens Nyholm, Ruth Rutzen, Marian D. Tomlinson, and Leon Carnovsky, chairman.

The annual report of the Committee for the period of 1944-1945 was as follows:[1]

> With the approval of the ALA Executive Board and Council the committee formulated a statement, "On defending the Freedom to Read in Libraries," and requested its publication by national and state library periodicals. The response was excellent and the statement received wide publicity. Through this statement librarians were invited to report to the committee incidents of attempted interference with the provision of books or periodicals, and it was hoped that such reports would make up the bulk of the committee's annual statement.
>
> Up to the present time very few incidents have been reported, and the committee has been requested not to publicize them. The lack of information about such incidents may mean that they do not exist—that librarians are generally free from interference in their book selection practices. On the other hand, it may mean that librarians do not care to report interference. Or, finally, it may mean that librarians are so cautious in policies of book selection that they avoid "incidents" before they have a chance to occur. Whatever the meaning, the fact remains that the committee has received very little indication of interference with the freedom to read in libraries. . . .

The statement referred to above is interesting still. It appeared in the Wilson Library Bulletin of December 1944:

ON DEFENDING THE FREEDOM TO
READ IN LIBRARIES

Every librarian hates censorship. His decision to add
a book or periodical to the collection is not arbitrary but
is based on the conviction that the book is of value and
interest to his patrons. Once he has made his decision
in accordance with that policy, he should not be overruled by persons who want to prevent others from reading what they themselves disapprove of. This type of
interference in library operation is frequently accompanied by threats so serious as to force the librarian
to accede to it. Whenever he does accede he reluctantly
restricts the freedom to read. Such action is directly
contrary to the principles he believes in; that's why he
hates censorship. . . .

No report seems to have been issued by the committee for 1946.
The annual report for 1946-1947 stated:[2]

The past year has been one of continuous activity for the
committee though it has not been productive of significant
results. It has served to show, however, the basic difficulty in operation for such a committee as this. Mobilizing
opinion and formulating group ideas into statements or
recommendations for action through the tedious process
of correspondence is a particularly ineffective way of
dealing with issues as complex as those which are referred to this committee.
The attention of the committee was called to H. R. 263,
"A bill . . . to declare certain papers, pamphlets, books,
pictures, and writing nonmailable. . . ." The belief of
the members was that though the purpose of the bill was
commendable, such legislation would set a bad precedent and was therefore against the public interest. A
statement to this effect was sent to Paul Howard, then
director of the ALA National Relations Office. No further
action was necessary since the bill died in committee.
An executive order of December 5, 1946, established
the President's Committee on Civil Rights whose duty
is to prepare recommendations for "more adequate and

effective means and procedures for the protection of
the civil rights of the people of the United States." The
Committee on Intellectual Freedom was asked to co-
operate with the President's committee by describing
its program of activity in the field of civil rights, reporting any specific findings, and making recommendations.
Efforts to do this emphasized the fact that while a basic
policy for free public libraries was established by the
Council's adoption in 1939 of the Library Bill of Rights,
the professional concern of all librarians, for the protection of "the first freedom" has not been converted
into a plan for procedure. Such a program is urgently
needed in cases when this specific civil right is threatened.

Acting on a request from the committee, the Council
approved a change in its name from the previous long and
cumbersome form to the Committee on Intellectual Freedom. Whether the statement of committee function should
also be revised to make it more comprehensive is an
open question.

On the current agenda of the committee are these
matters which have been referred to it for consideration:
proposal of the D. A. R. to keep public libraries "free
from false and insidious doctrines"; the so-called decency
resolution of the Massachusetts Library Association—the
question being whether this should be adopted by the
national association or one similar to it in purpose; H. R.
3970, a bill "to establish standards for education in the
Constitution and American history for the District of
Columbia . . ." a bill which provides a virtual censor
for schools and libraries in the District of Columbia;
and three resolutions adopted by the Library Unions
Round Table, referred by action of the Council on July
4, 1947. Members of the association are invited to contribute pertinent facts and opinions regarding any of
these matters. Appropriate recommendations and resolutions will be presented at the Midwinter meeting of
the Council.

Members of the committee were: Emily Miller Danton, Eudocia Stratton, Edna Elizabeth Gustafson, Donald
E. Thompson, Frederic G. Melcher, Marian D. Tomlinson, Doris Ellen Wilson, and Alice G. Higgins, chairman.

Between 1946 and 1949 the Committee on Intellectual Freedom of the ALA periodically pondered the warning of Oliver Wendell Holmes to Arthur Garfield Hays. Justice Holmes warned young Mr. Hays that whenever one becomes interested in a subject, data seem to be drawn from every direction around the magnetic point. In such a situation allowance must be made for one's special interest, and one's conclusion cannot always be trusted. The committee frequently considered the possibility that it had been making mountains out of molehills.

At Atlantic City in 1948 the committee reported that in Birmingham, Alabama, Senior Scholastic had been banned from all schools because of an issue devoted to the theme of human brotherhood. Newark, New Jersey, schools had banned the Nation for the allegedly anti-Catholic articles by Paul Blanshard. Building America was under attack by the Tenney Un-American Activities Committee in California, which objected to a magazine that, while picturing America's achievements, also admitted that some social problems were still to be solved. The New Republic was removed from the Champaign, Illinois, Public Library. Several books were banned from New York City high schools. An attack had been made upon the librarian of the Grand Rapids, Michigan, Public Library. The American Legion was on record as determined to clean all "subversive" literature out of schools and classrooms. The D. A. R. adopted a similar resolution in May 1947 and there were various other rumors of censorship or attempts to restrict Americans in their access to information. In brief, that was the situation in June 1948. Was censorship a mountain or a molehill? The committee was not sure. But it asked the ALA Council to reaffirm the Library Bill of Rights.

At this 1948 conference also the committee joined with the ALA Board on Personnel Administration to recommend a policy against the use of loyalty investigations. This resolution was adopted, but was the subject of debate through three succeeding meetings, until finally the matter was resolved at Cleveland in 1950. This policy as finally adopted reads:

> We, the Council of the American Library Association, strongly protest loyalty programs which inquire into a library employee's thoughts, reading matter, associates, or membership in organizations, unless a particular person's definite actions warrant such investigation. We ap-

prove the affirmation of allegiance to our government.
We condemn loyalty oaths and investigations which permit the discharge of an individual without a fair hearing.
We hold that in a fair hearing the accused is furnished
a statement of the charges against him, is allowed to see
the evidence against him, is given an opportunity to prepare and to present his defense and to question his accu-
sers with the aid of legal counsel, is presumed innocent
until proven guilty, and is given the opportunity, if ad-
judged guilty, of judicial review.

This is a summary of the first of three policies recommended
by the committee and adopted by Council. The Council at the
Cleveland conference also unanimously adopted a resolution recording its opposition to the Maryland Ober Law,

because we believe it to be a definite threat to the constitutional rights of librarians since it permits their
discharge on the principle of guilt by association in
lieu of direct evidence of subversion, and we support
the Maryland Library Association in its efforts to have
the law repealed.

These policies were adopted as expressions of belief that
routine investigation of all library employees is unnecessary
and weakening to the profession. Along with the American Association of University Professors, the library profession has consistently held that guilt is personal, and that an individual should
be judged by his acts, not his opinions.

If an American librarian acts to promote exclusively the ideas
sponsored by his organization, excluding contrary views from
the library, such an act would constitute a threat to free inquiry,
and ultimately to all freedom. Librarians are educators, and
educators must never be propagandists, for a single, exclusive,
orthodox view of truth.

At Atlantic City in 1948 the Council reaffirmed the revised
Library Bill of Rights, and in January 1951 the Peoria case involving film censorship caused a footnote to be added to make it
clear beyond any possible doubt that this official statement of
policy applied to all the media of communications collected or
used by libraries.

After 1949 the Committee on Intellectual Freedom had few doubts that censorship is a major problem. Many cases have been reported in library literature, the latest being Laurence Kipp's fine story of the attempt by the Boston <u>Post</u> to force the Boston Public Library to censor communist literature and the Blanshard books.

In September 1951 the Field Foundation set up a fund of $15,000 to be used by the committee over a two-year period. This fund made it possible to get the committee together at least once a year, thus removing the problem, noted in 1946, of conducting the committee's business by correspondence. The fund now pays a part-time executive secretary, and finances the committee's newsletter. The Field grant also made it possible for the committee to hold a two-day preconference institute on intellectual freedom at the Bar Association in New York in June 1952.

William Dix, committee chairman, opened this meeting by saying that the librarian's professional function is to disseminate information on all sides of every issue. At the same time, he declared, he would not want his library used as a tool by communists or by any other group which denied the fundamental thesis of a free society—that truth must have complete freedom to combat error in the market-place of ideas.

Mr. Dix also cited the Library Bill of Rights, which is, of course, the basic, official statement of ALA policy in regard to free inquiry. It has been studied in New Zealand, Great Britain, India, and Japan.

A third policy recommended by the committee is that on labeling library materials. This question of labeling was raised first by the Sons of the American Revolution in Montclair, New Jersey. It was also an issue in Burbank, California. It resulted in an ALA policy which states:

> Librarians should not use the technique of labeling as a means of predisposing readers against library materials. Although totalitarian states find it easy and even proper, according to their ethics, to establish criteria for judging publications as "subversive," injustice and ignorance rather than justice and enlightenment result from such practices, and the American Library Association has a responsibility to take a stand against the establishment of such criteria in a democratic state.

THE ALA INTELLECTUAL FREEDOM COMMITTEE

> Libraries do not advocate the ideas found in their
> collections. The presence of a magazine or book in
> a library does not indicate an indorsement of its con-
> tent by the library. . . . Although we are all agreed
> that communism is a threat to the free world, if mater-
> ials are labeled to pacify one group, there is no excuse
> for refusing to label any item in the library's collection.
> Because communism, fascism, or other authoritarian-
> isms tend to suppress ideas and attempt to coerce indi-
> viduals to conform to a specific ideology, American li-
> brarians must be opposed to such "isms." We are then
> anticommunist, but we are also opposed to any other
> group which aims at closing any path to knowledge.

This policy against prejudicial labeling of library materials
was recommended to the Council by the Committee on Intellectual
Freedom by Rutherford Rogers, chairman, in Chicago in 1951
and passed unanimously.

Now to complete the roster of earlier committee members,
in 1948 Emily M. Danton, Marion Hawes, Ralph Ellsworth,
Frederic Melcher, Evelyn Benagh, Doris Wilson, and David
Berninghausen, chairman, made up the membership. In 1949
Marion Horton and Hiller Wellman were added, and in 1950 Car-
roll C. Moreland and Rutherford Rogers became members of
the committee, with Mr. Rogers acting as chairman in 1950-1951.
William Dix became chairman in 1951, and Mabel Conat, Ralph
Hudson, Lachlan MacRae, and John E. Smith became new members.

After 1948, when more and more cases were reported to the
committee, there came a question as to whether the national
group should protest against censorious action directly or work
through local library organizations. There would certainly be
a risk in some cases that action by a national committee might
cause unnecessary resentment on the grounds that it was interference by an outside group.

This question caused the committee in 1948 vigorously to encourage state library associations to create state committees on
intellectual freedom. A letter was sent to every state association
and follow-up letters also went out. At one time about half of
the states and some regional associations had such committees.
California had one of the earliest and strongest committees – in
fact the national group learned much from California's experi-

ences. Recently Illinois, Iowa, and Massachusetts have had very active groups working to preserve free reading for library users.

Although the national committee strongly urged the states to appoint committees before an incident was known to have occurred in the state, some states did not recognize any need for a committee. For example, New Hampshire and Oklahoma were thus forced to rely on the individual courage of librarians who had no support from their state associations. In New Hampshire Keith Doms and Mildred Peterson McKay helped to defeat legislative censorship. In Oklahoma Ralph Hudson and Frances Kennedy performed noble service in investigating the Bartlesville affair. However, if a committee had already been in existence when Ruth Brown of Bartlesville was first under criticism, the results might have been different. In Massachusetts the state committee once had only twelve hours notice, but was able to send a representative to be heard on a censorship bill.

It has been the consistent policy of the Intellectual Freedom Committee to encourage action by state groups, with the national committee formally protesting censorious action only when invited in by local people or when no state group exists.

This chronicle has emphasized the early years of the committee because it is assumed that its early history is less well known. Since the 1948 convention library literature has given good coverage on the major cases requiring the committee's attention. For the stories of Los Angeles, Burbank, Bartlesville, or Peoria, the bibliography entitled "Library Literature" is a basic reference.

ALA's three basic policies on free inquiry have been summarized above. Perhaps the three following points about these policies should be emphasized.

The Library Bill of Rights was not drawn up to protect librarians. Its purpose is to preserve the right of every citizen to read whatever he wishes, forming his own private judgments. Librarians are keepers of books for their patrons, not from them.

ALA policy makes the responsibility of professional librarians clear. As members of ALA we are committed to resisting pressures to restrict the reading of American citizens, whether such pressures come from social, patriotic, religious, or any other groups.

THE ALA INTELLECTUAL FREEDOM COMMITTEE

These ALA policies were not imposed upon this organization of 20,000 librarians by any central government, or by any other <u>authority</u>. Such authority as they have derives from the <u>ALA</u> itself, a democratically organized professional association. These policies were drawn up by the ALA Committee on Intellectual Freedom, the duly appointed body of the organization, then submitted to the Council, the acting body of ALA, for full discussion and debate. The committee has always held that no document is above criticism. This includes all ALA policy statements.

At the beginning of this narrative, it was suggested that there might seem to be a paradox in the picture of conservative librarians resisting censorship. But is there any real paradox? Is it surprising, really, for this conservative profession to seek to preserve the freedom of every citizen to read what he wishes and form his own opinion?
No, it should startle no one to find that librarians recognize the validity of Alfred North Whitehead's two principles. This distinguished philosopher noted two principles which he considered inherent in the very nature of things – the spirit of change, and the spirit of conservation. Professor Whitehead said:

> There can be nothing real without both. Mere change without conservation is a passage from nothing to nothing.
> . . . Mere conservation without change cannot conserve.

By accepting the challenge to act as conservators of the American heritage of free inquiry, librarians have recognized and accepted <u>both</u> of Professor Whitehead's principles – the spirit of change <u>and</u> the spirit of conservation. They have – at one and the same time – preserved the most precious of our traditions – freedom of inquiry – and yet stood ready to welcome the new concepts, the new theories, the constructive thought of future creators. Librarians have thus helped to provide the opportunity for the continued advance of knowledge and the growth of individuals. Upon these two factors depends the future of our democracy, and indeed, of all humanity.

[1]<u>ALA Bulletin</u>, 10/15/45, p. 391-2. [2]Ibid., 10/15/45, p. 393-4.

PERSONALITIES BEHIND THE DEVELOPMENT OF PAIS

Marian C. Manley

> Marian C. Manley (Mrs. Gerald H. Winser) was supervis-
> ing business librarian, Newark Public Library, Newark,
> New Jersey from 1926 to 1954; she retired on November
> 1st, 1954, and now lives in Summit, New Jersey. The es-
> say here reprinted is a paper read before the American
> Library History Round Table during the 1954 Midwinter
> conference of the American Library Association in Chicago.

This year, PAIS is forty years old. The subscribers to its
weekly Bulletin,[1] its cumulations, and its annual volumes have
grown steadily since the first forty were enrolled in 1914. The
quantity of material to which it is the key has increased even
more. The annual volumes have expanded from the first in 1915
with its 344 pages to the current volume numbering 827. Yet
PAIS is perhaps unique among library expenses in that the coop-
erating libraries are still paying $100 annually, as they did when
the service first appeared in printed form in 1915.

PAIS is a notable achievement, invaluable to libraries large
and small. Yet it is probably one of the least discussed of library projects. In a professional world where hundreds of pages
are devoted to the pros and cons and many facets of any library
development, this quiet but steady progress is in itself a phenomenon. To what can such progress be attributed?

Frankly, PAIS can be considered the lengthened shadow of
three men: John A. Lapp, Charles C. Williamson, and Rollin A.
Sawyer. Each one has been the directing head at a time when
his special gifts have been of infinite value to the development
of a great bibliographic tool. Each one has given unsparingly of
his ability and interest. The debt owed them by the library profession is great.

When we read in "Who's Who" of the long list of achievements
of the distinguished labor arbitrator, Dr. John A. Lapp, it comes
as a surprise to realize that we owe this major index to his ef-

Reprinted from College and Research Libraries, 15:263-270+, July,
1954, by permission of the author and the publisher.

forts. We can be proud that in those early years he saw the outlines and ramifications of an increasing problem and through
his leadership a solution was found.

PAIS was first discussed in 1910. A number of elements had
combined to focus attention on the stream of special publications
for which there was no general listing or guide. Legislative reference libraries had come into being. The six years' development of the Newark Business Library had helped to focus attention on many sources of information hitherto receiving little
library attention. The Special Libraries Association, formed in
1909, had brought together a group of lively minds and afforded
a meeting place for those who had had occasion to realize both
the amount of specialized information in print and its relative
inaccessibility.

In such a climate, Dr. Lapp, then with the Indiana State Legislative Reference Bureau brought up for discussion at the 1910
meeting of the Special Libraries Association the possibility of
an index to public affairs publications. As chairman of the new
Association's Public Affairs Committee, he stressed the need
for such an index covering city and state reports, those from
many national associations in the field of public affairs, and the
countless other sources of information untouched by the existing
indexes. At succeeding conferences there was further discussion
of the needs, but no method of meeting the problem was defined.

At the Kaaterskill Conference in 1913 no formal action was
taken by the Special Libraries Association, but a group including
Guy Marion, Arthur D. Little, Inc., Boston; John Cotton Dana,
Newark Public Library; Robert H. Whitten, Public Service Commission, New York; George Godard, Connecticut State Library;
Daniel Handy, Insurance Library Association, Boston; H. H. B.
Meyer, Library of Congress, and Dr. Lapp, in informal discussion felt that no more time should pass without action. Dr.
Lapp said, "The way to begin is to begin", and that if the major
special libraries would each pledge $25 annually, and would co-
operate in supplying material, he would undertake the work of
assembling information at the Indiana Legislative Reference
Bureau and distribute the lists in mimeographed forms with the
bibliographical notes. As Dr. Lapp was also editing Special Libraries at that time, he had a supplementary source of material.
He believed that the benefit to the Indiana Bureau in becoming
the clearing house for the materials justified the use of staff

time in the project. The payments from the cooperators covered the mimeographing and distribution costs. Lillian Henley of the staff of the Legislative Reference Bureau took the major job of managing the work and Ethel Cleland, then librarian of the Bureau, gave much assistance. Dr. Lapp took as his share of the venture the determination of types of material and priorities. It was on this basis that PAIS first came into being and went on for one year.

At this point another of our library geniuses came into the picture. H. W. Wilson with his gift for the development of the current printed index saw the potentialities of PAIS and went to Dr. Lapp with a proposal that the material be printed cumulatively in the form of other Wilson publications. He proposed to take it over as a cooperative enterprise and publish it on a "cost plus" basis. The cooperators agreed and Dr. Lapp was enlisted by Mr. Wilson to go to White Plains to help organize the new bulletin and to secure the minimum number of cooperators. Orrena Louise Evans became the first editor. Expenses were covered by the 70 or so cooperators who were now paying $100 a year.

With the printed weekly bulletins and the frequent cumulations, PAIS became even more useful to the cooperators. An Advisory Committee was established consisting of Dr. Lapp, George S. Godard, and Charles C. Williamson, then librarian of the New York Municipal Reference Library. Under the editorship of Miss Evans and later Lillian Henley, the growth was satisfying. Innumerable problems incident to the development of the publication were solved and the format that has proved so satisfactory was evolved. Dr. Lapp's interest was unabated and he served as a member of the Advisory Committee, but his active direction was discontinued after he had done this major task of organization. Dr. Charles C. Williamson became chairman.

Dr. Williamson had served on the Advisory Committee of PAIS since 1915, but while he was Municipal Reference Librarian, his interest in the growth of PAIS was not too acute. But when he became chief of the New York Public Library Economics Division in 1919, he had immediate reason to become more deeply interested. From the vantage point of the Economics Division two problems became clear. Comparatively few of the materials that should be indexed in PAIS were flowing naturally into the Wilson offices for use in such an index. On the other hand, the

PERSONALITIES BEHIND THE DEVELOPMENT OF PAIS

New York Public Library had an abundant intake of valuable material from all over the world, both free and purchased. In normal library processes such material could not be as fully analyzed as it should be for good service. In Dr. Williamson's eyes a desirable method for meeting such a situation was the transference of the editorial office of PAIS from the H. W. Wilson Company to the Economics Division. This would give the editor a chance to select material for inclusion from the wealth of publications received by the library. The prompt analysis and listing of such material in PAIS would not only give the users of PAIS prompt information on hundreds of publications, it would give the New York Public Library a much more detailed and promptly issued printed guide to its resources in this field than could be financially and administratively possible under any other circumstances.

At this time the Advisory Committee consisted of Dr. Lapp, Mr. Godard, Mr. Hicks, Mr. Wheeler and Dr. Williamson. Service on the Committee had been a pleasant and not too strenuous responsibility. Dr. Williamson's new slant on the future possibilities of PAIS changed this for a while. The revolutionary idea led to much discussion and produced some masterly and detailed memoranda. It was not surprising that the editor and the publisher were disturbed at the possibility of difficulties developing in what had become a smoothly running operation. Where the library was concerned Dr. Williamson had other problems. He had to convince the naturally dubious Director, Mr. Anderson, that the precedent set by letting him run a "commercial" service in the library building would not be dangerous. Too, the Acquisitions Department of the library could not be expected to be altogether happy about letting PAIS have the first chance to go over the material that came to the library. However, in time Mr. Anderson was convinced. The Advisory Committee and the publisher discussed all angles. Eventually the soundness of the Williamson proposals was recognized and the plan accepted. As a result, the library cooperators in PAIS now have the tremendous advantage of consulting what amounts to an acquisition list of the New York Public Library's resources in the fields of economics and public affairs. Too, the opportunity for selective indexing of the extensive collection of periodicals in the same fields has immeasurably increased the value of the Bulletin.

Another important step taken at this time as a result of Dr.

Williamson's study was a clarification of the organization of PAIS itself. Until that time it had operated on an informal basis with no clearly defined lines of responsibility. Just <u>who</u> decided <u>what</u> had never been stated and machinery for making suggestions by the cooperators effective, for example, with the publisher was nonexistent. With this general study of the status of PAIS it was apparent that its future progress demanded some definite basis by which the cooperators could, through their representatives, the Advisory Committee, control the service. As a result of this study, Dr. Williamson, as chairman, was asked to draw up articles of agreement and after their study by the members and adjustment of details, they were submitted to the cooperators for vote. These articles have since then been the basis for the operation of PAIS. Briefly stated, they outline the procedure by which the cooperators who are the libraries paying $100 for the service, elect the Publications Committee of five members and that Committee, formerly the Advisory Committee, is responsible for the management of PAIS.

In the development of PAIS, Dr. Lapp was responsible for originating the plan and for starting the service on its long and successful career. Dr. Williamson, in the period in which he guided its destinies, had greatly expanded the usefulness of the service by bringing the editorial work to the New York Public Library. Under his auspices the formal organization of PAIS had been clarified. Annual revenues for PAIS had grown from $7,378 in 1915 to $12,794 in 1919. PAIS was now a well established entity.

When Rollin Sawyer became chief of the Economics Division in 1919 he succeeded Dr. Williamson as chairman of the Publications Committee for PAIS, a position he has held since that time. The editorial policies had been established, a formal organizational procedure had been defined. But in 1923 another major change took place. Until then, the financial management had been in the hands of the H. W. Wilson Company as publishers. At that time Mr. Wilson asked to be relieved of the responsibility and it was assumed by the Publications Committee while the H. W. Wilson Company continued as printer. This shift in management was a logical move as it placed all managerial responsibilities with the Committee. Since 1923, the chairman has been editorial advisor, general manager, salesman, and bookkeeper, a combination of duties carried out with remarkable success by

PERSONALITIES BEHIND THE DEVELOPMENT OF PAIS

Mr. Sawyer.

PAIS, a library sponsored and library managed project, is a business success. A non-profit organization, it has published for forty years a bulletin which has become a foundation reference tool in all but the smallest libraries. In 1953 its 663 contributors received weekly bulletins of 24 pages covering some 700 entries each and an annual of 827 pages. This has been done without any increase in the annual contribution of $100, first established in 1915. In this period the cost value of the subscription list has grown to be four times as large, or from $12,367 to $53,430. The revenue for 1953 covered a payroll of $31,174 and printing costs of $20,910 as compared with the corresponding costs of $5,700 and $4,500 when Mr. Sawyer took over in 1921. This change can be attributed in part to a growing understanding by librarians of the need for this tool. To a far greater extent it must be attributed to the quiet systematic work of its able chairman.

To the editors who, in the forty years of its growth, have facilitated the use of the flood of publications, the library world is greatly indebted also. The list includes only seven names, but their contributions are diversified. While Lillian Henley edited the mimeographed sheets that appeared when PAIS was issued from Indianapolis, Orrena Louise Evans was the first editor of the printed bulletin published by the H. W. Wilson Company. The first annual cumulation appeared with Miss Evans as editor in 1915 and in its introduction she summarizes the development of PAIS and the problems met in its progress. She passes lightly over the difficulties but they must have been many. Although Miss Evans had the great advantage of drawing on the experience of the H. W. Wilson Company in the solution of indexing and format problems, there were still the questions created by the special peculiarities of the varied types of material included in PAIS. It is a tribute to her powers of organization and editorial ability that the current format of PAIS so closely follows the pattern which she set.

But editorial problems were not the only ones encountered in these early days. A system of obtaining material to list had to be built up almost from the bottom. In this the cooperators were supposed to assist but with the loose organization it was natural that their aid was intermittent. Much correspondence was required to insure accuracy in the entries. All in all, the first volume can be considered a monument to Miss Evans' diligence and enterprise. In writing of these early days, Miss Evans says: "Your letter has set me thinking of those early days of Public Affairs Information Service when the H. W. Wilson Company was housed in a big garage on Mamaroneck Avenue in White Plains. The front end of the building had a second floor and this is where PAIS was housed. From the editorial and printing standpoints the H. W. Wilson Company was a wonderful place for PAIS, as was the access to conventional books and periodicals; but for the real purpose for which PAIS was organized – to call attention to pamphlets, reports, ephemeral material, notices of meetings, digests of legislation, and the like – it was anything but a fertile field. I remember what a feeling of helplessness I had in trying to issue a Bulletin without access to the needed information. Mr. Lapp and his Bureau of Legislative Information were most helpful in the early days in sending notices of information to be included.

"Our staff began busily writing letters to government agencies (federal, state and local), universities, associations and other sources and received enough material to issue the Bulletin from week to week. But I used to wish the work could be done in New York where access to publishers and libraries would make it possible to cull only the best. When I learned the compilation of material for the Bulletin was to be taken to the New York Public Library I considered it a wise move.

"During my association with PAIS the form of publication was worked out, decision was made to include the various key lists in the front of the Annual, editorial policy and office routine adopted, and a start made in turning the vast tide of ephemeral material toward the H. W. Wilson Company for listing. Mr. Wilson and the editors of the other H. W. Wilson publications were most helpful, both by making their review publications available and by suggestions as to form and methods. Mr. Lapp made frequent visits to New York and came out to see how PAIS was getting along. He was full of optimism and enthusiasm and had a keen grasp of the field. His advice and suggestions were of the greatest assistance".

After two years as editor, Miss Evans left to become librarian of the Bureau of Public Roads in Washington, a position with which we all associate her. Lillian Henley, who had handled the preliminary issues of the Bulletin, came on from Indianapolis to be the next editor. In her first annual, 1916, she pays tribute to Miss Evans for her work. Miss Henley in turn dealt with the problems of expanding the content of the <u>Bulletin</u> until 1919, a period in which publishing problems diminished with the close cooperation possible through its location at the Wilson plant.

Experimentation in different lines was tried in this period and it was at this time that one noble experiment was finally proved to be impractical. When PAIS was first projected, one service attempted was its use as a clearing house for these special publications so that cooperators could use the <u>Bulletin</u> as a checklist placing orders through PAIS. Such work had clogged the machinery of the publication to such an extent that the prompt listing of useful material was impossible. With the general reorganization that took place and the study of the work of PAIS, it was decided to eliminate all order work for cooperators and confine the efforts of the PAIS staff to the development of the <u>Bulletin</u> itself. As a result there was immediate improvement in the varied content of the <u>Bulletin</u> and the promptness with which material was listed.

When in 1919 the editorial offices of PAIS were moved from the H. W. Wilson Company to the Economics Division of the New York Public Library, Miss Henley left to become research secretary of the National Municipal League. Alice L. Jewett took over in her place and served as editor for two years. This again was a period of adjustment. The editor now had the advantages of contact with the resources of a large reference library. Through the courtesy of the library, incoming books, pamphlets, and documents were examined each day so that everything which fell within the scope of the service was immediately available. Too, there was the great advantage afforded in the opportunity to examine many economic and trade periodicals not elsewhere indexed. This system made possible not only greater promptness in listing material, but also much more discriminating selection than was possible when money and so much of the editor's time were consumed in acquiring material which, once listed, was of no further use to PAIS. The great advantage of prompt examination, held to this day, has meant that the weekly bulletins can carry information on publications received shortly before going to press.

Under these three editors, the problems in the development of PAIS as a serviceable index were to a great extent solved.

Under Miss Evans and Miss Henley the format was evolved and the scope of the entries was decided. In Miss Jewett's term, the problems of working with the facilities of the library were encountered and a procedure satisfactory to the library personnel and effective for PAIS was found. The path for future editors to follow was clearly defined.

Miss Jewett served as editor from 1920 to 1922 and Harriet Burcholdt, who followed her, from 1922 to 1925. Then came the long period of service as editor of Mary Elizabeth Furbeck, who kept the service moving smoothly for twenty-two years, 1925 to 1947. By now the problems of organization and scope had been solved. Close contact with the users of PAIS was invaluable in noting new trends and adjusting headings and entries to changing conditions. Rollin Sawyer with his wide knowledge of the field and intense interest in the development of the service, was at hand for consultation. The chief objective of the service now was adequate coverage and prompt publication. Miss Furbeck, quiet, systematic, and persevering, was well equipped for the work that she carried on so satisfactorily until ill health forced her retirement in 1945.

The position of editor of PAIS is not an easy one to fill. While it offers the advantage of at least a brief opportunity to scan the varied publications growing out of the changing trends and demands of the whole field of economics and public affairs, it calls for the patience to participate in and oversee an immeasurable amount of detail. Yards of galley press must be read and thousands of entries must fall into their appropriate place. While the machinery for handling this detail is established, the human element is always present and its weakness must be anticipated. Only those with special qualities can spend long hours happily engaged in this work and the library world has been fortunate that so far PAIS has been able to find people of this calibre.

When Miss Furbeck retired, her long time associate, May Mellinger, retired also and the chairman had some difficult years in continuing a smoothly running publication. The shortage in library personnel in the years from 1945 on made it difficult to fill the position. Fortunately, Mary E. Bartley, who had come up through the ranks of PAIS proved to be adaptable and resourceful. PAIS continued to prove its worth, but with many hectic moments for the chairman and for Miss Bartley as editor. In 1952 Miss Bartley asked to be released as soon as a successor could be found, and after some months, the present editor, Robert S. Wilson, was appointed. With a background of professional training, with experience in the Acquisitions Department of the New York Public Library, and with his real interest in the opportunity to note the progress of world affairs through the flow of print, the editorial future of PAIS has brightened considerably and the Publications Committee and its Chairman may feel more at ease about the immediate future.

In the growth of PAIS the respective chairmen and editors have of necessity carried the full burden but the parts played by the other members of the Committee and by the cooperators have their important aspects. The cooperators with their substantial financial contribution through the years made the growth of PAIS possible. In their varying degrees of expressed interest they have helped to develop the scope and editorial value of the service. Each year they receive a report of progress of their project and each year they vote for one member of the Publications Committee of five serving for a term of five years. Always the chairman and the different members of the Committee have welcomed suggestions for the development of the service and to the extent they have been forthcoming the cooperators have made direct contributions to the increased service of the bulletin.

The members of the Publications Committee have been distinguished for length of service rather than for their number. Of the original group of three, Dr. John A. Lapp served from the beginning until 1929. His contribution to the service both as the first chairman and as a member of the Committee cannot be measured. Dr. Williamson, who clarified the organization of PAIS and brought it to the New York Public Library, served until he left that institution for the Rockefeller Foundation in 1921. George S. Godard, State Librarian of Connecticut, the last of the original three, served until his death in 1936. While less active than the other two, his thoughtful consideration of the organizational problems and his sound advice made his service of special value.

At the Louisville meeting of ALA in 1917 the original committee of three was expanded to five and Joseph L. Wheeler, then at Youngstown, and Frederick C. Hicks, at that time law librarian of Columbia University, were asked to serve. Mr. Wheeler served until 1922 when he resigned because of ill health. In 1929 Mr. Wheeler again came on the committee in place of Dr. Lapp, whose many other activities had forced him to give up the contact with PAIS. Mr. Wheeler brought to his service on the Committee the experience derived in a medium-sized library such as Youngstown and again in the large Enoch Pratt Free Library in Baltimore. Writing of his contacts with PAIS he says:

> I was librarian at Youngstown, a hustling industrial
> city of smoke and steel, where the word "library" had
> been associated in the public mind with Shakespeare and
> children's books, rather than as a vital help in solving
> the daily vocational, civic and personal problems of the
> adult Tom, Dick and Harry. PAIS was a tremendous lift,
> a new well oiled key to a vast realm of everyday com-
> munity topics, and a stimulus to every library to get
> busy, beat the bushes, and introduce library materials
> and services to great groups of busy men who had no
> idea it could help them. I still think PAIS should have
> ten times as many subscribers, and that the libraries
> using it should keep up a stream of publicity about it . . .

Mr. Hicks served for slightly more than thirty years as a member of the Publications Committee, most of the time as its secretary. Always methodical and thorough, his contributions were greatly missed when ill health forced his retirement in 1948. Though seriously handicapped, his interest is still keen and his generosity in sending on his PAIS files is responsible for much of the data presented here.

When Mr. Wheeler resigned from the Publications Committee in 1922, he was succeeded by Dorsey W. Hyde, Jr., at that time engaged in civic research for the American City, and later librarian of the New York Municipal Reference Library. In these and later positions he both used and was useful to PAIS. Now in the retirement which brought his resignation from PAIS in 1952, his recollection of what PAIS meant in his work is still as keen. In writing of this he says:

> In New York City I called PAIS to the attention of vari-
> ous city officials who learned for the first time of the re-
> search background of various civic problems. While with
> the National Chamber I compiled some sixty-odd technical
> and statistical reports on major civic problems, which

104

were distributed to requesting members of commerce
throughout the country. The compilation of these reports was made possible by the use of PAIS. Because
of PAIS I was able to write reports with information
no where else obtainable. All who heard it congratulated
us upon the performance of a widely needed public service.

So for its first twenty-odd years, only seven people, the
three successive chairmen, Dr. Lapp, Dr. Williamson, and Mr.
Sawyer and four Committee members, Mr. Godard, Mr. Wheeler, Mr. Hicks, and Mr. Hyde were responsible for the administration of PAIS. The death of Mr. Godard in 1936 and my appointment as his successor were the first major changes since the appointment of Mr. Sawyer in 1921 and Mr. Hyde in 1922. Now with
the appointment of Donald Clark, associate librarian, Baker Library, Harvard, in 1948, Charles F. Gosnell, state librarian,
New York, in 1949, and Eileen Thornton, librarian, Vassar
College, in 1952, succeeding respectively, Mr. Wheeler, Mr.
Hicks and Mr. Hyde, the founding fathers are no longer at the
helm. But the years of experience of the chairman, Rollin Sawyer, and the regard for the standards set for PAIS held by the
Committee members, insures its continuance along the lines
that have given so much satisfaction.

So much for the personalities that have guided and produced
PAIS. Has its use increased with the same steady growth? On
this, comments from two of the earliest subscribers throw light.
In speaking of PAIS, Margaret Bonnell, librarian of the Metro-
politan Life Insurance Company Library, one of the great special libraries of the country, says:

> Our Insurance Research librarian tells me she found
> PAIS extremely useful in library research for a company
> staff which made an extensive study of Social Insurance
> and prepared a series of monographs published by the
> company in the 1930's. She has continued to use it for
> reference questions involving Social Insurance and Pen-
> sions — especially to keep informed about current legis-
> lation and International Labour Office reports. In refer-
> ence work for the Business Research bureaus of our
> company we rely heavily on PAIS for information in fields
> of wholesale and retail trade and finance.

Its use from another angle is reflected in a letter from Esther Schlundt, head of the Readers Division of Purdue University Libraries:

> With the growth of our graduate school program we have found that the demand for the special services which PAIS can render has increased and that we now also acquire many more of the special studies and series which are included in this index. From a practical point of view we consider it a very satisfactory social science index and invaluable when it comes to finding pertinent state, federal, and now United Nations documents from a subject approach. We, of course, use with great frequency, the Directory of Publications and Organizations as well as the bibliographical data given in the Key to Periodical References.
>
> I well remember having helped a student in aeronautical engineering try to find material on the transportation of pharmaceuticals by air. We searched through the engineering and aviation literature indexes with little success and then went to PAIS to find there just about what he wanted in a Wayne University Study in Air Transportation on the air cargo potential in drugs and pharmaceuticals.

While the chairmen of the Publications Committee have carried the administrative burden, and the demands on the members of the Committee has been slight, we find an enduring satisfaction in our relationship to a financially sound institution that quietly and without fanfare has served so effectively as an aid to research.

---

[1]Bulletin of the Public Affairs Information Service

THE CARNEGIE CORPORATION AND THE
LIBRARY RENAISSANCE IN THE SOUTH

Robert M. Lester

Robert M. Lester is Executive Director of the Southern
Fellowships Fund and retired Secretary of the Carnegie
Corporation of New York. The essay here reprinted is a
paper read before the American Library History Round
Table during the 1956 conference of the American Library
Association in Miami Beach, Florida.

The rebirth of the South as a strategic and dominant part of
the nation may well be dated from about 1885-1890, a period in
which, strangely enough, Andrew Carnegie, in 1889, in an article published in the North American Review, declared his opinion that it was a shame to die rich, and Henry Grady in his famous speech on the New South, in 1886, stirred the visions and
ambitions of men.

The wealthy southern planter in pre-civil-war days was not
a bookish man, and the small landowner had little time for books
and study. Despite romantic illusions, the typical plantation owner was not a Thomas Jefferson. Scholars and scientists were
few; public libraries were almost unknown; notable personal collections of books were rare; academic libraries were hardly
worth the name; manners were more important than learning. . . .
Actually, anything like a new South did not begin to emerge, and
that beginning could be seen only as it were through a glass darkly, and not openly declared, until Henry Grady, putting together
an equation of human effort and ambition, made his eloquent prophecy of the new South that was about to be.

The Latin poet, Virgil, in the second book of the AENEID has
his hero, Aeneas, recount at length to Queen Dido the story of
valiant deeds on the plains of Troy, of his later wanderings, and
of strange happenings which he had witnessed by land and sea —
things which later, the poet could sing, had led to the building
of the high walls of Rome and the beginning of the Latin race.

Reprinted from Wilson Library Bulletin, 31:255-259, November,
1956, by permission of the author and the publisher.

So, with a notably inaccurate parallel, in this story of library development in the South, I can truly say that in my thirty years of going up and down the land, trying to help in some small way in the task of distributing the surplus wealth of Andrew Carnegie and John D. Rockefeller, I have seen great things happen to the library movement in the South, and in some of these great things I myself have been privileged to play a small part. Certainly now in 1956 it is possible for me, having arrived at an age when men and events may be viewed in historical perspective, to discern a pattern outlined by many activities which may once have seemed disconnected and unrelated. The emergence of the public and academic library as a social force in the South has been truly a phenomenon of the twentieth century.

What has happened in the first half of this century in libraries in the South is the result of a combination of interlocking efforts, primarily on the part of enlightened and devoted librarians aided by funds given by Carnegie, Rockefeller, Rosenwald, Phelps-Stokes, Jeanes, Slater, and Peabody. These remote funds, in turn, may be translated happily into their southern representatives: men like Wallace Buttrick, and Wickliffe Rose, James H. Dillard, Jackson Davis and Leo Favrot, Fred McQuistion and Thomas Jesse Jones, Curtis Dixon and S. L. Smith, who as philanthropic circuit riders made their rounds, even in the byways and hedges, proclaiming the gospel of books and learning to town and gown alike. For these brave men, and for many others who worked not for foundations but with foundation money, we today now can say truly, with Pindar, the noble Theban poet, "The long toil of the brave is not lost in darkness."

When Andrew Carnegie, sincere in his wish to dispose of his surplus wealth, began his world-wide program of providing free public buildings to communities which would stock them with books and maintain them in perpetuity from tax funds, there was a notable effort on the part of enterprising communities to secure Carnegie library buildings. Nearly two thousand such structures were made possible. Let it be said here that Mr. Carnegie never asked that his name be used in the designation of a free public library building; more than two-thirds of the library buildings erected through his generosity were not christened with his name. During thirty years after 1865, the Carnegie gifts ran their course, and the free public library became an object of pride throughout the land. It was distinctly an American institution.

THE LIBRARY RENAISSANCE IN THE SOUTH

Since few persons at that time had any idea of what a public library building should be, or how a free library should function, or what a public librarian should be, the architects drew memorial buildings with steps and columns and domes; the librarian often regarded herself as a keeper of rows of beautiful unsoiled, unstolen, and alas only too often unread books. Library service as we know it today was not even in its infancy.

This urge towards free library buildings, however, prevailed less in the South than in the North and East and Middle West. Southern towns, struggling with problems of municipal life; of police, fire, and sanitary protection; and of providing pavements, streetcars, electric lights, piped water, and public schools, and hospitals – matters already cared for in other sections not devastated by war and reconstruction – could not concern themselves enthusiastically with the matter of getting a public library to be maintained at public expense. Consequently, Carnegie libraries, though not rare, are not today so frequently found in the South as elsewhere.

As for education, it must be said that college instruction in the South, as in the North, during those years was based chiefly on the text book; university library research facilities, except maybe in the classics, were practically unknown. Academic reading rooms were visited by students only in extreme emergency, when monthly allowances had been spent or when boredom or bad weather prevailed.

The period of library building and acquisition of scanty reservoirs of books, with collections good in some instances but more often indifferent, may be said to have come to an end during the years 1914-1918. By 1914 it had become evident to Carnegie officers that many pledges of tax support of libraries made to secure buildings in the South and elsewhere were not being kept, and that many so-called librarians had no idea of what could be done with a library. Librarianship was regarded by and large as a dismal occupation, not a lively profession.

In my home town of Birmingham, Alabama, about that time were two young and imaginative librarians, then unknown to me, whose influence was later to become nationwide and international, Carl H. Milam and Emily Van Dorn Miller, in each of whom some fifteen years later I was to find a lasting and devoted friend. Professional librarians of their type, however, were then few and far between in the South. Even Birmingham, hustling steel city that it was, had not cared to get a Carnegie building.

In 1915 the Carnegie Corporation of New York engaged Dr. Alvin S. Johnson, once a Columbia professor, later to be director of the New School for Social Research, to make a study of the results of the wide provision of free public library buildings. His report, in 1917, was the first library survey ever supported by Carnegie funds. It was the forerunner of many others during the long run of years ending with the comprehensive study made a few years ago by Robert D. Leigh and his highly skilled staff of investigators.

Among other findings, Alvin Johnson reported that a time seemed to be at hand when public interest would demand that public funds be used to provide library buildings and service; that library service could be sufficiently well organized for public administration; that philanthropic funds might well be employed no longer for buildings but for working out problems of library service and standards of efficient performance. He mentioned the then-struggling American Library Association as an agency which, with more funds, could offer a better and more practical service to libraries. Assisting Dr. Johnson were librarians Matthew S. Dudgeon, W. H. Brett, and George B. Utley, who exercised their best judgment and tact in conducting what they described as a very delicate but exceedingly necessary investigation as to delinquency on the part of many communities.

This Johnson report, when carefully circulated, brought a halt in Carnegie giving, and directed public attention again to the library. Just then came World War I, with its thirty-two cantonments, or camps, with millions of boys in strange environments, with too much to do at some hours and too little to do at others. Somebody wisely thought up the idea of having a camp library in each cantonment, and to give a tangible shape to this, Carnegie Corporation of New York provided funds to build and stock thirty-two library buildings. In one of these at Camp Gordon, Georgia, I first encountered the American Library Association, since on each camp library was a sign ALA LIBRARY. Being from Birmingham, I wondered why the state of Alabama should provide a library for a camp in Georgia. On wandering in, I found that ALA meant more than Alabama, and from that day hence my admiration for the American Library Association, enriched by later experiences with the association and its members, has known no bounds.

In the meantime, the Carnegie trustees were taking stock. They determined to end the practice of making grants for library buildings, and to try thereafter to change librarianship from a haphazard way of making a living to a university-trained profession. A report on library training, prepared by C. C. Williamson in 1918, and his later report, TRAINING FOR LIBRARY SERVICE, in 1921 and published two years later, gave a fresh and accurate conception of steps that might be taken to improve library training. In this study, as one adviser to Mr. Williamson, was Chancellor James H. Kirkland, of Vanderbilt University, an early and persistent advocate of excellence in all fields of education. Then, William S. Learned, a Carnegie staff member, in 1924 published an epoch-making treatise under the title, THE AMERICAN PUBLIC LIBRARY AND THE DIFFUSION OF KNOWLEDGE. This book, still in demand, became almost overnight a guide book to a new world of librarianship.

By this time Carl Milam had become executive secretary of the American Library Association and with a few vigorous and enlightened associates had begun to make the American Library Association a vital agency in promoting libraries. In 1926, the year in which I resigned my teaching and administrative positions at Columbia University, where earlier as a graduate student I had been a night-shift librarian, to enter upon my long and pleasant career as a philanthropoid, the Carnegie Corporation made a notable ten-year library service grant for financing the association, for transferring library schools to university auspices, and for many strategic library demonstrations.

In initiating and carrying out this program, Southerners, Northerners, and Westerners alike worked to win a new degree of respect for the American public and academic library. A few names will not be out of place here: Linda Eastman, Tommie Dora Barker, Charles Belden, W. W. Bishop, Harrison Craver, Milton Ferguson, Mary Rothrock, H. M. Lydenberg, L. L. Dickerson, Dorothy Rowden, Charles Rush, Louis R. Wilson, Judd Jennings, Joseph L. Wheeler, Milton Lord (librarian and folkdancer), Sara C. N. Bogle, Charles H. Brown, Harold Brigham, Julia Wright Merrill, Anita Hostetter, Florence Curtis, Susan Akers, and Helen Harris. And who can ever forget that cheerful and ubiquitous Kentuckian on the ALA staff, Cora Beatty. These evangelists of the library by advice, visits, and persuasion contributed hugely to the southern program. If I have failed to name other equally devoted, and especially the successors to those whom I have listed, please look about you in this and other sessions of this conference. They are probably here, and are entitled to equal praise.

In all of this renaissance, the South was a full partner. Library schools at Columbia, Chicago, and Michigan, at North Carolina, Emory, and Louisiana State, at Hampton and Atlanta, at Peabody and Florida State, soon began to attract and turn out men and women with professional attitudes, high purpose, and missionary zeal. They shifted library interest from acquisition of books and structures, from mass production in book reading to the proper utilization of reading matter and equipment, to quality circulation and community educational service. Librarians now tend to regard themselves as actual or potential intellectual leaders in their communities and campuses, rather than as highly efficient handlers and keepers of books. In bringing this change about, Carnegie funds made possible some of the initial steps, which were later supported widely and wisely by other foundations, with added present strength from the Ford Foundation.

Many Carnegie supported and far-reaching library projects in the South must be passed with only a reference. Flood relief for small libraries, surveys of southern library schools, library extension work in Tennessee and Louisiana, aid to the Southeastern Library Association, adult education demonstrations—all have had Carnegie funds. One far-reaching demonstration was the work of the League of Library Commissions in Louisiana, from which grew the Louisiana Library Commission, under the dauntless leadership of Essae Martha Culver and her hand-picked cohort of persuasive and personable young ladies who, as library workers in the parishes, set a pattern which has been imitated in other lands and areas.

Carnegie funds to young librarians for graduate study have gone to Southerners and Northerners, black and white alike, who in their later careers have made ample use of their opportunities to render public service even beyond the range of their profession.

Many are the library contributions of that great southern librarian and scholar, my neighbor and fellow honorary member, Louis Round Wilson, in training and inspiring many of the leading librarians in service today. Mr. Wilson's use of Carnegie money at the University of North Carolina, and for ten years at the University of Chicago, is a matter of pride to all who like to see philanthropic funds well spent. The influence of the library training provided by the University of Chicago and Columbia University through major Carnegie grants is beyond estimate in all sections of the country.

It is not meet for me to attribute credit to Carnegie influence for the changes in college and university library development in the South. These were a part of the academic awakening in the southern region beginning about 1925. About that time librarians at North Carolina, Tulane, Vanderbilt, Virginia, Duke, Louisiana State, Texas, and a dozen other universities began to secure means of getting private and public funds to erect buildings, to acquire research collections, to develop expert staff members, to devise schemes of purchase and exchange, and to assume positions of educational influence. Some of this resulted from Rockefeller funds, under an informal agreement between Raymond Fosdick and Frederick P. Keppel which largely confined Rockefeller library grants to universities during the years 1929-1938, while Carnegie Corporation was completing a program of helping colleges in the South and other sections of the country to build collections of books adequate for general undergraduate reading. We must not omit the widespread effect of Professor J. G. deR. Hamilton, who set state and university librarians on their ears by building up at the University of North Carolina the extraordinary collection of southern historical documents.

In the development of southern undergraduate libraries, we can not pass over the effect of the visits, writings, and advice of W. W. Bishop of Michigan; of William M. Randall, in his meticulous detailed surveys and reports to the corporation; of George A. Works, in his study of academic library problems; of James T. Gerould, in his book on planning and equipping college library buildings; of C. B. Shaw, in his list of books; of Hugh Gourlay, Foster Mohrhardt and Thomas Barcus, as assistants to W. W. Bishop, in the centralized purchasing office, in training college librarians how to order books under Carnegie grants; of Harvie Branscomb, now chancellor of Vanderbilt, in his learned exposition of teaching with books; and Wheeler and Githens, in their monumental work on library buildings.

As far as academic buildings are concerned, I well recall speaking on the same platform with Adam Strohm, of the Detroit

Public Library, then president of the American Library Association, at the dedication of the new library at Fisk University in November 1930, when that library, made possible by Rockefeller money, was probably the most modern academic library building in the South. As far as I can recall, that building was not excelled, at least in the lower tier of southern states, until December 1941, when the Joint University Library in Nashville, which was known even then, as now, by the revealing short title of Kuhlman's Show, was opened. With Dr. Wilson, I, as a Carnegie representative, spoke at the dedication of that Rockefeller library. In each of these Rockefeller enterprises the Carnegie Corporation, I must confess, had some recognizable financial part other than paying my expenses to appear on the program. Today practically every southern college has a modern library building well stocked with books and librarians and students, and university libraries from Virginia to Florida and Texas are wonders to behold.

Through all this academic library upsurge, pervasive influence has come steadily from the competence, vision, friendly association, and informal operations of the members of the Association of College and Reference Librarians, many of them Southerners.

This account might well go on forever. Little mention has been made of how the regional and state library associations served as vehicles for spreading knowledge of the results of every study and demonstration.

As might be expected there has been through the years much discussion and criticism of libraries and librarians. Some critics complain of the multiplication of library chores, the scarcity of well trained and educated personnel, the refinements of technique, the development of professional jargon, the sometimes vociferous claims for professional recognition, the missionary zeal for conversion of the multitude to reading, the emphasis on statistics, the lack, at times, of a suitable ratio between quantitative and qualitative effort, and so forth.

Many of these things, we know, are the result of a young and growing profession which has devoted much of its energy to meeting pressing needs and demands. We have reason to believe, however, that librarians in the South are constantly seeking steps to make libraries more useful and fruitful to their constituencies, especially in light of changes in civic life, in social and industrial organization, and in education.

Whatever renaissance may have occurred in the South can be traced to devoted men and women, not initially to any foundation. These persons have been gifted with educational vision; their labors have transformed southern public and academic libraries into well established centers of learning. Their names are names of note, worthy to be remembered. Through them, foundation money, a necessary but secondary element, has been made useful. To use time-honored words, these librarians were "renowned for their power, giving counsel by their understanding, wise and eloquent in their instructions; they were the glory of their times". For them, we may say that the long toil of the brave is not lost in darkness. The library renaissance is their doing. It is their living monument.

STOP THIEF!

Lawrence Clark Powell

> Lawrence Clark Powell — first recipient of the Clarence
> Day Award which is intended for librarians who have done
> "outstanding work in encouraging the love of books and
> reading" — is Dean of the School of Library Service, Uni-
> versity of California at Los Angeles. The essay here re-
> printed is a paper read before the June, 1953, meeting of
> the American Library History Round Table at the Los An-
> geles conference of the American Library Association.

First, a word or two about the telephone — an angelic instrument during the working day, a devil at night when, through deep
slumber, its bell rings like a summons from hell!

At 1:30 o'clock in the morning of Saturday, March 5, 1949,
I was enjoying the deep sleep of a librarian whose week's work
is done — all cards checked, all orders placed, all books cata-
loged, all readers served, returns all shelved — a most sweet
Islandian sleep, conscience at rest, dream free. When, ah when,
the phone rang. Blindly I reached out and picked up the little
bedside radio and said hello. Then I knocked the lamp over. Our
two Siamese cats jumped up and began to purr for their milk.
My wife slept on.

At last I found the phone and said hello into the ear-piece.
"Is that you Larry?" a voice asked, then said, "This is the other
Larry."

I recognized the voice as that of Laurance Sweeney, Superintendent of Buildings and Grounds at U.C.L.A. "Good morning,
you so and so", I said.

"Good morning to you." he replied. "We've had a little trouble — thought I ought to call you."

"Water pipe break in the stacks?" I asked.

"No, it's that book."

Reprinted from A PASSION FOR BOOKS by Lawrence Clark Powell
(World Publishing Company, 1958, ©1958 by Lawrence Clark Powell, pp. 85-91) by permission of the author and the World Publishing Company.

STOP THIEF!

"The book?" I asked.

"Someone tried to steal it." Sweeney chuckled. "We caught him!"

"To hell with him." I said. "Where's the book?"

"Right here in my hand."

"Sweeney, you Irish angel! I'll be there in ten minutes."

I never dressed so fast in my life. By then my wife had an eye open. "Someone tried to steal the BAY PSALM BOOK", I said. "And Sweeney caught him."

"So what?" she asked and turned over.

Driving through the empty streets to campus, I recalled the events which had led to a copy of the BAY PSALM BOOK — the first book printed in the English colonies, in the Massachusetts Bay Colony in 1640 — being on exhibition at U.C.L.A. It was the Rosenbach copy — the one that had toured the country on the Freedom Train — and the Rosenbachs, the doctor and his elder brother Philip, had loaned it and the other Freedom Train documents to us for a Washington's Birthday exhibit. It was a good arrangement for U.C.L.A., fledgling library that we were then, lacking all the great early Americana, and it was not without publicity value to the Rosenbach Company.

Another copy of the BAY PSALM BOOK had made international headlines the year before when Doctor Rosenbach paid $151,000 at auction, for the benefit of Yale — the highest price ever paid for a book at auction. Yale objected to the price, as having gone beyond the commissioned figure. In any case the Yale Library has the book — and both the doctor and Philip are dead — the latter here in Beverly Hills last March, aged nearly 90 — and that is why I am free to recount this nocturnal episode in library history.

The Rosenbach copy was said to be insured for $100,000, a story which the Los Angeles press had not overlooked. We had taken security measures. What had gone wrong?

The campus was deserted, the library dark — only the police headquarters was lit up. Sweeney met me at the door.

"Where's the book?" I asked.

"Right here in my pocket", he said, bringing the calf octavo out and putting it in my hands.

"Good man. I said. "Very good man."

"Not me." Sweeney said. "Officer Frush. He's having a cup of coffee and will be back soon. Come see the crook."

He led me down the hall to a room where a student was sitting alone at a table, pale and haggard, his hands on the table. He was wearing handcuffs.

My first feeling toward him was of pity — his scheme, whatever it was, had failed, and he was due to sleep in jail. Not a good place for anyone to be. I suppressed this tender emotion and asked, "Are you a student library employee?"

"No, sir."

"What was the idea?"

Sweeney spoke up. "He says it was a fraternity prank — an initiation stunt — and that he was going to put the book down the return chute in the morning."

"What fraternity?" I asked the kid. "Not Phi Gam, I hope."

"A secret fraternity", he replied. "It was an initiation stunt."

"It didn't pay, did it?" I said.

"No, sir. I'm sorry I tried it."

"Come along", Sweeney said. "We're going to take you down for booking."

"Sweeney, you wit", I said. "You should be writing plays; that's worthy of Oscar."

The student got up and was driven away to the West Los Angeles police station.

Officer Frush returned then and I shook his hand in one of the warmest handshakes one man ever gave another. If Paul Frush was not an ex-cowpuncher, he looked like one — tall, thin, sandy-haired, blue-eyed man, of few words and those in a southwest accent.

We went to the library and he showed me what had happened. We had arranged the exhibit in one end of the reserve book room on the second floor, the windows of which had been sealed. The exhibit was shut off from the rest of the reserve room by a temporary plywood partition, which ran just short of the ceiling. We had the carpenters leave about a foot for cross ventilation when the front doors were opened. Crowds had attended the exhibition, including thousands of school children. Doctors Andrew Horn and Edwin Carpenter of our Department of Special Collections had compiled a handlist in record time and Ward Ritchie had printed it even faster.

The books and manuscripts were housed in several dozen exhibit cases which the aforementioned staff members had scrounged from all over the city. The BAY PSALM BOOK was in a little mahogany case all by itself — a case without a lock, but closed by two invisible set-screws.

Invisible to all save this crafty student, who had studied the lay of the land. At closing time of ten P.M., he had concealed himself in the adjoining reserve area and lurked there for two hours while the janitors cleared the public rooms. At midnight they left. About an hour later, when he thought the building was cleared, the student somehow scaled the ten-foot plywood wall, squeezed through the crack at the top, and dropped down into the exhibit room. At one A.M. Officer Frush looked through the glass front doors and shone his flashlight about the room. He saw nothing amiss and left. Whereupon the student whipped out his trusty screwdriver, opened the case, took the BAY PSALM BOOK, and put in its place — of all things — a paper-bound Army language manual — PORTUGUESE MADE EASY. With the loot in the pocket of his tweed jacket, the thief scaled the wall again, squeezed back through the crack, and dropped down into the reserve room. Here the windows were not sealed. He opened one. It squeaked slightly — and at precisely the moment when Officer Frush was leaving the building by the west side door, directly beneath the reserve room, on his way to circle the outside of the building. The student hoisted himself over the sill and dropped twelve feet into a bed of scarlet hibiscus. Soft and muddy earth broke his fall. He got up at once and made off.

Officer Frush approached at that moment and suggested he stop. The student began to run. Whereupon Frush drew his 45, and called "Stop! or I shoot." Fortunately, for himself, the student heard the frontier quality in that voice — and also the click of the cocked gun. He stopped. Frush marched him to the station where he was searched and the book found. The captain was called. He then called the superintendent, who in turn called the librarian.

After hearing Frush's story and returning the book to the case, I went home and slept a few hours, then was back at the library, prepared to greet a thousand members of the California Library Association who were meeting on campus, with the Rosenbach exhibit as a special documentation for a program on intellectual freedom. I shuddered to think of the student having successfully made off with the book on the very morn of the meeting.

I did not believe his story of a secret fraternity prank. I was anxious also that there be no publicity.

The day went well and I thought everything was nicely back under control — until toward the end of the afternoon. I was in the exhibition room with visitors, when one of the staff told me there was a man asking for me.

He identified himself as a reporter from the Los Angeles Examiner — a Hearst paper — as if that wasn't exactly who he resembled!

I drew him aside.

"What do you want?"

"The story", he replied.

"What story?"

"About the stolen book."

"What book?"

"O.K., Doc." he said. "I've read the blotter at the West Los Angeles station. I'm going to break the story. Wouldn't you like to have the facts straight?"

"You win." I said. "Let's go up to my office."

I gave him the whole story, and then I phoned the rival Los Angeles Times. Of the two papers, I prefer the Times, and wanted to see them get an even break. Their reporter and photographer reached the library within half an hour.

At home that evening the Associated Press phoned for the story; and I did some phoning, too, to get word to President Sproul and Provost Dykstra before the Sunday morning papers appeared.

What happened to the student? What was his real motive? Through preliminary hearing and probation investigation, he stuck to his story of a secret fraternity stunt. I never believed it nor do I now. From what I learned of his background, I believe that he intended to shake down the insurance company for the few thousand dollars they would have paid for a no-questions-asked return of the book.

I didn't like the kid — who was actually not a kid at all, but a twenty-eight-year-old graduate student who had once changed his name — and liked him least of all the day he came to my office, when out on bail, and begged me to intercede on his behalf. I did eventually recommend probation — which he got — but that day I was ready to throw him out. He had come a little too close to making a monkey of me.

Two amusing footnotes. . . . At the student's preliminary

hearing in court, old Philip Rosenbach was put on the stand, white carnation boutonnière, perfumed handkerchief, patent-leather shoes, and all.

"About this so-called Boy's [sic] Psalm Book", the defense attorney began. "Is it not true that there are facsimile editions of it? What proof have we that this book in question is an original and not a facsimile?"

I thought Philip would have a stroke and die at eighty-three! He spluttered a full minute before he managed to say:

"I'll have you know, sir, the Rosenbachs don't deal in fac-similes!"

And the other footnote: the student was actually a transfer to California from the University of Oregon — and once, later, at dinner with a distinguished elderly friend of the University, I mentioned this fact, that the thief had been from out-of-state.

Quick was the comment: "See what happens when we let these foreigners into California?"

THE MULTILATERAL APPROACH REQUIRED
OF FRENCH-CANADIAN LIBRARIANSHIP

Jean-Charles Bonenfant

> Jean-Charles Bonenfant is Librarian of the Library of the
> Legislature of the Province of Quebec. The essay here re-
> printed is a paper read before the American Library His-
> tory Round Table during the 1960 joint conference of the
> American Library Association and the Canadian Library
> Association in Montreal.

For us, a few million French-speaking Canadians, the fact of
living within an Anglo-Saxon America, creates many intellectual
problems with both good and ill consequences. In most branches
of learning and in the practice of many professions, French Canadians are under manifold influences emanating from Paris, London, New York, as well as from Toronto and Montreal. Since the
end of the eighteenth century, our parliamentary chiefs have used
English constitutional law to improve our political status – but
this has been expressed in the French language. It is in French
that our lawyers plead before courts where English Criminal
Law is the rule or where Common Law melts with French Civil
Law. Our physicians, our architects, our engineers, our scholars in every field of the social sciences face intricate influences.
These influences are not easy to digest intelligently, but they do
form a great wealth that is unique. Life at a cross-roads is sometimes difficult but in the long run, it can be "a gift from the gods".

It would have been amazing if such a learned and extensive a
profession as librarianship had escaped the multilateral approach
required of other French-Canadian intellectual activity. The librarian indeed, according to his training and his work, is not
bound to a country or a language and he is, more than anyone,
a citizen of the world.

I would like to emphasize the situation of the research-librar-
ian because this is the part of librarianship where the multilateral approach is most evident, but I think that my observations

Reprinted from Canadian Library, 17:190-193, January, 1961, by
permission of the author and the publisher.

would apply "mutatis mutandis" to other types of French Canadian libraries.

The multilateral approach required of French-Canadian Librarianship may be studied under three headings: the technical aspect; the cultural aspect and the specialized aspect in the field of law.

Librarianship in French Canada has been for a long time under European influences, mostly French. There was the tradition that libraries were large museums with locked showcases. They were managed, or rather, supervised by learned old gentlemen with a fondness for books but with no special training. The best qualification for the job of librarian often was poor health that prevented the earning of a living from other sources. A library situation was a sinecure and the librarian was annoyed when anyone invaded his sanctuary.

This ancient continental concept of a librarian as an old and learned gentleman without professional training has faded, but it has been very often replaced by another dangerous concept: the idea of a librarian as one whose vision of books stops at their covers, or title-pages, as one who looks at books with the eyes of a grocer facing the cans of peas on his shelves. Nevertheless, it appears that today the French-Canadian librarian is in the process of synthesizing culture and technique; technique of which I intend to speak immediately, with the purpose of coming back later to the problem of culture.

In the gathering of professional knowledge and in the use of technical processes, a French-Canadian librarian is obliged to choose constantly between data coming from France, his natural and traditional source of knowledge, and the overwhelming material from the United States. I think that the American influence is breaking through and this is for the best, but it has to be accepted and digested in a French context. Many French-Canadian librarians use professional books such as MANUEL PRATIQUE DU BIBLIOTHECAIRE by Leo Crozet or PETIT GUIDE DU BIB-LIOTHECAIRE by Charles-Henri Bach, but often they are overshadowed by American Library Classics such as TECHNICAL SERVICES IN LIBRARIES by Tauber.

The most difficult problem for the French-Canadian librarian is to use tools, instruments, techniques from the English language without losing what he wants to preserve in the French language. Many problems are above language distinctions, but it is quite difficult, for example, to compile a catalogue without giving prominence to our own language. Many French-Canadian libraries buy catalogue cards from the H. W. Wilson Company and from the Library of Congress. These save time and money. They do not raise difficulties for English books in the author or title catalogues but they do in the subject catalogue where it is necessary to respect uniformity of language and to make entries in French according to patterns from Biblio. With respect to French books, since it would be incongruous to have them catalogued in English, the cards have to be prepared in the French language since none are available by sale. This is one example of how a perpetual mingling of French and English, or more precisely American methods, complicates our work.

But in return, we truly profit by two great cultures. In our large French-Canadian libraries, we move equally between French and English. We peruse with equal interest catalogues issued in Canada (English and French Canada), France, the United States and England. For us, The Cumulative Book Index is as important as Bibliographie de la France and on our shelves stand the Catalogues of the Library of Congress, of the British Museum and of La Bibliothèque nationale. Important libraries do the same all over the world, but for us, it is not only a display of wealth but also it is a necessity of professional life. Our libraries are among the most generous subscribers to the Wilson indexes which are more useful for us than French indexes of the same kind. We use the GUIDE PRATIQUE DES BIBLIOGRAPHIES by Calot and Thomas and the well known works of Maclès but, living in America, we have also the STANDARD CATALOG FOR PUBLIC LIBRARIES and the GUIDE TO REFERENCE BOOKS.

As you know, the main source of information in a library, in a general library and more precisely in a reference library, is found in encyclopaedias and dictionaries. It has been said by Thomas Landau, in his ENCYCLOPAEDIA OF LIBRARIANSHIP that we have to "look on the reference library as a living encyclopaedia". In this very large and important field, in the province of Quebec, we equally use works in French and in English. We have to buy the latest editions of the best sets from Paris, London, Chicago, and Ottawa to name only a few cities where the best reference material is sold. In our libraries, LAROUSSE, and QUILLET face the ENCYCLOPAEDIA BRITANNICA and the AMERICANA and without partiality. For the purpose of finding the truth we use them in a kind of rivalry. We are so used to such a practice, that often we do not remember if the information has been obtained from an English or French source but, as we usually relay it in French (spoken or written French), there is the danger of poor interpretation because the translation is often, of necessity, hasty. It is a universal danger for French in the Province of Quebec and, as it was said by a French-Canadian politician, defending the quality of our language against Paris critics, "perhaps our French is not very good and is a wounded language, but, do not be cruel, if it is so wounded, it is because it had to fight".

Everywhere in a French-Canadian library, French and English are neighbours. We keep the international publications in both languages; the government publications from Ottawa and Quebec are bilingual – in separate parts in Ottawa and usually with both texts side by side in Quebec; we have to preserve Canadian newspapers in French and in English, and we are as much interested in important newspapers from France as we are in those from the United Kingdom and the United States. So, a good library keeps on microfilm, Le Monde, The Times of London and the New York Times.

But to give you a detailed demonstration of the multilateral approach required of French-Canadian Librarianship, I shall speak of a law library as it relates most particularly to my own professional knowledge and training.

The law system of the province of Quebec is intricate. It is the product of many age-old influences and it is under the jurisdiction of both the provincial and the federal authorities. During the French regime, our ancestors were, of course, subjects of the king of France and lived under the French private and public law, the law that disappeared with the French Revolution. In 1763, by the treaty of Paris, New France was ceded by France to England and according to international law, English public law was automatically introduced on the banks of the St. Lawrence River. So, our public law, our constitutional law and our administrative law, is of English origin but during two centuries it has been deeply transformed by Canadian statutes and conventions. A public law library possesses every Canadian public law book but it would be dangerously incomplete without the numerous English public law works which influence our constitutional, administrative and political life. But, this is not enough. We

live, for better or for worse, beside a great country with political institutions different from ours but which have an influence
upon our political behaviour. So, we have to include in our libraries the excellent public law books coming from the United
States without, of course, being obliged to buy all the Ph.D. the-
ses on the subject. And after all, as we express ourselves in
French, we find in French constitutional works very useful phras-
ing, as well as good ideas.

But it is in private law, civil and commercial law, that a
French-Canadian library, even a small library for practising
lawyers, becomes quite complicated. During the French regime,
New France was under the old law of Paris. After the conquest,
in 1774, the Quebec Act was passed to encourage the subjects to
remain faithful to the King. When Americans revolted against
him, it was enacted that "all His Majesty's Canadian Subjects
within the Province of Quebec, may hold and enjoy their Property
and Possessions, together with all Customs and Usages, relative thereto, and all other of their Civil Rights, and that in all
Matters of Controversy relative to Property and Civil Rights,
Resort shall be had to the Laws of Canada".

And so the basis of our private law is French law, not the
modern French law, but the old French law, which was in major
part destroyed by the French Revolution. This is the reason why,
in our libraries, we have to keep old French treatises of law
that have no use in France. A great French author of the 18th
Century like Pothier, a kind of Blackstone for us, is more often
referred to before our courts than he is in France. But old French
law is not completely forgotten by French modern law and further-
more, our private law was codified in 1866 on the model of the
Napoleonic Code. This situation has made it necessary for us to
use modern French commentators, the authors of great treatises
of civil law like Aubry and Rau and Planiol and Ripert. Incidentally, the treatise by Planiol and Ripert was translated into English a few months ago for use in the State of Louisiana, the law
of which is based, like ours, on French civil law and this translation will be useful also for citation before our English judges.

Our French private law has been affected with law expressed
in statutes adopted by our parliaments — statutes which very often
are inspired by English, American or Anglo-Canadian statutes
and judicial precedents. Common law has invaded our French
civil law and today our commercial law has very little of its

French origin. So, we have to use in our libraries not only the authorities from France but also old and new treatises from England, from the United States and from English Canada. And of course, we have also our own authors. It is amazing to see the hundreds of feet of shelves required for storing the many and diversified law reports even in a small library. These reports range from the United States Supreme Court reports to the Dalloz and Sirey sets from France.

This is an example of our complex situation. We live at a cross-roads between the French and Anglo-Saxon world, between Europe and America. It is for us a perpetual challenge with its advantages and also with its difficulties. But for a librarian, it is the best invitation to that universality which is our true vocation. In the ideal library indeed, there should be no barriers of language, no preference for a country. Everything should be used and, as it has been said by the English essayist and poet Edward Thomas in CLOUD CASTLE, "the ideal library is the library in which no book would have disdained its neighbour".

In our libraries, French and English books do not disdain each other; they do not live "in two solitudes", as it has been said by pessimists about husbands and wives, but they stand side by side in friendliness with the best spirit of co-operation.

A NATIONAL LIBRARY FOR CANADA:
A RECORD AND A PROMISE

H. Pearson Gundy

H. Pearson Gundy is University Librarian, Queen's University, Kingston, Ontario, Canada. The essay here reprinted
is a paper read before the American Library History Round
Table during the 1960 joint conference of the American Library Association and the Canadian Library Association in
Montreal.

Long before its birth, the National Library was a gleam in
the eyes of Canada's first Prime Minister, the redoubtable Sir
John A. Macdonald. Had the Joint Committee on the Library of
Parliament caught that gleam our story might have been very
different. We go back to the year 1882, fifteen years after the
scattered provinces of Canada had united, with some misgivings,
to form the new Dominion. The members of Parliament are proud
of their stately Gothic buildings, the architectural gem of which
is conceded to be the buttressed lantern of the Parliamentary
Library, perhaps the only library in the world to have been featured on its country's currency.[1] The Librarian, of whom the
members are somewhat in awe, is one of Canada's most distinguished scholars, Colonel Alpheus Todd, C.M.G., LL.D., world
famous authority on constitutional law and parliamentary practice.

In his own domain Librarian Todd is supreme, subject only
to the will of Parliament as expressed by the library committee
jointly representing the Senate and the House of Commons. For
several years now the wily Dr. Todd has exceeded his meagre
budget by the simple expedient of buying books on credit and
forcing the hand of the government to make supplementary grants.
Again the library budget has come up for debate,[2] and some of
the members have decided it is time for a showdown. The former Liberal Prime Minister, Hon. Alexander Mackenzie, com-
plains that the last grant was spent almost entirely on law books,

Reprinted, with minor changes by the author, from Canadian Library,
17:170-177, January, 1961, by permission of the author and the publisher.

and his colleague, Hon. David Mills, points out that because of
this the library is "not keeping up with the literature of the Empire". Sir John A. Macdonald hopes the library committee will
look into this and consider what the library should be. "At present", he says, "it is neither one thing nor the other. It is too
large for a parliamentary library and too small and confined for
a public and general library." Sir Hector Langevin is sharply
critical: "The Librarian", he protests, "continues to do year
after year what we have been complaining of year after year, exceeding the sum placed at his disposal." Clearly he must be
brought to task. A full enquiry is left to the Joint Committee of
seventeen members, over half of whom, including the rising hope
of the Liberal party, Mr. Wilfrid Laurier, are lawyers by profession.

One year later, on April 16th, 1883, the published report[3] of
the committee is brought before Parliament for the concurrence
of the House. Regrettably the Chairman, Mr. C. C. Colby, the
honourable member for Stanstead, is absent, but speaking for
the committee is the leader of the opposition, Hon. Edward Blake,
unrivalled for his forensic brilliance.

Although the Prime Minister had suggested that the Committee consider the purpose of the library, this question is evaded
in the report. The chief recommendation is that the law books,
with some necessary exceptions, be transferred to the Supreme
Court Building to form a new and independent library under the
Department of Justice.

Sir John opens the debate by pressing to its logical conclusion
his former observation on the purpose of the Library of Parliament: "Our library", he repeats, "is neither one thing nor the
other just now. It is not a British Museum or a Canadian Museum
or a National Library. It falls as it were between two stools . . .
It is assumed from the number of the volumes that it has the
character of a national library, yet it is commonly and technically merely a Parliamentary library . . . In England a member
of Parliament wanting information on any possible subject to
which his attention may be called as a legislator, will find it in
the Parliamentary Library; but the general collection of books,
and the Library of the Nation, is the British Museum. We will
have to face that subject very soon . . . The Dominion of Canada really ought to have a National Library, containing every book
worthy of being kept on the shelves of a Library, but we cannot

be continually adding to these buildings and to Parliamentary Libraries. It ought to be a quite separate and distinct question, which should be taken up at an early day".[4]

The proposal so aptly put falls, however, on deaf ears. Other members turn at once to the question of a new law library removed from the responsibility of Dr. Todd. On this point the lawyers have their innings. Sir John is not opposed, but he rises again and by directing a question to Mr. Blake, tries to focus the debate on the national issue:

"I would like to ask the Hon. gentleman whether the Committee have really considered the question of having a National Library as distinct from the Library connected with the Buildings."

Mr. Blake replies, "I am not the spokesman of the Committee. My honourable friend from Stanstead acts as its spokesman; but I may say that the Library Committee did not think it was within its province to propose the creation of a National Library."[5]

And in this reply the idea of a National Library for Canada received the kiss of death in the House of Commons for over half a century.

The first decade of the twentieth century had passed before a single voice was raised in Canada in support of Sir John A. Macdonald's singular ambition to create a Library for the Nation.

The second voice of one crying in the wilderness was that of a librarian whose father had been a personal friend and parliamentary opponent of Sir John, Mr. Lawrence J. Burpee, Chief Librarian of the Ottawa Carnegie Library. A historian of note and a Fellow of the Royal Society of Canada, he was a man whose opinions commanded attention and respect. In the University Magazine for February 1911, he published an article entitled "A Plea for a National Library"[6]. His thesis was that such a library would be "the keystone of a broad and efficient system of education" in Canada. It could make available on loan to provincial, public and university libraries throughout the country the resources of "a noble collection of books" embracing the whole range of human knowledge. "Canada", he pointed out, "enjoys the dubious distinction of ranking with Siam and Abyssinia in at least one respect—none of the three possesses a National Library' And he underlined this by commenting on a dozen or more national libraries throughout the world, some of them in countries smaller and less developed than Canada. From all of these we could borrow "those features that would most readily adapt themselves to our own peculiar needs".

The article had far-reaching repercussions. It received favourable, even enthusiastic editorial comment in the Canadian press from coast to coast. The Toronto Globe ran a feature article on March 4, "For a National Canadian Library" by Agnes C. Laut, popular journalist and historian of the Canadian North West. "Every intelligent Canadian", she began, "will endorse the plea put forward by Mr. L. J. Burpee for the creation of a National Library for the Dominion."[7] And from her own experience in being obliged to turn to American Libraries for source material on Canadian history, she branded our lack of concern "a national disgrace".

In the spring of 1911, the Ontario Library Association elected Mr. Burpee President and voted unanimously to petition the government of Sir Wilfrid Laurier to appoint a Royal Commission on the need for a National Library. Sir Wilfrid himself had more than a passing interest in this project and had suggested Nepean Point as a suitable location for a National Library. But the time was inopportune, for a general election was impending, and the petition of the OLA went unheeded. Because of the uncertain political situation the submission of the Royal Society of Canada, approved by the annual meeting of 1911 on the same terms as that of the OLA, was deferred. When the matter came up again in 1913, the Council of the Society "doubted whether it would be expedient to make a specific recommendation".[8]

With the outbreak of the first World War in 1914, the question was again shelved, but a year later the Royal Society finally submitted to the government a watered-down resolution urging "the importance of expanding the present Library of Parliament into a national institution".[9] This was a very different proposal from those of Sir John A. Macdonald and the OLA. It was duly acknowledged, filed away, and never brought before Parliament.

Librarians, not easily discouraged, kept up the agitation in the Ontario Library Review. Mr. J. D. Barnett, in the issue for May, 1918, suggested the end of the war as an opportune time to begin "this great and useful institution", and with more force than elegance described the National Library as "a circulating turbine pump with a pulsating delivery".[10]

The end of the war came, but not that "turbine pump", though reconstruction was the watchword. Mr. Burpee returned to his theme in the pages of the newly established Canadian Historical

Review,[11] repeating the points he had made nearly ten years earlier –a "noble collection of books", yes; but the National Library
must also classify, catalogue, issue bibliographies, answer reference questions, and aid other libraries. Now, however, Mr.
Burpee was preaching to the converted, for the circulation of the
CHR was limited largely to historical scholars all too well aware
of our library shortcomings.

The decade of the twenties saw little advance toward the fulfilment of the national library ambition. There was, however, one
hopeful sign. In 1926 Dr. George H. Locke of the Toronto Public
Library was elected President of the American Library Association, and the annual meeting for 1927 took place in Toronto. Canadian members present made plans to organize a Canadian Library Association. The project fell through for lack of financial
support, but the first need was seen to be a comprehensive survey of library conditions in Canada. To carry this out, the ALA
obtained a grant from the Carnegie Corporation and appointed
three Canadian members to make the survey: Dr. G. H. Locke,
Miss M. J. L. Black of Fort William, and Mr. John Ridington,
Librarian of the University of British Columbia.

Between June and September, 1930, they visited every province in Canada and discussed library affairs with prime ministers
provincial and national members of parliament, judges, civil
servants, teachers, professors, newspaper editors, business
men, labour leaders, and, of course, "librarians of all sorts
and sizes of libraries".[12]

The report was published jointly by the American Library
Association and the Ryerson Press, Toronto, in 1933. Chapter
ten dealt with "The Need for a National Library Policy". Several
broad suggestions were made: appoint as National Librarian a
scholar-librarian-administrator with large powers and wide dis-
cretion; turn over to the National Library all books in the Library
of Parliament not needed for legislative reference and books deposited under the Copyright Act; build a new library designed for
indefinite growth on a central site; staff the Library with trained
librarians who are also specialists in various subject fields as
in the Library of Congress.

The report made a considerable stir — in library circles;
otherwise it was largely ignored. Even the university quarter-
lies failed to give it passing notice. Canada was still struggling with the depression and libraries throughout the country

could do little more than mark time.

Fighting a rearguard action against unemployment, the Bennett government went down in defeat in 1935 and was succeeded by a Liberal administration under the Rt. Hon. W. L. Mackenzie King. Before undertaking widespread measures of reform, the government appointed a Royal Commission on Dominion-Provincial Relations to make an impartial investigation of the Canadian economy.

Here was one more opportunity for librarians to state their case for a National Library, and they rose to the occasion. There was still no national organization, but the two strongest provincial library associations, Ontario and British Columbia, both submitted briefs prepared by committees on which Miss Elizabeth Morton served for Ontario and Dr. W. Kaye Lamb for British Columbia.[13]

Both briefs placed the primary stress upon the bibliographic and allied services which a national library could render, and the valuable assistance it could offer to libraries in every province — a demonstration on the intellectual level of good Dominion-Provincial relations. These submissions were made in the spring of 1938, two years before the Commission's report was published. Meanwhile, librarians continued to propagate the national library gospel. At the annual conference of the Ontario Library Association in April 1939, Mr. E. C. Kyte, my predecessor at Queen's University Library, gave a bracing address[14] on the subject and was promptly elected Convener of the National Library Committee.

Again Fate intervened, for by the time the Royal Commission Report appeared, and Mr. Kyte was due to present his first report to the Ontario Library Association, World War II had broken out, and government action on domestic issues was postponed for the duration. Nevertheless, advised Mr. Kyte, "we should continue by word and pen to keep alive an enlightened interest in the National Library . . . more at the moment we do not think can be done; less we will not do".[15]

Surprisingly, this continued agitation began to bear fruit even in wartime. In his annual report for 1943, Mr. Felix Desrochers, the General Librarian of Parliament, summed up his views:

"Let the government adopt the policy of a National Library, erect a suitable building for its accommodation in some central locality; and remove from the Library of Parliament to the Na-

tional Library all books and library material that would properly find a place in such an institution but which serve no very useful purpose in a purely legislative library. Of the books at present crowded into the Library of Parliament probably two-thirds
could be removed to the National Library. This would leave, say,
150,000 volumes in the Library of Parliament, embracing all
material which could have any definite value as legislative material."[16]

The joint Committee accepted this proposal and recommended
to Parliament that "as soon as circumstances permit, the Government should consider the desirability of creating a National
Library, and the maintenance of the existing library as a parliamentary library for the use of the Honourable Senators and Members of Parliament".[17]

Shades of Sir John A. Macdonald and Hon. Edward Blake! After sixty years, the Joint Committee on the Library of Parliament found that, in point of fact it did come within its province
to propose the creation of a National Library.

By this time Parliament was in a more receptive mood. The
turning point came in August 1944 when the Canadian Library
Council under the chairmanship of Miss Margaret S. Gill presented a brief to the Reconstruction Committee of the House of
Commons. No immediate action was taken, but it was a portent.

In 1946, under Dr. Freda Waldon, the energetic first President of the Canadian Library Association, a brief was drawn up
jointly by the CLA and representatives of four other Canadian
learned societies.[18] This was no hasty effort; it represented the
combined thought of a group of distinguished scholars, the burden of which was "NATIONAL LIBRARY SERVICE can be started
now".[19] In its final form it was sponsored by no fewer than seventeen organizations across Canada, including the Trades and Labour Congress and the Canadian Congress of Labour.

In January 1947, at the invitation of the Prime Minister, a
delegation from the five societies which had drawn up the brief
met in Ottawa to discuss it with the Secretary of State, Hon. Co-
lin Gibson. Asked whether the delegates had in mind a suitable
candidate for the office of National Librarian, Professor R. G.
Trotter, Head of the History Department of Queen's University
representing the Royal Society, proposed Dr. W. Kaye Lamb, librarian of the University of British Columbia.

This time the brief was not conveniently pigeon-holed, but

duly reported to the House of Commons where, by resolution, it was referred to the Joint Library Committee for consideration and report to Parliament, along with any further representations which might be made on the National Library.[20]

For the CLA this was only the beginning. Later in the year Dr. Waldon gave a talk on the subject over the national network of the CBC which brought an encouraging response.[21] Copies of a paper to the OLA Reference Workshop on "Bibliographic Centres and the Situation in Canada" by Miss Marie Tremaine were sent to the Prime Minister, and all members of Parliament. The Secretary of State was deluged with articles and newspaper clippings on the National Library — seventy-six in one year. These were passed on to the Joint Library Committee with good results.[22]

More ammunition came from an outside source. Since 1944 the Humanities Research Council of Canada had been conducting a survey on "the state of the humanities in Canada" under Dr. Watson Kirkconnell and Dean A. S. P. Woodhouse. Their report, published in 1947, reviewed the arguments for a national library, outlined its proper functions, and concluded: "It is conceivable that no other single project could contribute so much to the intellectual and cultural integration of Canadian life".[23]

This, too, was sent to the Joint Library Committee. That long suffering body reported to the House of Commons June 11, 1948, and recommended:

That as a first step toward the creation of a National Library, the planning of a Bibliographic Centre be commenced by the selection of a competent bibliographer and secretary; and that this matter be referred to the Secretary of State, with the recommendation that a special committee be set up to supervise such work; and that sufficient funds be supplied to meet expenses.[24]

At this opportune time the vacant position of Dominion Archivist had to be filled, and the Prime Minister, Mr. Mackenzie King, made the inspired appointment of Dr. William Kaye Lamb, Librarian of the University of British Columbia, former Provincial Archivist, and newly elected President of the CLA. The terms of appointment included the special assignment of establishing a National Library Advisory Committee. A small staff was also authorized to begin the work of compiling a National Union Catalogue.

As yet there was no National Library, but the ghost of old Sir John could now repeat with assurance: "We will have to face that subject very soon." In 1949 the Hon. Louis St. Laurent became Prime Minister. One of his first acts was an Order in Council appointing a Royal Commission on National Development in the Arts, Letters and Sciences under the Chairmanship of Rt. Hon. Vincent Massey, to investigate among other things, "the eventual character and scope of a National Library".[25]

Once again the CLA went into action. Briefs on the National Library were by now such a familiar exercise that they almost wrote themselves. Nevertheless, a committee was appointed for this purpose, on which I had the honour to serve, under the Chairmanship of the late Dr. Charles R. Sanderson of the Toronto Public Library. At the Winnipeg Conference of the CLA in June 1949 we put the finishing touches on our brief,[26] confining our submission to points not already under consideration by the National Library Advisory Committee. We advocated photocopying rare Canadiana known only in collections outside Canada; amendment of the Copyright Act to make the National Library the legal depository; use of the National Library as a distributing centre for government publications; the microfilming of Canadiana ephemera; collection of recordings of Canadian dialects, folklore and music and of Canadian films. The library site we submitted, should soon be selected and the building planned on functional lines.

The brief was presented at a hearing in the Supreme Court Building, Ottawa, on August 18. To all of us present it was apparent that the Commission was already well informed and wholly in favour of the National Library.

On May 1, 1950, the Bibliographic Centre was officially established and began at once the task of compiling the now familiar current national bibliography Canadiana, ably edited by Dr. Jean Lunn. Miss Martha Shepard was already doing yeoman service on a union catalogue, compiled from photographic enlargements of microfilm reproductions of some thirty-five card catalogues in various government libraries in Ottawa, a programme since extended across Canada.

With this impressive start, it was no surprise, therefore, when the Massey Commission Report finally appeared in 1951, to find a categorical statement that "the time had now come for the creation of a national library". The major points were cogently set forth in a series of seven recommendations.

On Tuesday, May 20, 1952, a resolution to provide for the establishment of a National Library was introduced in the House of Commons by the Prime Minister. The ensuing debate takes up some twenty pages of <u>Hansard</u>.[27] Nine members spoke to the resolution. Their questions and comments showed how well the groundwork had been prepared. Not a single voice was raised against the project. Mr. St. Laurent made it clear that it was the intention of the government on approval of Parliament, to continue the policy of developing the National Library under the supervision of the Dominion Archivist, without prejudice to possible future separation of these two services under independent heads. Hon. George Drew, Leader of Her Majesty's Loyal Opposition, spoke for the House when he said: "All honourable members will welcome the first step in what would appear to be the fulfilment of a dream that has engaged the imagination and the hopes of Canadians for a very long time."[28]

The resolution was approved; the Prime Minister moved for leave to introduce Bill No. 254 respecting the establishment of a National Library and the bill was read for the first time. Second and third readings followed later and Canada had on paper her long-awaited National Library.

One crucial step remained, the appointment of a National Librarian. Mr. John Ridington and his collaborators, as far back as 1933, had stressed the vital importance of choosing the right man for this high position.

"On the wisdom or otherwise of that choice would depend, in large degree, the success or failure of the whole enterprise. He should be broadly educated and professionally trained, yet young enough to look forward to a quarter century of active effort; a man of ripe scholarship and wide sympathy, of faith and vision, of tact and tenacity; whose character and abilities would command respect and inspire confidence; who could plan, organize and administer, who could select, assemble, and lead a competent staff, and deserve and secure their co-operation, loyalty and devotion."[29]

There was only one man in Canada who met every one of these exacting qualifications, the Dominion Archivist, Dr. William Kaye Lamb, and to the very great satisfaction of his professional colleagues throughout Canada he was appointed our first National Librarian on December 22, 1952, the appointment to take effect on the first day of January 1953.[30]

At the same time, the National Library Act went into force, under which an Assistant National Librarian, Dr. Raymond Tanghe, formerly Librarian of the University of Montreal, was appointed on June 1. Architects also were appointed to design a modern building which would house both the Public Archives and the National Library. This fine building would now be in construction had it not been for a disastrous explosion in a near-by government building on October 25, 1958. A home had to be found for the refugee staff who, pending re-location, were installed in a wartime temporary building, due for demolition, on the site of the National Library. Meanwhile it was imperative to find shelf-space for the rapidly accumulating national book collection. The Public Archives had recently constructed a large new Records Centre in Ottawa West. An acre of floor space was made available to provide the National Library with a local habitation until its new home was built. Out of site out of mind. Instead of proceeding with demolition of the Temporary Building on Wellington Street when the refugee civil servants were re-located, the building was promptly commandeered for other government purposes.

Pressure on Parliament thus continues. The Executive CLA met with the Prime Minister, the Right Hon. John G. Diefenbaker, to plead for action in 1959. Resolutions were again drawn up and in November 1960 were presented to the Hon. David J. Walker, Minister of Public Works, by a joint delegation of the CLA Council and the National Library Advisory Committee. The issue is far from dead, for the expanding book stock will soon outgrow the Records Centre. The government has a firm commitment and despite exasperating set-backs a National Library building in which all Canadians can take pride is a prospect bright for the future.

A NATIONAL LIBRARY FOR CANADA

NOTES:

1 Canadian dollar bill, issued by the Canadian Banknote Company, 1923.

2 Official Report of the Debates of the House of Commons of the Dominion of Canada (Hansard), Ottawa, 1882. See debates April 5, May 12.

3 Journals of the House of Commons of the Dominion of Canada, Session 1883, pp. 178-90.

4 Hansard, April 16, 1883, pp. 630-1.

5 Ibid., p. 631.

6 Lawrence J. Burpee, "A Plea for a National Library", University Magazine, vol. 10 (1911), pp. 152-163. (The University Magazine was published by a committee representing McGill University, the University of Toronto, and Dalhousie University).

7 Toronto Globe, Saturday Magazine Section, March 4, 1955, p. 6.

8 Royal Society of Canada, Proceedings and Transactions, 3rd ser., May 1913, p. xxxiii.

9 Ibid., May 1916, p. xviii.

10 J. Davis Barnett, "A National Library for Canada", Ontario Library Review, II, 4 (May 1918) p. 108.

11 Lawrence J. Burpee, "A Plea for a Canadian National Library", Canadian Historical Review, vol. 1 (June 1920) pp. 191-194.

12 John Ridington, Mary J. L. Black, George H. Locke. LIBRARIES IN CANADA: A STUDY OF LIBRARY CONDITIONS AND NEEDS by the Commission of Enquiry. Toronto & Chicago, 1933, p. 5.

13 Royal Commission on Dominion-Provincial Relations. Brief submitted . . . April 1938, by the Ontario Library Association . . . Also: Brief submitted . . . March 1938, by the British Columbia Library Association.

14 E. Cockburn Kyte, "A National Library for Canada: the Place of a National Library in National Life", Ontario Library Review,

vol. 23 (1939) pp. 181-4

15   E. Cockburn Kyte, "Report on a National Library for Canada", OLR, vol. 24 (1940) pp. 124-5.

16   Journals of the Senate of Canada . . . 1943-44, Ottawa, 1944, p. 333.

17   Ibid., p. 334.

18   Royal Society of Canada, the Canadian Historical Association, the Canadian Political Science Association, the Social Science Research Council of Canada.

19   "A National Library for Canada", A brief presented to the Government of Canada . . . December 1946. Text in OLR, vol. 30 (1947) pp. 3-6.

20   Hansard, May 20, 1948, p. 4188; Journals of the House of Commons, 1948, p. 951.

21   Text in CLA Bulletin, vol. 4 (1947) pp. 41-3.

22   "Report of the National Library Committee", CLA Bulletin, vol. 5 (1948) p. 16.

23   Watson Kirkconnell and A. D. P. Woodhouse. THE HUMANITIES IN CANADA, Ottawa, 1947, p. 166.

24   Journals of the Senate of Canada, LXXXIX, June 14, 1948, p. 398.

25   REPORT OF THE ROYAL COMMISSION ON NATIONAL DEVELOPMENT OF THE ARTS, LETTERS AND SCIENCES, 1949-1951, Ottawa, 1951. p. xviii.

26   Text in CLA Bulletin, vol. 6, (1949) pp. 31-33.

27   Hansard, May 20, 1952, pp. 2370-2390.

28   Ibid., p. 2376.

29   LIBRARIES IN CANADA, op. cit. p. 110.

30   The Canada Gazette, January 3, 1953, p. 19.

PART THREE — BIOGRAPHICAL ESSAYS

AMONG THE FOUNDERS

Frederic G. Melcher

Frederic G. Melcher is Chairman of the Board of the R. R.
Bowker Company, New York City. The essay here reprint-
ed is the text of an address given on National Library Day,
October 4, 1951, at Drexel Institute, Philadelphia, at the
celebration of the 75th anniversary of the founding of the
American Library Association.

The nation was certain to celebrate in the year 1876, and it
was certain to celebrate in the city where the nation had begun
a century before. The United States had just weathered its se-
verest internal test and was starting confidently on the task of
expanding across a great continent, to populate and more fully
use it. The anniversary could have fallen, however, in days
more happy for democracy, political corruption was rampant
and commercial chicanery had been only slightly halted by the
devastating panic of '73.

Yet, in retrospect, a most significant aspect of that decade
was to be the upsurge in education, bringing new standards and
new ideas. It was the period marked by the leadership of Charles
W. Eliot, Andrew D. White, Daniel Coit Gilman, and others; it
was the day of the Morrill Act with its well-financed land-grant
colleges; it was the period of the establishment of colleges for
women.

Of equal importance in this new educational activity was the
coming together of American librarians, both public and college,
in recognition of their common interests and to form a permanent
national organization. They outlined a plan for expansion and
new usefulness which was to keep pace and companionship with
the programs of the other cultural agencies of the country. As
always, with cultural agencies, its ambitions were always just
beyond its grasp, its dreams of usefulness always ahead of realization, it had to see hopes deferred until support caught up.

The story of the founding of the American Library Associa-

Reprinted from Library Journal, 76:1959-1963, December 1, 1951,
by permission of the author and the publisher.

tion is a familiar one, which I am permitted to be the one to re-tell at this seventy-fifth anniversary, because the initial steps toward the organization came from the Office of the Publishers' Weekly—which was located then, in an old building in lower New York—steps which went forward side by side with the establishment at the same office of the Library Journal.

I shall base this retelling of the ALA's beginning on brief outlines of the contributions of three men, men of background and energy who had an unselfish devotion to a cause, the importance of which each very clearly recognized. These three men were Frederick Leypoldt, the eldest, 41 years of age, with some twenty years of bookselling and publishing experience behind him; Richard Rogers Bowker, Salem born, 28 years of age, then finding his way into book trade journalism, who was to consider the development of libraries his chief vocation throughout a long life; and Melvil Dewey, then 25, a creative genius of the first order who was turning his energy and amazing inventiveness to the library field. It was the coming together of these three in the spring of 1876 which brought it about that a group of leading librarians decided that there should be a convention and this convention was called by the sending out of formal invitations. The meeting was set for October 4, 5, and 6 at the mecca of all the conventions of that year, Philadelphia, where the great Centennial Exhibition was being held.

The full story of the successful fruition of this plan would include the separate story of each of the delegates to that meeting and of those pioneering men and women who had been developing the American conception of the library into something that could claim its true place, both in the formal educational processes of schools and colleges, and in informal education for both young and old to which no other agency was so completely devoted.

Public libraries were busy with the effort to lift their clientele out of too great absorption with sentimental fiction; college libraries were trying to justify and fill a place in the very center of new curriculums; the Library of Congress was raising its head from national neglect; and state agencies for encouraging the growth of libraries had begun to appear.

Frederick Leypoldt, from whose Office of the Publishers' Weekly issued the first moves toward organization, had come from Germany 21 years before and, in his adopted country, had promptly exhibited marked ability in both bookselling and publishing, first in New York, then in Philadelphia, and then again in New York. He had sold out his book-publishing interests to a young partner, Henry Holt, in order to devote himself exclusively to serving the field of books through improved tools. With untiring energy and fertile imagination he had planned and published the Literary Bulletin, the Literary News, Publishers' Weekly, Publishers' Trade List Annual, the annual American Catalogue, and American Educational Catalogue. The majority of these enterprises were so sound in their conception that even to this day they continue to serve the purposes for which he planned them.

Not the least evidence of his foresight was his marriage, in 1867, to Augusta Harriet Garrigue of Brooklyn (she was a sister of Mrs. Thomas Garrigue Masaryk), who was not only his steady support in a greatly overcrowded career but who for thirty years after his death carried on in the same office with the bibliographical programs he had begun.

It was not inappropriate, it would seem, that a call for library organization should have been issued from such an office as this, and it has been said that the idea for its calling may have been suggested by the experience of the book trade in its convention of the previous year and again in July of 1876, in which both he and Mr. Bowker had important part. It will also be remembered that the call for the one previous national conference of librarians, that of 1853, presided over by the distinguished librarian, Charles C. Jewett, then of the Smithsonian Institution, was issued from the office of a 28-year-old New York publisher and bookseller, Charles B. Norton.

Mr. Leypoldt supplied, then, the focal point where the discussion began which led to the launching of a library periodical and the simultaneous calling of the conference in Philadelphia, which he attended. He became the publisher of the Library Journal, which was the official organ of the ALA until 1907. He took most of the financial losses of the publication, which were considerable, and in 1880 when the continued handling of its deficit seemed impossible, a wide expression of regret from the profession caused him to reconsider his announced plan to cease publication, thus continuing this necessary chain of communication between libraries.

Mr. Leypoldt was also in 1876 beginning the work on his monument as a great bibliographer, the American Catalogue, was con-

tinuing and extending the scope of the Publishers' Weekly and of
the Trade List Annual, and taking on the responsibility of publishing the Index Medicus. He was, with his eager enthusiasm,
burning up his strength in the ambition to bring the American
book trade into the habits of a profession; and, while neither he
nor his successors have achieved that aim, the trade tools which
he developed and his concept of trade responsibilities have helped to point the direction for such a development. He must, too,
have had satisfaction in seeing librarianship begin its evolution
into a well-rounded and competent profession. He died in 1884
at the age of 49, to be succeeded as director of the many enterprises by Richard Rogers Bowker, who, while active in business,
politics, and reform, was finding in book trade and libraries his
deepest interest.

Mr. Bowker, after being graduated from the College of the
City of New York in 1868, immediately entered the field of journalism. He provided the Evening Mail with New York's first
newspaper gossip column on books and, in 1875, after a few
years as contributor, he made a permanent connection with the
Leypoldt office as associate editor helping with the editorial work
and in the business office of the Publishers' Weekly. Both he and
Mr. Leypoldt had an instinctive understanding of the close relationship that must always exist between book trade and libraries,
a subject which they often discussed, so that the January 10,
1874, Publishers' Weekly carried a department called "The Library Corner", which was continued through January 30, 1875.
On November 6, 1875 (p. 714), "Library and Bibliographical
Notes" appeared as a department, [and was continued] until September 16, 1876. This column may have been noted by Melvil
Dewey who was soon to leave Amherst for Boston and who had
also for sometime been stirring with the possibility of a periodical which should serve to give fresh impetus to the library profession by providing a place for the discussion of library practice and the exposition of new library ideas.

In May of 1876 there was a conference on this possibility in
the Publishers' Weekly office, and, as Mr. Dewey conceded some
advantages to New York and the Leypoldt office equipment for
the publishing of such a periodical, plans were laid for issuance
from there of an American Library Journal. It was recognized
that an all-important function of the new periodical would be to
help bring about the organization of American librarians into a

broadly conceived national association.

The American Library Journal came to its first issue of September 30 just as the American Library Convention was about to open. (The word "American" was dropped from the periodical title a year later.) The editorial direction was in Boston, with Mr. Dewey; the publishing office was in New York, at 37 Park Row. The associate editors included some of the most distinguished names of those who were about to gather at Philadelphia: William F. Poole, of Chicago, Charles A. Cutter of Boston Athenaeum, Justin Winsor of Boston, L. P. Smith of Philadelphia, John S. Billings, and others. Mr. Bowker, who was later listed as general editor, must have had much to do with easing the burdens of the publisher, who was obligated to pay an editorial allowance to the Boston editor which the periodical, though enthusiastically welcomed, failed to earn.

Mr. Bowker, like Mr. Leypoldt, was a man with a great sense of social obligation, and the development of the library system in America made a strong appeal to him. After an absence of two years in England in the interest of Harper's Magazine, he returned in 1882 to the work of the Leypoldt office and for fifty years thereafter directed its management and policy. Successful in other business, his heart was with the world of books. Year after year he was a striking figure at library meetings, well-informed, quick to analyze, eloquent in espousing causes once determined, internationally minded but strong in support of local and regional organization. Probably no one outside the profession has made greater contributions to its development. As his eyesight gradually failed, his grasp of details and his decisiveness on principles were as keen as ever. From a close contact with him for fifteen years, I can say that his part in aiding the growth of American libraries was to him the greatest satisfaction of a long life.

After the May meeting at the New York office, letters and telegrams were sent to various librarians asking them their thought as to organizing a convention, the possibility and need of which were soon agreed upon. Later, invitations to attend were sent to the profession in general, to public, college and governmental librarians. The response was highly favorable. The three sponsors liked to relate that only the distinguished William F. Poole of Chicago, on receiving the invitation, made cautious inquiry as to the standing of a plan coming from two men in a publishing office and one young man only recently out of college.

The Historical Society of Philadelphia offered a hall for the meeting, and L. P. Smith of the Philadelphia Library completed the local arrangements. Ninety men and thirteen women registered on October 4, including Mr. Leypoldt, Mr. Bowker, and Mr. Dewey. Justin Winsor, then of the Boston Public Library, presided; Mr. Dewey was elected Secretary.

If ever a new movement was blessed at its start with an organizational genius it was the library profession. Mr. Dewey's enthusiasm was unbounded, his creativeness unlimited, his vigor unflagging. That year he had been working in the Amherst College Library after finishing his courses and had already begun those lines of thought which were to revolutionize library practice, give value to professional training, and invigorate library discussion and library programs at every level.

The development of librarianship was happily resting on strong men, on Winsor and Poole, on Fletcher, Cutter, and Spofford, on Evans and Green. Librarianship was now secure as a profession, but the force that spurred it as an organization, tempted it with mechanical ideas, and augmented its ranks with trained recruits was the young man who began his work from a desk in Boston (giving sponsorship to the metric system and reformed spelling on the side), who then moved to Columbia, to Albany, later to withdraw into innkeeping at Lake Placid. Mr. Dewey carried on the affairs of the new association under a continuing series of distinguished presidents and served as secretary of a Cooperation Committee which existed to bring concrete benefits to far-scattered members.

Mr. Bowker and Mr. Dewey spoke together here at Philadelphia before the ALA twenty-five years ago; Mr. Bowker spoke of the past, Mr. Dewey of the future of librarianship, and it was said of them then in pride that after fifty years "their eyes were not dimmed nor their natural force abated".

These three men are here grouped together in retrospect as they were together in council seventy-five years ago. I have spoken of two projects that grew out of that counciling. But even beyond that, for library progress, 1876 was annus mirabilis. Not only did the Library Journal reach the Philadelphia conference with its first issue containing Mr. Dewey's remarkable forecast for "The Profession", but there was then issued the first Government Report on Libraries from the Bureau of Education, an event of far reaching importance; the first trial presentation of the Decimal System of Dewey's was ready; and Leypoldt's monumental <u>American Catalogue</u> of 1876 was announced.

That spreading of library usefulness, and the demand for librarian organization, coming so soon after the exhausting Civil War, and, when corruption, both governmental and commercial, showed up the undermining of our ethical and cultural standards, gave evidence of the recuperative powers of a people in finding for themselves new aims and powers.

Can it not be hoped, then, that things that we are witnessing today, as we review our library heritage, our heritage of men and women and of books and buildings, may be pointing toward a new quarter century which can be made by our efforts to show fresh significance and power?

This decade of ours also has felt, and is still feeling, the depletions of war, the scrambling selfishness of reconstruction, the frustration of idealism. But <u>are</u> we not as ready, as was the library world of seventy-five years ago, for fresh, significant developments — for an all-out effort to make books available to every last sector of this country; for programs which will tie library service so firmly into the educational needs of the country that from childhood to old age our people will not be without the books to inform and inspire; for zeal to continue and expand the recognition of the uses of books and libraries in all governmental activities, for defense, for industrial and cultural needs; for confidence that we can all still further confirm the place of books in international relationships and understanding on the long road to one world — a healthy and literate, self-sustaining and peaceful world.

A WORM'S-EYE VIEW OF LIBRARY LEADERS

Marian C. Manley

Marian C. Manley — author of BUSINESS INFORMATION:
HOW TO FIND IT AND USE IT (1955) — was at the time of
her retirement on November 1st, 1954, supervising business librarian, Newark Public Library, Newark, New Jersey, a position she had filled since 1926; she now lives in
Summit, New Jersey. The essay here reprinted is a paper
read before the American Library History Round Table
during the 1952 conference of the American Library Association in New York City.

Enlivening memories are among the rewards for the minor
aides in daily contact with leaders in any field. In the flippant
title of this paper I have tried to show how, as a very, very minor character, I had the opportunity to meet frequently people
who gave color and impetus to the library movement as it took
on momentum in the 1910's and 1920's. Because I was fortunate
enough to be the watchdog at the office threshold for John Cotton
Dana and Beatrice Winser, I have had contacts not normally the
portion of a library assistant at the bottom rung of the ladder.
But then, nothing about the Newark Public Library when those
two dynamic people, John Cotton Dana and Beatrice Winser,
were its leaders could ever be considered routine.

Perhaps the way in which I joined the Newark library staff
is indicative of the unpremeditated manner in which it expanded.
Like most girls of that pre-1915 period, I had grown up without
any plans for a career. On the other hand, I was caught up in
the campaign for women suffrage, waged in 1915 in New York,
Pennsylvania, Massachusetts, and New Jersey, and was a frequent street-corner speaker in the suburbs. That unusual preparation for a library career brought me into happy association
with Louise Connolly, then serving as educational expert and
consultant for the Newark Public Library. Miss Connolly learned
that Mr. Dana and Miss Winser had been consulted about some-

Reprinted from Wilson Library Bulletin, 27:229-235, November, 1952,
by permission of the author and the publisher.

one to fill a special job on the Newark 250th Anniversary Committee. She suggested me, so I was called in to discuss this possibility. Later, as I saw the many demands on their time, I appreciated even more the friendly interest and consideration they gave then to a rather shy girl. Indeed, instead of that other job, Mr. Dana asked me if I would like to work in the Newark library! So I began five strenuous and happy years in the immediate orbit of these stars.

Miss Winser had asked for me as her assistant in a job that combined errand girl, chief cook and bottle washer, schedule artist, and in odd moments docent for any museum exhibits that might be on. It involved the usual occupation of a combination receptionist-secretary and generally useful mortal, but it had the added tension of centering between the offices of two vigorous people with a hundred irons in the fire. At frequent intervals they would erupt from their respective quarters in rapid transit one to the other, commenting on details in stentorian tones as they passed by.

And what was the world of the Newark Library back there in late 1915? For one thing it gave close, if lowly, association with two people who, for zest in living and vigorous leadership, will not soon be surpassed. That they should have worked together so long and in a partnership that afforded full play to the best qualities of each was great good fortune for the library world and particularly for those in the sphere of their influence.

It is easy to recall them and their distinguishing characteristics. Mr. Dana, slender, long-legged, slightly stooped, broad forehead, piercing eyes, and with a smile that brought instant response. Miss Winser, tall, vigorous, with a deep voice unmistakable in any crowd, eyes into which the sparks could come rapidly because her reactions were swift, but with the most enchanting dimples and a hearty laugh.

The whole atmosphere of the institution reacted to the vim, vigor, vitality, and vision that marked their every day's existence. To this partnership in administration Mr. Dana brought creative imagination, the gift of seeing relationships in wide areas, extraordinary powers of communication and interpretation, and intense concentration on the development of the broad aspects of librarianship and of library service in Newark and everywhere. In their association, Miss Winser was the immediate director of the library. The details of administration were

151

in her hands, and they were closely held. Department heads had authority for management and for recommendations, but Miss Winser, of the English autocrat school, directed every detail. While initiative was encouraged, action must be ok'd. Four of the most important letters in Newark library activity for many years were "O.K. B.W."

These comments indicate a highly centralized authority and that was the case, but it was a centralized authority that was constantly subjected to the interplay of individual consultation. The members of the Newark library staff, whether assistants or department heads, all felt part of the flow of creative library activity. Carrying on the work of the Newark library was an enterprise in which friends worked together in a highly enlivening atmosphere and with frequent discussions.

There was enthusiasm and gaiety in the Newark library and there was no even tenor to our days. Miss Winser was always around the building, observing activities, eliminating bottlenecks, exchanging comments with the staff, and stimulating everyone by her human but decisive admonition. Mr. Dana might pass through the institution more rapidly; on the other hand, he had a trait for suddenly noticing some detail of mechanics and promptly working out an effective revision. All the members of the library staff had reason to know the qualities and characteristics of this directing team. The annual Christmas parties, with their varied central themes, were special opportunities for mutual enjoyment with their informal gaiety accented by Miss Winser's spontaneity and Mr. Dana's wit.

Each day for the staff was both a strain and an adventure. One never knew where the lightning would strike next, but the process would be stimulating. The program for the day could never be anticipated. This was hard on methodical workers and in some cases they could not stand the pace. For those who enjoyed ingenuity and enterprise it was an engrossing experience.

As it happened, in my first years in Newark, Mr. Dana and Miss Winser were especially close to the city authorities. Miss Winser had just been appointed a member of the Board of Education, the first woman so to serve, and had thrown herself into that work with all the energy of which she was capable. Mr. Dana was a member of the City Plan Commission. In fact, he had suggested such a commission to Mayor Haussling, and Harland Bartholomew, now the outstanding authority in the country on city planning, then secretary for that City Plan Commission, has spoken fervently of what he owed to Mr. Dana for his constructive influence on reports and studies. The successor to Mayor Haussling, Mayor Raymond, an extraordinarily gifted man and a close personal friend of both Mr. Dana's and Miss Winser's, was much interested in the library and came frequently to board meetings. There was close contact with different parts of the city's administration and Mr. Dana's advice was sought constantly in any effort to interpret the city to its citizens through print. Mr. Dana was a member of the executive committee of the Committee of 100 that planned the city's 250th anniversary, and influenced its publicity and design. The library, in the persons of Mr. Dana and Miss Winser, was a positive element in the city's administration, just as library resources were used in the city's work.

Of course, there was always a close friendship between the publishing and editorial staff of the Newark News and other papers and the library administrators. The library was newsworthy. Its interests were wide. The pulse of the city's intellectual and civic development was felt through its halls.

What were some of the developments in the Newark library in those days? One was a special emphasis on the use of ephemeral material. From his earliest days in the library world, Mr. Dana had been conscious of the great mass of the information outside of books per se. In the vertical file, now information file, with thousands of newspaper and magazine clippings, government publications, association pamphlets, such ephemeral material was made available to a greater extent than had so far prevailed in library circles. A defined program for the development of such a tool appeared in the American Library Economy pamphlet, The Vertical File, printed in 1915. Interest in the organized use of ephemeral material was one of the factors that lead to the development of the Special Libraries Association, of which Mr. Dana was the first president.

This period saw the intensification of the work of the then Business Branch, now Business Library. Probably the first formal library cooperation with a business group lay in Mr. Dana's contacts with the Associated Advertising Club of the World. This led to intensive work in assembling information on the resources of business print. One result was the compilation of 1600 Business Books and its successors. During the same period the important part that libraries could play in business research was recognized by The Nation's Business. That magazine, for nineteen months, carried a "White List of Business Books" prepared by the business library staff and edited by Mr. Dana.

Always Mr. Dana's appreciation of art in its relation to everyday life was reflected in the library collection. Mr. Dana had introduced the idea of a picture collection in Denver. This was carried to greater lengths in Newark and in that period the art department expanded, the collection of fine prints grew enormously; a collection of pictures and frames lent for home use was a supplemental development. Too, Mr. Dana's interest in museum development and his constructive criticism as represented in his essays, "The Gloom of the Museum", found fruit in the growth of the Newark Museum.

Nor was life dull in other ways. The question of the library's responsibility to assemble material on both sides of controversial subjects had already touched Mr. Dana. In Denver during the "free silver" days he was accused, as a gold bug, of spreading propaganda, and at that time he replied, "Yes, I have distributed the literature to those who I thought would be interested. . . . I consider that it was entirely within my province as librarian to keep and circulate literature on both sides of the money question. . . ." The same willingness to accept public attack for a principle was shown again during the First World War. One of the emotional developments of that period found outlet in the Vigilantes, a society of poets and artists that became excited over the fact that the Newark Library had books on German developments and requested their elimination. Among other outbursts, the New York Journal had an editorial urging that Mr. Dana be awarded the iron cross. Of course, the books remained on the Newark library shelves.

Library development over the lunch table was an important part of the Newark library's growth. This had two distinct phases. One was the luncheon for the distinguished visitor. The round table could hold twelve and still allow for easy conversation. Because of Mr. Dana's slight deafness, Miss Winser sat always at his right. On his other side might be Bruce Rogers, the famous book designer; or Harland Bartholomew, the city planning authority; Tom Raymond, gifted collector of fine books, port developer, as well as mayor of Newark, might be there; or Rudolph Ruzika, whose beautiful wood cuts are famous. Leading advertising men such as Ernest Calkins or David Gibson; editors, writers, artists, countless numbers of those who had the gift of creative imagination were drawn to the Newark library as a result of Mr. Dana's broad interests and capacity for understanding. They came from Europe and from all corners of this country, even from such remote areas as Tibet.

The liberal education provided by these visitors was a constant stimulus to the staff. Each luncheon would have varied staff representation depending on the interests of the guest. It might include Margaret McVety, then head of the lending and reference department; or Blanche Gardner, head of the art department; Marguerite Gates, at that time in charge of publications; Catherine Van Dyne, a young and brilliant assistant in the lending and reference department; or other younger members of the staff. Usually I was lucky enough to be there as I had the job of seeing that the simple lunch moved smoothly and I must be available for Miss Winser if she needed an errand done.

Conversation was usually dominated by the guests, Mr. Dana, and Miss Winser, but the staff members were expected to contribute their quota to the conversation, in itself a beneficial experience. Those that could not contribute were recognized also. I remember Miss Winser saying to me, "We will have Blanche Gardner today. I can always count on her light touch. I wish some others would not simply sit and listen."

Of course, library personalities were frequently among the guests. Richard R. Bowker and the editors of the Library Journal; Mary Eileen Ahearn of Public Libraries, whose spicy comment broadened the horizons of librarians in smaller communities; George Utley, then quietly dealing with the problems of ALA; Frank P. Hill and Emma Baldwin from Brooklyn, always a part of astute ALA thinking; or Tessa Kelso of Baker and Taylor, whose bracing and original approach to library problems startled the unwary; Melville Dewey; H. W. Wilson; and librarians from England, the south, and the far west all beat a path to Newark's door. There was rare education for the staff members who through these occasional luncheon experiences encountered people from many different areas and participated in the discussion of varied topics. Such encounters added zest and stimulus to work in the Newark library.

Then there were the other, the staff luncheons. Into that democratic gathering entered the assistant, the branch librarian, and department heads. The dominating quality in the guests that came to the library and in the staff members who appeared most often at the luncheons was the ability to respond to the stimulus of an idea and to contribute to its development. An incidental comment might result in plans for an exhibit of library relationships with the advertising world or in the step by step exposition of a method of teaching the classics. The growing demand for certain information might be noted and plans for a new publication to meet the need would take shape.

Preparing for an ALA would always bring entertaining development. I remember when plans for the 1918 conference at Asbury Park were under way, we were involved in the work of a committee that prepared a four-page newspaper that was distributed at the conference. This was printed daily on an Asbury Park press. Before that we had prepared much material for fillers and we rushed through copy covering the meetings. This was a gay occupation rather than a serious one.

But more often the ALA interest was serious. Mr. Dana was vitally interested in the program of the American Library Association. He felt that it could be a tremendous power for good and he wanted to see its potentialities realized. This made him a keen and discerning, if sometimes disconcerting, critic. Much of the pervasive interest that I have had in the work of the association goes back to the long letters on ALA policies that Mr. Dana exchanged with so many throughout the library world. Mr. Hill, Mr. Legler, Mr. Utley, Mr. Brett, Mr. Bishop, Dr. Putnam, all were correspondents or visitors in discussions of library policy. Mr. Dana's library friends were legion. Only recently I saw in the Times the obituary of George Parker Winship, first librarian of the John Carter Brown Library and later of the Widener Collection at Harvard. He and Mr. Dana had been close friends from Mr. Dana's Springfield days and letters passed between them often, not on problems of library policy, instead on their reading or new interests.

Of Mr. Dana's professional correspondence, I believe that on the ALA reflected the most sustained, constructive, and farsighted interest. My years in the library "office" — 1915 to 1920 — were years in which he served on the executive board, on the Enlarged program committee, and was most often in attendance in ALA. But his interests and views then were founded on his years of experience — starting with his first Denver days and intensified with his presidency in 1895-1896. It lasted through continued interest and through many addresses that cut through pleasant platitudes and concern with multitudinous detail, to open the way to a wider understanding of the place of the library in a fast changing world. Mr. Dana, as a constructive critic, has had a great influence on the growth of ALA, far more than many realize. In many ways, we are only now catching up with his recommendations of thirty to fifty years ago. He was a frequent and often caustic critic of current American Library Association activities, but it was because of his fervent belief in fundamental values of libraries and of his desire to see the association's sights lifted.

As library trends and thinking of today are weighed in the light of Mr. Dana's recommendations of many years ago it is evident that great progress has been made toward his goals. His emphasis on a shift from concentration on hoarding and recording books to recognition of the necessity for using the many forms of ephemeral information is completely accepted now. In one of the heated council meetings in which recommendations by the Enlarged program committee and others were discussed at length, he said: "We do not need a survey of library activities. We do need a study of the place of the library phenomena in a print-using society." The Public Library Inquiry nearly thirty years later provided the study for which he asked in 1919.

The liberal education offered by work in the Newark library meant much to the intellectual growth of the staff. It had these several aspects. First came the remarkable gift for recognizing individual abilities shown by Mr. Dana and Miss Winser and the stimulus they gave for the development of these abilities. Staff members at every level came into frequent contact with them both and individual abilities registered to an extraordinary degree. Then there were the broadening contacts through the people that visited Newark and what was done in relation to their visits. There was still another channel of enlightenment through Mr. Dana's engrossing correspondence. With his incredibly wide range of interests he noted developments in many fields and would write discerning comments to those concerned. Out of that came many contacts and new interests. These letters were passed around to many and often staff members became involved in the correspondence.

A fourth great educational device resulted from Mr. Dana's

passion for the use of print. One illustration was the Newarker, a journal published by the library to "introduce a city to itself and to its public library". Another was the American Library Economy series in which the services of the Newark library were described in minute detail as aids to other libraries in establishing similar practices. The last formal development in a regular publication under Mr. Dana's direction was The Library, which appeared in the twenties and early thirties. In the columns of these publications were contributions from authorities in outside fields and from staff members. These last contributors learned much of the art of precise writing through these efforts. It was an agonizing experience to have one's carefully prepared prose go to Mr. Dana and be ruthlessly edited, but it brought growth.

It was Mr. Dana's conviction that expended effort should bring the greatest possible return. By making library experience available to many through publication, such experience could be used as a basis for modification and development. He believed that much of the work done in libraries could reach a wider audience and so be made to bring greater return on the effort involved. Seldom was a special index prepared solely for department use. Rather, when a need for compilation of certain information developed, the process of compiling such a tool and putting it into print was a logical result. In that, great contributions were made by Marguerite Gates and Catherine Van Dyne.

A positive attitude toward activities was perhaps one of the most outstanding characteristics of both Mr. Dana and Miss Winser. It was impossible for them to be passively interested in anything. When their attention was caught and interest aroused, immediate impetus to participate and contribute followed. That characteristic meant much for the Newark library and its growth in outside recognition and staff stimulus. The record of these activities is found in many sources with the sketches of Mr. Dana by Frank Kingdon and by Chalmers Hadley as excellent summaries. In Mr. Dana's own writings there is much that indicates the range of his contacts, but nothing yet written could convey the many facets of his interests.

There is little published record of Miss Winser's work. She wrote few articles, nor was she a prolific correspondent, as was Mr. Dana. It was the zest, generosity, and constructive energy with which she met life that meant so much to all about her. Her

more than fifty years association with the Newark library probably did at least as much to set the pattern for the vigorous life
of that institution as did Mr. Dana's years there. Miss Winser
had a genius for working with people. As assistant librarian to
Mr. Hill and again as assistant librarian to Mr. Dana she gave
constructive balance to their work. Like Mr. Dana she had an
intuitive sense for abilities and did much to bring out latent
qualities in the members of the staff. She knew the individual
characteristics of them all, from the youngest page to ranking
heads, and the details of the building, from the bowels of the
engine room to the roof. The janitors adored her because of the
vigor, decisiveness, and sympathetic understanding that she
gave their work. Her passionate interest in books and her constant zeal for the quality of the collection made the library resources a monument to her powers of selection.

Probably one of the most delightful records of someone of
her capacities is found in a unique volume, "B.W. by her Staff",
a book compiled for her from letters from the hundreds who, as
staff members, remembered her dynamic qualities, her vigorous leadership, and her extraordinary warmth and human understanding. In its pages is the reflection of her influence. Her
great contribution to Newark as a city, to the public library's
growth, and to the development of its staff can never be measured. The records in print can only to a small degree reflect this
influence but what she was and did will live on in the lives and
hearts of those who knew her.

Newark has been extraordinarily fortunate in its librarians.
First it had the gifted administrator Frank P. Hill. He was followed by John Cotton Dana, recognized as the library genius of
his era and whose work was supplemented for so many years by
Beatrice Winser who carried on after his death in his tradition
but in her own vigorous and zestful style. The library under the
guidance of these people had developed extraordinarily but as
health had suffered and years had taken their toll, it was within
a framework that was strained and in the need of sound renova-
tion. When the time for this arrived, the Newark library was
again fortunate in that, fourth in the line of its administrators,
came John Boynton Kaiser, its present director. His sound knowledge of library and personnel administration has done an immeasurable amount to strengthen the organization's framework,
while carrying on the tradition of service for which Newark has

always been recognized. Few people could have been so well qualified to carry on that tradition and yet to reinforce and develop where development has been needed. There has been rare good fortune for those of us who have had the opportunity to work under three such notable directors.

JOHN LANGDON SIBLEY, LIBRARIAN

Clifford K. Shipton

Clifford K. Shipton is Director of the American Antiquarian
Society, Worcester, Massachusetts.

Because of that jade Clio's preference for entertaining, gos-
sipy tales, John Langdon Sibley has been remembered chiefly
as the antiquated and absurd figure he cut in the stories which
members of the Eliot administration told about him. In reality
he was one of the wisest and ablest librarians of his time, and
it is a blessing to the entire world of scholarship that it was he
who was in charge of the Harvard Library during its swift development into an institution of world-wide importance. In his full
personal diary, his many bound volumes of library correspondence, and his annual reports, he has left a detailed record of
the development of library policy which is interesting, and amusing, to all good librarians who today struggle with similar problems.[1]

Sibley was born in the year 1804 in the town of Union in the
District of Maine, and was fitted for college at Exeter. He came
to Cambridge to enter the Freshman class in the fall of 1821.
During the next spring vacation he began working in the College
Library, the only employee besides the Librarian, Joseph Green
Cogswell, and his successor, Charles Folsom. Chiefly by this
means he worked his way through college. A few days after his
graduation in 1825 he was crossing the bridge into Boston when
overtaken by a chaise driven by President Kirkland, who nearly
frightened him into the river by pulling up and addressing him
as "Mr. Sibley". It was the first time that John had ever been
addressed by the title, but, as he observed, old customs were
passing. One of these was that the librarian's assistant should
be an undergraduate. Kirkland told him that it was proposed to
appoint a full-time assistant librarian at a salary of $150 a year,
and offered him the place.

This was a golden opportunity which Sibley eagerly grasped.

Reprinted from Harvard Library Bulletin, 9:236-261, Spring, 1955,
by permission of the author and the publisher.

He had his room free, and as his only duty in the Library was to obtain books for readers, he had plenty of time in regular hours to do copying, which brought him in as much again as his salary. When Folsom left in 1826, Sibley was acting Librarian for a month; but then his job as assistant was abolished in order to provide a more adequate salary for the new Librarian, Benjamin Peirce. There being nowhere else in America any prospect of a career as a professional librarian, Sibley turned rather unwillingly to the Unitarian ministry, at which he was not a conspicuous success. Nor in four years spent as editor of the American Magazine of Useful and Entertaining Knowledge did he attract much attention.

Sibley happened to be in Cambridge and at leisure in March, 1841, when the University faced the problem of removal of the Library from Harvard Hall to the new building, Gore. Employed temporarily as an assistant, he managed so well that it took only eleven days to make the change, and during that period every book was accessible by means of a marked copy of the printed catalogue. The fact that the new building was a long, high, narrow hall in which pillars effectively shut off vision from any one point made a second full-time employee a necessity. So Sibley was appointed Assistant Librarian and launched a second time on his life work.

With a new building and two full-time employees, the Harvard Library quickly began to improve its service. In the old library in Harvard Hall there had been an effort since 1765 to keep up an open-shelf collection for undergraduate use, but borrowers who wanted books from the alcoves had to put in a call-slip one day and return the next to obtain the volume – or to find that it was out. In Gore, Sibley provided reasonably fast service for alcove books. The main hall, or "Librarian's Room", provided space for an open-shelf collection of three thousand volumes, which at first seems to have satisfied all usual undergraduate need. But with the improvement of methods of instruction in the forties and fifties, more and more undergraduates began to ask for alcove volumes for research and supplementary reading, making the question of reader access to the rest of the Library a subject of warm debate. In general, any student who wanted other books than those on the open shelves was admitted to the locked alcoves, where he could sit at a table and help himself to the books around him; but this was a matter of special privi-

JOHN LANGDON SIBLEY, LIBRARIAN

lege and not of right. In the fifties, both undergraduates and
Faculty began to complain that the books in the open-shelf collection, having been selected by the college officers many years
before, were out of date, and that alcove access, hours, and
borrowing rules were inadequate. Sibley answered some of these
criticisms by weeding the open-shelf collection and keeping special shelves for latest and most popular books. By changing these
seasonally with the courses he increased the number of volumes
readily available to undergraduates, and prevented the charging-
out of books needed for course work. In addition he instituted the
practice of overnight charging-out at closing time.

These changes, made by Sibley without much more than the
indifferent consent of the Librarian, Thaddeus William Harris,
did not still the demands of the Faculty for longer library hours
and freer access to the shelves for themselves and the students.
Particularly troublesome was the growing habit of the students,
and even of the Faculty, of remaining in Cambridge during the
long winter and summer vacations and expecting to have access
to the Library. Although Sibley willingly put in much voluntary
overtime, he and Harris expected the long vacations which academic men had enjoyed since universities began. In term time
Sibley's hours for some years were from 9 until sunset or 4,
whichever came earlier, with Friday afternoons and Saturdays
off. In 1847 the Corporation enraged him by voting, at the be-
hest of his Faculty critics, that his hours in term time be from
8 to evening prayers, with the dinner hour and Saturday afternoon off. During vacations he was to work Monday mornings.
If he worked overtime, he was to be paid for it. Bitterly he protested the eight-hour day for librarians: "Is there any man,
whose constitution, with such confinement, would not in time be
seriously injured if not ruined?" As for having to work Monday
mornings during vacations: "Is it not a hard life, when a man
in vacation is deprived of a great part of the relaxation and opportunities for journeying, which the stringency of the requirements for term time renders the more necessary. . . . The ex-
actions made by these votes he considers oppressive. His time
has not been spent in reading, or frittered away, but conscien-
ciously devoted to labor." It was not that Sibley was lazy, or
even set upon having the traditional academic freedom of time,
but that he resented being ordered to stay in Gore Hall waiting
on undergraduates when he might have been traveling around

gathering books for the Library. The Corporation heard his protest and recognized its point by voting that he should have half
of each vacation period entirely free.

When Harris died in 1856 certain members of the Faculty,
who were entirely mistaken as to the quality of the service rendered by the Harvard Library in earlier years, and by European
libraries in their own generation, were pressing for further privileges of access which could not possibly be granted by such an
institution with such a staff. When Faculty members broke library rules, Sibley applied the sanctions with such gusto that
there were a number who were determined that a new and more
amenable man should be brought in as Librarian. There were
many applications for the job, but a number of prominent people
wrote in on behalf of Sibley. According to him, Louis Agassiz,
determined "to get a scientific control over everything", tried
to influence the situation by starting the rumor that the one man
whom the Corporation would not accept was Sibley. The latter,
however, convinced President Walker that the purpose of the
Faculty critics was to get a Librarian under whom they could
"set aside the laws pertaining to the government of the Library".

Sibley's friends won out, and on 18 February 1856 he was
unanimously chosen Librarian by the Corporation, and given a
salary of $1,300. Ezra Abbot was appointed Assistant Librarian.
The Overseers approved Sibley's appointment by a vote of fifteen to two. Now, after years of chafing at the elbow of a Librarian who was content with old-fashioned library ways, he
was free to put into effect his own ideas. He was the first Harvard Librarian to realize that the University drew its nourish-
ment from the Library, which in turn must grow in order to
supply that sustenance. Some of his ideas were simply too advanced for his generation. Among these was a proposal which
he made to the Corporation in 1847 to appoint a "Builder up of
the Library", or "Library Professor", or "Professor of Bibliography", who would lecture on libraries, and on the contents
of Gore in particular, in order to breed up in the student body
future book lovers, book collectors, and library donors. This
new appointee should familiarize himself with the Harvard collections so that he could intelligently correspond with authors
and collectors, and attract donations from them. He should also handle the book orders to guard against the purchase of duplicates; should complete imperfect series, exchange duplicates,

attend auctions, read catalogues, and travel in order to search bookstores and garrets. This proposal is the best summary of the important things which his predecessors had not done, but to which, during the next two decades, he devoted every moment which he could squeeze from the traditional routine of the Library. For this larger outline of the functions of the University Library and the work of its Librarian, he was indebted only to his own comprehension of the problem. For many of the details of the essential improvement in library machinery, he drew on the ideas of such friends and acquaintances as Jewett of the Boston Public and Dewey of Amherst. His conversations and correspondence with them are reflected in his decisions that public catalogues should be as simple as possible, that call-numbers should denote subjects rather than shelves, and the like.

Neither the details of the librarian's craft, nor the theories as to his function, interested Sibley as much as books themselves; and it was in the gathering of them that his greatest contribution lay. During his first term as Assistant Librarian, the accessions of the Harvard Library amounted to twenty-five or thirty volumes a year, of which he himself gave about half. When he returned in 1841, he found accessions increased about tenfold, but still, to him, absurdly small. Harris watched with indifference the increased flow which resulted from the efforts of the Assistant Librarian, and complained that the government documents which he was bringing in only "lumbered up the Library". After a verbal clash on this subject, Sibley reviewed his argument in his private diary:

> Are we to say to the public we do not want your books
> unless they are such as we think are very excellent? Be-
> cause we are afraid we shall fill the shelves too full, when
> we have in Gore Hall, one hundred and forty feet long
> from window to window, but about 50,000 bound volumes?
> Let the library be filled. If trash comes let it come.
> What is trash to me may be the part of the Library which
> will be the most valuable to another person. Numbers
> give consequence to a library abroad.

Ignoring the position of Harris' eyebrows, Sibley during his tenure as Assistant Librarian dunned all and sundry so well that he brought into the Library by donation, he reckoned, 7,000 volumes and between 15,000 and 20,000 pamphlets.

When Sibley became Librarian the funds available for book purchase amounted to three or four hundred dollars a year, not enough to buy even the books which the professors requested. As the energetic editor of the Triennial Catalogue for many years and as Commencement Marshal and the leader of the singing of the Seventy-eighth Psalm on that occasion, he was well known to the alumni body, a fact which he proposed to utilize. At the first Commencement after his elevation to the librarianship, each graduate sitting down to the dinner in Harvard Hall found at his place a circular asking his personal assistance in obtaining for the Library a copy of every book, map, or pamphlet written or published in the United States, or pertaining to America. The collection in Gore Hall should be made, he declared, a "National library". The plea had immediate effect. The Alumni Association formed a library committee, and the Harvard Club of New York gladly afforded him the opportunity of meeting and influencing the great book collectors of that city.

The most unexpected result of the Commencement circular of 1856 was the gift of nearly a hundred volumes from Ticknor and Fields. That firm instituted the policy of giving Harvard a copy of each of its publications, and a few years later Oliver Ditson & Co. adopted the same policy for its musical publications. Macmillan & Co. was equally generous, if not as regular in its giving. But Sibley kept his eye on the small donor as well, and popularized the idea that every graduate should give the Library at least one book a year. Soon, he estimated, one in every fifteen living graduates was contributing. He made a practice of inviting the Senior class to Gore Hall, where he exhibited interesting books and manuscripts and in this connection installed, in 1860, the first exhibition cases. The undergraduates became interested; the Advocate gave $200, and other student organizations, lesser sums. Further enthusiasm to give was engendered by Sibley's introduction of the practice of listing donations in his annual reports, which were usually printed at length in the Boston newspapers and which obviously interested both the Harvard community and the public. Before his appointment as Assistant Librarian donations were running to about 160 volumes a year; in 1864 they numbered 2,000. By 1868 the donors had become so numerous that the list of them had to be relegated to an appendix in the report. In these lists, incidentally, Sibley chastely segregated the names of "female donors".

The new Librarian's field of interest extended beyond the usual printed books to contemporary ephemera in every form. He urged men interested in special fields, such as the war in Texas, to make it their duty to build up the Harvard collection of printed material relating to them. Brigham Young yielded to his importunings and sent a collection of Mormon books. Harvard men marched to the Civil War carrying his instructions for collecting. Even the facsimile Confederate script he thought to be worthy of special attention. But for plunder he had no use. By means of his annual report of 1863 he addressed his collectors:

> Personal communications speak of plates torn out of
> books by vulgar or besotted Soldiers, volumes trodden
> under foot, magnificent works torn to fragments, and
> collections tossed about in sport, burnt or carried off
> piecemeal by officers as well as soldiers. In the seced-
> ing States this Vandalism ought to have been prevented,
> and in many cases would have been, if the Federal of-
> ficers had done their duty. A very few of these volumes
> have found their way into Gore Hall. I am glad they are
> here. They were rescued from immediate destruction
> by persons who felt that they should be saved. I regard
> them as deposits to be sacredly kept, and shall gladly,
> if possible, restore them hereafter to the former pos-
> sessors.

He showed no such resentment at the liberation of the human property of the South, but in his determination to disprove the calumny "that colored people are incapable of high intellectual cultivation" he conducted a "Books for Liberia" campaign. After the war he made an effort to enlist the aid of the ex-Confederates in the student body to collect Rebel material for the Harvard Library.

Nothing in the Civil War pained Sibley more than the sight of piles and cartloads of books and pamphlets on the way to the paper mills, drawn by the prices offered for waste. "The havoc is terrible; of many books and pamphlets not a single copy will be left." To forestall it he spent long hours with cloak and lantern in wet cellars which yielded treasures for the Library. Once he heard of a large pile of Baltimore newspapers lying on the sidewalk in Water Street in Boston and dashed over to save them, only to find that they were on their way to the Boston Athenaeum rather than the paper mill.

Usually Sibley was without competition in his search for newspapers; and, indeed, no successor of his in the Harvard Library has felt that he could continue the space-consuming policy of gathering such material. However, no one has regretted the fact that Sibley made a point of collecting early California newspapers and regularly subscribed for a dozen others during the Civil War. Other files came in from the libraries of the Harvard Clubs. Directories, city documents, and schoolbooks were other materials which he industriously gathered and defended against the protests of Faculty members who regarded them as so much junk. But where else, he asked the examining committee of 1858, will "some American Hallam or Sismondi" find "the schoolbooks of the last and present centuries to obtain a general idea of their character and of the early education of the country?"

To Sibley it was the most sacred duty of the librarian to preserve a copy of every printed item for the use of posterity. No one else in his generation did more to spread the idea of the importance of ephemeral material for history. To the newspaper printings of his report for the year 1861 he added this paragraph, typical of his campaign:

> One of the greatest favors to the future historian would be to collect all the books, pamphlets, maps, files of newspapers, engravings, photographs, caricatures, ephemeral publications of every kind, even to printed notices, circulars, handbills, posters, letter envelopes, and place them beyond the reach of destruction. . . . If I could, I would appeal to every inhabitant of the continent to send me everything which could be obtained, in order that every phase of mind in every section of the country, North, South, East, West, for the Union and against the Union, for secession and against secession, might be represented.

With members of the Faculty taking a cynical view as to the value of preserving even pamphlet material, Sibley had to become really eloquent to convince Examining Committees that the whole of the printed word was the scope which the Harvard Library

should try to cover in order to fill its proper function. Although
he talked most frequently of American material, he welcomed
the great expansion of the foreign collections which occurred
in the fifties, particularly after the Henry Ware Wales gift of
1,500 volumes largely in Sanskrit, Hebrew, Turkish, Arabic,
and Persian. In 1865 he bought the musical library of Levi Parsons. Nor were his interests confined to printed material, for
he rejoiced to obtain a Latin manuscript which he believed to
date from the eighth century and to be the oldest in the country;
and he welcomed such special collections as the photographs of
members of Harvard classes, and urged every alumnus to send
in his own photograph.

The result of Sibley's ideas and labors can be read in the accession figures of the Library. In his first year as Librarian,
accessions hit a new peak of 3,906 volumes and 2,498 pamphlets.
Within three years the figure for volumes was doubled again,
although it later leveled off at around 5,000 a year. In spite of
his willingness to accept junk, this was no mere crow's nest
accumulation; in 1876 he began to issue a library bulletin, the
ancestor of this present publication, in order to call attention
to interesting and important accessions. When he became Librarian he found about 100,000 volumes in the several libraries
of the University. On the eve of his retirement this figure had
grown to 230,000, of which some 164,000 were in Gore Hall.
The bulk of the Library's holdings had increased about fourfold.
The figures are deceptive, for the "library count" did not cover
unbound pamphlets, maps, and the like, which in a moment of
excessive enthusiasm for this kind of material he estimated to
exceed in bulk the bound volumes which were formally counted.

When Sibley took over in 1856 one of his first steps was to
provide shelving for the books which were already stacked on
the floor and stored in out-of-the-way places, but this did not
deter his campaign to obtain "any and everything" in print. By
1863 he had come to the conclusion that the Library would double every twenty years, but he never really faced the arithmeti-
cal consequences of this fact, for he estimated that a century
hence the Library would contain only 750,000 volumes, and in
his later reports he even reduced that figure to half a million.
Since he would never contemplate serious weeding, one can only conclude that his subconscious mind was taking this means of
solving the space problem for him. Had his successors main-

tained his policy of collection, the Library would by now dwarf
the rest of the University.

When Gore Hall was built it was assumed that it would provide ample room for growth for a century, but within twenty
years it was crowded. President Quincy refused to permit the
sale or exchange of duplicates, but after his retirement Sibley
gained some space in this manner. When he became Librarian
he nearly doubled the capacity of Gore by the use of movable
shelves, some of which were installed so as to divide each alcove in two. President Walker and the architect complained bitterly that his new shelving destroyed the beauty of the building,
but he silenced them with the question, "For what was the library built—for books or for looks?" Sibley did not defend the
division of the alcoves on any other grounds than of the most
painful necessity, for he was the one who suffered most by it.
The architects of Gore Hall had made no provision for offices
or work space. Sibley himself had no room of any kind in the Library into which he could retire for private conversation, or in
which he could leave his papers spread out free from the risk
of having some undergraduate pick them up and start reading.
Indeed he had no more privacy, he said, than he would have had
in a barroom. The only working space for the staff was on the
tables in the main reading room, or in the alcoves; but now that
the latter were divided, when there was a call for a book in one
of them the staff member working there often had to come out
and bring his chair with him to make room for the ladder. By
1868 Sibley was piling books on the floor in front of the showcases, and by the end of his administration he was piling them
on the floor in front of the alcoves in which they belonged.

To combat this space problem Sibley tried all kinds of shifts.
In 1862 he gained a hundred shelves by shelving by size, a laborious process because it involved the changing of all of the
shelfmarks in the books. Three years later he began to double-
row the books on the shelves. The Overseers proposed weeding
the Library, but found the Librarian prepared to die on this
particular barricade. President Eliot was a strong advocate
of the storage of little-used books, but Sibley held him off and
reported with glee his experience when the enlargement of 1877
compelled the sending of some 20,000 volumes temporarily to
Boylston Hall, a few yards away. These volumes were selected,
he said, because they were "considered so worthless as to be

fit only to be ground up, since no person could possibly want them for any purpose whatever"; yet he found himself obliged to send to Boylston for volumes from five to twenty times a day. Although he would never admit it publicly, the problem of space finally shook his creed of universal collection. In his diary for 29 March 1874 he wrote:

> What is to be done with books? Till the beginning of the present century, and even later, it was not inexpedient for public libraries . . . to gather in copies of every book or pamphlet that could be got. Now, the facilities for printing, the passion for reading, which in America was greatly quickened in the late war . . . with various other causes, will make it necessary, both to use books to advantage and to facilitate investigations, and to keep library buildings within reasonable and convenient limits as to size and attendants, to adopt, quite generally, a system of libraries for specialties or particular subjects.

Although there were practically no funds earmarked for library use when Sibley's services began, he never found it difficult to obtain the money he needed for book purchases. As soon as he became Librarian, he began to urge that some individual obtain immortality for himself by endowing a book purchase fund. For a decade he campaigned for $150,000, or better $500,000, which would, he said, so overshadow all other gifts that by the judicious use of bookplates it could make the donor's name synonymous with the institution, which with such a wealth of research material would draw students from the entire world! This letter, addressed to A. A. Lawrence, was typical of his fund campaign:

> The leading men of the Revolution, the Otises, the Adamses, Hancock, Quincy, and others, caught the spirit of liberty and patriotism from the education and books at Old Harvard; and how many of the valiant defenders of our country in the field and in her councils during the recent Rebellion were moved by the consideration of subjects to which their attention was called and which they looked into among the tomes in Gore Hall! Shall the Library which sends out such influences be chilled for want of

funds? God forbid! Give us the money and we will give
you back the power of doing good to the whole world.

This particular plea had no results, but from various sources
the funds available for book purchase grew during his regime
from $250 a year to the yield of an investment of $170,000.

Another problem which the Sibley administration met with
success was that of staff. When Ezra Abbot was appointed Assistant Librarian the Librarian was informed that the new appointee was specifically given entire charge of classification
and cataloguing. Sibley did not resent having the Assistant Librarian autonomous as much as he resented the fact that Abbot,
who later became Bussey Professor of New Testament Criticism and Interpretation, tended to side with the Faculty in its
disputes with the Library. Abbot's successor, John Fiske,
played curiously little part in library affairs.

The energy with which Sibley attacked his job when freed
from the incubus of Harris brought an increase of mail amounting in 1858 to a thousand letters, and compelled him to add a
third member to the library staff, a clerk. But that year is
more momentous in the history of American libraries for the
fact that in it Sibley "for the first time employed females to
clean small books". These employees were, of course, in the
tradition of that ancient institution, the college goody; but on
11 April 1859 Woman really got her nose into the tent, and the
retreat of the male librarian commenced: "Began to employ female help in the Library. Miss Caroline Louisa and Miss Ellen Maria, daughters of the late Samuel Sawyer, M.D., of Cambridge (Class of 1827) began copying lists of books to be bought,
which have been brought in by Professors. Compensation six
cents per hour for the present." Sibley tapped this source of
library help at a moment when his activity piled up a mountain
of work which could not have been cleared away had it been
necessary to pay male wages. The girls wrote a beautiful hand
which is blessed by everyone who has to read through the earlier
records in Sibley's miserable scrawl. The advantages of the beautiful hand were so obvious that after two months the girls were
put to work assisting Abbot on the catalogue. That same month
a daughter of James Winthrop Harris was engaged to help read
the alcove shelves, and the next year her sister was brought in.

Almost immediately Sibley encountered the other perennial

problem concerned with the employment of women–girls will
be girls and get married. When the supply of daughters of deceased Harvard graduates ran out, he turned to that ever flowing spring, the Cambridge High School, and engaged the first
scholar in the graduating class. In six years the staff of the Library had increased from two to eleven: "Thus we now have employed in the Library, five young ladies, besides the Librarian,
Assistant Librarian, Mr. Cutter the 2d Assistant Librarian &
T. J. Kiernan, the Janitor; and John Maccarty a boy, and J. W.
Harris when not employed as Presidents Clerk." It had been
Sibley's custom to control the entrance to Gore Hall by hiding
the key in a niche by the door, but in 1867 he gave up this practice so that the girls might come and go as they wished. In 1873
he appointed Annie E. Hutchins "head of female assistants" with
a salary of $700. This was, however, not an entire solution, as
this entry from his diary suggests:

> Chiding one of the Library assistants for attempting to
> tyrannize over the others whom she was directed to in-
> struct in cataloging. . . . Stormy time in the Library
> about my finding fault with one of the girls. I told them
> all were equal and that all should behave and all should
> be treated as ladies.

In spite of such troubles the girls were such an obvious success
that President Eliot, Sibley complained, tried "to get away
library female assistants to help the College Treasurer".

Those were the days in which boys were glad to come to work
in the Library on trial without pay, and when proved were glad
to take $1.50 a week. However, the lads under twelve may not
have been worth much more. Sibley first tapped another great
source of faithful library help when on 5 December 1859 he
hired "John Maccarty, an Irish lad, not thirteen years old . . .
for one dollar a week, on trial". When John grew older he left
the Library and learned the bookbinder's trade, but remained
within Sibley's ken. In 1856 the Library had 246 volumes bound
and 42 repaired, but the flood of accessions which resulted from
the new Librarian's efforts quickly changed that statistic. Sibley himself checked shipments for the bindery and after their
return, sending back all defective pieces with specific complaints.
With octavos in half sheep costing as much as 50 cents a volume to

bind, expenses mounted. Sibley realized that pamphlets should
be bound separately and sought inexpensive ways to do it; this
was critical, because the Faculty did not want to keep pamphlets at all. John Maccarty seemed to be the ideal solution for
the problem of binding. Sibley attempted to obtain a college
room in which John could set up his shop, doing all of the college work for a stipulated wage and having the privilege of supplementing it by taking in outside work. Before the space could
be found, Maccarty died, and the Harvard University Bindery
receded into the future.

In the sixties the increased activity of the Library compelled
Sibley to begin the printing of various forms. Irked by printers'
prices, he bought a press and equipment in 1863 and on that did
the small printing of the Library until the college printer took
over ten years later. He introduced the familiar "Harvard College Library" letterhead in 1871. So far as possible, supplies
were homemade. His library paste was made of buffalo glue and
thick molasses. The year before he hired the first female he
bought a secondhand lounge for the Library, but usually he could
depend on discards. From the Brattle house he obtained three
dining tables and twenty-five cane-bottomed chairs. He never
squandered, and never overlooked details, down to the gift of
two penwipers and the purchase of two penpoints. Quick to de-
tect the usefulness of penny postcards, he purchased the first
to appear. He quarreled with the Postmaster General over the
institution of a charge of a cent for newspapers delivered by
mail to the Library, and rowed bitterly with the Adams Express
Company, which refused to follow his directions about forward-
ing what it called his "little stinking bundles" of books.

Civil War inflation upset wage and salary scales as well as
supply costs. As Assistant Librarian, Sibley had received a
room, $500 a year, and 40 cents an hour for the period between
4 p.m. and the prayer bell. As Librarian he received $1,500 a
year in a period of rapidly rising prices. In 1867 he asked for
a 50 per cent increase on the ground that his work had doubled,
but the Corporation gave him only $10 a quarter more, which
he rightly said was "pretty mean". Still, he was well off by contrast with the other employees. Students who dusted books got
$1.25 a day. In 1860 Morris O'Conner took a contract to clean
all of the books in the Library for $40, and with this employed
a crew which finished the work in a month. The next year John

Donovan, a lad fresh from Ireland, was hired to dust the books for $2 a week. During the War, the pay of female help was increased to a scale of from 11 to 14 cents an hour. Sibley insisted that the girls be kept on an hourly basis, although there was steady administrative pressure to have them paid by the week. In 1873 the pay of the three skilled female assistants was raised to 20 cents an hour.

It was during Sibley's administration that there occurred the revolution in library hours which so profoundly affected employee and user alike. Because he opposed a liberalization which would have been administratively impossible, funds and staff considered, he has been unjustly classed with the antediluvians. When he became Librarian the College Laws provided one hour a week in which Freshmen and Sophomores might charge out books, and two hours for Juniors and Seniors. This schedule being unreasonable, he had been accustomed to let students take out books at other times. Finding that this service interrupted his other work, he proposed to President Walker that the official hours be doubled and enforced. After some discussion he extended the undergraduate borrowing hours to from 2 to 4 on each of the four secular days of the week that the Library was open. During his first years as Librarian he himself presided at the charging desk, but later he assigned the job to an assistant. In 1860 the delivery hours were increased from 9 to 1 and 2 to 5. Monday through Friday, except when the sun set earlier.[2] Saturdays and college vacations must, Sibley insisted, be kept for tasks, such as cataloguing, which had to be done without interruption. In 1863 he offered "to allow access of Professors and Tutors to the Library from 3 to 4 o'clock when I am in town on Wednesday and Fridays this vacation". With these expansions there was not enough call to justify keeping an assistant at the delivery desk during the hours that it was open, so there was installed a spring bell by which the visitor might summon help. In 1864 Gore was opened Monday mornings during college vacations, and the next year it was opened three mornings a week. In 1867 Sibley voluntarily abolished the noon-hour closing and for the first time opened the Library to readers on Saturdays. The next year he kept it open during the winter vacation and the spring recess, but in his annual report bitterly protested having to keep it open a part of the summer recess:

> So far as I know, there is not a college or university library in the world where so much is exacted of its library officers. "Outrageous" is the word which more than any other, I hear applied to it, and the epithet is sometimes accompanied with very strong qualifying adverbs.

He obtained some satisfaction by defiantly closing the Library on 1 January 1869, claiming that New Year's was considered a holiday.

One subject on which Sibley and his readers agreed was his reform of the Library catalogue. The volumes transferred from Harvard to Gore in 1841 bore numbers according to alcove and shelf, and were, so far as possible, so shelved in their new home. Gradually they were reclassified and renumbered, although not much progress could be made until Sibley became Librarian. In 1860 he proposed that, instead of printing a supplement to the catalogue of 1830-34, there be made a public card catalogue of books added to the Library since that date. The suggestion found favor, and the first cataloguing desk and trays were purchased. Then in 1861 the Library Committee asked Abbot to submit a plan for a classed catalogue of the entire Library. The plan was drawn and accepted, and Sibley was authorized to hire three additional female assistants to write the cards. He obtained the girls from the Cambridge High School, and they began work in May 1862. Although the accompanying reclassification was properly Abbot's work, Sibley did much of it himself. There were to be two catalogues. That for the public was short-title and on 5 by 2 cards, including both authors and subjects. The "Librarian's catalogue" was to be full-entry, on long cards, and was eventually to cover the entire collection. The first cases for the public catalogue were bought in July 1862. The work was pushed through with speed. In the first year 35,762 cards were written. In 1875 Annie E. Hutchins was appointed cataloguer, and she was reported to have made more than 75,000 cards in the first year of her long career.

The newspaper collection represented a difficult cataloguing problem, for in the Ebeling volumes the papers are bound in a roughly chronological order. In 1870 Sibley put his attention to the task and devised a geographical, alphabetical, and chronological catalogue which was a wonder for its day, and a much better tool than is now available for finding newspapers at Harvard.

Early in his career Sibley laid down the rule that pamphlets should be catalogued as thoroughly as bound volumes because, he said, they were the most valuable part of any library which "had reference to posterity". For years this was the subject of a running fight with the Faculty, which in 1873 through the Library Council ordered the cataloguing of pamphlets suspended to permit the more expeditious cataloguing of books. After three years Sibley succeeded in having this modified to permit the cataloguing of important pamphlets.

More than most librarians Sibley realized that a public catalogue is a tool and not primarily an exercise of the art of logic; that a poor one which provides access to the books is better than an elaborate one which the ordinary user cannot fathom. In 1867 he printed for the use of students a seven-page pamphlet describing the catalogues.

When Sibley became Librarian the number of volumes stolen was running to about three dozen a year. In his report for 1857 he said:

In relation to the Public Library it is painful to be obliged to say that among the many who are permitted to use it there are a few who are guilty of violating the Eighth Commandment. During the year thirty-seven volumes have been abstracted from Gore Hall.

To check this loss he forbade readers to take books from the alcoves without permission, and, as he expected, there followed a sharp drop in the number of books stolen. This restriction, however, gave new currency to the charges made by the men who had opposed his appointment, to the effect that his policy was antiquated and that it discouraged the use of the Library. In June 1859 the Faculty suggested to the Corporation that all persons connected with the University be given practically free access to the Library, and the Corporation referred the matter to Sibley. To this he replied, referring obviously to book collectors and possibly to Faculty members:

Dr. Cogswell of the Astor Library, says, a person who has a specialty is not to be trusted without very great

caution in the department in which he is particularly
interested, for he will almost infallibly abstract the
rarities.

Admitting the undergraduates to the alcoves would, he said, result in the loss of books by misplacing. In the Law Library students had access to the stacks, and "Law Students sometimes
tell me in very rough language that they cannot find the books."
Experience, he reported, showed that American college boys
always wrecked a library when given the opportunity. At Harvard
a Benjamin Franklin autograph had been cut from a book six
months after it had been given to the Library. As a substitute
to opening the alcoves, he proposed that the latest and best books
be placed in the open-shelf collection in the main hall of Gore,
and that there be prepared for the students an author and subject
catalogue in which they could find what they wanted much more
quickly than by browsing the shelves of the alcoves.

To the demand for free access Sibley replied by placing on
the open shelves 200 periodicals, the material most wanted by
the students, which had previously been kept locked; and he did
give freer access to the alcoves. The latter policy, he believed,
was responsible for an unparalleled outbreak of stealing. One
valuable book was taken within twenty-four hours of its arrival,
on the day of the annual inspection of the Library, while the Visiting Committee was at dinner! The stealing of valuable books
like this he laid, not to the students, but to visitors who knew
the worth of the volumes. In his annual report for 1862 he said:

> From the pocket of one person who had received special
> favors at the Library, but whom for some time I had
> suspected, I drew with my own hand a periodical which
> he was surreptitiously carrying off without having it
> charged. . . . The ideas of liberty are so latitudinarian
> with some persons that they do not reflect on the base-
> ness or iniquity of such acts, or their liability to be ar-
> raigned before the civil authorities and punished as
> thieves. Death has more than once within my knowledge
> been the means of exposing such conduct.

In 1863 the problem of theft came to a head. The pilfering
of books by the students reached a new high just as a Library

Committee report bitterly attacked the Librarian because Gore
Hall was not open longer hours and the access to the alcoves was
not easier. The attack, like the one a decade earlier, was based
on a totally unfounded idea that the rules had been more liberal
in some golden age of the Library. It ignored the fact that Sibley had been responsible for great improvements, and that there
simply was not the staff or room to permit the adoption of the
proposals for liberalization. Sibley replied that the Harvard
rules were the most liberal among American colleges, and that
the partial opening of the Library during vacations provided statistics to show that the demand for this reform was greatly ex-
aggerated. He defied the Committee, held his ground, and as a
final insult omitted the critical report of the Committee from his
bound file.

In the late sixties and seventies the problem of theft by the
students was dwarfed by that of professionals seeking material
for the collectors then bidding frantically for the great rarities
of American colonial history. Winslow's GOOD NEWS FROM
NEW ENGLAND, Harris' VIRGINIA, and lesser rarities were
stolen and the theft concealed by mutilating or hiding the bound
alcove catalogues which served as shelf-lists. What appeared
to be Harvard's copy of Cushman's DISCOURSE turned up in the
library of Henry M. Dexter, who took (for such a religious man)
a very unreasonable attitude, and blamed Mr. Sibley:

> I will not say here — what I think one might almost be
> justified in saying — that [if] Harvard College keeps
> the choice books in its library in as careless a man-
> ner as Mr. Sibley represents to be the case, in ac-
> counting for the disappearance from it of its copy of
> this Discourse, it ought to lose them, but I will say
> that . . . it ought to expect to lose them.

So Sibley was criticized by the Faculty for not being liberal
enough and by the collectors to whom he looked for gifts for being too liberal.

Much of Sibley's time had to be given over to negotiations
on administrative subjects which are today recognized as being
within the sole jurisdiction of the Librarian. For example, he
felt that he had to ask the President or the Corporation for permission to exchange duplicates. He had to fight to stop the trans-

fer of books from Gore Hall to the Law Library where, he said, experience had proved that they would be stolen by the students. His assistants assumed the right to bypass him in contacts with the Library Committee and the Corporation, and were so careless as to lose three years in succession the list of donors for his report. Encouraged by Abbot, Faculty members tried continually to change library policy, and Sibley regarded them, and even treated them, like the natural enemies of the Librarian. His diaries contain such notes as "Charles Folsom in the Library prying into Library affairs", and:

> Difficulty with Prof. Bowen, whose disposition always is to exact every possible privilege and to avail himself of all (though in violation of the laws) that he can get. I peremptorily refused to let him take out a volume entitled "Waverly," because it did not come within the class relating to the "department of instruction," the books for which the Professors are allowed to keep out longer than the others. He made complaint about it in the Faculty meeting in the evening. He had defied me, before he brought the book, to keep back any book that he wanted saying if I did he should lay the matter before the College Corporation.

Because of such clashes and the growing misunderstandings, a Library Committee consisting of President Walker and Professors Felton, Child, and Eliot began meeting in the President's Office in 1859. Young Mr. Eliot was first secretary and then chairman. This committee concerned itself chiefly with seeing that the library funds were disbursed in accordance with the wishes of the donors, and with the collection of lists of desiderata from the professors, which were passed along to Abbot and Sibley with instructions to buy the books on them. Policy matters were largely ignored.

However, the need of a policy committee became obvious in 1866 when Sibley put his hand into his own pocket and laid out $100 for a private edition of his annual report of 1864, in which he lashed back at a Library Committee report of the previous year which had indeed reflected severely on his administration because he would not accept Faculty demands as to an extension on library privileges. The startled committee replied that they had not intended to reflect on Mr. Sibley. For twenty years the Administration had avoided taking sides in the battle over library policy, but on 18 January 1867 a special committee of the Overseers proposed the creation of a Library Council which would, besides taking over the functions of the Library Committee, assume the responsibility for the management of the Library, and exercise various administrative functions which would normally fall within the authority of the Librarian. This report did not mention Sibley or his office, but came out strongly for the increased service which his critics demanded, and urged the stringent weeding which he feared:

> Books, superseded by more recent and more thorough works, may be positively mischievous to persons not sufficiently versed in the subject to know their relative value. Officers of the college speak of the rubbish and chaff which ought to be removed from the collections in their department.

Against this proposal for weeding Sibley marshaled so much adverse comment in the Harvard community that when the Corporation set up the Library Council early in 1867 it unanimously rejected this part of the report of the special committee.

To the new body was granted authority far beyond that exercised by the old Library Committee:

> It shall be the duty of the council to see that the laws and regulations of the library are enforced, and to propose from time to time to the corporation such changes in them as may be for the interest of the University; to direct the purchase of books to the extent of the funds appropriated for that purpose; to appoint all persons employed in the library excepting the librarian, the assistant librarian and the janitor, and to fix the rate of compensation to be paid to such persons from the funds provided for that purpose.

Sibley was invited to attend the first meetings of the Library Council, but he was so obviously hostile that it formed the habit of consulting with Abbot on library matters and using him as its agent. In his twelfth report as Librarian, in 1867, Sibley formally relinquished to the new body his campaign to obtain an endowment and a new building for the Library, but on other matters he clashed with it.

One of the Council's first acts was to raise the wages of female employees to a range of 15 to 21 cents an hour. This Sibley bitterly protested because the old rates were based on the going scale in Boston, and any change should have been calculated on the increased cost of living instead of being arbitrary. But the major clash came over the question of binding in the covers of periodicals. Professor Gibbs, Dean of the Lawrence Scientific School, who thought that the volumes were spoiled by the binding in of covers, carried through the Council and the Corporation a vote that the Librarian be requested not to bind in covers of periodicals unless they contained information not in the pages. At the time Sibley was not informed of this vote; which is not surprising, for his only contact with the Library Council was the receipt of its occasional directives by mail. A year later Gibbs found that the covers were still being bound in, and he verbally attacked Sibley, giving him the impression that it was ordered that no covers be bound in. "I was somewhat annoyed", said the Librarian, "to be so treated by a man who knew no more about the Library than I did about his gallipots." As for the Library Council, he said, it acted "as if they knew nothing about a library except to get the greatest privileges with the fewest restraints and without regard to the getting of things prepared for use". Without difficulty he obtained from leading librarians and book dealers letters explaining the importance of binding in covers, and turned these over to President Eliot with remarks which he repeated in substance in his diary:

> It seems very small business for the Library Council to spend their time on such matters but as one notion after another was broached by persons who knew little or nothing of the practical or working part of a library, I thought it well enough to do something to check their crude ideas.

The Council and Corporation were too proud to back water in the case of the periodical covers, but they let it be understood that if Sibley made no fuss he could do what he wanted in the matter.

Eliot, convinced by this case that there was a good deal of

JOHN LANGDON SIBLEY, LIBRARIAN

validity in the Librarian's criticism of the Library Council, urged Sibley to accept appointment to that body. Although admitting that this seemed to be the best solution, Sibley held off for seven awkward years, until on 31 January 1877 the President simply informed him that he had been appointed to the Council. It was too late in Sibley's administration for this reform to bear fruit, but it made the work of his successor much simpler.

That Sibley's administration ended peacefully was largely due to the fact that Charles William Eliot was an administrator who could keep above petty bickering and see details in perspective. Unfortunately Sibley is known to a majority of those who have heard his name only by a story which Eliot, and his sons and friends after him, used to tell with amusement. It told how the President one day met the Librarian hurrying across the Yard and asked where he was going. Sibley replied: "The Library is locked up and every book is in it but two, and I know where they are and I am going after them." The generation of Eliot's sons assumed that this story illustrated Sibley's primitive ideas about libraries and books. In fact, the Harvard rules, like those of many other libraries in that day, ordered the Librarian once a year to get in every book and to lock the Library for a formal check and visitation, performed by a committee of the Overseers. Until 1854 this Examining Committee itself counted the books on the shelves of Gore and checked the count against the alcove catalogues, but that year they gave up after an hour. Sibley's accessions soon made the annual check a great chore; in 1859 it occupied two persons for three weeks.

After each annual check the titles of all missing books were posted on the bulletin board. The story of Sibley's going after the two missing volumes probably had its origin in an incident during Eliot's tutorship, for in 1858 there were only two books out on loan at the time of the visitation. But in the first three years of Sibley's administration book circulation about doubled. Students and Faculty were using more, and scholars from the outside world, some of them attracted by Sibley's library reports in the newspapers, were asking for books. The result was that at the time of the annual count of 1860 there were no less than fifty volumes out, in spite of the fact that the Librarian had advertised in all Boston newspapers for their return. The worst offenders among the outside borrowers were ministers. At one time Sibley proposed to advertise a delinquent in the Philadelphia

newspapers and would have done so had not a Boston friend of
the culprit taken the train to recover the volumes and save the
offender from public indignity. In general, Sibley's experience
with outside borrowers was bitter and will explain, if not justify,
his refusal to make a reasonable inter-library loan to the Library
of Congress in 1874.

Within the University it was not the undergraduates who were
the seriously delinquent borrowers. At the annual examination
of 1861 every book charged to a student had been returned except one that had been left in a Boston horsecar. The Faculty
were another matter; unlike the students, they used books during the summer vacation. When the Examining Committee re-
provingly pointed out to Mr. Sibley the gaps on the shelves of
Gore, he knew whom to blame. One of his first acts as Librarian was to take the question of delinquent borrowers among the
college officers to the Board of Overseers. To the modern researcher who suffers from the egotism of professors who for
years sequester in their own offices all books which they think
that they might have use for sometime, Sibley's report to the
Examining Committee of 1857 may not sound too stringent:

> Delinquencies of this nature are not common; but they
> are so dishonorable, to use no stronger word, that I
> consider them deserving of public exposure and repre-
> hension. They teach us the unwelcome lesson that we
> cannot extend even to all who have the reputation of
> being gentlemen and scholars unrestricted privileges
> in the use of the Library.

In 1868 he asked the Corporation to allow him to cut off the
library privileges of Faculty members who would neither return
books called in for the annual examination nor pay the fines for
overdue books. The Corporation replied by reminding him that
the College Laws gave Faculty members special privileges.
Probably it thought that his request was in part motivated by the
fact that, as he often pointed out, he was kept at the Library
during vacations while the other college officers were "luxuriat-
ing in relief from their duties". He still took up with the Corporation special cases like that of Professor Dennett, who obstinate-
ly refused to return twenty-five books or to pay the fines on them.

By 1870 the closing of the Library for the annual examination had become quite impractical, so Sibley substituted the system of beginning the shelf-reading some months ahead, and of checking returned books off the list of those not on the shelf. In this way the count was taken without either a shutdown or an unpleasant struggle to get books in by a certain date. This new practice made the gathering of the committee for the annual examination quite perfunctory. In 1874, having no list of the members of the committee, Sibley sent out no notices. The next year Ralph Waldo Emerson, the chairman of the committee, was to have sent out the notices, but failed to do so. So died an outgrown institution which had its origins in the seventeenth century.

So far as Sibley was concerned, no institution, building, or practice was sacred because it was old; he welcomed any change which was an improvement. The longest and bitterest battle of his career was to have Gore Hall, which was "unfit for a library from the first because erected in ignorance of the wants of a library", replaced by a functional building. It was gloomy Gothic, and what little light came through the narrow windows could not, because of a taboo quite general among libraries in that generation, be augmented by artificial means. Before the building was a dozen years old stones had begun to fall from its high pinnacles, to the great danger of life and limb. By 1872 large pieces of stucco were falling from the interior arches, menacing the readers and creating a grit which got among and into the books. The cellar was too wet to be used for book storage. For several weeks a year water ran through it, a situation remedied only when Sibley had a drain constructed in 1860. The towers, which had to be used for book storage, were nearly as damp as the cellar. Throughout the building the walls were only one stone thick, with the result that in winter frost formed on the inside unless there was, by chance, enough heat from the furnace to melt it off. A few days after the furnace was let out in the spring, green mold formed on some of the walls. In some parts of the building books had to be taken from the shelves and opened to dry after each damp spell. Sometimes they were so wet that they visibly steamed when brought near the heat.

The steam boiler which was installed when Gore was built never adequately heated more than the first alcove, and never warmed the damp drafts which swooped among the arches and pillars. During the winter readers had to wear their hats and overcoats. When Sibley employed females to do the writing he had to bring blinds from Holden Chapel to serve as cold-weather screens around them. The girls created another problem which he called to the attention of President Walker on 21 October 1859:

> All the persons who are employed in Gore Hall suffer from want of a water closet and appurtenances. The young women have no accommodations nearer than their homes. The inconvenience and the injury to health will be greater when the weather is colder and the ground covered. I take the liberty of asking you to lay the subject before the Corporation, and hope that accommodations of the best kind may be provided as early as practicable, not only for the comfort of us workers but that library visitors may not be obliged to wash their hands at the nose of the pump, as is now the case, or in an old rotten sink, which had served out its time in Harvard Hall before it was removed to Gore Hall more than eighteen years ago.

Whatever the sufferings of that winter may have been, spring brought relief. Fresh Pond water was piped into the cellar of Gore Hall and the conveniences were ready for use on 27 June 1860.

The Gore staff suffered almost as much from lack of work space. Boxes had to be opened and unpacked in the area used as a reading room. Since the building was a perfect whispering gallery, the noise distracted the readers and drew their attention to the new books, to which they helped themselves before the accession records were made. These drawbacks to Gore, and its great unusable and unheatable spaces, made Sibley the advocate of functional library buildings in which he foresaw most of the improvements introduced by the architects in the next century.

In 1863 plans of the Corporation to build a new dormitory close to the north side of Gore created a new menace, of which Sibley complained:

> Students coming from carousals in the night, as they sometimes do, would not be likely to go much out of their way to let off their high excitement, but if on their way to the new building they were to pass so near the Library,

untenanted, they would be very likely to do mischief
by breaking doors, perhaps entering through the windows.

As it was, they broke windows while trying to knock down horse-
chestnuts. Sibley's protest staved off the threat of the dormitory,
and his report of 1863, in which he eloquently argued that Gore
would never be a satisfactory library building, finally brought
agreement that a new structure should be erected. The plans
provided that it should go up on the site of the present Grays.
Sibley deeply regretted that the rent which the University received from Wadsworth House prevented that from being torn
down so that the library building might go on the line of the
street. He should have been forewarned by the fact that President Hill, after looking at the plans for the new library, took
off his coat and hat and wielded a spade diligently to plant ivy
and trumpet vines around Gore. They were indeed venerable
before Gore came down.

The dormitory which Sibley had shooed away from Gore went
up on the site behind Wadsworth House where he had expected
to put the new library. Attention was then shifted to the site of
Lamont, where by 1865 it was agreed that the new library building should go. Sibley drew plans for a plain, unostentatious,
functional building, built for the centuries, with double or triple
walls. Because of the elimination of waste space the building
was to be relatively small, but designed to facilitate external
expansion when the first unit was filled. Just when all were agreed that this building should be erected, the agitation for a Civil
War memorial began. Although Sibley regarded the plans for
Memorial Hall as "beautiful", he was terrified by the implication
of competition for building funds: "The excitement about it is a
great strain on my nerves."

When Eliot came into the Presidency in 1869 he informed Sibley that his solution of the library problem was an improvement
of the heating system and an enlargement of Gore. Bitterly the
Librarian fought for a new building and opposed the "improvements". He argued that the President's proposed structural alterations to combat dampness would make the building sag. The
proposed wooden sheathing would reduce the size of the alcoves
and create a fire hazard. When he heard that Eliot had asked the
college carpenter to find a large hot-air furnace to go into the

main room of Gore he protested vigorously that it would spread dirt and dry out the books; but it went in, and was lighted on 1 January 1874.

Before each step the President invited Sibley's scorn by asking his advice on the successive plans for alterations; but unfortunately the plans for the enlargement of the building were not shown to the Librarian until they had been drawn in detail by men who obviously knew nothing about libraries. Sibley walked into Boston on hot afternoons to beg members of the Corporation to scrap these plans in favor of a new building designed to house a million volumes. He went to Saratoga and sought funds from the millionaires gathered there. Finally he offered to will the Corporation $20,000 which was to accumulate until it would provide a new and functional library building. Meeting defeat everywhere, he turned to Eliot's plans and revised them to provide the new addition with iron stacks and shelves, steam heat, low ceilings, and plain window glass. His passion against library Gothic had already eliminated that danger. In his annual report of 1876 he formally registered his protest against the extension, which had been begun, insisting that in the end a new building would have been far less expensive. In April 1877 he moved into the new wing and his office, but within the month he told Eliot that he intended to resign.

Sibley had some difficulty in preparing his final annual report because his sight had so failed that even with all aids he could not see his own handwriting.

> It is not without a feeling of sadness that I leave a situation in which I have spent so many years. More than half of a long life has been devoted to its duties. It has taken precedence of all other pleasures and employments. But the recollection of the scenes and enjoyments I have had here will continue when my connection is dissolved. I cannot divorce myself and go forth as a stranger from what has been the home of my heart for so long. The Library will continue to be like an old home as long as I live.

He was content to surrender the administration to so able a man as Justin Winsor, and to him he handed the reins on 31 August 1877. The first two acts of the new administration were to put a "lady" (not a "female assistant") at the charging desk, and to begin moving into the new wing. The last entry in Sibley's library journal is: "Old library entrance closed and all admitted to the new entrance." The entrance was new but the goal was the same. The Winsor administration did not, as tradition would have it, mean long-delayed progress, modernization, and revolutionary changes, but rather the acceptance of library goals which fell considerably short of the unobtainable ideal for which Sibley had fought.

NOTES:

1   Besides these sources this sketch relies chiefly on the minutes of the Library Council, the Corporation, and the Overseers, and on certain reports made to the Overseers. All these sources are preserved in the Harvard University Archives.

2   For a full account of the movements which terminated with this reform see Kimball C. Elkins, "Foreshadowings of Lamont", Harvard Library Bulletin, VIII (1954), 41-53.

WILLIAM FREDERICK POOLE, LIBRARIAN-HISTORIAN

Sidney H. Kessler

Sidney H. Kessler is Assistant Professor of Social Studies, Glassboro State College, Glassboro, New Jersey.

Most librarians remember Poole as a nineteenth-century pioneer of the periodical index. Others may recall Poole as a genius at organizing libraries and librarians, a spokesman for the ladies in the profession, an expert on library architecture, an inventor of the dictionary catalog principle, or as an associate editor of the Library Journal. Few librarians are aware, however, that Poole was also a historian of such repute that he was elected president of the American Historical Association in 1888. Although considered primarily a librarian, Poole actually represented the perfect merger of the librarian-historian. As Carl B. Roden concluded in the DICTIONARY OF AMERICAN BIOGRAPHY:

> There is some basis for the surmise that Poole's earliest ambitions lay in the direction of historical writing and, perhaps, teaching, and that his first connection with library work was formed rather from necessity than from choice.

Characteristically, Poole's historical productivity was most often expressed in periodical articles, many of which were frequently privately reprinted. He never wrote a full-length book. As in library matters, Poole loved controversy. Once equipped with facts, which he uncovered by an amazing amount of unflagging creative research, his caustic pen was willing to take on all contestants — from the distinguished historian George Bancroft to the obscure young politico, Theodore Roosevelt.

Poole's historical writings began with a paper on the Massachusetts Popham Colony, published in Boston in 1866. This was a sarcastic, critical reply to an address by Professor J. W.

Reprinted from Wilson Library Bulletin, 28:788-790, May, 1954, by permission of the author and the publisher.

Patterson, delivered at Popham, Maine, the year before. Patterson claimed that the Maine colony antedated the one at Massachusetts, and Poole attempted to refute this theory. This disagreement launched Poole into a running three-way controversy with Rev. Edward Ballard and Frederick Kidder which peppered the pages of several contemporary periodicals.

It was his articles on Cotton Mather, however, that gave Poole his reputation as an historian, writer, and critic. As a descendant of Puritans and a native of Old Salem, he was long interested in the Salem witchhunts, and accumulated a wide range of knowledge on the subject. Poole observed that most historians, including Bancroft and Lossing, charged Cotton Mather with complicity in the persecutions. This attitude Poole traced to Charles W. Upham, who in 1831 published his LECTURES ON SALEM WITCHCRAFT. Poole tried to absolve Mather from guilt by showing that the Salem lawyers and judges, following English legal precedents, were responsible for the 1692 executions. Mather and the clergy shared in these only insofar as they supported the theory of the personal devil. Poole minimized the thirty-two Salem murders by pointing to more than 200,000 similar cases throughout the world.

Poole's first article on the subject, "The Mather Papers; Cotton Mather and Salem Witchcraft", was printed in the Boston Daily Advertiser for October 28, 1868, and later appeared both as a privately-printed pamphlet and in the COLLECTIONS OF THE MASSACHUSETTS HISTORICAL SOCIETY, volume eight, fourth series. When Longfellow that same year paid high tribute to Cotton Mather in the NEW ENGLAND TRAGEDIES, surprising historians and scholars, few realized that for his facts he consulted Poole, who was then the librarian of the Boston Athenaeum.

At the request of James Russell Lowell, Poole wrote his second article on Mather for the North American Review of April 1869. John Fiske once stated that for a correct estimate of Cotton Mather's character and influence, historians were indebted to Longfellow in 1868, and Poole in 1869. Poole's views were also accepted by many later historians, and his articles remain as important chapters in American historiography.

While Poole was organizing the Cincinnati Public Library, he naturally became interested in the history of the area. He noted that many historians compared the Thirteenth Amendment with the Jefferson-inspired sixth clause of the 1787 Northwest Ordi-

nance, which excluded slavery from the Northwest territory.
Poole concluded that the ordinance had no moral origin, but was
purely a matter of business. After the American Revolution, the
young, financially weak federal government took up large tracts
of land in Ohio. Poole theorized that by banning slavery, the
government could stimulate the sale of these lands to New England settlers, who reviled the slave system. In Marietta, Ohio,
Poole found the diary of Dr. Manasseh Cutler, an agent for the
New England land companies. Cutler was an early lobbyist who
spent a winter in Washington attempting to secure the approval
of the ordinance by inviting congressmen to elaborate meals at
his boarding house. In his diary, Cutler constantly referred to
the ordinance as a means to secure land sales. His diary also
revealed that many supporters of the anti-slavery ordinance were
from the Southern slave-owning group. Poole reasoned that since
these Southerners represented the wealthier element of the nation, their self-interest demanded a stable economy, free of national debt. Since the passage of the ordinance tended to lessen
the national debt, many Southerners gave the bill their full support. With this thesis, first proposed by Poole in 1876, and
later widely accepted, Poole anticipated by nearly fifty years
the sensation-creating economic interpretation of the federal
period by Charles A. Beard.

Once more Poole entered into continuous, volatile debate to
defend his point of view. As late as January 1892 he penned an
acid article for The Inlander which dealt out heavy blows on one
Henry A. Chaney, who committed the mistake of challenging
Poole's Northwestern thesis. Poole chose "The Early Northwest"
as his presidential address to the American Historical Association in December 1888. This paper was the epitome of Poole as
a librarian-historian. It dealt with areas of research in Northwestern history, with the purpose of showing what the sources
were, and suggestions as to how they might be improved upon.
Poole closed his address with a plea for Congress to set up a
Department of Archives so that scholars would not be forced to
go abroad and at their own expense translate and transcribe foreign documents relating to America. Here again he anticipated
by half a century the photostating of these documents by the Library of Congress.

Another standard for specialists is Poole's "Anti-Slavery
Opinions before the Year 1800", an address to the Cincinnati

WILLIAM FREDERICK POOLE, LIBRARIAN-HISTORIAN

Literary Club that was later printed as a pamphlet. The address began with a discussion of George Washington's private library, part of which was housed in the Boston Athenaeum, where Poole served as librarian. Partisans on either side of the slavery question could not fail to be impressed by Poole's painstaking scholarship, restraint, and objectivity. At the same time, Poole made it plain that his sympathies were with the opponents of slavery. The fact that Poole was not compelled to write polemical pamphlets and articles defending his ideas is indicative of the pamphlet's immediate acceptance.

As an organizer of librarians and director of his cooperative, nonprofit periodical index, Poole knew the value of scholarly collaboration. He contributed a section on witchcraft in Boston to the MEMORIAL HISTORY OF BOSTON, written in 1881 by a fellow librarian-historian, Justin Winsor. Seven years later, when Winsor saw his NARRATIVE AND CRITICAL HISTORY OF AMERICA in print, Poole's chapter on the West from 1763-1783 appeared in volume six.

When Poole's fame as a historian spread, he became an important critic, and was frequently asked to write reviews for newspapers and periodicals. In 1889, William Dean Howells, editor of the Atlantic Monthly, asked Poole to review THE WINNING OF THE WEST, a new history by a young politico named Theodore Roosevelt. Poole's unsigned review appeared in the November 1889 issue, and outshone all others in grasping the implications and complexities of the subject. In general, Poole approved of Roosevelt's work, but took him to task for overlooking certain primary sources. Because of this review, the two men entered into a correspondence over historical matters, and later met in Washington, D.C., before the historical novice assumed the presidency. Roosevelt's first letter to his anonymous reviewer began:

> My dear sir;
> I do not know whether it is usual for an author to write a reviewer; but yours is the first criticism of my book from which I have learnt anything, and indeed the first which I felt was written by a man who really knew the subject.
> I must frankly acknowledge the justice of some of your criticisms. . . .[1]

Poole brought a historical perspective to his many writings and addresses on library science. For example, his influential Phi Beta Kappa address "The University Library and the University Curriculum" emphasized the study of classical languages by prominent persons of the past, including the Mather family.

Throughout his lifetime, Poole was an active member of the American Historical Association. In addition, he belonged to the American Antiquarian Society, the Essex Institution, and the state historical societies of Massachusetts, New York, Pennsylvania, Maryland, Wisconsin, and other states.

On March 1, 1894, the "Good Doctor" passed away, leaving his wife, four of their seven children, and a world of learning to reflect on the beneficence he gave to humanity. Since that time, the invaluable, multi-sided life of Poole the librarian-historian has not been recorded in a definitive biography. May this long need soon be met!

NOTE:

1   Utley, George B. "Theodore Roosevelt's The Winning of the West: some unpublished letters". Mississippi Valley Historical Review vol. 30 no. 4:499 March 1944.

FREDERICK M. CRUNDEN, LIBRARY STATESMAN

Bertha Doane

> Bertha Doane, a member of the St. Louis (Missouri) Pub-
> lic Library staff for more than fifty-seven years, died at
> the age of eighty-two on October 5th, 1960. The essay here
> reprinted is a paper read before the American Library His-
> tory Round Table at the 1954 conference of the American
> Library Association in Minneapolis.

Carved on the pediment of Cass Gilbert's beautiful portal
are these words:

> The Public Library of the City of St. Louis. Recorded
> thought is our chief heritage from the past. The most
> lasting legacy we can leave to the future. Books are
> the most enduring monument of man's achievements.
> Only through books can civilization become cumulative.
> Frederick M. Crunden

This quotation from one of his own addresses, chosen by an
appreciative committee, is the true and lasting memorial to
that library statesman whose vision, initiative, and administrative acumen brought this institution into being.

His friend, Dr. Herbert Putnam, said in his speech at the
formal opening of this building on January 6, 1912:

> Of such a service as his, memorials are rare —
> or rarely visible: for the task of an administrator is to
> merge himself in his work; and his success as an ad-
> ministrator will in a way be proportioned to the success
> of his effort to do so. He is endeavoring to shape some-
> thing larger than himself and more lasting: to embody
> an ideal which he does not possess, but which possesses
> him. If he succeeds — in proportion as he succeeds —
> his own personality, his own identity, will be lost in

Reprinted from Wilson Library Bulletin, 29:446-449+, February,
1955, by permission of publisher and the author's sister, Mrs. Dorothy D. Stewart of Glendale, California.

that which it has created.

But if this must in the nature of institutions be so, it is humanly and professionally speaking unfortunate: for it deprives the community and the profession of the example and the stimulus of a life which is itself a lesson. And it must be a deep satisfaction to us librarians, that in gathering here to declare the future of this institution you insist upon recalling and paying tribute to the wise, open, gentle, persevering, unselfish spirit whose devotion has gone into its past.

It is said that little is known of Mr. Crunden in the A.L.A. Yet the record of his services and his numerous writings on library matters are available in the professional journals and his personality vividly written about by his associates throughout America and Europe. The most valuable source of his life and work is Dr. Bostwick's MEMORIAL BIBLIOGRAPHY, a fine piece of research, published by the St. Louis Public Library. In this volume are gathered the many tributes and memorials from various sources at the time of his death, together with a list of all his papers, articles, and addresses, with an explanatory note about each. Katharine Twining Moody, for many years chief of our reference department, published an excellent paper in Public Libraries, 1925, in which she gives a faithful picture of Mr. Crunden during her sixteen years of work and friendship with him. It is from these sources I must draw my paper, as I was associated with him for only two years as an apprentice and junior clerk. Although I was too young and inexperienced to recognize at the time my great opportunity and privilege, I remember him vividly and he has never become a shadow to me in my fifty years' service in the St. Louis Public Library.

Frederick Morgan Crunden, says W. E. Foster, was one of "a notable group of men who, when the founders of the American Library Association were passing off the stage, took the torch from their hands and carried it forward with vigor and effectiveness". He was born in Gravesend, England, September 1, 1847, the son of Benjamin Robert and Mary Morgan Crunden. Coming to St. Louis as a child, he was educated in the public schools of the city. He graduated from high school as valedictorian of his class and entered Washington University on a scholarship, working in vacations to support himself, as his father was no longer living. He graduated from the course in arts and sciences in 1868 with a degree of B.A., taught in Smith Academy, and later held the position of principal in Jefferson and Benton Schools. Returning to Washington University, he instructed in mathematics and elocution while working for his master's degree, which he received in 1872.

During his college course, Mr. Crunden had taken a vital interest in library work and in January 1877 became librarian of the St. Louis Public School Library. This library had few books (about 39,000 volumes) and a very small membership; in fact, it was not a free library, for it charged its members for the use of its books and these sums, with a small amount paid by the public school fund, constituted all it had for support. It was scarcely a library in more than name and it was not a public library at all. It is interesting to note at this point that the newly formed American Library Association disapproved of the appointment of a young man, inexperienced in library affairs and unknown to them, to the headship of a library in the leading city ("The Athens") of the west at that time. Mr. Crunden, however, entered at once into the activities of the association, won the devoted friendship and respect of those critics and was chosen president of the Association in 1889, within twelve years of his entrance into the library profession. His friend, Mr. Melvil Dewey, wrote in Public Libraries, December 1911, at the time of Mr. Crunden's death:

A little after we founded the ALA in 1876, there came to us from St. Louis the brain and big heart that won instant recognition and enduring leadership. For years he has been our senior living ex-president. For a third of a century I have worked intimately with the rare man who has just left us. We have discussed a thousand matters but never once have I heard from his lips an argument or suggestion based on selfishness. His thought was ever the greatest good of the greatest number and for that he was always ready to sacrifice his own interests in a way sadly rare in these days of self-seeking. Those who shared his friendship are better men and women; the ALA is stronger and has higher ideals . . . because of the influence of his earnest life.

Although not technically the founder of the St. Louis Public Library, when Mr. Crunden became librarian of the Public School Library he wasted no time in trying to give the city all the benefits of a free, public, and well conducted library and to place it in a suitable building. John Lee, chairman of the building committee, said in his address at the formal opening of this building in 1912:

All the great changes which have since taken place have followed the initiative of Mr. Crunden.

For many years the progress was slow; at times it halted altogether, but he was ideally formed for the task which he had assumed. He was capable of great labor; he loved his work and he gave himself to it without limit. His talents were of a high order and the range of his learning was wide.

His nature was gentle and loving, but where principle was involved he was inflexible. He had no rancor; he was not embittered by opposition, or even by defeat, but he considered defeat only as another reason for another effort in another direction.

So deep was his sincerity and so strong the belief he held as to the uses of a public library, that many a man has been led to his support because of his sympathy with Mr. Crunden.

When he began his library work it was not the sentiment of a majority of our citizens that a library filled a public want or met a public duty. He set himself to work to build up the sentiment in its favor, which is so overwhelming today.

In fact, during the more than thirty-two years for which he was librarian, he was the life, the soul and center of every great advance it made.

The most important steps taken by Mr. Crunden to create the free public library were, first, to draft a bill authorizing cities, towns, and villages throughout the state to tax themselves for the establishment and maintenance of free libraries. This was presented in the Legislature and approved April 10, 1885. In 1893 Mr. Crunden and his committee decided to avail themselves of this law and after a vigorous campaign obtained

FREDERICK M. CRUNDEN, LIBRARY STATESMAN

1/5 mill library tax by vote of the people at the election in April.
The library was now "free" from the school board, which was
delighted to be relieved of its $20,000 yearly burden. Shortly
after this happy event, Mr. Crunden received the following letter from his board of directors:

> The election of a librarian of the new Public (Free)
> Library will take place in Jan. 1894. The undersigned
> members of the Board of Directors desire to secure
> the services of Mr. F. M. Crunden for that position.
> Having learned that he has had offers from another
> city we desire to inform him of our intention, as stated
> above, and to say that it is the intention of the under-
> signed to attach a salary of $4500 a year to that position.

All signatures of board of directors were attached.

There followed eight years of the struggle for growth, expansion, development of new methods and ideas in the library
world. Miss Moody writes of this time:

> No man ever more conscientiously conserved the
> people's money. The habits of cheerful economy he
> inculcated in the members of his staff were so firm-
> ly rooted that no one of those assistants may today
> discard a slip of paper unmindful of it. For 30 years
> he struggled with a very limited appropriation and
> against obstacles that seemed insurmountable — never
> for a moment showing discouragement, if he felt it,
> making the most of every resource, everywhere
> showing absolute faith in the institution he represented.

Sam Waller Foss might well have had in mind such a "head
librarian" as Mr. Crunden when he graphically pictured him as

> Trying to spend a dollar when he only has a dime
> Tailoring appropriations and how deftly he succeeds
> Fitting his poor thousands to his million dollar needs

During this period not only was Mr. Crunden indefatigable
in his own library but also attended all meetings possible which
discussed library matters, local, state, national, and interna-

tional. Although English born, Mr. Crunden was American through and through, yet he was very much pleased to be invited to attend the International Conference of Librarians in London in 1897 to make an address, the title of which was "Books and Textbooks, The Library as a Factor in Education" and, of course it was the reiteration of his deep conviction that the library was the always open door to education.

> Complete living is the highest possible development of all the human faculties physical, mental and moral: it is success in life. . . . Now, what are the means adopted to accomplish this end? It is the education received by the masses of the people that make the progress of the nation. . . . A nation is like a railway train which can go no faster than its hindmost car.

Few librarians have contributed more effectively with talks and papers and addresses on this subject than Mr. Crunden. Indeed, he had attained international fame when, in 1897, he was made the vice-president of the International Library Conference at London. He was also a member of council of the American Library Association and of the American Library Institute. To quote from the resolution adopted by the ALA at its annual conference held in Ottawa, Canada, June 1912:

> Mr. Crunden's public services were by no means confined to the distinctively library interests of his community and the country. He was particularly interested in the mutual relations of schools and libraries, developing them in St. Louis in a manner which served as a model for others, and contributing largely to the evolution of the present official relations of the National Education Association and the American Library Association. . . .

Out of these difficult years of expansion and insufficient funds grew Mr. Crunden's idea of applying to Mr. Carnegie, who was also firmly convinced of the importance of public libraries as educational institutions. Mr. Carnegie responded with $1,000,000, provided the city would make an appropriation of $150,000 annually for the maintenance of the library system and, after another vigorous campaign, the people of St. Louis voted a library tax of 2/5 of a mill at an election held April 2, 1901. Mr. Dewey's comment on this transaction was, "One gave a million dollars, the other gave his life."

Mr. Crunden was one of the leading citizens of St. Louis and his interests were wide. He belonged to the University Club, the Round Table, the Artists Guild, the Missouri Historical Society, and numerous other organizations. To quote Miss Moody again:

> He was what may be called a charming man and it should be remarked that his ability to arouse enthusiasm in others extended far beyond the members of his staff — it was felt by all who came in contact with him: members of library boards from small cities came to him again and again to urge him to present the library cause to the citizens of their respective towns — to give advice as to the conduct of financial campaigns and the general management of their libraries. This confidence in him could be traced not merely to his culture but to his absolute genuine belief in the work itself and the latent influence of books throughout the community.

In 1889 he was married to Kate Edmondson, a beautiful young English woman who also was an accomplished reader. Together they took great interest in amateur dramatics and readings and formed a group of library assistants which met regularly in the librarian's office to read the plays of Shakespeare. Mr. Crunden knew personally many of the great actors of his time — Henry Irving and Beerbohm Tree, Southern and Marlow, for instance, who, when in St. Louis, gave Mr. Crunden tickets to their plays for distribution to his staff. In fact, Mr. Crunden seemed to know personally most of the eminent people who came to St. Louis — lecturers, musicians, artists, authors, American and European — and it was his delight to bring them to the library to meet and say a few words to the staff. (I remember especially John Fiske.)

His staff always came first with Mr. Crunden. His relations with us all were kindly, friendly, and helpful. He, with Mrs. Crunden, enjoyed having spreads for us in his office and often arranged pleasant evenings in their home, where we could talk freely and come to know him and each other. His was an engaging personality. While sometimes seeming reserved and austere, there was always a whimsical twinkle not long out of his eyes, for he had a delightful sense of humor. He also loved to tease. If he found someone reading on duty he would say sternly "Remember, the librarian who reads is lost" (a quotation from someone I have never been able to locate), remembering that he continually urged us to read, but not on duty. Another whimsy was "Whatever is is wrong, i.e., it is safe to assume that we have not yet achieved the best." If his entire staff did not finally achieve the best, it was not his fault. Mr. Crunden thought that Tennyson, whom he admired greatly, stated his convictions perfectly:

> I held it truth with him who sings
>> To one clear harp in divers tones
>> That men may rise on stepping stones
> Of their dead selves to higher things.

He loved quotations and had a fund of appropriate ones for all occasions.

[The year] 1904 was indeed strenuous for the St. Louis librarian. It was the year of the World's Fair — the Louisiana Purchase Exposition — and the American Library Association decided to show a "model public library" there. A committee was appointed with Melvil Dewey at its head and many libraries and librarians collaborated to make this exhibit possible. It was established in the Missouri building and the St. Louis Public Library collected and prepared the books and the card catalog and maintained and conducted it as a branch. Mr. Crunden was keenly interested in this exhibit. He had been largely instrumental in securing the space and best of all, the good will of the fair's commission. He simply could not keep away from his show and brought in many visitors, distinguished and otherwise, from all over the world. I remember especially Cobden-Sanderson of the Dove Bindery at Hammersmith, who brought with him boxes of his beautiful books and set up a stunning display of bindings such as was seldom seen in this part of the world.

Mr. Crunden addressed the library section of the International Congress of Arts and Science, held in connection with the Louisiana Purchase Exposition, and closed with a summary of the pub-

FREDERICK M. CRUNDEN, LIBRARY STATESMAN

lic library's functions which I will abridge:

> But not last, if an exhaustive list were aimed at —
> at least it supplies a universal and urgent craving of
> human nature by affording to all entertainment of the
> highest and purest character, substituting this for the
> coarse, debasing, demoralizing, amusements which
> would otherwise be sought and found. Further, it
> brings relief and strength to many a suffering body
> and cheer and solace to many a sorrowing heart. It
> is instruction and inspiration to the young, comfort
> and consolation to the old, recreation and companion-
> ship to all ages and conditions. Education is the great-
> est concern of mankind; it is the foundation of all hu-
> man progress. The library is an essential factor in
> all grades of education; and it is the agent plenipo-
> tentiary in the betterment of society and the culture
> and cheer of the human soul.

Mr. Crunden made the address of welcome to the ALA at the conference in St. Louis at this time, as well as the farewell remarks, and entertained and guided hosts of his old friends of the association through the mazes of the great exposition. Though tired beyond his strength, he saw with regret the crowds depart and the World's Fair dismantled. He had had the time of his life and loved to relive it all over again and again.

During the year 1905 Mr. Crunden was engrossed with the plans for this building, as the time had come to prepare for its erection. The board requested him to report as to the library's requirements and his report was submitted and approved.

Very shortly after, Mr. Crunden's illness fell upon him and his mind became a blank. After a year, there was a brief recovery, when he was able to inspect the plans which Cass Gilbert had perfected and realize that the dream of his life had come true, that his library had a great and beautiful building with six branches scattered over the city. Then the darkness descended and the light of his mind went out forever. He died October 28, 1911.

It was not ordained that he should enter into the promised land. He was never within these walls. He

was called to his reward when his work was done, but
he fell in the hour of victory.

I wish to repeat the closing statement of the resolution adopted by the ALA at its conference in Ottawa in 1912: Mr. Crunden
"had the sense of the real librarian which has been said to be an
intensive perception of the needs of the present and a prophetic
insight into the needs of the future". It is true, as has been re-
iterated by his colleagues, that he did clearly see the needs of
his time; but who, fifty years ago, could foresee the needs of
our institutions of the present day or the circumstances with
which they have to struggle? The shifting population, the new
ideas on buildings which require remodeling or rebuilding, the
rising tide of labor-saving devices, audio-visual departments,
and new facilities for distribution of books you all know too well
and I have only mentioned them as an introduction to a curious
coincidence which recently occurred, indicative of our time.

On May 19, the Crunden Branch of the St. Louis Public Library was sold to a financial firm and the name of Crunden disappeared from the list of branches for the time being. It will
be rebuilt, it is hoped soon, in a more suitable neighborhood,
for on June 4, 1954, the board of directors passed a resolution
that the Frederick M. Crunden Branch be restored "as soon as
a suitable branch can be erected in the future". Meanwhile, the
Crunden name did not disappear altogether. A charming new
young people's room was dedicated at the central library on May
18th with great pomp and ceremony and in each of the beautiful
new books is this plate:

Frederick Morgan Crunden Collection
Books for Young People
Given by
Kate Edmondson Crunden
In Memory of their Son
Frederick Edmondson Crunden

FRANK AVERY HUTCHINS:
PROMOTER OF "THE WISCONSIN IDEA"

Alan Edmond Kent

Alan Edmond Kent is an historian with the Branch of Museums, National Park Service, Washington, D.C. The essay here reprinted is a paper read before the American Library History Round Table during the Minneapolis conference of the American Library Association in 1954.

In the last years of the nineteenth century and in the first few of the twentieth the Badger state became renowned for what has been termed "The Wisconsin Idea", a concept that involved bettering the lot of the ordinary citizen through bold state action. No single individual can be acclaimed "Father of the Wisconsin Idea", although the names Robert Marion La Follette, Charles McCarthy, and C. R. Van Hise are most often presented as personifying its spirit. Others are mentioned less frequently, but in the annals of the promoters of the "idea" no one has been relegated to the footnote more often than has Frank Avery Hutchins, probably "the most obscure big man" in the history of Wisconsin.

Hutchins' obscurity is a tremendous curiosity. The fruits of his labor are still among us. His associates—among them some of the great men of the time—thought him a remarkable creator and builder. And yet he remains on the fringes of recorded history, waiting for recognition that is long past due.[1]

Frank Hutchins was literally born among books. His father, Allen Sabin Hutchins, was teaching Latin and Greek at a small Norwalk, Ohio, academy when son Frank was born on March 8, 1851. The family moved to Wisconsin a year later and settled on a farm near Sharon, Walworth County. Allen Hutchins shortly associated himself with Wayland "University", as it was known in its first years, and Frank spent his early life at Beaver Dam, the site of the school, and at Baraboo. He attended Wayland and later took two years at Beliot College (1871-1873). There followed a period of teaching school at Fond du Lac under

Reprinted from Wilson Library Bulletin, 30:73-77, September, 1955, by permission of the author and the publisher.

the superintendency of his uncle, Charles A. Hutchins, another pioneer in Wisconsin education, and a position traveling in the interests of a book concern.[2]

Ill health stalked him constantly and curtailed many activities, but by 1884 he was ready to work in earnest toward creating a better life for Wisconsin's citizens. In the summer of that year he purchased an interest in the Beaver Dam Argus, a Democratic weekly run by Benjamin F. Sherman. While acting as editor of the paper Hutchins also served the community as city clerk. Viewing his function of editor as the carrier of information he learned as city clerk to the people, he was struck by the lack of community spirit. Sensing the necessity of interesting the citizenry in some one vital need, he began a campaign for a public library. Together with other interested townspeople, Hutchins formed, on August 30, 1884, the Beaver Dam Free Library Association, conducted at first on a private basis in a room turned over to it in the city hall. Through Hutchins' influence, the library was one of the first in the country to provide "open shelves". The city assumed support of the organization in 1885, and in 1890 a $25,000 bequest from the local banker, J. J. Williams, provided a large library building to house the rapidly growing collection.[3]

Frank Hutchins' life work was set. He often quoted the saying "God made the country, man the city, and the Devil made the small towns." He particularly wanted to save the youth of the smaller communities from temptations he thought were especially acute for them. A library, good books, and an understanding librarian were the remedies he suggested.[4]

In 1891, his uncle, Charles Hutchins, then assistant state superintendent of public instruction, persuaded him to assume the duties of township library clerk in that office. Frank worked tirelessly to extend library facilities to school areas not previously served. In 1891 also, shortly after his arrival in Madison, he joined with other leading librarians to found the Wisconsin Library Association. He was the organization's first secretary and during the period 1894-1897 served as its president.[5]

At the Chicago Fair in 1893, Hutchins heard of the pioneer efforts being conducted in New York by Melvil Dewey with the traveling libraries. Dewey hoped to stimulate the formation of libraries in small towns by shipping groups of books, which could be rotated from community to community. Hutchins seized upon the idea, but added his own peculiar twist. Knowing that large libraries were not practical for small towns, he chose to use the system merely for what its name implied; he would see that books became available to rural areas and villages on a permanent basis and not merely as a stimulus for the creation of a library building.[6]

Unfortunately, it was impossible for the state to undertake such a venture, and Hutchins did not possess the funds to organize it on a private basis. Accordingly, he formed a partnership with James H. Stout, a state senator, which was destined to make Wisconsin one of the leaders in the country's library movement. Stout, a Menomonie, Wisconsin, lumberman, supplied the capital; Hutchins took care of the ideas and their implementation.[7]

The first step in this joint venture occurred early in 1895. Lutie Stearns of the Milwaukee Public Library had just returned from the east where she had seen the state library commissions in action. She urged the idea upon Hutchins, who proceeded to write the bill which Senator Stout introduced into the state legislature in January of 1895. After some difficulties the measure was passed in April of that year. A woefully inadequate appropriation of $500 for expenses (but not for salaries) was provided. Appointments to the Free Library Commission were not made until November; at which time Hutchins was named chairman.[8]

Due partly to the delays involved and the small sum appropriated, Hutchins and Stout decided to start the traveling libraries on a private basis. And so, in December 1895, the Stout System of Traveling Libraries was inaugurated in Dunn County. The same year saw the establishment of a summer library school at Madison, the cost of which was met by Senator Stout. Stout's generosity also enabled Hutchins to devote full time to his position as chairman of the Free Library Commission.

In 1897, the legislature increased the commission's appropriation to $4,000, and Hutchins stepped down as chairman to become the salaried secretary of the agency. Senator Stout moved into the chairmanship.[9]

The growth of public libraries was phenomenal. When the commission commenced operations in 1895 there were only twenty-eight free public libraries in Wisconsin, of which only six were housed in their own buildings. During Hutchins' nine-year tenure almost 100 more were added, for by June 1904 some 126 public libraries had been established, 55 of these occupying separate buildings.

The traveling library record was equally impressive. In 1895 there were no traveling libraries in the state. In 1904, the number stood at 350, including 186 circulated by the commission, 77 in county systems supported by taxes, and 87 in county systems with private support.[10]

The record for library training was equally good. Only one library in Wisconsin employed personnel with library school training in 1895. By 1904, there were 20 libraries with staff members trained in such courses and 89 librarians and assistants who had attended the summer school conducted by the Commission.[11]

Frank Hutchins was not idle. While serving as secretary of the commission he also began what became the most unique feature of the Wisconsin library system: the Legislative Reference Library. Hearing about developments in New York which aimed at the systematic collection of materials to enable the passage of better legislation, Hutchins drew a bill providing for a department in the Free Library Commission:

> (1) to make a check list of the public documents of Wisconsin; (2) to prepare catalog cards for such documents, as published, and distribute them to public libraries; (3) to maintain a reference room in the capitol for use of state departments, legislators, and public men; (4) to loan from its working library books of permanent value to students throughout the state.[12]

This bill passed early in 1901. Due to Hutchins' illness, the job of seeing the measure through the legislation fell to his assistant, Cornelia Marvin. As a reward for her work, he allowed Miss Marvin the privilege of going east to select the right man to head the newly created department. After looking over the field she hit upon the man she thought best qualified: Judson T. Jennings of the New York State Library.[13]

Mr. Jennings never came to Madison. Professor Frederick Jackson Turner of the University of Wisconsin saw to that. Turner told Hutchins about one of his graduate students, Charles McCarthy, who had just been granted his Ph.D. Turner did not feel that certain personal peculiarities which McCarthy possessed fitted him for academic life, but urged that Hutchins interview him for the legislative reference post. A conference was arranged. Hutchins detected a slight cough that indicated McCarthy might be suffering from tuberculosis. After an examination proved these fears groundless, Hutchins made the appointment.[14]

Charles McCarthy has always been credited with Wisconsin's Legislative Reference Library, but neither in its origins nor in its initial development was the legislative reference idea in Wisconsin the work of McCarthy. Such features that later came about, such as the bill-drafting service, were doubtlessly originated by McCarthy, but the role of Frank Hutchins in connection with the Legislative Reference Library has too frequently been glossed over. Not that McCarthy ever denied his debt to Hutchins. In a letter written to Lutie Stearns in 1912 he had this to say:

> I am glad from the bottom of my heart to be able to acknowledge the great debt of gratitude which I owe to the noble-hearted idealist, Frank Hutchins. The work that he has done in this state, and for that matter, in the nation, cannot be appreciated. It seems too bad that his very self-sacrificing nature, his modesty, and his very idealism has made it impossible to do full justice to him. . . . I say without hesitation that I think he has been the most valuable man in this state in all the great work which has recently been undertaken here. . . . Frank Hutchins has been going about this state unnoticed with packages of good germs and he has been throwing them into dark corners and these good germs have certainly worked their way into the entire social and political structure. . . .[15]

In 1903, Frank Hutchins became seriously ill and found it necessary to spend several months at Asheville, North Carolina. The rest was made possible by gifts from his many friends, the largest bequest ($1,000) coming from John D. Rockefeller, Jr., as a response to a letter written by his friend Charles McCarthy. Hutchins officially resigned his position as secretary of the Free Library Commission in 1904. Although not at his best in an executive capacity, Frank Hutchins managed to give Wisconsin in less than a decade one of the most progressive library systems in the nation.[16]

One of Hutchins' greatest contributions to the library world was the "booklist" which the American Library Association later took over. In a letter written some years after his resignation from the Library Commission, Hutchins outlined his ideas on booklists:

> I have some crank ideas with regard to bibliographies and lists of books and articles recommended by experts and associations for purchase by public libraries or by individuals. The subject is one which I fought out in the American Library Association and in which I think I finally won out against the big men of the association. The general feeling in all that matter was that it is best to be modest and not tell people what to buy, just give them a list of publications that can be secured and let them use their own judgment. Now, personally, I have not much use for an expert in whom I have confidence who treats me in that way. . . . The man whom I like when I go for assistance is the man who says "This book is the best book for you and your purposes", "This is the second best book", possibly giving me a line or two of description which shows the line in which each book excels. Now in the case of a list of books for public libraries where one library could purchase only one book or two . . . and another might be able to purchase five or six, double star the best one, put one star for the second best, and let the others go, giving a line of description to each book showing their strong points. With such a list as this the librarians and book committees who have no special knowledge of the subject will sit down and make their list and buy the books that they can afford when with the longest [unannotated list], they will end up with doing nothing or fumble around and probably get second rate stuff.[17]

By 1906 Frank Hutchins had recovered sufficiently to begin another phase of his fight to bring education to the people. Hutchins had long been interested in the possibilities of university extension and had talked to many persons about the failures of past attempts in this field. In 1905 his friend, Charles McCarthy, convinced Charles Van Hise, president of the University of Wisconsin, that an attempt to revive extension work was warranted.

McCarthy managed to secure Hutchins the post of field organizer in the spring of 1906, and until the arrival of the extension dean, Louis Reber, late in 1907, Hutchins and Professor W. H. Lighty laid the groundwork for an extension division that became a model of its kind.[18]

In 1907 Mr. Hutchins was named head of extension's department of debating and public discussion. Here his genius for ingenuity brought forth the "package library" idea. Realizing that books were not current and at best could give information a year old, he began the practice of surveying the periodicals and newspapers, clipping items which touched on important questions of the day and collecting them into little "package libraries" which could be mailed to interested parties throughout the state. The idea became so popular that even President Van Hise, who had looked with some misgivings on the extension revival, began calling on the department for clippings. This loan package library, "a tool for implementing adult education in a democracy", as it was called in a recent number of The Library Quarterly, is still an important feature of the University of Wisconsin's Extension Division.[19]

Besides his labor on behalf of the library and university extension, Frank Hutchins was a prime mover in other fields. He was one of the organizers of the Wisconsin Anti-Tuberculosis Association and suggested many of the educational devices, plans, and exhibits which made its work in Wisconsin so effective. He was also interested in the state parks and conservation movements in Wisconsin and the story of his role in these developments has yet to be written.[20]

He died at Madison, Wisconsin, January 25, 1914, of cerebral thrombosis. At memorial services held in his honor the following May, Jane Addams of Hull House interpreted Hutchins' career:

> He was an unquestioned leader of the humanitarian movement. . . . He wanted to give to every community great themes to discuss. He thought that something of the higher things of life should be brought into the small village. . . . He wanted all to be leveled to one plane by education.[21]

All of which indicates that Frank Avery Hutchins can rightfully claim rank with the promoters of "The Wisconsin Idea", might well be styled "father of the free library movement in Wisconsin", and should receive some attention as one of America's foremost librarians – acclaim which has long been denied.

NOTES:

1 A good summary of Hutchins' achievements may be found in the Wisconsin Library Bulletin, 10:1-4, January-February 1914.

2 Letter, A. Avery to Allen S. Hutchins, November 13, 1852 (in possession of writer); Madison Democrat, January 27, 1914; Who's Who in America, 1899-1900 (Chicago, 1899), 366; Wisconsin Library Bulletin, 9:3-4, February 1913.

3 Interview, September 7, 1951, writer with Messrs. James and Arthur Sherman, publishers of the Beaver Dam Argus; Cornelia Marvin, "The Spirit of the Wisconsin Pioneer", Public Libraries, 30:182-90, April 1925; "Record Book, 1884-1914", Secretaries of the Beaver Dam Public Library Association, later Williams Free Library (Hutchins was secretary from 1884 until 1891 and part of the record is in his hand); J. W. Stearns, ed., THE COLUMBIAN HISTORY OF EDUCATION IN WISCONSIN (Milwaukee, 1893), 416-19. Just which library was the first in the country to provide "open shelves" has not been settled. William Howard Brett of the Cleveland Public Library has often been credited with originating the idea in 1890, but L. Quincy Mumford, recent head of the Cleveland library informed this writer that the idea was being debated as early as 1876. Cleveland's was probably the first library of any size to provide open shelves. Letter, March 18, 1952, Mumford to writer.

4 Wisconsin Library Bulletin, 10:13, January-February 1914.

5 Wisconsin Library Bulletin, 5:76-79, October 1909; Interview, October 2, 1951, writer with Lucy Curtiss, Madison, Wisconsin.

6 Frank A. Hutchins, "A New Philanthropy", The Outlook, 53:752-53, April 25, 1896; First Biennial Report of the State Library Commission of Wisconsin, 1895-96 (Madison, 1896), 79-85.

7 Interview, July 15, 1951, writer with Mrs. Burr W. Jones, Madi-

son, Wisconsin; Letter, August 15, 1951, W. H. Lighty to writer; M. M. Quaife, WISCONSIN, ITS HISTORY AND ITS PEOPLE (Chicago, 1924, 4 volumes), 2:422-23.

8   Wisconsin Library Bulletin, 5:74, September-October, 1909; Kathryn Saucerman, "A Study of the Wisconsin Library Movement, 1850-1900" (M.A. thesis, University of Wisconsin, 1944), 75.

9   Second Biennial Report of the Free Library Commission of Wisconsin, 1897-98 (Madison, 1898), 1.

10 Quaife, op.cit., 424; Charles F. Smith, "Wisconsin Libraries", South Atlantic Quarterly, 3:16, January 1904; Wisconsin Library Bulletin, 5:75, September-October 1909.

11 Quaife, op.cit., 424; Wisconsin Library Bulletin, 9:4, January-February 1913.

12 Fourth Biennial Report of the Free Library Commission of Wisconsin, 1901-02 (Madison, 1902), 18-20.

13 Letter, September 16, 1951, Cornelia Marvin Pierce, Salem, Oregon, to Mrs. Burr W. Jones, Madison, Wisconsin; Interview, July 15, 1951, writer with Mrs. Burr W. Jones; Interview, October 2, 1951, writer with Lucy Curtiss, Madison, Wisconsin.

14 Letter, August 15, 1951, W. H. Lighty to writer; Interview, Mrs. Burr Jones with writer; Edward A. Fitzpatrick, McCARTHY OF WISCONSIN (Morningside Heights, New York, 1944), 27.

15 Letter, May 12, 1921, Dr. Hoyt E. Dearholt to Irma Hochstein (Hutchins Memorial Volume, State Historical Society of Wisconsin Manuscript Division); W. A. Titus, "The Hutchins Family in Wisconsin", Wisconsin Magazine of History, 16:250, March 1933; The Review of Reviews, 49:275-76, March 1914; Letter, May 6, 1912, Charles McCarthy to Miss L. E. Stearns (Hutchins Memorial Volume, State Historical Society of Wisconsin Manuscript Division).

16 Fitzpatrick, op.cit., 202-03; Letter, August 15, 1951, W. H. Lighty to writer. Reuben Gold Thwaites, head of Wisconsin's State Historical Society, declared that Hutchins "had absolutely no executive ability despite his many other good qualities". Letter, Thwaites to J. M. Perles, October 9, 1909 (State Historical Society of Wisconsin Archives). Hutchins' coworkers refute this

statement, however.

17   Letter, Frank A. Hutchins to Dr. Hoyt E. Dearholt, March 17, 1910 (Correspondence, Wisconsin Anti-Tuberculosis Association, Milwaukee). Mrs. Burr Jones recalls that Hutchins began by publishing the "Suggestive List", a list of twelve hundred titles – known later in every part of the country where small libraries sprang up – and later supplemented it with the "Buying List", a list of current books suitable for little libraries. The demand for this kind of aid led ultimately to the publication of the <u>ALA Booklist</u> by the American Library Association.

18   Letter, <u>op. cit.</u>, W. H. Lighty to writer; Interview, <u>op. cit.</u>, Mrs. Burr Jones with writer; Interview, August 20, 1951, Dr. W. D. Frost with writer.

19   Merle Curti and Vernon Carstensen, THE UNIVERSITY OF WISCONSIN, 1848-1925 (Madison, 1949, 2 volumes), 2:554-70; Karl B. Weinman, "The Package Library", <u>Wisconsin State Journal</u> (Madison), October 17, 1914; LOUIS EHRHART REBER: BUILDER OF UNIVERSITY EXTENSION (Madison, 1944), 11-15; W. H. Lighty, "A Sketch of the Revivification of University Extension at the University of Wisconsin", (Madison, 1938, mimeographed), 7-15; Martin P. Anderson, "The Loan Package Library", <u>The Library Quarterly</u>, 20:119-26, April 1950.

20   A series of letters from Hutchins to Dr. Hoyt Dearholt in the files of the Wisconsin Anti-Tuberculosis Association, Milwaukee, record Hutchins' part in the early history of that organization. See also Harold Holand, REHABILITATION AT LAKE TOMAHAWK STATE CAMP (New York, 1945), 2-8; Louise Fenton Brand, "Epic Fight: Wisconsin's Winning War on Tuberculosis" (unpublished manuscript in the State Historical Society of Wisconsin Manuscript Division); Letter, May 3, 1912, E. M. Griffith, state forester, to Hutchins (Hutchins Memorial Volume, State Historical Society of Wisconsin Manuscripts Division); Conrad E. Patzer, PUBLIC EDUCATION IN WISCONSIN (Madison, 1924), 292.

21   Titus, <u>op. cit.</u>, 251; <u>Wisconsin Library Bulletin</u>, 10:148, June 1914.

JAMES LOUIS GILLIS, WESTERNER AND LIBRARIAN

Peter Thomas Conmy

Peter Thomas Conmy is Librarian of the Oakland Public
Library, Oakland, California. The essay here published is
a paper read before the American Library History Round
Table during the San Francisco conference of the American
Library Association, July, 1958.

Among schools of historical method there are divergent points
of view regarding the manner in which the facts of history should
be evaluated. There are eight accepted interpretations of history,
the one of which is most popular currently is the economic. The
great interplay of conflicts which the industrial revolution and
the development of science have brought about in the modern
world have caused historians to recognize in these movements
and events a background of economic motive. Notwithstanding
the ascendancy of this type of interpretation, it would seem that
the older idea of the predominant influence on affairs by great
men should not be discarded entirely. Within the framework of
the economic interpretation there must be human actors, some
of whom appear to have influenced tremendously the movements
of the modern world. Ambition for economic supremacy may have
caused the South to secede on the one hand, and provoked the
North's determination to retain the rebellious areas on the other,
but the part played by Lincoln cannot be disregarded. That public librarianship fits in with the educational pattern of modern
America, in the development of which may be discerned the economic factors of the development of the individual and his contributions to society, is quite clear. Yet without vigorous leaders
like James L. Gillis, the library would have lagged far behind.
In his professional contributions, therefore, may be seen the extent to which an individual may influence society, that the social

Grateful acknowledgment is here made to the author for providing the
compiler with a copy of the complete text of this paper and for granting permission to include it in this volume. A shorter version of this
paper appeared in Wilson Library Bulletin, 34:272-280+, December,
1959; permission to reprint has been granted by the publisher.

environment not entirely is governed by the application of such concepts as the acquisition of wealth, the filling of needs and the law of supply and demand. On the contrary, there must be human agents who import leadership and direction, infusing with the economic, the spiritual, the idealistic and the aesthetic. Appointed State Librarian of California in 1897 and continuing in office until his death in 1917, Gillis served in a state that was emerging from the pioneer stage.[1] The California of this period was one in which the stress was on building. This included the development of agriculture, the planning of highways, the dredging of harbors, the inducement of capital and industry and the extension of transportation and communication. Education was favored, of course, on the basis of a traditional belief in schools rather than any desire to disseminate culture, and that particular part of education known as the public library was not in a position to compete with the heavy movement for economic growth, had it not been for the influence and leadership of a single man, James L. Gillis. His position in California librarianship in his day fits in with the typical American pattern, wherein men took leadership as advocates, and then sensing their own inadequacies, sought the professionalization of their cause. Gillis, not well educated, and certainly not trained professionally, first advocated public libraries, and then came to the realization that trained workers would be necessary to carry out successfully the system which he launched. Hence, in common with many other pioneer American leaders his work included the founding of a training school. In this respect California public librarianship enjoys a development parallel to American public education generally. Witness such men as Horace Mann, an attorney, first advocating public schools, then seeking for them greater financial support, and finally urging the founding of normal schools so that the work might be professionalized. Placed in such a comparative light the status of Gillis becomes identified with the entire American pattern whereby the frontier produced its leaders who in turn effected the refinements that were necessary. Thus does the mind of the individual and his personality influence an evolving economic society.

James Louis Gillis was born in Richmond, Washington County, Iowa, on October 3, 1857, the son of Charles and Emily Eliza (Gelatt) Gillis. When he was three and a half years old his parents left that state by ox team for California. A journey of three months brought them to Empire, Nevada, and here they opened a hotel remaining until 1863. In that year the family moved to Carson City where the father engaged in mining interest (this was the era of the silver rush) and the six-year-old James started school. In 1864 the Gillis family moved to the Antelope Valley, but in 1866 left for California, arriving in Placerville in December 1866 and settling in Sacramento a month later, remaining until 1870. Here James continued grammar school. In 1870 the family took up residence in San Jose but within a year returned to Sacramento. Now James continued his studies in a Lutheran school conducted by Rev. Mr. Goethe. However, at age fourteen years and ten months, on August 12, 1872, he left school and became a messenger for the Sacramento Valley Railroad Company. For the next twenty-two years he engaged in railroading, working up to the position of Assistant Superintendent from which he retired in 1894.

On December 25, 1881, age twenty-four, he married Kate Petree of Sacramento. Of this union came the following children: Mabel Ray, Emily G. and Ruth M. The oldest, Mabel R. Gillis, graduated from the University of California in 1902 and shortly thereafter entered the service of the state library taking charge of the work with the blind. She served the State Library until 1951, just a few years short of a half century. She served as State Librarian for twenty years, 1931-51.

In addition to his connection with the railroad Gillis had affiliations with other corporations. He was at one time president of Sacramento Oil Company, and Vice President of Acme Development Company. He also had banking interests and was an active member of the Republican Party. In this latter connection he made many warm friends and soon after his retirement from the railroad was the recipient of political appointments. One of his friends was Hon. Judson Brusie, Assemblyman from Sacramento, who in 1895 became chairman of the Ways and Means Committee of the lower house. Mr. Brusie appointed Gillis chief clerk of the committee, one of the most important in the legislature. At the close of the session he became keeper of the archives in the office of the Secretary of State. Here he served until the 1897 legislative session when again he was appointed as chief clerk of the Ways and Means Committee. After this tour of duty he again took up his work as keeper of the archives, holding this until his appointment as State Librarian.

Gillis was a man who made friends easily. Living in an age

when political non-partisanship was not in vogue, and when the line of cleavage between Democrats and Republicans was drawn tightly, it is not surprising that his close supporters were in the Republican party in which he was very active. In his years in Sacramento he had enlisted the friendship of a number of influential men who not only backed him for appointment as State Librarian but who thereafter added their moral support to the ambitious legislative program which sagely he proposed and successfully had adopted. It is not possible to list all of Gillis' friends but some of them may be mentioned here. Among them were Lewis H. Brown (Secretary of State 1895-99), Grove L. Johnson (Assemblyman and Representative in Congress, and father of Governor Hiram W. Johnson), Governor Henry T. Gage, Lt. Governor Jacob H. Neff, Charles F. Curry (Secretary of State 1899-1911), Alfred J. Johnston (Superintendent of State Printing), Frank L. Coombs, (Assemblyman, United States Attorney, Congressman and his immediate predecessor as State Librarian), Judge of the Superior Court, C. N. Post, Frank D. Ryan (District Attorney of Sacramento County and President of State Library Board), Elijah C. Hart (Superior Judge and later Justice of the District Court of Appeals), Senator Charles B. Bills, Lt. Governor Alden Anderson, Assemblyman W. W. Greer, William C. Van Fleet (Superior Judge of Sacramento County and later United States District Judge), Assemblyman E. L. Hawk, Senator F. R. Dray, and Assemblyman Elwood Bruner. These, and dozens of other leading California men were the friends of James L. Gillis, and gave him the entre which he needed to advance the cause of librarianship in California.

Appointment as State Librarian. In April 1899, James L. Gillis was appointed State Librarian succeeding Frank L. Coombs, who resigned to become United States Attorney for the Northern District of California. Gillis was the ninth State Librarian since 1861. The State Library was established on April 9, 1850 with the Secretary of State as ex officio librarian. In 1861 responsibility for the library was divorced from the Secretary of State and vested in a Board of State Library Trustees who were charged with the appointment of a librarian. The first, William C. Stratton, served for nine years. The second was in the office only two months but Robert O. Cravens, the third, was in charge for twelve years. His successor, Talbot H. Wallis, served for eight years. Commencing with the appointment of W. Dana Perkins in

1890 the tenure of California's state librarians was short. He
served six years, dying in office. His successor, William P.
Matthews, resigned after less than six months' service and was
succeeded by Edward D. McCabe, who completed the unexpired
term of four years. Frank L. Coombs took office on April 7,
1898 and because of his appointment as United States Attorney
resigned at the close of one year. In the early decades of its
existence the State Library gave its greatest attention to law
books, because it was the library of the state supreme court.[2]
Its holdings were by no means limited to the legal, however, and
as a matter of fact one hundred volumes donated by John C. Fre-
mont in 1850 served as the nucleus of the collection, these including books on medicine, travel, exploration and government reports as well as law. Indeed in the years that followed many
valuable books found their way into the state library. Use, however, was limited to the Supreme Court and state officials. That
the collection was regarded highly by those who had studied it
is evidenced by the following excerpt from the Daily Alta California of December 28, 1863:"Let the citizens of our state frequent
this institution, become better acquainted with its utility, and
lend their aid to its further advancement and prosperity."

Obviously the people of the state did not heed the advice of
the editorial. The years following the gold rush were characterized by short periods of prosperity but long cycles of depressed
economic conditions. It was neither an era of governmental expansion nor of high taxes. The one exception appears to have
been in the field of public education where a more liberal support
was noted largely as a result of the leadership of John Swett.
The State Librarians from 1860 to 1895 carried on as well as they
could and notwithstanding adverse criticism by some writers
did a relatively good job. If they did not make the institution
popular and gain for it greater support, at least they built up a
good collection; and when Gillis was working in the archives of
the Secretary of State, he is reported to have viewed the library's
collection and to have said, "What would I give to be in charge
there and show what really could be done."[3]

The immediate predecessor of Gillis was Frank L. Coombs,
a man of great vision. He held the office a scant twelve months
but recognized the value of the collection and the immense potential of the library. Writing the report for 1896-98 he said,

The great study of the library, however, lies in the
question of its utility. It is supported by the State, yet
it is simply the State's storehouse of art and literature.
If such is its design it surely fulfills its purpose. If, on
the contrary, it is supposed to become useful alike to
the people generally of California, it falls short of the
object.[4]

It will be accepted that Coombs saw that the destiny of the
library lay not in its capacity as a storehouse of books, but in
what modern librarians call the communication of ideas. Continuing he wrote,

I find in the discussion of this subject that several
ideas are involved. One is to maintain it as a reference library; and another is to so amend the laws as
to bring it in contact with the several town and city
libraries, and to inaugurate a system of exchanges
with them, which would enable it to furnish them with
books otherwise beyond their control. Even this plan
would not contemplate the shipment of works of art,
or rare and costly editions, yet it would enable the
reader to receive the benefit of valuable matter now
beyond the reach of his own library.[5]

Retiring State Librarian Coombs thus presented the challenge
and it was met and answered by entering State Librarian James
L. Gillis. He brought to his new position very little formal education. He did possess a high native intelligence.[6] He had had
many years of experience in handling people, and in politics.
Above all he had a great vision. This was born of his long life
in the west, his childhood in Nevada, the old Sacramento and
the quaint San Jose. He grew up on the frontier, and associated
with men who had lived on the frontier. He was imbued with the
spirit of the West. That is the spirit of progress. That is the
spirit of moving forward. That is the spirit of recognizing what
is needed and then filling the gap. The leaders of the frontier
knew that the romantic life, the halcyon days, the rough and
ready attitude, the break with polite conventions which had been
in vogue for centuries, could not endure permanently. The pioneer west they discerned might thrive for a few decades in its

rough state, but they realized that culture must come in the end. The educators were the first to arrive at this conclusion. Gillis saw it, too, and accepted the challenge posed by Coombs. He answered it by eighteen years of undaunted efforts. His efforts and achievement now will be described. For convenience it seems best to present the story under the following major headings; namely, (1) reorganization of the state library, (2) extension of the library and the county library system, (3) professional education, (4) professional organization.

Reorganization of the State Library[7]

Immediately following his appointment Gillis spent much time in studying the state library, its history, its current purposes and its potential. Having found himself in relation to the office to which he had been appointed, his great vision began to assert itself and a plan transcending both the past of performance of the institution and the political motives behind his appointment began to unfold. An article appearing in 1917 after the death of Gillis had this to say,

> There has been little question but that Mr. Gillis' appointment in the first place was made because he had shown efficiency and obtained without criticism, results which were appreciated in the field of California politics. But after his appointment, as he himself told the writer, in examining the situation in which he found himself and the duties pertaining to the position to which he had been appointed, he found that in his hand was a great machine for building up an institution which could bring to the people of the state, abundant sources of helpfulness.[8]

Eight years after his appointment as State Librarian, Gillis wrote an article on administration in which he stressed the necessity for the administrators having vision. Part of this is quoted herewith,

> Successful administration requires a grasp of the library movement as a whole; it is not sufficiency [sic], nor is it always essential, that the administrator of a library should understand the technical part of the

work, but he must see the ends to be reached, and the relation of each part of the work to the other and to the whole.[9]

The task of reorganizing the California State Library was not an easy one, however. There was so much to be done on both the intrinsic and extrinsic levels that one wonders how he was able to face the task at all, for as Holt writes,

> The first problem was reorganization of the library itself. On hand was a mass of unclassified and uncata-loged books, documents and miscellaneous materials. Patronage was limited to occasional use by legislators and state officials. Gillis soon acquired the enduring conviction that the library was for all the people and it was his job to see that library services were avail-able to every person in the state. This meant topnotch organization and Gillis proved to be gifted with admin-istrative ability equal to the task. His uncanny flair for judging people enabled him to organize a competent staff to man a departmentalized library designed by Gillis to facilitate library service.
>
> His political skills worked overtime on a legisla-tive program which would provide legal structure to place his concept of state-wide library service into operation. Personality and know-how were the keys to political action and Gillis was well equipped for the legislative fray.[10]

During his first three years in office Gillis spent much time in studying his institution and librarianship generally. He also worked on a revision of the public library laws and in 1901 an amended statute relating to public libraries was passed.[11] On May 2, 1903, the Trustees of the State Library voted him a trip to visit the important state libraries of other states. Among those which he observed were the state libraries of Iowa, Wis-consin, Michigan, New York, Connecticut, Massachusetts, Rhode Island, Indiana, and Mississippi. He visited also the Li-brary of Congress and the public libraries of Boston, New York and Chicago.[12]

Reorganization proper. The plan of reorganization of the

222

State Library employed by Gillis was that of the establishment of departments that perfected a more workable form of organization on the one hand, and enabled the institution to give an expanded service on the other.[13] A more business-like method of ordering books was installed. A dictionary catalog was set up and a book repair department instituted. One of the most important new units was the California History Department to which were assigned not only books on the history of California, but books on California as well, and all back files of California newspapers. In 1904 was inaugurated the most important service to the blind under a Books for the Blind Department. These new departments would have meant little, however, had not the legislature in 1903 amended the law so as to authorize the trustees to grant the use of the state library to persons other than those enumerated in the law, that is, public officials of the state.

It was in the field of extension, however, that Gillis made the greatest advances for the state library. He was long of the opinion that the resources of the library should be open to everyone. This was fulfilled in part at least in 1903 when the legislature liberalized the use of the library and the subsequent action of the Trustees taking advantage of this authority. The action of the legislature and of the trustees which followed merely opened up the library to people. The matter of distance still remained unsolved. By two means was this problem attacked. First, at Gillis' insistence the trustees of the State Library permitted the public libraries of the state to borrow its resources for their own patrons.[14] Second, traveling libraries were sent into remote sections of the state upon petition of five inhabitants. Thus did the great library in Sacramento extend itself to the people in all parts of California. This was good public relations for the State Library and Susan Smith explains how aid to women's clubs brought much support for Gillis' legislative program.[15] A later development was the filling of subject requests, especially for schools, which at that time either had libraries that were poorly equipped, or in most instances no library at all. The summation of all this activity was to make the people of California more library conscious. Writing in 1905 Lauren W. Ripley, Librarian of Sacramento Public Library stated,

> California has no library commission; it is doubtful
> if the lawmaking power could be induced to establish one,

223

except under undesirable conditions. But in the state
library we have an agency already established not
only capable but desirous of fulfilling its obligations
and broadening its scope until it shall become in all
things a library for the people of the state. The ever
increasing number of its traveling libraries widely
scattered gives proof that libraries of some kind are
wanted.[16]

In addition to the extension services that have just been described there was inaugurated in 1904, a Department of Public
Libraries. The purpose of this was twofold. On the one hand,
the department offered an advisory service to public libraries
assisting them to solve their problems, while it gathered from
all of the public libraries of the state statistical and other pertinent information.

The California Library Association was interested in the matter of bringing library service to the rural areas. In May 1899
Public Libraries devoted an issue to the libraries of California.[17]
A little later there was a movement in CLA to have established
a state library commission that would provide extension service
including traveling libraries. To this proposal Gillis was opposed.
He felt that the state library should be the extension agency
rather than a commission. In a conference that ensued Judge
Van Fleet suggested that the law be amended so as to permit the
trustees of the state library to name the classes of persons who
might use the State Library, and thus perform the duties suggested for allocation to the proposed commission. This met the
approval of the CLA committee and was enacted into law in 1903
as pointed out previously.[18] This action although not following
the pattern of other states did satisfy the best thought in political science referring to a consolidation of efforts rather than a
multiplication of governmental agencies.

In the eighteen years which he gave to developing the State
Library, Mr. Gillis is not to be credited with each and every accomplishment. Genius though he was in suggesting improvements,
he possessed the greater talent for enlisting the thoughts of others. This is brought out by Susan Smith who advises,

It must not be assumed that Mr. Gillis was the only
one responsible for every plan that developed. Ideas

came from many divergent persons, his library staff
in particular, but his was the foresight to select and
put into operation those that would accomplish the best
results. It was team work that counted.[19]

No discussion of Gillis' work in the State Library would be
complete without reference to his creation of the Department
of Legislative Reference and Statistics and to his establishment
of a state library periodical. The former was the second of its
kind in any state library in the United States. The first was at
Wisconsin State Library and Gillis was much impressed with
the service when he visited that institution. The Department of
Legislative Reference and Statistics rendered very valuable service to state officials and to the legislature itself. In May 1906
there was issued the first number of the periodical, a state library magazine in the sense that it emanated there, but by its
title, News Notes of California Libraries, dedicated to information about all of the libraries in the state. The first issue
comprised forty-eight pages. It listed under location all free libraries in California. It contained an article on the state library
itself, and listed the officers of California Library Association.
The second number June, 1906, followed pretty much the same
pattern, but the third was dedicated to library buildings, and
included the plans and buildings of a number of representative
California libraries. Each issue, of course, listed the accessions of the state library, thus informing local librarians of
what might be obtained from Sacramento. News Notes continued
during the remaining eleven years of Mr. Gillis' administration,
and now is in its fifty-third volume having been a most valuable
aid to California State Library administration and leadership
during the administrations of his three successors, Milton J.
Ferguson, 1917-1931, Mabel W. Gillis, 1931-1951 and Carma
R. Zimmerman, 1951 to date.

State Library Legislation, 1897-1917. One of the first steps
taken in the Gillis administration was that of increasing materially financial support of the library. In 1901 a new law ordered
that the first $2500 received in fees each month by the Secretary
of State be deposited in the State Library Fund.[20] This assured
a minimum of $30,000 annually. Ten years later, the amount
to be transferred monthly by the Secretary of State was increased
to the first $3,500, thus producing from this source $42,000 an-

nually.[21] In 1913 and 1915 the legislature made biennial appropriations of $190,000, and in 1915 allocated $250,000.[22] The 1903 amendment authorizing the State Library Trustees to "permit persons other than those mentioned in <u>Political Code</u> Section 2296, to have the use of books", already has been mentioned.[23] At the same time, another change in the law gave the State Librarian power to distribute to the State University, to Stanford University, to each incorporated college and to such institutions as he might select one copy of all state publications. He was authorized also to exchange California state documents with other states and countries. At the same time he was empowered to requisition the Secretary of State for a sufficient number of copies to make this program possible. In 1907 this law was implemented by an amendment requiring the State Printer to furnish the State Librarian with fifty copies of all state publications, except those printed from day to day during legislative sessions of which he was to supply as many copies as the librarian might request.[24] The matter of discarding books was legalized in 1913 by an amendment giving the State Library Trustees authority to sell or exchange duplicate copies of books.[25] At the same session they were empowered to establish deposit stations in various sections of the state. The State Printer by a 1913 amendment was required to furnish the State Librarian two hundred and fifty-six copies of all reports and state publications. In this year also, the State Librarian was made ex officio Secretary of the State Library Trustees. The legislature in 1915 authorized the trustees to accept the gift of the Sutro collection in San Francisco, and to establish it as a branch of the State Library.[26] As part of Gillis' policy of gathering data for local history preservation, the <u>Political Code</u> in 1917 was amended by requiring the County Clerk of each county annually to transmit to the State Library one copy of the general index of voters.[27] As part of his policy of gathering statistics on public libraries, legislation passed in 1905 required each public library in the state to make an annual report and to file a copy thereof with the State Librarian.[28]

Extension of the
State Library and the County Library System

The efforts which Gillis made to extend the state library have been discussed above in that they were restricted to (1) traveling

libraries and (2) assistance and advice to public libraries. There
were other lines in which he worked to obtain library coverage
for the state. The most notable was the establishment of the county library system. Of lesser importance must be mentioned the
obtaining of legislation which encouraged public libraries.

The genesis of the county library. The first plan for library
coverage was that of extending the state library through various
spheres of influence, the sending out of traveling library service
at first, and ultimately the founding of branches. Several years
experience with the problem, however, convinced Gillis that this
could not be done. California was too vast an area for a state unit
of library service. After almost ten years of experience as State
Librarian, Gillis concluded that the best way in which California
might obtain full library coverage was by a system of county libraries. This is well explained by Miss Harriet G. Eddy, who is
quoted at this point,

> But the big idea that Mr. Gillis had first conceived
> on that memorable day back in 1898 was to bring the
> entire State Library within the reach of every person
> in California from the Oregon line to Mexico. The en-
> tire State Library must be extended. How could it be
> done ? Some intermediate library unit must be found
> between the State Library and the little boy in Modoc
> County; study clubs and traveling libraries were not
> sufficient to reach the ranch woman in Imperial County.
> Many libraries clung to the municipality as the answer.
> One prominent library worker from the East, who had
> come to live in California, hoped to see "the entire
> state dotted with municipal libraries, just like Massa-
> chusetts". But it was not the answer for California,
> which had a greater number of people living outside
> of towns than inside. Other librarians thought the town-
> ship was the correct unit. But there were too many
> townships and their assessed valuation was too small
> to furnish adequate funds for library support. . . .
> The answer was the county. California had fifty-
> eight counties, all of them small enough to operate
> as a unit, and most of them large enough to give
> adequate support. And with the counties organized,
> California would be covered with a network of librar-

ies, so unified that they would satisfy the hope <u>for equal</u>, <u>economical</u>, <u>complete library service</u>.[29]

<u>The first county library</u>. Once Gillis was convinced that a system of county libraries best would serve to give California the desired library coverage, he prepared legislation which was presented to the legislature in 1909. In advance of that year, however, he was able to persuade the Board of Supervisors of Sacramento County to establish a county library by following a never before invoked provision of the Municipal Libraries Act. This section permitted the Board of Supervisors of any county to make a contract for library service with a city in the county that had a public library. The supervisors and the trustees of the Sacramento City Library entered into such a contract and the Sacramento County Library came into being on its effective date, October 1, 1908.[30] Shortly thereafter the principal of Elk Grove High School sought a branch in her school and this request was granted. The Branch came under the administration of the school and this is how its principal, Harriet G. Eddy, later county library organizer, came to be interested in the library movement. Gillis now worked assiduously preparing for the coming legislative session. Opinion he mobilized through articles in the <u>News Notes</u> and elsewhere and by addresses at meetings of librarians and citizens. Miss Eddy was invited to address CLA in the Spring of 1909 describing the success of the Sacramento County Library's Branch in her school. In fact Gillis enlisted the assistance of the State Superintendent of Public Instruction and stressed in his utterances his desire to establish a system of public libraries parallel to the schools. In one article he wrote, "It would seem that the time is ripe for the institution of a large library system, covering the state with the thoroughness of the public schools."[31]

The task was by no means easy. The California of 1908 was a very conservative one. Tax money was difficult to obtain. Only the grim determination of a James Gillis saw the project through. Writes Susan Smith,

> The establishment of the county free library system turned his vision into a practical reality. Much work had to be done before success was attained. The interest of the people had to be aroused, supervisors won over,

legislators answered. Mr. Gillis' political acumen was used to good advantage.[32]

The long awaited county library law was enacted in 1909.[33] It will not be possible to summarize it completely here but some of its salient provisions were the following:

(a) Boards of Supervisors may establish county libraries upon a majority vote of the electors of the county.

(b) Only the property of those parts of the county participating in the county library system might be taxed for its support.

(c) A committee of Board of Supervisors shall appoint the county librarian for a four year term. Eligibility for appointment depended upon a written recommendation from either the State Librarian, or the University of California Librarian, or the Stanford University Librarian.

(d) The State Librarian shall have general supervision of county libraries, and may call annually a convention of county librarians. It shall be the duty of the county librarian to attend said convention.

(e) County Librarians shall make an annual report in July.

(f) A tax not to exceed one mill on the dollar may be levied.

(g) Boards of Supervisors may contract with city librarians for county library service.

In the year 1910 eight county libraries were established pursuant to this legislation. The Attorney General objected legally to certain provisions of the law, and there was an ambiguous implication that its provisions intended that county libraries should be operated by contract with already existing city libraries. To correct this situation a new law was enacted in 1911.[34] Some of the new features were the following:

(a) One county may furnish library service to another

by contract.

(b) The Board of Supervisors (not a committee thereof) may appoint the county librarian.

(c) Eligibility for appointment was on the basis of certification. An ex officio Board of Library Examiners was created to establish and administer certification standards.

(d) The government of the county library to be by the Board of Supervisors, but the administration to be by the county librarian.

(e) Bonds for county libraries might be issued in accordance with Political Code, Section 4088.

County libraries multiplied rapidly and by the time Gillis died more than half of the counties had availed themselves of the provisions of the law. Under the State Library Miss Harriet G. Eddy was engaged as county library organizer. The work was arduous and was a great strain on Gillis. This was a novel step in California. In 1910 eight county libraries were organized, two in 1911, eight in 1912, four in 1913, three in 1914, seven in 1915, and two in 1916.[35] Barmby and Provines explain the multiple problems:

> Widely extended library service required new and different means of handling finances; of controlling central, branch and school records; of solving problems of transportation; and of providing adequate reports. Securing, furnishing and staffing branch quarters was an enormous and continuing operation. The legal and physical difficulties of giving service to rural schools had to be surmounted, and this aspect of library work Mr. Gillis believed to be of primary importance. As a county officer the county librarian had to learn to work with and through county boards of supervisors, without whose co-operation his efforts were unavailing.[36]

As the county libraries, notwithstanding their specific legal status as county institutions, virtually and morally were a part of the state library, Gillis had to extend his efforts to assist greatly the county librarians with their many problems. It was this aid from him that for all practical purposes saved the county library. Says the CLA historical account,

> Out of it (traveling libraries) grew the county library system, California's greatest contribution to library development. For this system we are indebted to James L. Gillis, then state librarian and president of the California Library Association, for without his political knowledge and skill, his ability to overcome obstacles, his courage, energy and persistence, the project never would have been carried through to a successful conclusion.[37]

It should be recalled that at the time of the enactment of the county library law in California, library schools were not as numerous as they are now, and stressed the techniques of librarianship in their courses, rather than administration. The result was that few librarians knew very much about government. As library administration becomes more professionalized, that is to say, as it becomes the subject of systematic and scientific study, administrators trained in the problems of government as well as library science, will be able to function alongside of the political scientists in other branches of public management. It was this lack of knowledge of city, county and state government that made operation difficult, and that caused the librarians constantly to seek Gillis' assistance. He himself recognized the special nature of this problem when he wrote,

> The necessary legislation for promoting and fostering the literary interests of the state must be secured, and a close watch kept that no detrimental legislation is passed. This part of the work requires a personal acquaintance with the leaders of the legislative body, and certain administrative qualities that have no direct relation to library work.[38]

The county library law provided for an annual meeting of County Librarians at the call of the State Librarian. Gillis, of course, lived up to this provision of the statute which was permissive and not mandatory. The second annual meeting was held at the State Library October 10-14, 1911. The program appears to have centered around relations between the state library and the county libraries. One sentiment from Gillis' keynote address is worthy of reproduction here,

> The one thing to make it a success is the service rendered. . . . Service was the keynote of our meeting a year ago, and still remains our motto. We must not spend too much time on methods; we must get results by the methods best suited to the needs of each county. The only result which counts is service to all.[39]

As this is a paper on James L. Gillis and not a study of the development of California's system of county libraries, it will not be possible to list every step in the growth of these institutions in the years 1909-1917. Suffice it to say, however, that the records bear witness to the fact that Gillis gave of himself unselfishly to effect an efficient system, and deserves well the appellation "Father of California's County Libraries". In 1947, thirty years after Gillis had passed on, one of California's outstanding historians, Robert Glass Cleland, had this to say about the system of county libraries, and although he is not mentioned, it is a tribute to his endeavors for the welfare of society,

> The growth of library facilities in small towns and rural communities throughout the state also constitutes a form of educational and cultural leaven of incalculable value in the body politic. County libraries, for example, that maintain units in thinly populated regions offer opportunities to the isolated but often reading-hungry settlers that were utterly unattainable — indeed, almost undreamed of — a generation ago.[40]

Professional Education[41]

The multiplication of county libraries brought a need for trained librarians. The 1911 amended library law created a Board of Library Examiners charged with the responsibility of certifying eligibles for appointment as county librarians. Pursuant to this legislation in April 1911 News Notes printed the text of the County Library Law followed by a circular of information by the Board of Library Examiners.[42] The desired background for county librarians was presented in terms of qualitative suggestions rather than quantitative requirements such as graduation from college and library school. Applicants were urged to spend time in the State Library studying the collection and routines. The first examination for the county librarian's certificate was scheduled for May 22, 1911 at Pasadena.

At this period there was an expansion of public libraries. There were two library schools in California. One of these was in Los Angeles Public Library and dated back to 1891. The other was the Riverside Library School founded in 1910. In 1909 at Gillis' request a Library Training School Committee was appointed by CLA. After a few years of observation it was decided that the State Library should open a library school. This was announced in 1913 and commenced instruction in January 1914.[43] This class graduated in December of that year. A new class started in September 1914 and graduated in June 1915 and thereafter there was one class annually following the school year calendar. Between 1914 and June 1917, a total of forty-one persons were graduated from this school. After 1919-20 the school was closed for the reason that the University of California at Berkeley had established a Department of Librarianship. Although the existence of the California State Library School was brief, a number of its graduates became the leading librarians of California. Here again the work of Gillis is to be seen because the school was stamped with the imprint of his influence. In a recent article Mrs. Post writes,

> In establishing and operating the state library school during those years before the University of California took over the work, Gillis did more than train librarians. Once again he showed his ability to envision a need, organize the necessary program and select the right kind of people to train and be trained. His other contributions to libraries in California were greatly enhanced by the successful training of competent librarians equipped with the skills and attitudes necessary to pioneer the county library system.[44]

Professional Library Organization

Although there was a professional library organization in California as early as 1895, and there was founded on March 11,

1898, the Library Association of California, the society was not a potent agent in library affairs until in 1906 James L. Gillis became president of California Library Association, as it was then known. He served as president 1906 to 1909 and again from 1911 to 1915. In the early years of Library professional organization the state library as Rowe points out had remained aloof. A few publications had been issued but there was no regular periodical. At the same time that Gillis became president of California Library Association, the State Library began publishing News Notes of California Libraries. This was broadened to include a printing of all proceedings of CLA, and of all its committees and sections. News Notes was sent to every member of the association. In this way Gillis brought a knowledge of the state library and of what his office was doing to practically all librarians in California on the one hand, and a record of what their professional organization was doing on the other. The result was twofold. The efforts of all librarians in the state were enlisted in his cause of library extension. On the other hand, the morale of the professional was raised to a high level.

A close co-operation between the State Library and the association was needed in those days to bring the many divergent library interests into unity.[45] In an article written in 1950 Howard Rowe advises

> In 1904 Mr. Gillis addressed the Association on "The State Library and its Work". Mr. Joy Lichtenstein (in a wire recorded interview, February 17, 1950) recalls that while he was President (1904 and 1905) he visited Sacramento for the purpose of encouraging Mr. Gillis to participate more actively in the affairs of the Association. In 1906 James L. Gillis became President. This cinched close cooperation between the State Library and CLA, which has continued to this day. Mr. Gillis' personality, his political knowledge, courage and energy, and his intense interest in developing libraries in California, backed by the California Library Association, set up the County library system as an effective means of providing state-wide library service.[46]

Perhaps the greatest contribution made by Gillis to CLA was not that of officer, committeeman or plain member, but rather

his contributions to librarianship in general which brought a
professional pride to librarians and prompted them to join the
association. Henderson quotes Rowell in connection with Gillis
as follows:

> In July 1917 the Association mourned the death of
> State Librarian James L. Gillis. Later at the 30th
> annual convention, Joseph C. Rowell, first president
> of the CLA, said in praise of Mr. Gillis, "The directing
> of the State and the inauguration and development of the
> wonderful county library system by him and his able co-
> workers unified the entire field and brought many hun-
> dreds into our numbered ranks."[47]

Miscellaneous Contributions

Hereinabove has been presented Gillis' contribution to the
State Library, in the founding of the county library system, in
the California State Library School, and to California Library
Association. No treatment of his career would be complete without reference to his contributions to public libraries and to librarianship in general. As these were largely in the field of
legislation they will be presented under those headings:

Legislation affecting public libraries. Notwithstanding his
interest in the state library and the proposed county system,
Gillis found time to prepare legislation benefiting the public library. The first public library law had been enacted in 1878,
and amended in 1880. Thereafter for a score of years it was
dead letter. Gillis studied the needs for revision and in 1901 a
new municipal library law was adopted.[48] With little change this
remains to-day as the basic legislation affecting city public libraries. In 1901 also an amendment to the Penal Code denounced
the mutilation of books and other public library materials as a
misdemeanor.[49] In 1905 the Municipal Libraries Law of 1901
was amended by providing that trustees must meet at least once
a month, and may hold special meetings.[50] An amendment adopted in 1909 provided that municipalities of the first, second and
third classes might levy a tax for public libraries not to exceed
two mills on the dollar, whereas those of the third, fourth and
fifth classes were permitted to tax up to three mills on the dollar.[51] In 1909 also another law permitted the establishment of
public libraries in unincorporated towns and villages through

the formation of library districts.[52] Bonded indebtedness in these localities was authorized also. In 1911 the possible multiplication of public libraries was aided by the new law providing for the establishment of public libraries by union high school districts.[53] It will be noted that these laws authorizing the establishment of public libraries in villages and districts, was a part of the entire plan to extend library coverage either through city, county, district or village library systems. As the laws now made ample provision for the establishment of public libraries their governmental status was recognized to a great extent in 1911 when the 1909 law was amended so as to extend the right of eminent domain to acquiring property for public library purposes.[54] In 1915 the possible extension of public libraries was aided further by the enactment of a law authorizing school district trustees or city boards of education, to operate libraries which "shall be open to teachers, pupils and residents of the district".[55]

Legislation affecting librarianship in general. The legislation heretofore described in this article deals largely with the organic structure relating to the establishment and government of California public libraries, ranging from the state library on the top to the village and district institutions below. In addition to these legislative contributions Gillis, of course, sought to maintain high professional standards. These usually are matters of administrative policy rather than the objects of legislation. Nevertheless a few found their way into legislative enactment. In 1862 County Records were required to maintain files of newspapers published in their respective counties. In 1909 they were authorized to deposit these files with the public library in the county seat, under an agreement between the Board of Supervisors and the Library Trustees to preserve the papers and have them accessible to the public.[56]

In 1911 the creation of a Board of Library Examiners with authority to establish standards for certification to the position of county librarian assured each county library a professional head. This was a tremendous step forward.[57]

In 1917 the professional nature of librarianship was recognized by certain amendments to the Political Code relating to educational institutions. One provided that no person might serve more than two hours a day as librarian of a high school library unless he held either a high school teacher's certificate, or a

special teacher's certificate in library crafts. At the same time
Political Code, Section 1771, was amended to provide for a
special credential a certificate in library crafts.[58]

His Passing

On July 27, 1917, Mr. Gillis was stricken by a heart attack
at the entrance to the capitol on his return from lunch. So he
passed quickly and without pain.

Greatly was he mourned.

Great and numerous were the tributes paid to him.

In 1957, forty years after his death, the centennial of his
birth was commemorated by the California Library Association.

Dead so many years, yet his fame lives on. His glory will
not fade, because his work has made him immortal.

NOTES:

1 For bibliography of materials on James L. Gillis the reader is
referred to Beaulah Mumm and Allan R. Ottley, comp., "James
L. Gillis in Print", News Notes of California Libraries, 52:4
(October 1957). pp. 654-58.

2 For a history of the California State Library, see Mabel W. Gillis, "California State Library, Its Hundred Years", California
Library Bulletin, 11:2 (December 1949), pp. 55-57, 77.

3 Harriet G. Eddy, COUNTY FREE LIBRARY ORGANIZING IN CAL-
IFORNIA 1909-1918. p. 2. (Berkeley: California Library Association, 1955).

4 "Report of Trustees of State Library", Appendix to Journals of
Senate and Assembly 33rd Session II, Document 1, p. 7.

5 Ibid.

6 "Abounding in energy, keen foresight, much intelligence and undy-
ing persistence made it possible for him to become a great worker and organizer," M. J. Ferguson, James L. Gillis, News Notes
(July 1917). p. 85.

7 The reader interested in a general sketch of the history of Cali-

fornia State Library will find interesting, Mabel W. Gillis, "California State Library, Its Hundred Years", Bulletin of California Library Association, 11:2 (December 1949). pp. 55-59, 77.

8 Public Libraries 22:8 (October 1917). p. 308.

9 James L. Gillis, "State Library Administration", Library Journal, 30:8 (August 1905). p. 34.

10 Raymond M. Holt, "James L. Gillis: Librarian in Retrospect", California Librarian, 18:4 (October 1957). p. 222.

11 For a treatment of library legislation in California during Gillis' tenure as State Librarian see Peter T. Conmy, "James L. Gillis and California Library Legislation 1899-1917", California Librarian, 18:4 (October 1957). pp. 227-31.

12 Biennial Report of the Trustees of the California State Library 1902-04, pp. 5-6. (Appendix to Journals of Senate and Assembly 36 Session, No. 1).

13 For a detailed account of the re-organization of the State Library the reader is referred to the Biennial Report of the State Library Trustees, for the years in question, 1902-04, 1904-06, 1906-08, 1908-10, 1910-12, 1912-14, 1914-16. These may be found printed separately or in the Appendix to the Journals of the Senate and Assembly for the legislative sessions 1901-1917.

14 James L. Gillis, "Inter-Library Loans", Bulletin of the American Library Association, 6:1 (January 1912). pp. 99-100.

15 Susan T. Smith, "James L. Gillis and the State Library", California Librarian, 11:4 (June 1950). p. 155.

16 Lauren W. Ripley, "Library Conditions in Central California", Library Journal 30:789-90 (October 1905). p. 790.

17 California Library Association, Historical Committee, California Library Association, Proceedings, 1895-1900 (Stanford University, 1930). p. 14, pp. 16-17. See also for Gillis' ideas on state library leadership, James L. Gillis, "Shall the State Library be the Head of all Library Activities in the State", Public Libraries, 16:7 (July 1911). pp. 287-88, and James L. Gillis, "A State Library System for California, a Suggestion", Library Journal, 33:8 (August 1908). p. 316.

18 The Report of the State Librarian, 1902-04 indicates that at the close of the first year of traveling libraries, a total of 85 had been sent out, representing 4250 volumes.

19 Susan T. Smith, op.cit. p. 156.

20 Statutes, 1901, p. 88

21 Statutes, 1911, p. 575.

22 Statutes, 1913, p. 1343; Statutes, 1915, p. 621; Statutes, 1917, p. 500.

23 Statutes, 1903, p. 363.

24 Statutes, 1907, p. 891.

25 Statutes, 1913, p. 1149.

26 Statutes, 1915, p. 822.

27 Statutes, 1917, p. 436.

28 Statutes, 1905, p. 296.

29 Eddy, op.cit. p. 3. See also James L. Gillis, "The California County Library System", ALA Bulletin, 3 (September 1909). pp. 152-54.

30 Eddy, op.cit. p. 3

31 James L. Gillis, "A State Library System for California", Library Journal, 33:8 (August 1908). p. 316.

32 Susan T. Smith, "James L. Gillis and the State Library", California Library Bulletin, 11:4 (June 1950). p. 156.

33 Statutes, 1909, p. 811.

34 Statutes, 1911, p. 80.

35 Biennial Report of the Trustees of the California State Library, 1914-16, p. 18. (Appendix to Journals of Senate and Assembly, 42nd Session 1917, II December 2).

36 Mary Barmby and Cornelia D. Provines, "James L. Gillis and the

County Library System", <u>California Library Bulletin</u>, 11:4 (June 1950), p. 157.

37 California Library Association, Historical Committee, <u>California Library Association, Proceedings</u>, 1895-1907 (Stanford University, 1930). Publication No. 30, p. 19.

38 James L. Gillis, "State Library Administration", <u>Library Journal</u> 30:8 (August 1905), p. 37.

39 <u>News Notes</u>, 6:4 (October, 1911). p. 425.

40 Robert G. Cleland, CALIFORNIA IN OUR TIME, 1900-1940, p. 148 (New York: Alfred A. Knopf, 1947). W. W. Ferrier, NINETY YEARS OF EDUCATION IN CALIFORNIA, 1846-1936, devoted pages 345-347 to the educational contributions of the State Library and gives the early statistics relating to the traveling libraries. (Berkeley: Sather Gate Book Shop, 1937).

41 For more complete information the reader is referred to Beaulah Mumm, "California State Library School", <u>News Notes</u>, 52:4 (October 1957). pp. 679-82. Also to Sydney B. Mitchell, "Education for Librarianship in California", <u>California Library Bulletin</u>, 11:4 (June 1950). pp. 159-162, 184.

42 <u>News Notes</u>, 6:2 (April 1911), pp. 146-150.

43 <u>News Notes</u>, 8:4 (October 1913). p. 448.

44 Miriam Colcord Post, "James L. Gillis: Educator", <u>California Librarian</u>, 18:4 (October 1957). p. 238.

45 Grace Murray, "James L. Gillis and the CLA", <u>California Librarian</u>, 18:4 (October 1957). p. 233 says, "It can be seen that from the very beginning of this professional association, there was an awareness of the place it should take in statewide library development, involving coordination of activities between CLA and the State Library."

46 Howard Rowe, "The Genesis of the California Library Association", <u>California Library Bulletin</u>, 11:4 (June 1950), p. 185.

47 John D. Henderson, "The CLA since 1906: an Essay in Retrospection", <u>California Library Bulletin</u>, 11:4 (June 1950). p. 186.

48   Statutes, 1901, p. 557. This with slight change is now Education Code 22201-222265.

49   Statutes, 1901, p. 99.

50   Statutes, 1905, p. 296.

51   Statutes, 1909, p. 823. This was a recognition of the greater wealth of the larger cities.

52   Statutes, 1909, p. 815.

53   Statutes, 1911, p. 467.

54   Statutes, 1911, p. 17.

55   Statutes, 1915, p. 272.

56   Statutes, 1909, p. 436.

57   Statutes, 1911, Chapter 68.

58   Statutes, 1917, pp. 1315, 1317.

WILLIAM H. BRETT

Carl Vitz

Carl Vitz is Director Emeritus of the Cincinnati Public Library, Cincinnati, Ohio. The essay here published is a paper read before the American Library History Round Table during the Cleveland conference of the American Library Association in 1950.

William Howard Brett was chosen Librarian of the Cleveland Public Library in 1884 and served continuously and with unabated vigor until his sudden tragic death on August 24, 1918. This one third of a century of his librarianship, 1884-1918, was most significant in the history of the American Public Library since it was during these years, that its present program and character were developed.

In 1884, only eight years after the founding of the A.L.A., the public library was experimenting with the basic methods by which to carry on its work. Even more, it was seeking to establish what was its proper area of work, and what should be its functions and services to the community. By 1918 these had been well determined and progress had become chiefly a refining of methods and policies, except where technological advances in mechanical processes or new media still made pioneering possible.

These years were a period of formulation and development. Among those in the forefront, initiating and guiding this public library development, was Mr. Brett in Cleveland. It is my personal opinion that of them all, he was easily the first in the number, variety and quality of his contributions. Even more important, whatever he did was so well thought out, so appropriate to needs and purposes, and so in harmony with the developing spirit of public library service that it has stood the test of time in the

Grateful acknowledgment is here made to the author for providing the compiler with a copy of the complete text of this paper and for granting permission to include it in this volume. An abstract of this paper appeared in Wilson Library Bulletin, 25:297-302+, December, 1950; permission to reprint has been granted by the publisher.

WILLIAM H. BRETT

Cleveland library and has found general acceptance elsewhere.

In a short paper, much must be omitted and taken for granted. One such omission must be a biography of our subject. This morning, as we are meeting as a Round Table on American Library History, I plan to devote my brief half-hour, largely to a statement of Mr. Brett's contributions to the development of librarianship. Fortunately we possess in the "American Library Pioneers" series, the excellent "Portrait of a Librarian: William Howard Brett" by Linda A. Eastman. Miss Eastman could base her account on twenty-five years of close administrative association with Mr. Brett, and on two decades more, during which, as his successor, she ably carried on his program.

My purpose will be to list and comment on his many contributions to librarianship and somewhat to relate them to the general stream of library development. This recital will, in itself help to bring Mr. Brett, the man, before our eyes, and enable us to see the growth in his thinking and vision.

At the outset we must stress Mr. Brett's originality and creativeness. Strange as it may seem, Mr. Brett did not think of himself as an inventor, originator or creator. He was not interested in doing anything just to be different, or to be first or to attract attention to himself or to his library. He was a modest man, in a very full sense of that term. He freely borrowed from others and freely shared. To him the important thing was to better library service in his community. Wherever anything promised to do a task better, he sought it out. Constantly he questioned others about what they were doing. When he did find and used an idea, he was always generous in giving credit, forgetful of the touch of genius, which he so often gave to it in the using. For him borrowing was not mere copying. His imaginative mind and his practical common sense made of it something that was better.

Quick to see the meritorious, his ready and sympathetic adoption of many an idea gave it an earlier and wider currency. This was especially important in the early days when library meetings, library publications and library schools played so small a part in the diffusion of library ideas and techniques.

I do not mean that he himself did not originate. What I want to emphasize is that when he saw a need, he was intent upon meeting that need. He sought for answers everywhere. He found them in his own mind, in the work of associates and outside of his own library. When found, he converted them by some sort of alchemy, into a solution peculiarly his own.

Mr. Brett came to librarianship from many years of successful bookselling. His love of books had developed in him a wide and rich acquaintance with the best in literature. Basic was his strong conviction of the importance of providing for people the books they wanted and needed. He had learned to "give service beyond the line of duty". When the city of Cleveland needed a new librarian, a discriminating board of trustees found in him a man who possessed the attributes to make a great librarian.

His motivation from the first was a strong desire to bring books, their books, to all the people of Cleveland. This impelling desire, combined with practical common sense, an open mind, patience, and application to his work, quickly improved the scope and the quality of library service to his city.

One more quality of mind is necessary to an understanding of Mr. Brett's success in creative librarianship and that was his unfailing and generous recognition of the help of staff and associates, which made every associate an enthusiastic co-worker, proud to contribute his share, no matter how minor, to the grand total result.

Mr. Brett was chosen librarian when no library school was in existence. Organized statements of library methods were not to be had. Techniques varied radically from library to library, and usually were cumbersome and inelastic. Few were the bibliographic tools. Buildings were dreary, drab and unimaginative and book collections dull and inadequate. Active users were few. There were, to be sure, stirrings everywhere in the public library movement, but the giant was just beginning to waken.

The Cleveland Public Library of the early '80s has been described by a Clevelander, reminiscing, and perhaps seeking emphasis by overstatement, as the "worst library in the world". Competition for this doubtful distinction was keen. We need not try to award the palm to any library. Suffice it to admit that libraries then were on the whole, mediocre and the one in Cleveland more so than many.

Mr. Brett certainly started from scratch. His first printed report, after ten months of service, reveals a prompt, practical and forward looking approach to his problems. We quote, "The question of how to make the library available to those in the more remote districts of the City is a very important

244

one . . ." Again, "Another matter of great importance, and one which need not be postponed, is the consideration of every means for making the library useful to the young people of the city both in and out of school."

The mechanics of the work required his first attention. He devoted himself to the problems of classification and cataloging. Melvil Dewey's Relative Decimal Classification was then new, and only partially developed, but Mr. Brett impressed by its advantages, adopted it for Cleveland, or rather adapted it, as he improved it considerably, at least for public library use. Some of his changes have become general, such as the alphabetical arrangement of fiction and of individual biography. Many years later, in some connection with the development of subject departments in Cleveland, Mr. Brett expressed to me his regret that he had departed from Dewey as a standard. My unexpressed regret was that Melvil Dewey had not realized the advantages in these changes and adopted them. But Mr. Dewey was not noted for a flexible mind, or a gift for learning from others.

In any event, Mr. Brett's choice of this new classification must have helped in its wide adoption, especially as he used it in the printed Catalog of the English books in the Circulating Department of the Library, begun in 1885. The better part of four years was devoted by him to compiling this dictionary catalog and to seeing it through the press. A "dictionary catalog" with all entries, author, title, subject and analytic in one alphabetical arrangement, was still much of an innovation, in the day of classed catalogs, of bibliographes and of author lists. The appearance of this catalog was met with interest and marked approval. For two decades it served many other libraries as a model and a tool. The newly organized New York State Library School used it as a model dictionary catalog although it preferred its own local classed catalog.

The long, arduous task of reclassifying and recataloging the books in his library made Mr. Brett unusually familiar with the book collection. Until his pre-occupation with a rapidly developing branch service, after the turn of the century, he found much time personally to make the library's resources available to readers. Even after the Library had developed into a large system and the central work into many departments, he still enjoyed the all too few opportunities left to him to give direct service to borrowers. He was thus in a position to guide and inspire

245

a staff with his ideals of service. His quick understanding and his efficient, courteous help to readers became a pattern and an incentive to all his staff. It became a tradition that no borrower must be permitted to leave without having had the full benefit of the Library's resources.

Out of his early close and direct contact with the users of the Library, developed three forms of service which are now so taken for granted that it is hard to conceive that at one time they were unproved experiments. I refer to open access, the use of the library by children and cumulative indexing of periodicals.

To take the last first, the Cleveland Reference department in common with all other libraries, found it difficult at that time to supply information on current topics from current periodicals. In the case of those recently issued, memory was the chief reliance. After the lapse of some time, a search through the many printed indexes to the individual completed volumes of the various periodicals was necessary. Ultimately, of course, a Poole Supplement would come along but until then many libraries depended upon indexing articles in important periodicals on slips and filing them.

It seemed however a pity to Mr. Brett that every library should of necessity perform this same time consuming chore. The invention of the linotype and the linotype slug suggested to him the possibility of printing and publishing an index on the now familiar cumulative formula and so, beginning in 1896, the Cleveland Public Library published the "Cumulative Index to Periodicals", unlocking promptly the contents of 70 and soon of 100 periodicals. As an index it was successful, but a public library could not well function as a publisher and so in 1898, the Index was acquired by the Helman-Taylor Co. of Cleveland. The editorial work, however, continued for a time in the Cleveland library.

It did not prosper under its new direction and was soon taken over by the H. W. Wilson Company and merged with its "Readers Guide" begun in 1898 in Minneapolis by Halsey W. Wilson who was to become one of the great bibliographers of all time. Though relatively unimportant in Mr. Brett's career, the "Cumulative Index to Periodicals" is nevertheless indicative of his direct, sensible and courageous approach to problems in need of solution.

To Mr. Brett, familiar with the easy access to books in book stores, it never seemed right for a public library to deny access to the books in the library to the real owners, the citizens. At that time in all of the larger libraries access to the books, except for a privileged few, was not permitted. Professional opinion was strongly against it. Because of his own strong championing, his board, after some years, and despite great misgivings, finally consented to open the shelves to the people, a daring step taken in 1890.

Cleveland was the first large public library to do so, if we may credit a statement in the Sept-Oct 1918 issue of the Library's happily named, The Open Shelf. Of all of Mr. Brett's contributions, free access to books in libraries, is the one most associated with his name. This is due to the fact that he himself was for so long and so often an ardent champion, at a time when his name was beginning to be widely known. For a full decade in library press and at library meetings, in England as well as in this country, its merits were argued strenuously pro and con. As late as in 1899, at the Atlanta Conference, an informal show of hands still indicated minority support from large libraries, but after this general acceptance followed rapidly.

Children and Mr. Brett always were friends. Understanding and trust were mutual. His own children, when young, found themselves much at home in their father's office and in the dusky recesses of the Library. It was inevitable therefore that he should wish that children might share the delights and benefits of a collection of books. In his first report (1884-1885), he urged the immediate consideration of their needs. In 1886 he pleaded for a reading room and library for young people, a need which he persistently presented until 1898, when the first separate accommodation for children in Cleveland was arranged by enclosing a part of the Main Library Circulation department. Prior to the opening of this room, however, children had not been neglected. Books of literary quality and suited to their age and interests had been freely bought. Children were made welcome in the building and friendly service was given to them, especially when Mr. Brett could wait upon them in person. At times they were even invited to come back into the stacks to make personal selection.

After the establishment of this first separate room, with equipment, books and staff, all selected to provide the best possible service to children, progress was rapid. Cleveland, however, was not the first library to have a separate children's room. The honor of a first, perhaps goes to Minneapolis. Other early rooms were at Denver, Milwaukee, Pratt Institute, but with great variation in the necessary factors of separate space, carefully chosen books, a special staff and books lent for home use. The animating spirit was, however, more important than what was actually possible to do in the greatly overcrowded libraries of the time. It was because of this that Mr. Brett's name belongs easily and naturally in the roster of pioneers in work for children.

Acceptance and development of children's work was amazingly rapid in the nineties. Mr. Brett's great contribution to work with children was due to the fact that he considered it of major importance. When he could provide facilities for it, he helped to set high standards. The very best in training and personality was required of workers with children. Books, wholesome, beautiful and generous in supply must be provided, and surroundings attractive and comfortable.

Cleveland's many new branch buildings in the early years of the new century made a rapid and rich development possible. By 1910 children's work was on a firm basis with carefully chosen collections of books, adequately prepared children's librarians, attractive and comfortable children's rooms, story hours and reading guidance generally assumed.

At the time of his death he was called "the greatest Children's Librarian" by Anne Carroll Moore. In a letter recalling his last visit to the Children's Room of the New York Public Library, she wrote, "It was the anniversary of the opening of the Central Building and we sat for a long time speaking first of the Robin Hood pictures and then England and France. He loved our Children's Room so much that I shall always think of him as having left in it, on what was destined to be his last visit, a very beautiful token of his love of beauty, his belief in childhood, his reverence for women and faith in such work as ours."

That people, no matter who they were, or where they lived, should have the benefits and help of the library, was fundamental in Mr. Brett's library philosophy. Out of this belief there developed in Cleveland a wide ranging extension service, through branch libraries, service in and to schools, and stations in factories, business houses and institutions, and even in individual homes, if thus a means could be found for getting books to borrowers beyond the reach of other library agencies.

There is not time to trace in any detail this development from the first station opened in 1890 in a manufacturing plant and the first branch library in 1892, but quotations and personal reminiscence or two will indicate the extent and rapidity of its development.

The Librarian's report for 1891, includes this paragraph, "Another great need is the establishment of branch libraries or delivery stations, or of both. The city is so widely extended that a large part is out of reach of the Library and can only be reached by branches" and again, many years later in 1914, deploring the uneven distribution of Library facilities, he says, "The branch library is of great importance to the child. It is possible for older people to go farther for books, but unless the library is in walking distance of their homes, as the school is, most children cannot use it."

My connection with the Cleveland Public Library goes back 52 1/2 years to February 1898. Not until at work on this paper did I realize that in beginning as a part time page at the South Branch, it was my good fortune to begin in the first branch library in Cleveland planned and built to serve as such. It was opened February 22, 1897. Though not Library owned, it was built to meet the needs and ideas of the Library and made available on a long term lease. Simple and inexpensive, it was nevertheless spacious and inviting, as revealed by an interior view in "Public Libraries and Popular Education" by Dr. Herbert B. Adams, a 170 page bulletin published at Albany in 1900. Mr. Brett's gift for planning an attractive building is already apparent. The branch buildings built during his librarianship, a total of perhaps nineteen, and the many more in rented quarters greatly influenced branch building design. It is to be regretted that the small town Carnegie Library could not have had equally good patterns to follow.

The realization that South Branch of Cleveland was an early example of branch planning, made me wonder what others there might be. In a hurried and incomplete check I could find few. Floor plans for the first branch in Pittsburgh to be built out of a Carnegie gift of $300,000 are shown in the Library Journal for Sept. 1897, a half year after the completion of South Branch. In the accompanying text, Mr. E. H. Anderson, Librarian, is still uncertain as to open access or closed shelves and whether or not to shelve books in the reading room for children, while this Cleveland Branch had already solved both questions essentially as they would be today.

Several Baltimore branches were planned and built before this time, but they were so uninviting and "closed" that they were without influence. Many cities had no branches, e.g., Chicago which still favored delivery stations, or housed them in buildings without benefit of planning.

Children can most easily be reached through the schools. This was first done in Cleveland in the '80s and early '90s, through class room libraries to individual teachers, supplemented later with grade school stations. Some of these ultimately developed into branch libraries in their own buildings. I myself worked for a time in 1899 in one such school station which also gave general neighborhood service.

An early example of a high school library was the one established in 1896 in Central High School. The early recognition in Cleveland of the great value of school libraries on all levels and the generous financial support available had developed by 1918 a school library service then unequalled elsewhere in the country. It greatly influenced school library service after school men recognized its value and devoted school funds for support.

To me it seems regrettable that the Cleveland pattern of a public library directed school library service, costs fairly divided between the schools and the library, has not become general. In this plan the strength, skills and approach to education of the library can contribute to creating a service not only richer in content but also freer from the regimentation so common in our schools, but financial and administrative difficulties have brought about the present solution.

Cleveland is a city of many and large foreign populations, most of which came from southern and eastern Europe during the years of Cleveland's rapid growth as an industrial city. To Mr. Brett, these foreign born residents also were people to be reached through the Library. Unable to read books in English, obviously the only way they could be reached was to supply them with books in their own language. Large collections of books were built up, Polish, Czech, Italian, Hungarian, supplementing an earlier German collection. Lesser collections in other languages were provided to a total of more than thirty languages.

This service to the foreign born, well under way in the first years of the century and fully developed before World War I, contributed greatly to making Cleveland an outstanding city for loyalty and war participation despite its very polyglot population. The Americanization movement, born in world war days, was surely more understanding in its program because of library pioneering in work with the foreign born. We may add also that much of Cleveland's popular support of its Library is due to this recognition of the reading needs of immigrant groups.

Next to open shelves, the development of subject departments in the central library is most definitely associated with Mr. Brett's name. An arrangement of the central library, under which resources should be grouped together in a number of subject departments, had been in his mind, for sometime. A necessary removal to temporary quarters, gave the opportunity for a testing out. This occurred in the late summer of 1913, upon the removal into the Kinney and Levan Building, whose spacious 6th floor with 36,600 sq. ft. of floor space provided excellent conditions for the experiment. Of this, an area of about 27,000 square feet of unbroken floor area was allotted to the Main Library, the name given to this grouping of subject departments.

This experiment is of especial interest to me. Though I participated little in the planning, I did for the first six years function as head of the Main Library. The original organization included the following subject departments known as divisions: Philosophy and Religion; Sociology; Technical; Literature; History, Travel and Biography; and Fine Arts. Other divisions were the Periodical and Foreign Language and the Popular Library, while General Reference had coordinating functions in the reference field, and Circulation; Shelf; and Branch Loan, respectively, cared for registration and lending matters; shelving and records to and from order, catalog and binding departments; and book requests from branches or other libraries. Thirty seven years and the planning of a new building have resulted in no basic changes in organization.

General adoption of full subject departmentation has been gradual. As in Cleveland, adoption seems to have depended upon the acquisition of new quarters or a new building. Los Angeles, also first in temporary quarters, followed it in its new building, as did later Baltimore, Rochester and Toledo. Libraries such as Toledo (before its new building), Minneapolis, Cincinnati, Detroit and others have adopted it for some subjects, some of them before Cleveland's complete adoption.

An early subject department, of the type under consideration, is the Useful Arts department of the District of Columbia Public Library established in November 1907. Minneapolis at about this time, created a similar department. Subdivisions of the reference function, as are those of the New York Public Library or the Technical department at Pittsburgh, are excluded.

In speculating about this important Cleveland change in organization, I have wondered how much the experiment in Washington, D.C. influenced Mr. Brett's planning. I can recall his interest in all that I could tell him of my work in the Public Library in Washington and especially about the recently formed Useful Arts department of which I was then head. No doubt he knew of experiments in this direction in other libraries and had discussed their advantages and disadvantages with many others.

It is interesting to note that the first and second heads of Washington's Useful Arts department, namely myself and Joseph L. Wheeler, who followed me at Washington, headed full dress rehearsals of this plan applied to all departments, in temporary quarters at Cleveland and at Los Angeles. The experiments were so successful that both libraries provided full subject departmentation in their new buildings.

Mr. Wheeler as librarian, provided, as is well known, for full subject departmentation in the highly successful and pioneering new Baltimore building. This solution influenced greatly the planning in Rochester and in Toledo. Current planning (1950) in Denver, Detroit, Milwaukee, Minneapolis, Seattle and elsewhere is taking this form of organization for granted. For Cincinnati, we are working it out with a somewhat reduced number of departments in a building planned with large unbroken areas, as it has always seemed to me that its one large room was an important factor in the success of the early Cleveland experiment in temporary quarters.

Mr. Brett made his influence felt in four other important areas upon which I will touch more briefly, but they must not be omitted in a study of a man notable for his many-sidedness.

Some mention has already been made of his work as a planner of library buildings. Because both books and beauty were important to him and because he wanted all to share them, he planned his buildings not only so that books would be easy and inviting to use but also that the buildings themselves and all details carried the message of beauty. And while he was glad to draw upon the skill and good taste of associates, he made the planning of these details, so important in their sum total, a special personal responsibility. To be invited by him to participate in the selection of just the right pictures, hangings, pottery, wall colors and furniture, was no uncommon experience but one always to be welcomed and valued.

In matters of legislation, national, but especially state and local, his counsel was often sought and always available. The libraries of Ohio, especially those organized as school district public libraries, owe much to his vision, skill and foresight. In direct contrast with legislative committees, he was singularly successful.

He was well acquainted with the library laws of other states as well as with those of Ohio. Mr. Carnegie, and later the Corporation, often consulted him on matters of library law as they did also on library buildings. His compilation of state library laws, made at the request of the Carnegie Corporation, was an amazing achievement for a man occupied so fully with the many and varied plans for improving the service in his own library. It was characteristic of the man, that this "Abstract of laws relating to libraries in force in 1915 in the states and territories of the United States" and published in 1916 was done and proofread almost entirely in non-office hours and, that the title page does not bear his name.

Immediately upon his first election as librarian, library association meetings became of importance to him because here he could learn and discuss how to make his own library more useful. He contributed much to programs and even more in personal discussion and exchange of opinion, where he was at his best. He served as president of the A.L.A. in 1897 and was one of the founding group of the O.L.A. and its first president. He so encouraged staff members to attend and participate in meetings that few libraries were better represented at the annual meetings than was Cleveland.

Training for librarianship also owes much to his enthusiastic interest. He began his work as librarian with a small untrained staff. A high school education was an exception. It was his full conviction that adequate library service to Cleveland implied a staff with a liking for and a knowledge of books, and enthusiasm for the work, a broad general education and special preparation for librarianship. His first step was to raise requirements for entrance to the staff in terms of schooling and by an entrance examination. By 1890 the President of the Board could state proudly "the fact that all now were graduates of the high school".

Soon normal school and college graduates appeared. I quote here from Miss Eastman, "Mr. Brett so imbued these young women with his own zeal and enthusiasm that for a time a group of them met voluntarily once each week, to discuss books and their use with him, at the forbidding hour of seven o'clock in the morning. The library opened at eight, and there was no other time when working schedules made meetings possible. It took zeal to get them there in the cold gray of a winter's morning, when it meant working steadily thereafter until five-thirty, six, or even until nine o'clock — for twelve or thirteen-hour working days were quite frequent — with only brief respites for meals."

In 1896, 1898, 1900 and 1903 lecture courses in librarianship or institutes were provided, lasting two weeks, then six weeks and the last for five months, drawing into his "faculty" men and women from other libraries and cities to supplement his own staff. Miss Katherine L. Sharp of the Illinois Library School directed the first of these.

His influence was important in securing an endowment from Andrew Carnegie for the Library School of Western Reserve University of which he was Dean from its beginning in 1904 until his death. A training class for children's librarians was begun in 1909 to help in the adequate staffing of the increasing number of branches. This class is now a part of the University's Library School.

Mr. Brett's skill in selecting staff members has often been commented upon. And with him it was indeed a process of selection. Of course he expected education and training, but more important to him were the personal qualities of leadership, loyalty, enthusiasm for books and for people and capacity for team work. When any of these were lacking, his interest in the person as an applicant, ceased.

Once when discussing this subject with him, I learned his secret in part. As he told me, he was less concerned with filling positions than in adding people who could meet high standards of character and personality and had the capacity to contribute and to grow. When he found such a person an important task would inevitably develop.

WILLIAM H. BRETT

And when the opportunity did develop, fortunate was the staff member, as initiative and creativeness were recognized and encouraged by him, with full credit and evident pleasure and in an atmosphere where all were working together for desired, common goals. As a result almost everyone responded with the best that was in him.

Mr. Brett was a man of deep patriotism. It was an integral part of his character and was indissolubly linked with his service as a librarian. I believe he felt that in his work and in that of all librarians, a most important service to the nation was being rendered.

When World War I broke out and the librarians of America made their great contribution of books and libraries to the men in the service, Mr. Brett was not content with any service by proxy — he wished to make his personal contribution and to range himself as it were, in service to his country alongside of his four soldier sons.

This service he rendered in many ways but outstandingly at the Newport News (Va.) Library and Dispatch Office which demanded great organizing skill and tactful contacts with a great number and variety of military agencies and personnel. The long hours, difficult living conditions, arduous travel, heat and hard physical toil involved, would have taxed the physical powers and the courage of a young man. But he, a veteran of seventy-two years, whose courage and enthusiasm continued strong, had an energy and strength which seemed never to flag.

On August 24, 1918, he had just returned from Newport News to Cleveland. Though he had not had a vacation himself, he was characteristically desirous that Miss Eastman and I should have a fort-night of vacation. Saturday afternoon had been spent in going over things that might need attention. At the close of the afternoon, Mr. Brett accompanied me to the door. As I departed, he waved a friendly goodbye to me and said "Carl, have a good time and forget all about the Library while you are gone." This is my last and lasting memory of him.

Words, moving and enlightening as they often can be, are none-the-less feeble things with which to recreate the sense of a great and rich personality. There are gathered, however, in Miss Eastman's "Portrait of William Howard Brett" many tributes from those who knew him. Their very number and variety, here skillfully brought together cannot help but recall to those who knew him and to portray for others, something of his rich personality. His gift of inspiration, will thus be handed on to many future generations of librarians.

We close with the appropriate lines on the pedestal of the memorial bust in the Library's Brett Hall:

> "The worker pays his debt to Death;
> His work lives on, nay, quickeneth."

MARY FRANCES ISOM: CREATIVE PIONEER
IN LIBRARY WORK IN THE NORTHWEST

Bernard Van Horne

Bernard Van Horne is Administrative Assistant, Contra
Costa County Library, Martinez, California. The essay
here reprinted is a paper read before the American Library History Round Table during the San Francisco conference of the American LibraryAssociation, July, 1958.

In June 1901, Pratt Institute Library School had at least one
very promising graduate. Mary Frances Isom at 36 was somewhat older, more mature and poised than the average graduate.
She had come to the school two years before on the urging of
Josephine Rathbone, a longtime friend then on the faculty of
Pratt. Miss Isom's education at Wellesley had been interrupted
after only one year by the need to return and care for her father,
a prominent Cleveland surgeon. Her mother had died some years
before and Mary Frances took her place as hostess and buffer.
Dr. Isom, a former Army surgeon, was a cultivated and highly
disciplined man who reserved his warmly human side for his
witty, capable, and attractive only child. They were very close.
His death in 1899 left her financially independent but personally
lost.
    Her two years at Pratt must have been stimulating and re-
warding. The vision of service, that she always acknowledged
she had caught from Miss Rathbone, permanently filled the void
left by the death of her father. Any attempt to find the clue to
her great accomplishments must take into account those two
strong influences. Her own sparkling intelligence, boundless
energy, and creative imagination did the rest. From the time
she left Pratt until her death she was fully receptive to ideas
but worked always as partner or as leader, never as a follower.
    Her break with the past was dramatic and complete. She ac-
cepted a position as cataloger for the then recently accepted
Wilson collection at the Library Association of Portland, a pri-

Reprinted from Wilson Library Bulletin, 33:409-416, February, 1959,
by permission of the author and the publisher.

vate subscription library in the farthest corner of the country. The Pacific Northwest was sparsely settled and had only recently been reached by rails. Certainly the distance from Cleveland was an attraction, as was the absolutely virgin character of the region, so far as public library service was concerned. One can only speculate that the crafty pair — missionary teacher and star pupil — knew what an awful dilemma had been posed the Library Association by the acceptance of the Wilson collection. The gift was too valuable to refuse but the donor had specified that, if accepted, the books would have to be available free to the people of Portland. There was no tradition for this. The board and the librarian had on many occasions, when faced with suggestions to seek public support, expressed the belief that if the library were wholly free its readers would cease to value its privileges. The costs of membership were low, but the memberships were few — just a thousand or so in 1900.

The Library Association had been founded thirty-six years before by a group of Yankees who had done well in the new country but missed the cultural advantages of New England. In the face of rising costs the growth of the collection had slowed and more and more often financial crises had to be met by substantial gifts from the directors and founders. Now came the Wilson gift, and with misgivings the board set about opening the library to the public without charge. A free public library had been founded in the city hall a few years before, but was weak in both books and service though it had a small city subsidy. This library and its subsidy were absorbed by the association.

Miss Isom never got around to cataloging the Wilson collection. She started on it but was soon involved in every aspect of the preparations for opening the library to the public. It was woefully unprepared. There was no catalog, the librarian tended to every item of business himself and was making feeble motions to gird the library for the onslaught. The feeble motions became furious activity in the winter, and in the midst of it the librarian, Davis P. Leach, packed up the carpet slippers he habitually wore in the library and departed at the end of January 1902.

Without hesitation, the board named the new young assistant as librarian, and Mary Frances Isom found herself at 37, in the first year of her first employment in charge of a public library just perilously launched, financially shaky, unorganized, and expected to do the impossible. She calmly set about doing it.

MARY FRANCES ISOM

There were assets. Her board consisted of the most powerful and influential men in the city or even the state. Her bibliophile predecessors had accumulated a collection of 40,000 well-
chosen books. A strong reference service had been established.
The city subsidy was a beginning toward financial stability. The
library, thanks to a windfall bequest, had its own two-story building in the heart of town on an increasingly valuable piece of land.
The association had tremendous prestige and from its first day
as a public library was able to provide services of a quality that commanded respect and made access to them a valued privilege.

Within a month of her appointment Miss Isom had moved the
small children's collection from a remote corner to a favorable
spot near the front door, not, however, without first discarding
Alger, Optic, Castleman, and Finley from the collection. Her
concern for the children and their reading was always to remain
a major point in her philosophy of library service.

The period 1902 to 1911 was the time of the unfolding of the
grand design. One cannot but believe that, except for the adjustment to the circumstances of her situation in Portland, it was
a design and a method matured in her days at Pratt. This was
the attainment of a goal which would see a strong central library
reaching out through a multiplicity of outlets, branches, sub-
branches, stations, schools, and organization halls so that
books and reading might become a part of the lives of everyone
in the area served. The method used would be to take advantage
of every opportunity for placing books, well-chosen books, near
the people; straining and overstraining the institution to the utmost and then by enlisting every person, every device, every
organization, to strengthen the institution to meet the call. Lack
of buildings, lack of time, lack of staff, lack of books were never factors that led to passing up a chance. These were used later as arguments to build the strength needed to take advantage
of still other opportunities.

Eleven months after opening as a city library, the association opened its services to county residents by contract with the
county. Trunks of books went immediately over nonexistent
roads to remote corners of the county. There was no library law
in Oregon so the board and Miss Isom went down to Salem and
one was passed allowing the county to do what had been done —
contract with a private association and pay a subsidy for public
library service. The legislature was to see much of Miss Isom

259

and her notable ally on the board, Winslow B. Ayer. Mr. Ayer was a lumberman of great influence and wealth. He had been an early convert of Miss Isom's and during most of her administration was president of the board. The strength reached by the county library system was the result of their close alliance and their ability to marshal strength where and when needed. They had many able allies but they were the generals. The clear understanding each had of his role and their evidently clear agreement on strategy and tactics was a great credit to their intelligence, their dedication, and their respect for each other's individualism. For them both, the building of the county library system was a life work. Both died in harness.

They were concerned not only with Multnomah County. In the spring of 1905, a law was passed establishing a state library commission modeled on the Wisconsin plan. Miss Isom had no illusions that the Portland Library Association could remain an exotic flower in a desert of library service. There were no public libraries in Oregon except for feeble associations in Salem and Eugene. The law established a commission including ex officio the librarian of the Portland Library Association (Miss Isom), various officials of the state, and an appointive member (Mr. Ayer, of course).

This move was important for another reason. It brought another great figure on the scene, Cornelia Marvin, then secretary of the Wisconsin Library Commission. Even before the law was passed Miss Isom, in a series of elaborately contrived letters, spun a web into which Cornelia Marvin walked with her eyes wide open and probably amused. Describing the excitement of working in such a fertile if unplanted field, Miss Isom described Miss Marvin in every detail as the person to take the job and, without naming her, asked her to recommend candidates. Her surprise and pleasure when Miss Marvin suggested herself were most touching. Miss Marvin came, labored mightily in the fertile field until her marriage to Governor Walter Pierce in 1927, and died very recently.

I am going to take the unusual step here of introducing excerpts from four letters from Miss Isom to Miss Marvin since they convey so much about that period so much better than I would tell it. The first three date from May after the passage of the law, the last was written shortly after Miss Marvin's arrival in August 1905.

. . . The bill establishing the State Library Commission emanated from this library and Mr. Ayer was really the man who put it through. . . . The bill met opposition in committee. . . . I went down and also Mr. Miller,
Speaker of the House and trustee of this library, Mr.
Ackerman, state superintendent of instruction, and Mr.
Linthicum, a very able lawyer in Portland had charge
of the bill. The committee decided to drop it but after
three quarters of an hour of conversation they not only
voted to work for the bill but to increase the appropriation from $1,500 to $2,000. — May 1905.

So far as I know I shall stay in Portland if I continue
to please and to be pleased. I can ask for nothing better.
I am very fond of the life out here and one can't live here
and not be intensely interested in its prospects and the
development. The state is large and thinly settled. . . .
It will be hard work but it is bound to succeed and you
can make it your work and stand or fall by it, which is
the best part of it. I must not say too much. I have so
much enthusiasm and optimism but we have weathered
through so much here the possibilities ahead of us seem
unlimited. It must be so for the state. — May 1905.

. . . You certainly would have infinitely more to
start with than I did when I came to Portland four years
ago, for not only was there no knowledge of public libraries but a tremendous amount of prejudice against
them that has been overcome in large measure by our
work here. . . . I feel sure . . . that the secretary
would have freedom to work out her own ideas without
interference. I have insisted upon that in my work here
from the beginning and I hope it will be an established
precedent in library work. — May 1905.

. . . You are not to get nervous, it doesn't pay.
. . . I wonder whether men out here are like men in
other places, these amuse me tremendously, and now
that I am accustomed to the workings of the animal I
am not troubled. My early experiences nearly planted
me in my grave. I must tell you about them sometime.
— August 1905.

Miss Isom was not only concerned about the state but about the region, about the nation, about the world. Anxious to bring recognition to the area and to give it pride and interest in library matters, ALA was invited and met in Portland in 1905. She had issued a call for a meeting of people in Oregon interested in libraries in 1904 and at that meeting organized the Oregon Library Association. In 1909 she was a prime mover in the organization of the Pacific Northwest Library Association. Because it is interesting and because this paper is being read at an ALA conference I am going to quote the following excerpt, in full recognition of the fact that it has little pertinence in the light of the later development of ALA and ALA headquarters. I might mention, too, for the local committee who might be present, that two weeks before the conference in 1905 Miss Isom disappeared from Portland. In a letter to Miss Marvin she said she couldn't bear any more and had gone for two weeks solitude on the coast!

> . . . You know I am still a Philistine as regards the
> ALA. I think it is pleasant to go and meet the people
> but so far as the association being of any value I fail
> to see it. I feel the same way about ALA headquarters.
> I think it is money sunk in the bottom of a well. I have
> never asked a question yet that has been intelligently
> answered. Perhaps they do some sort of work but I
> fail to see that too, and I think that a small association
> that is alive is more important for our people than the
> larger one. I firmly believe that every living library
> mortal in Oregon must belong to PNLA. I burn with
> missionary zeal. — March 30, 1911.

Toward the end of the first decade as a public library there were increasing signs that something fundamental would have to be done about the housing and the financial base of the association. The Stark Street building was hopelessly overcrowded, even though the art museum had been persuaded to relinquish its hold on the second floor. The city was niggardly and carping about its contribution and the county limited its contribution to matching the city. Carnegie funds were available nationwide but not to the association because of its lack of firm tax support. Plans were carefully laid. Back to the legislature went the board, and the present library laws were written. A contract with the county was entered into in 1911. This contract still governs the relationship between the Library Association of Portland and Multnomah County, modified only by the removal of the millage limitation. This unusual instrument embodies wise compromise and has been the basis of a cordial, beneficial relationship for nearly fifty years. The association retained its identity and its freedom to act creatively and enterprisingly. The association provided a valuable city block and the county agreed to erect a building and set a tax rate determined by the needs of the association expressed in an operating budget submitted to the county commissioners. The proceeds of the tax levy are turned over to the association and the county is relieved of all policy and administrative responsibility with regard to the library.

With the new central building assured and the contract in hand, Miss Isom went back to Mr. Bertram to loosen the Carnegie purse strings. Somewhat grumpily they were opened, but not as wide as Miss Isom would have liked. Mr. Bertram said Mr. Carnegie thought she would pamper the people with her eight large branches and cut it to five. She was privately elated but did not relax her efforts to get the other three until she succeeded.

Now there was another period of furious creative activity. The roadblocks had been removed and in the period 1911 to 1918 the jerry-built public library system, strung together with baling wire and glued with optimism, was replaced with a sound county system well-planned, well-housed, well-financed, well-stocked, complete with a thorough-going school library service and a highly respected training school for librarians. One can imagine that the staff, while pleased, must have groaned a little too at the prospect of Miss Isom and Mr. Ayer with little to impede the breakneck speed to which by nature they inclined.

During 1912 the central building was constructed. North Portland, Gresham, and Vernon branches were built and opened, St. Johns was planned and started, two other branches were in preparation by the architects, five deposit stations were opened, and libraries were opened in the high schools!

The planning and building of central was for the library and for Miss Isom the major work and responsibility of the time. That it was done so quickly is evidence of the fact that much thought had been given to it for some years. Miss Isom's great talent for creative collaboration was again in evidence in her work with Albert E. Doyle, a local architect of national repute.

This was for him, too, his great work, and his speech at the dedication is evidence of the major role played by Miss Isom in planning. The architect and librarian went on a cross-country trip to visit and talk with librarians and architects responsible for the major buildings, including Denver, New York, and Boston. The stamp of Doyle is on the exterior particularly, that of Isom on the functional parts of the interior. This central building, still in use and serving well a much larger population, is a tribute to the taste, the foresight, and the creativeness of its collaborators. The central stack was Miss Isom's idea. She bowed to Doyle on the inclusion of the grand stairway. The building, one of the most handsome public buildings of the country, has grace, beautiful proportion, and warmth of texture and decoration. It belongs to neither the railroad-station nor department-store school of library architecture, but is strictly Isom-Doyle. The interior spaces were left in large units — there are five reading rooms of 4,600 square feet each. There are no corridors. Criticism can of course be made of it, and it has not been imitated except by Richmond, Virginia, but the fact that the people of Portland have felt so at home in it, that it can be so easily understood from the moment of entering it, and that it could be effectively modernized many years later makes such criticism seem minor. Consider the fate of other, even later central buildings.

No funds had been asked of the county for branches. That impressed the county. Carnegie was impressed by the fact that Portland asked for no funds for central — a very adroit maneuver! Local citizens were encouraged to give or give toward sites and all were donated for the Carnegies. Mr. Ayer had to reach for his checkbook frequently to provide come-on funds for these efforts. In fact, without Mr. Ayer's checkbook for emergencies and Mr. Ayer's White Steamer and chauffeur to take Miss Isom with her books and her crusading spirit to every crossroads and school in the county, progress toward the goal would have been slow indeed. The Carnegies were now widely spaced and among them some ten smaller branches were installed in rented quarters, staffed by librarians rather than the volunteers of the earlier days.

Mary Frances Isom was by conviction a person of liberal democratic views. The war in Europe disturbed her profoundly. She threw herself with her accustomed vigor into war work; supported the Liberty Fund drives and personally organized hospital and camp libraries in Oregon and Washington. The strength of her convictions was put to the test by events of 1917-1918. Every effort was made to encourage active participation by the staff in war work. The assistant librarian, M. Louise Hunt, was, however, by conviction a pacifist and conscientiously refused to buy war bonds. This quickly became a raging public issue. Whipped on by superpatriots and especially by Mr. Woodward, one of the county commissioners and an ex officio member of the board, the attacks on Miss Hunt and, through her, on Miss Isom and the library, mounted. Miss Isom stood firm by her convictions that Miss Hunt's conscience was her own concern and rejected every cry for her resignation. The county commissioners had not before then or since actually attended board meetings. They did attend in the spring of 1918. In April, after listening to Miss Hunt's explanation of her views, the board voted unanimously, except for the ex officio members, that Miss Hunt was a valued employee who had the right to act in accord with her minority opinion. At another special meeting, Miss Hunt submitted a letter of resignation as follows:

> Because I do not wish in any degree to hamper the
> usefulness of the library, and because I am unwilling
> to place upon the library board the burden of a conflict
> to maintain its brave stand for freedom of conscience,
> I hereby tender my resignation as assistant librarian
> to take effect at once.

Mr. Woodward moved that it be tabled, that she be dismissed, and he also stated that he considered Miss Isom disloyal to her country. The board voted to accept Miss Hunt's resignation and then, on motion of the president, Mr. Ayer, passed a strong vote of censure of Mr. Woodward's statements and actions. Remember, the county commissioners were wholly responsible for setting the library's tax rate. The action of the board in this crisis was an example of dignity and courage for any board and a matter of great pride for ours.

The years had told on Miss Isom and recent events as well as her war efforts had taken a toll, but she was to make a last supreme effort. She volunteered for service in France in the ALA unit under the Red Cross. There is strong evidence that she knew before she left that she had an incurable and inoperable cancer. She labored from September of 1918 until April of 1919 against the impersonal indifference of Army red tape, under conditions of physical discomfort that must have been particularly hard for one of her fastidious temperament, and in failing health, setting up hospital libraries.

Her letters addressed to "my dear library family" are a delight and should be published. Witty, thoughtful, burdened with the pain of what she saw, taking on her own shoulders the frustrations and hopes of the broken man, she must have been a source of strength for many who had none left.

On her return she was exhausted and dying at the early age of 54. She came to the library as long as she could, then part time, and finally by phone and letter from her bed until her death on April 15, 1920.

This then was her life. But what of Mary Frances Isom as a person, as a friend, as a colleague, as an administrator and, yes, Mary Frances Isom as a mother — because she had adopted a child, Berenice Langton, daughter of a Cleveland friend. Her work is written — large and bold — in the history of library service and on the face of the region of her choice. What was her philosophy, her approach, her method? This aspect of Miss Isom is elusive. There is the story, probably apocryphal, of the assistant in the children's room who answered the phone and heard, "This is Miss Isom", and promptly fainted. There are the stories of her trips through the library, pad and pencil in hand, making the perfect grand entrance in every room, and the fear of the hapless assistant who had to state the reasons for observed infractions. There are personal accounts of the terrors of giving book reviews under the watchful eyes of the head librarian or being called on to discuss books read, because books charged to staff were kept separately and Miss Isom frequently consulted the file.

But then there is the story told me by a distinguished librarian who as a young trainee was assigned to work on Christmas Eve in the old Stark Street building. Miss Isom came down to take her place saying, "You have a family. I have none. Go home and enjoy the holiday." And there is the story she told on herself of a somewhat fuddled patron in the reference room when Miss Isom was on the desk — an assignment she took when she could. He was getting the usual first-rate, top-flight, Isom

service and suddenly said, "Look here, girlie, you don't need
to shine up to me, it won't get you nowhere."
Every account, reminiscence, and clue in her correspondence seems to prove that Mary Frances Isom was by nature an
autocrat and by deep personal conviction a democrat. She was
of the time when Trojan labors were the order of the day. She
was of the generation of librarians that Ralph Munn refers to as
the Era of Crowned Heads. And remember she was a woman in
a world of men — both in the library world and in the community.
She believed in women's rights and the vote for women, but she
deplored the fanaticism of the suffragettes. She cultivated a mien
that equated the standing of the institution and of her profession
with her own as representing them. First names were never
used in the library during her administration but she strove for
informality and simple friendliness as keynotes for the service.
Her notes of sympathy to bereaved staff members of all levels,
her helpful hand for the hard pressed, her concern for the un-
derprivileged and for the foreign born were heartfelt and sincere.
We have to remember that many of the stories about her
come from then young assistants and during a time when Miss
Isom was already a living legend in the community and was in
poor health. She had a temper that sometimes put her to bed.
It was most often aroused by sloth, mediocrity, or self-seeking.
She was not a patient woman except with the weak and helpless.
Despite her best efforts one must conclude that her staff respected, admired, and were proud of her to an inordinate degree,
but did not feel a personal affection for her. They wanted desperately to do what she wanted because she inspired them. Her
attempts at informality were not always successful and she probably did not herself realize her unapproachableness.
With her colleagues and intimates she was witty, gay, and
relaxed. She was a woman of medium height and somewhat plump,
which made her seem shorter. Her movements were brisk, her
approach direct. She was fastidious in her grooming and dress.
She was a gracious hostess. Her at-homes every other Sunday
were salons of good conversation, music, and gourmet food.
People of every degree frequented them and enjoyed them. She
was able to renew herself in solitude and particularly enjoyed
the cottage on the coast designed for her by Albert Doyle in the
shadow of Neah-kah-nie Mountain. This cottage is, thanks to
the generosity of Miss Isom's daughter, Berenice, owned by

the library and used by the staff for the relaxation enjoyed by
Miss Isom there. She loved to walk on the shore in the early
morning with Bunker Hill, her bull terrier from whom she was
almost never parted. Bunker walked to the library with her every day and sat in her office. It is said that among his privileges
was any trouser leg he favored except Mr. Ayer's. To this day
the Library Association has no rule against dogs but they must
now leave all trouser legs alone.

Perhaps in spite of her apparent complete self-possession
Mary Frances Isom was shy. In fact, that might have been the
reason for her sternness. In 1911 when she was president of
PNLA she wrote Miss Marvin:

> I dread it very much because I never presided at
> a meeting and I know I shall make a perfect fool of
> myself. If I were only in the habit of fainting it would
> be so convenient.

There are so many things to tell on the human side of Mary
Frances Isom — the fun she had in Paris on Armistice Day with
her arms hooked in those of soldier boys who joyfully ran interference for her and protected "mother" from the unruly mobs;
or the time she won over the juvenile delinquents at one of the
branches to become avid readers and regular visitors to her office; or her love for animals — but we haven't the time. I should
like, however, to let her speak for herself as she wrote Miss
Marvin on the passing scene:

> . . . Mrs. Stallings has just been in to see me. She
> seems to be an aged party but quite bright. . . . I am
> in perfect despair over my applicants for tomorrow.
> I have few under 85 and in some cases whole families
> to take the examination and join us in a body. I am
> thinking of giving up library work and establishing a
> home for eastern people left over at the Fair. Have
> you heard that Mr. Anderson has taken the Albany
> School and state librarianship. . . . He is a gentleman
> with some culture and polish and we cannot say that of
> all our library friends unfortunately. [1905]

> . . . her letter did not make a pleasant impression.

MARY FRANCES ISOM

She impressed me as being truly Middle West, a young person with much information and no taste or real culture. . . . — July 12, 1909.

. . . The Oregonian you will find hard to convert because the opinions are Harvey Scott's even when not written by him. He simply pitched into our library and me too when we were first free and I thought it was all over with us, but we are still here. . . . The Oregonian is not the power it was four years ago. I'd like to claw Mr. Scott. — August 21, 1905.

. . . Teachers have to be persuaded books are good or necessary. School authorities are apathetic. . . . I have come to the conclusion since I have had Berenice that most schools are abominable and all teaching is poor. . . . I think I am quite dull when it comes to these modern educational fads. — September 22, 1911.

Mary Frances Isom personally chose the many inscriptions for the stone work of central library. The many friendly benches in the balustrade are named for novelists. Miss Isom disapproved of fiction generally, but loved Sir Walter Scott. The bench named after him is therefore three times as long as the others! At the most prominent point where it can be seen by all approaching the building from the center of town there is this inscription:

Come, go with us. We'll guide thee to our house and show thee the rich treasures we have got, which with ourselves are at thy dispose.

For all of us who enjoy the fruits of her greatness and her devotion, I can only say

They were
You were
We are.

A DEDICATED LIFE: MEMORIES OF A GREAT LIBRARIAN — ELECTRA COLLINS DOREN

Virginia Hollingsworth

> Virginia Hollingsworth read the essay here reprinted before the American Library History Round Table during the Midwinter meeting of the American Library Association in Chicago in 1954. At the time she was Head Cataloger in the Dayton Public Library, Dayton, Ohio. Miss Hollingsworth died in 1955.

It is not possible in a paper, which must confine itself within the limits of a morning program, to give a full picture of the career of Electra Collins Doren. I can touch only the high points, with the hope that a more adequate treatment may be given later. Harry Miller Lydenberg, former librarian of the New York Public Library, who began his career as an associate of Miss Doren, has an excellent sketch of her life ready for publication. There is also other biographical material which should appear in print.

Miss Doren's father, John Gates Doren, was born at Athens, Tennessee in 1834. Because of objection to slavery, the Doren family moved to a community near Xenia, Ohio, when John Doren was a lad. From a material point of view, the move was a costly one. John and his brothers had to earn their livelihood while obtaining an education. John worked at the printing trade and later became a student-teacher in Latin at the Xenia academy.

In 1861 the family moved to Columbus, Ohio, and Mr. Doren entered the offices of the Ohio Statesman at a time when such men as William Dean Howells and Whitelaw Reid were on the staff of the paper. After a varied journalistic, legal, and political career, Mr. Doren was for twenty years owner and publisher of the Dayton Daily Democrat, predecessor of the Dayton Daily News. He was a crusading editor, free in his comments on social and political affairs, and outspoken in his criticisms of his own party, when he felt such criticism was needed. He championed woman suffrage and the participation of women in public affairs.

Reprinted from Wilson Library Bulletin, 28:782-787, May, 1954, by permission of the publisher.

ELECTRA COLLINS DOREN

John Doren married an Ohio young woman, twenty-three-year-old Elizabeth Bragdon, who was of Puritan ancestry on her father's side and of Quaker and Methodist ancestry on her mother's. She lived her early life partly in Kentucky and partly in Southern Ohio. In Maysville, Kentucky, she and her widowed mother made their home with an uncle, Richard Collins.

Electra Collins Doren, their first child, was born December 4, 1861, in the little town of Georgetown, Ohio, east of Cincinnati.

Mrs. Doren was a deeply religious woman and a woman of warm sympathies. Miss Electra once said of her, "Although bearing a full share in church and philanthropic activities, her family always found her bright and loving in a home made comfortable by her own hands. Her reading aloud was one of the delights of the family circle and her daily prayer with them a benediction."

We see here two formative influences in Electra Doren's life — the courage of the fearless, forward-looking father, and the tenderness of the warm-hearted, deeply religious mother.

In outlining the career of Miss Doren, I am confining myself to her library activities and chiefly those relating to the Dayton Public Library. I am omitting the details of her personal life and of her civic contributions, other than her librarianship, which were many and varied.

In September 1879, just out of high school, she began her career as assistant librarian of the Dayton Public Library. At this time the library was housed in rooms over the market house. The books were under lock and key. There were very few assistants.

In 1880, Miss Doren started an analytical dictionary card catalog, one of the first four in the United States. It was completed in 1884 — the work of a young woman between the ages of 19 and 24. Once completed, it had to be kept up on cards and with printed supplements. Five supplements came out between 1884 and 1895.

In 1888 the library was moved to its present location in Cooper Park.

In 1896, after refusing the offer twice, Miss Doren was made chief librarian.

Interesting data concerning the first year of her librarianship is given in annual report of the Dayton Public Library for 1896-1897, which, in Miss Doren's words, is called: "Report for the year ending August 31, 1897, being my first year as librarian and 37th in the history of the library."

Dayton Public Library reports extant, prior to this one, were made up of statistics. In the report for 1896 there is considerable text — concise and meaningful. Here are recorded and foreshadowed the things this young librarian was doing and the things she hoped to do for the Dayton Public Library. It tells of the organization of the work into departments; of a training class opened for applicants for library positions (the second of its kind in the United States); of the continuation under the direction of Esther Crawford of the reclassification of the library according to the Dewey Decimal System; and of the continuation of recataloging begun in 1895.

It tells also of the formation of a school library department in which carefully chosen selections of juvenile literature were distributed for home use by means of libraries sent out to public schools — forerunner of our classroom libraries of the present day.

Gone are the days of the lock and key. The report tells of the "rearrangement of the interior of the building to give readers ready access to books".

A new idea emerges in the plea for a "branch and a delivery station for persons debarred from library privileges because of lack of time, cost of car fare, and distance from the library" — an idea which was to bear fruit in the establishment of branch libraries and in book wagon service, the first city book wagon service in the United States.

I quote the closing paragraphs of this report. They must have given food for thought to the gentlemen who composed the contemporary board of trustees:

> It is needless to remind you of the projects already almost full-grown in our thoughts, but which must await the increase of means before they can be executed. It would seem a pity that any of these things, each so full of good for the people, be lost to them for the lack of a small increase in our present appropriation.
>
> As the executive of the board, I therefore ask that the advisability of an addition to our present tax levy be taken into consideration by your honorable body, with a view to securing action in the matter at the opening session of the state legislature.

ELECTRA COLLINS DOREN

I hear in these words the opening guns in her long battle for adequate library funds.

She was librarian of the Dayton Public Library from 1896 to 1905, during which time there were leaves of absence for intensive study of libraries in the East, in Europe, and in the Western United States.

From 1905-1906 she was the first director at the School of Library Science, Western Reserve University, Cleveland. There were few library schools to which she could look for precedent. According to a faculty statement:

> She laid a firm foundation. The first class was so well grounded that their subsequent careers as librarians have been a matter of pride for the school.

From 1906-1913 she was in retirement, during which time she built her beautiful home, Morningside, four miles north of Dayton.

In the midst of this peaceful interval, she was called to the rescue of the Dayton Public Library which was staggering under the impact of the disastrous flood of March 1913. Here an enormous task awaited her — a building warped and undermined by flood damage, a book collection cut almost in half, and a reduced staff. Money was needed for building reconstruction, for restoration of the book collection, and for a more adequate staff. Steadily rising costs for materials and labor complicated the problem. The institution was slipping backward and even its existence seemed threatened. As the years brought no adequate relief, Miss Doren saw that a battle for funds was inevitable. She accepted the challenge and steeled herself for the task.

Like a general she planned the campaign waged in 1920. Every member of her staff was called into service. A street directory was compiled from the borrowers' file. Armed with sheafs of petitions, staff members visited these borrowers in their homes, secured petition signatures, and often volunteer workers. Properly chaperoned, the younger girls were stationed with petitions at all of the city's places of amusement, to secure signatures from departing audiences. Another group toured the factories.

My assignment was the downtown district. With a stalwart page as helper and body guard, I was instructed to call at every

office and every store in every building, to ask to see the manager, to tell him of the library's needs, to get his signature to
our petition, and to get his permission to interview his employees and get their signatures also.

Meanwhile Miss Doren held the home front. This was the
hardest task of all. Every threat, short of physical violence,
was made to compel her to withdraw the petitions. Loud-voiced,
angry men stormed the librarian's office. They could be heard
from the adjoining offices, though Miss Doren's voice was in-
audible. She never mentioned these encounters, but we knew
about them, and we grieved for her.

I looked eagerly for the account of this campaign in the library report for 1920. There is this brief, dispassionate statement. After outlining the dilemma at the library, Miss Doren
says:

> Relief could come only through securing a larger
> tax levy for the fiscal year of 1921. . . . The issue
> was squarely faced. Due notice was published . . .
> and we set forth to explain why the stigma of a closed
> library should not be allowed to fall upon Dayton.
>
> The city, the schools, and the county were also
> seeking large funds at this time to meet their obliga-
> tions. For eight months the decision hung in the bal-
> ance. Finally, yielding to the logic of the situation
> and the widely manifested interest on behalf of the
> public as expressed through the pulpit, the press,
> and by individual petitions, the budget commission
> saw its way to granting, for the first time in five
> years, an increased budget for the immediate needs
> of the library.

As a direct result of this campaign, library funds rose from
$65,000 in 1919 to $225,000 in 1927. Thus was laid the foundation
upon which the finances of the Dayton Public Library have been
built.

In addition to the library services which I have mentioned,
Miss Doren, with Linda Eastman and William Brett, was a
founder of the Ohio Library Association, and was its president
in 1906. She was vice-president of the American Library Association; member of the ALA Executive Committee, 1917-1920;

member of the ALA Council; member of the American Library
Institute; member of the ALA War Camps Community Service
Committee, and contributor to Library Journal and Public Li-
braries.

Her philosophy of librarianship is characteristically expressed
in her address as president of the Ohio Library Association:

> To read and out of it to yield to another's need out of
> what one has himself absorbed with true understanding
> is the finest end of librarianship. The magnetism bred
> of knowing one's books and, as it were, by a finer divi-
> nation, feeling where lies the point of contact between
> them and the unspoken ways of a human soul, lies near
> to the solution of that primary problem in man's educa-
> tion and regeneration which Phillip Brooks calls "the
> problem of bringing the power of ideas to bear upon the
> will of man. . . ."
> The great discoverer in library science will be he
> who finds a fair economic basis upon which to justify
> as a part of the higher education the maintenance of
> the reading librarian resident in each library official
> from chief to messenger boy.

I would like to present some of my personal memories of
Miss Doren as an executive, and as a woman.

She was a disciplinarian. Always her staff had the feeling
that library affairs were administered by a firm hand. For the
reference and circulation staffs the dictum was "Absolute deco-
rum when before the public." Personal conversation between assistants was forbidden. "The library must present a dignified
front at all times." Concentration and absence of irrelevant conversation was expected also behind the scenes. This discipline
hurt none of us. More of it is needed in the world today. How
bitterly it is needed is seen when, with dismay, we view the
vicious and senseless crimes of vandalism perpetrated by the
undisciplined children of undisciplined parents.

Miss Doren believed in an atmosphere favorable to study
and concentration.

There are various attitudes toward silence. The Quakers
felt that it was beautiful, fruitful, and holy. To men like Thoreau
and Emerson, it was a delight. To some, like Miss Electra, the

silence in which the mind of the reader meets the mind of the author is a living thing — potent with possibilities. There is a present-day feeling among some people that libraries are not sufficiently gay. This is a problem which we may have to consider. But surely, no matter how jovial we may become, there will always be islands of refuge for those who wish to use the resources, which we gather with such thought and care, for serious study and research.

I have seen appreciation of the quiet atmosphere in the old days. I can give you a rather striking example.

When I was on reference duty, I sometimes observed a certain tall young man, with a rather stern cast of countenance. He habitually sat in the quietest corner of the reading room. He never asked for help. He knew just how to find what he wanted, and having found it, book or periodical, he read for a long time with great concentration. The only help I gave him was to see that the room was quiet. I viewed him with respect, but not sufficient respect. I did not realize that here was a man who was to become known all over the world, and who was to be the honored guest of kings and princes. If you have noted on your program that I come to you from Dayton, Ohio, you may have guessed his name — Wilbur Wright.

One of Miss Doren's most lovable qualities was her absolute and unconscious democracy. Her warmest welcome was for our humblest patrons. The same democracy extended to all members of her staff. In those days we had one janitor. He was a wiry, little man, with snapping black eyes, and the worst temper I have ever seen. But he had a knowledge of plumbing, electricity, carpentry, and building repair which made him worth many times his salary. Most of us found him pretty difficult. Miss Doren saw no difficulty at all. She had great respect for knowledge in any field.

I have a memory picture of the two of them. . . . Miss Doren is listening with absorbed and respectful attention, while Mr. X, with such courtliness as he can muster, is telling her what had "orter be done" in regard to a certain building difficulty.

This janitor had a hobby, which was fostered by Miss Doren. It was amateur photography. In his more genial moments some of us were asked to pose for him during the noon hour. On one occasion I was sent with a message to his quarters — a tiny room near the furnace. As he was not there, I looked about a bit. I was not surprised to see above his makeshift desk an enlarged, framed picture of Miss Doren.

We of the staff always felt that we were very close to Miss Doren in her thoughts, plans, and even prayers. She sought to develop the best that was possible in each of us. If discipline was necessary to do this, such discipline was forthcoming. She never scolded. Discipline was given in advice, admonition, and often unconsciously through her own force of character.

Her ideals of librarianship were joined by constant efforts to improve the education and status of the staff and to provide helpful privileges.

A first effort was the securing of a half-day off, with pay, for each one of us. Later in 1919, when the time was ripe, she established a forty-hour week. Sabbatical leave granted to staff members after ten years of service was an achievement and an innovation in library administration. It is still an innovation — and we still have it. It exists today on the lines which she established:

> Eight weeks and four days on pay to be added to the regular vacation and to be taken for extended travel or study which will increase the assistant's ability to serve the community. An additional leave is granted after five additional years of service.

Pensions were considered as early as 1916.

The Dayton Public Library Staff Association (called when organized "Friends of Reading") was formed through her advice and encouragement.

In common with every other individual on Miss Doren's staff, I have my special reasons for gratitude to her. In 1923 I was seriously ill. So ill in fact that I felt that my career at the library was ended — and possibly my career on the planet. Miss Doren came to my home to cheer and encourage me. Through the long months when I was bed-fast she held out the life line which enabled me to pull back to shore. When at last I could stand on my feet, she allowed me to work at the library two hours a day until I fully recovered. Through this privilege of feeling my way, I was finally able to give full time. Thereafter I gave full time every day for twenty years — which brings me to the present day.

Early in 1927, the situation was reversed. It was I who sat by her bedside, powerless to give her the aid which she had given to me. It was our last time together. I had brought a notebook and I took notes of the things which she wanted me to do.

She referred to her illness in only one phrase. It was a slang phrase which I think came into circulation during World War I. It was the only slang I had ever heard her use. She was distinguished always for her use of pure and beautiful English. I think she intended to lighten the moment. As I rose to leave she said: "Just one more thing. After I have gone west, I want you to give the same loyalty to the new librarian which you have given to me. The board has chosen wisely."

She died March 4th, 1927, after a lifetime devoted to library service and to the advancement of the profession. The funeral took place at Christ Episcopal Church. In the hours before the service the senior members of her staff, two at a time, in one hour intervals, stood as her honor guard.

In the years that followed we came to think of ourselves as the "Old Guard", and of her as our fearless, little Napoleon. We still preserve this tradition. Each of us has some special memories of her love and kindness and each of us, I think, is pledged to be faithful to the ideals of life and service taught us through precept, and through example, by Electra Collins Doren.

WILLIAM E. FOSTER: LIBERAL LIBRARIAN

Clarence E. Sherman

Clarence E. Sherman is Librarian Emeritus of the Providence Public Library, Providence, Rhode Island. The essay here reprinted is a paper read before the American
Library History Round Table during the Philadelphia conference of the American Library Association in 1955.

The year 1876 is a memorable division of time in the history
of our country. Torn by the War between the States, national
economic recovery had only twelve years of peaceful reconstruction and development when the panic of 1873 struck a crushing
blow. With the spirit of the rebirth of a nation, however, and
an optimistic view of economic and educational growth, a great
exposition was held in Philadelphia. It was a symbol of confidence in the future of a country only a century old, still groping
along its way toward national unity, and determined to possess
a measure of cultural development.

To librarians, 1876 and the exposition were milestones in
the progress of bibliothecal techniques and library advancement.
The report of the United States Bureau of Education on Public
Libraries in our country issued the same year, brought together
summaries and accounts of progress in the history, condition,
and management of libraries up to that time. It was an encour-
aging record of growth and achievement. Moreover, Melvil
Dewey was in the foreground with his new DECIMAL CLASSIFI-
CATION AND RELATIV INDEX, fresh from the Amherst College
Library where he had created it.

It was an appropriate time for librarians to assemble for the
exchange of experience and the renewed strength and confidence
to be gained from a gathering of kindred spirits. Moreover, it
was the first general conference since the meeting in New York
twenty-three years earlier. A total attendance of 103 persons
was recorded at Philadelphia; 33 from public libraries. Among
those present were 13 women.

Reprinted from Wilson Library Bulletin, 30:449-453+, February,
1956, by permission of the author and the publisher.

In his book, THE PUBLIC LIBRARY MOVEMENT IN THE UNITED STATES, 1853-1893, Samuel Swett Green, librarian of the Worcester Free Public Library, refers to the distinguished librarians present at Philadelphia, among them, William E. Foster, a young man of promise, who represented the Turner Free Library of Randolph, Massachusetts, and who soon was to be called to the new public library in Providence, Rhode Island.

It is interesting to observe that in the late nineteenth century, the American Library Association was developing as a learned society and many of the leaders were scholars of distinction, such as Justin Winsor, William F. Poole, Charles A. Cutter, Henry Barnard, James Whitney, Richard R. Bowker, and Melvil Dewey.

Today, with the sights of public librarians directed toward the spread of reading, yes, but instead of scholarly research, emphasis on the spread of reading for information, recreation, and popular personal education, the place of public libraries in the American scene has strolled considerably from the paths of our pioneers of 1876. Now it's less of a learned society; more of an instrument for propaganda, but propaganda for a useful purpose.

So much for the professional environment of William E. Foster as he was preparing to fill an important post in public librarianship.

But first a flashback in personal history. Mr. Foster was born in Brattleboro, Vermont, June 2, 1851. His family later moved to Beverly, Massachusetts, where he prepared for college. He entered Brown University in 1869 and immediately gave evidence of an unusual intellectual foundation for college experience, particularly in the classics. He was of a quiet, retiring, and studious nature that found satisfaction and pleasure in the university library where he spent much of his free time. Indeed, it has been said that in one of his courses which had proved to be disappointing, he "cut" all the classes he could in order to read books in which he was deeply interested, in the library.

The attention of Reuben A. Guild, the university librarian, was drawn to young Foster. As a result, he was given some work in the library as a student assistant, and when he was approaching the end of his college course, he was advised by Mr. Guild to select librarianship as a career.

WILLIAM E. FOSTER

With his degree of A.B. in hand, young Foster accepted the librarianship of the Hyde Park, Massachusetts, Public Library where he remained until 1876 when he resigned to take the position of cataloger at the Turner Free Library in near-by Randolph.

The experience in these small libraries, where he had opportunity to study at close range the working organism of a public library was excellent preparation for a position of greater responsibility and promise.

But he was not content to confine his efforts to the limited requirements of his office. He wanted to grow professionally and without delay. There was no library school to enter in those days, so he took the next step. For nearly two years, he worked on a part-time schedule in the Boston Public Library where he came under the influence of perhaps the greatest librarian of his time, Justin Winsor. This program was in addition to the young librarian's regular duties in Randolph.

In the spring of 1877, there came to Foster just the opportunity that would appeal to an able and ambitious librarian — an invitation from the trustees of a public library that was just a-borning. Providence, Rhode Island, was not numbered among the earliest of the larger American cities to establish a common collection of books for all the people of the community — a free public library. The Providence Athenaeum, a proprietary or shareholders' library, tracing its genealogical line back to the founding of the Providence Library in 1753, was until the 1870's the only collection of books serving any considerable number of readers in the community. In 1871, a charter was issued to a group of interested citizens, by the State of Rhode Island, granting authority to establish and maintain a free public library, an art gallery, and a natural history museum. Four years later, the charter was amended to include one objective only, and that was the title of the Providence Public Library.

By 1877, the board of trustees had the assurance of the gift of approximately 10,000 books, largely transfers from several expiring local societies, and funds amounting to nearly $90,000. The cataloger of the little public library in Randolph, a young man in his mid-twenties, was highly recommended by the librarians of the Boston Public Library and Brown University to move to Rhode Island and to help establish and take charge of the new Providence Public Library. He accepted the appointment and in June 1877 assumed the duties of selecting, classifying, and cataloging the library's beginning stock of books.

On February 4, 1878, the Providence Public Library, not municipally owned and operated, not of and by the people, but a library dedicated by purpose and compelled by the dictates of its charter to be a library for the people, was opened in rooms on the second floor of a downtown office building, a library with many limitations — limited book stock, limited staff, limited funds — but with a librarian of unlimited optimism and vision.

Those were days when trails were being blazed in American librarianship. A librarian with a problem had more to do than scan the printed reports of several libraries, or to send out a questionnaire when in search of advice or precedent. Like other pioneers in a new land, he had to depend largely upon himself. Little of the structure of what may now be called "public library practice and procedure" had been codified. For example, when Mr. Foster approached the classification scheme for book arrangement, he proceeded to develop one of his own. The result was a system based on a numerical basis. He later explained that had he been better acquainted with the Dewey classification and especially its future possibilities, he would not have introduced his own plan.

Two years in the first home of the library made it necessary to move to larger quarters, this time on the sidewalk level of another downtown building. There, under humble conditions, he developed the public library into an important community institution and himself into a superior librarian. He soon decided that there must be segregation of activities in order to perform the services better. And so it was that his library was one of the first to set apart a section for children.

During those years of struggle in which victory rather than defeat was the usual experience, calls came to this progressively spirited librarian to transfer his duties to other cities; but he quietly declined them all. He never lost sight of the big and exciting task that was all around him, and he had the faith to carry on. Success was achieved when, in the late 1890's, the trustees made preliminary preparations for the building of a permanent home for the library. After discouraging problems and delays, the building was at last erected and opened to the public March 15, 1900.

In design and interior plan, it attracted attention both at home and abroad. In it many of the librarian's dreams came alive, for he was able to introduce features of which he had realized the need but that were impossible to establish in the old library. So it was that the Providence Public Library became one of the first to have an information desk; an art department with material for the general reader but especially for the professional artist and the commercial designer; a music division with scores and librettos for home or studio, with a piano in the department to try out music, and later, recordings and player-equipment; an industrial department to aid the mechanics and engineers of a great manufacturing city; a foreign department to serve not only the foreign language desires of cultured readers but also the foreign-born who have so densely populated New England. He introduced an untried feature, the standard library, a browsing room of the distinguished writers of all literatures, an idea reproduced with modifications in many other libraries, a forecast of the reading lounge of today. When public libraries became centers for informal adult education a program and the position of reader's advisor were established. Providence was among the first to act. Providence was early in establishing a business branch. It is now consolidated with science and industry in the central library.

There has always been a generous supply of light recreational reading in the library and there always should be. But from the very beginning, it has been the library's policy to devote a considerable part of its funds and its energy to the encouragement, but not the enforcement, of reading that propagates ideas; reading that expands vision; reading that develops an inquiring mind; reading that a person may live by.

The birth and early growth of carefully determined special collections in the Providence Public Library are traced back to Librarian Foster's administration: architecture, civil war and slavery, jewelry, textiles and printing.

Despite all this specialized library service, the librarian never forgot the needs of the general readers. The circulation department, the reference department, and the children's room received their appropriate share of attention and development.

Meanwhile, the librarian was not introverted. He had already considered the importance of activity outside the walls of the Library and had started to make the community conscious of its library, first through his monthly reference lists which, in a later form, came to be recognized as an organ of exceptional value. With the local newspapers, he established close and friendly relations. The Providence Public Library has had an article in the Providence Journal-Bulletin weekly for more than 50 years.

In understanding the importance of a public library's contribution to the work of the public schools and in their joint efforts to develop readers of significant books, Mr. Foster was again a pioneer. The practice of every elementary schoolboy and girl visiting the public library once during their school experience for instruction in the use of the card catalog and simple reference books was begun early in Providence. A cooperative plan of operating junior and senior high school libraries was a natural result of these close associations between the Providence School Department and the Providence Public Library which is an independent incorporated institution and not a municipal department.

During his long administration, an unusual spirit of liberalism influenced the library's policies. In the selection of books, Mr. Foster was among the first to invite and encourage the reading public to suggest or recommend books for the library's shelves. His own standards of choice were marked by a finely developed taste, tempered with broad and tolerant appreciation. Although the library is not owned and operated by the city government, it was his hope that people would develop a sense of partnership in its use and growth. We still decline to add books suggested by the public with more hesitation than we do with our own recommendations.

In the rules governing the use of books, his inclinations were away from the restrictive viewpoint. Easy access to books, permitting the adult reader to borrow "any reasonable number" of volumes, lending all except new publications for a period of one month instead of the traditional two weeks, an appropriate provision for the suburban resident in need of special library service beyond the scope of the suburban library — these are just a few examples of the spirit with which Mr. Foster surveyed the library's relation to the reading public and which he never surrendered. To him there came no conservatism with old age.

To increase the opportunity to read recent publications in lively demand, a pay duplicate collection was established and defended successfully in the Superior and Supreme Courts of the State against the claim of a book dealer that a library with a pay collection, no matter how small, is not a free public library.

In a life that was devoted to the systematic completion of each day's ordinary problems and never drawn away by the lure of an occasional spectacular task, Mr. Foster had the strength and the urge to write. During his hours at the library and at home, his pen was seldom idle. Dictation to a stenographer was never a satisfying experience for him. From his pen, however, there flowed freely clearly-phrased and often beautifully expressed sentences. He carried on an unbroken correspondence with a circle of friends, personal and professional, in America and overseas. He enjoyed writing letters and they often brought joy to those who received them.

Incidentally, another means of communication that bothered him was the telephone. Even within the library, he preferred to send a note by messenger to a department or another library official. It seemed a more natural way of transmitting his message.

Mr. Foster frequently, but always painstakingly, wrote for publication both in periodicals and in books. He believed in the free use of footnotes, so much so that a friend once referred to him as "Footnote Foster". Among his most important publications are: THE CIVIL SERVICE MOVEMENT, 1881; LIBRARIES AND READERS, 1883; STEPHEN HOPKINS, A RHODE ISLAND STATESMAN, 1884; TOWN GOVERNMENT IN RHODE ISLAND, 1886; THE POINT OF VIEW IN HISTORY, 1906; HOW TO CHOOSE EDITIONS, 1912. He lectured also at the New York State Library School.

Among the societies with which he was affiliated and in which his interest was ever alive, are the American Historical Society, the American Antiquarian Society, the Rhode Island Historical Society, the Massachusetts Library Association, and the Rhode Island Library Association. Of the two last-named organizations, he was at one time President.

In 1876, Mr. Foster received the degree A.M. from Brown University, and in 1901 his alma mater honored him with the Litt.D. degree.

He was married in 1886 to Julia Appleton of Providence. They had no children but he enjoyed the reputation of being an ideal uncle.

Mr. Foster possessed personal qualities that marked him as different from most of his fellowmen and yet, because of these differences, gave him a personality all his own. He dressed with a restrained dignity and except during the summer, wore white wing-collars. Some who did not know him well, labelled him as an extreme conservative, whereas he was a spirited liberal in library matters and in many other affairs — as to prohibition, for example. A small glass of wine was perhaps the limit of his contact with liquor or liqueurs, yet he resented the law that denied him that freedom.

While always alert to bring the library and its growing resources to the attention of the community, he slipped quietly into the background when he himself was concerned. This quality of self-effacement was shown on the occasion of the library's fiftieth anniversary in 1928, when it required a personal request of the trustees committee in charge to persuade him that he must appear on the program as speaker. He said it was the library's anniversary and not his, so he should not be too prominent. When a local newspaper requested a recent photograph of him and, finding that none existed, asked him to sit for a picture in his office, again the trustees had to invoke friendly intervention.

Though deeply interested in the fiftieth anniversary of the ALA — and he spent many hours preparing an exhibit representing a feature of his library's service to art and industrial designers — he did not attend the conference. He later told the writer of this paper that as one of the few surviving members of 1876, he would receive an unnecessary amount of attention if he appeared. And so the address that he wrote for the occasion — "Five Men of '76 — Winsor, Poole, Cutter, Dewey, and Bowker" — was read by another.

His descriptive characterizations of these notable pioneers in librarianship were: Winsor — "Well balanced wisdom"; Poole — "A mellow view of life"; Cutter — "Accurate scholarship"; Dewey — "Tenacity of purpose"; Bowker — "Clear-headed perception and patient cooperation".

He had little or no interest in office-holding. He declined election as secretary of the ALA in 1891. "Besides", Mr. Foster remarked at the time, "I prefer to sleep at home in my own bed." Compulsory absence at distant cities as secretary did not appeal to him. Perhaps that also is the reason why he was never honored with the presidency of the association. The question has been asked many times.

Apart from his library duties and his home, to which he was devoted, one of his most lively interests was his correspondence with intimate friends and his beloved collection of the works of Horace, with which he spent many happy hours.

And yet he played, and when he did, he played with the same analytical thoroughness with which he worked. His favorite outdoor recreation was walking, either through the busy streets of Providence or along the beautiful country roads of New Hampshire and up the trails of Mount Chocorua, in whose shadow he spent his vacation for many years. And as he walked, he moved along with every faculty he possessed actively alert. For he observed, studied, and thought about nearly everything that came within his range — people, houses, foliage, the sky in all its shades and color; and when he reached home it was often to follow up his simple adventure by dipping into a book that informed him as to the history of or the reason for something he had seen.

He also was fond of play-reading. As a member of a dramatic reading club, his efforts were frequently outstanding on account of his rare ability of interpretation, especially in the delineation of character parts.

A liberal education is attainable by several routes: through the classroom, by the reading of important books, by intelligent travel, or by association with a man like William E. Foster. Though reserved in manner and never one who could be called hail-fellow-well-met, scattering his friendship like handbills wherever he went, to those who knew him well he was one of the most rewarding companions that we are privileged to meet along life's highway.

Mr. Foster assumed charge of 10,000 books in limited drab quarters, with an income amounting to less than $10,000 a year. Aided and encouraged by a loyal board of trustees, who slowly added to those resources, he developed a library system which, when he retired, was composed of a collection of nearly 400,000 books, housed in the central library and twelve branches, with a book storage stack in one branch supplying space for more than 150,000 less-called-for books from central. The total annual circulation exceeded 1,300,000 books to 80,000 registered borrowers.

During his years as librarian, gifts and bequests exceeding $3,000,000 were received, impressive testimony to the approval of the library by the community.

When he laid aside his duties as Librarian in February 1930 and was honored with the title of Librarian Emeritus for Life, he had the rare distinction of having been the organizer of a public library but also its directing force for nearly fifty-three years, a record perhaps unequalled in the library history of our country. During his service to Providence, the institution became not only one of the vital informational, recreational, and educational influences in the community, but the vision of the librarian in the introduction of new practices and services, and the success with which older methods were improved, brought to the library and its librarian a reputation known across our continent and also across the Atlantic.

The blending of his fine qualities of scholarship with a practical sense of the importance of popularizing the use of the printed page by a city's heterogeneous population, ranging in reading appreciation from the child with a picture book to the intellect of the mature scholar, was possessed by him in an unusual combination. To William E. Foster, an inquiring mind and a book appropriate for that mind constituted one of life's happiest unions, and his long career was devoted to the task of bringing those elements together.

One of his contemporaries, Dr. Harry L. Koopman, librarian of Brown University, said of Mr. Foster:

> A superb university librarian was lost to fame when he dedicated his abilities to public library work. He is by nature a scholar. He is as much interested in the deepening, as in the diffusion of knowledge.

As the Providence Public Library left his hands, it was not a mere structure of bricks and mortar surrounding a collection of books, nor simply "a monument of vanished minds". It was a seat of learning for all the people of a great city, and a living memorial to the achievement of a clear thinker, a tireless worker, a notable librarian.

Mr. Foster retired in February 1930 and died in September of the same year.

Several months later, an informal ceremony, just as Mrs. Foster desired it, was held in the lobby of the central library where a handsome bronze tablet, designed and cast by Gorham of Providence, was unveiled:

WILLIAM E. FOSTER

To
William Eaton Foster
1851-1930
First Librarian
of the Providence
Public Library
1877 to 1930
He Created This Library
He Founded Its Traditions
He Gave It Worldwide
Influence

RECOLLECTIONS OF JOSEPHINE ADAMS RATHBONE

Nordica Fenneman

Nordica Fenneman is Chief, General Circulation Department of the Chicago Public Library, Chicago, Illinois. The essay here reprinted is from a paper read before the American Library History Round Table during the Midwinter meeting of the American Library Association in Chicago in 1949.

When the program of this conference arrived, one of my younger colleagues in the library said to me: "I see your name in the program — tell me, who is Josephine Adams Rathbone?" I was reminded of an interview with Somerset Maugham which appeared in a New York Times Book Review. Answering the question, "Why do writers write?" he said: "Some write for fame, which is a mistake. Fame is a will o' the wisp, here today, gone tomorrow. I've known a number of authors who were quite sure of their immortality. They're now, every one of them, alas, quite dead." And so I suppose I should not have been surprised that a young librarian did not know who Miss Rathbone was, for she devised no system or tool which made her name a library byword — as Cutter and Dewey and Poole — and she died eight years ago. Her influence as a pioneer trail blazer lives on, nevertheless.

I doubt that fame mattered very much to Miss Rathbone. She enjoyed the honors which came to her, to be sure, but personal ambition was not her motivating force. Faith in public libraries was; and the goal to which she directed all of her energies and all of her abilities for forty-five years was the training of young people to become effective instruments in the development of the public library movement.

Miss Rathbone was truly a pioneer in the history of the American library school, for she came to Pratt shortly after its founding when she graduated from the New York State Library School in 1893, first to work in the library, then in 1895 to teach in the library school under the direction of Mary Wright Plum-

Reprinted from Wilson Library Bulletin, 23:773-774, June, 1949, by permission of the author and the publisher.

mer. When Miss Plummer left in 1911, Miss Rathbone became
the executive and continued in that office until her retirement in
1938. Her achievements are a matter of record. Her philosophy
of librarianship is ably set forth in her presidential address,
"Creative Librarianship", before the New Orleans conference.
Her views on library school curricula appear in various library
periodicals where all who will may find them. These may still
be read with profit. I wish simply to tell you how she appeared
to me when I was her student. My impressions are general rather than particular, for it was a long time ago, and incidents I
remember are only those in which I was personally concerned.

The first time I saw Miss Rathbone was shortly before the
term started when I went to introduce myself to her, for I had
been admitted to the class without personal interview. She was
seated at her desk when I was announced — a small, trim, tailored figure, light brown hair dressed simply over a high forehead, rather plain looking but of distinguished presence. She
looked up from some papers as I entered, flicked off her pince-
nez with a movement of her nose which sent them flying to the
limits of the black cord she wore about her neck (a mannerism
with which I was to become very familiar), and scrutinized me
frankly. After a brief exchange she asked me where I was stay-
ing. I told her I was living in Greenwich Village with a former
student of hers, happily unconscious of the fact that this same
student, a rebel by nature, had been an enfant terrible while at
Pratt. Miss Rathbone was not pleased. She scented danger, and
she acted with characteristic promptitude to dispatch it. "You
had better move to Brooklyn", she said. I recognized command —
and I did!

We stood in considerable awe of her at first. We were to
learn that she had great social charm, but in her school relationships she was businesslike and brisk, and she knew how to
keep a proper distance between teacher and student. We realized at once that no nonsense would be brooked; we were there
to get all we could in our brief year, and a high standard of performance was expected of us, or else — ! No idle threat — for
before two weeks had passed one of our number was dropped.
As the year progressed and we came to know Miss Rathbone,
we found her warmly human and helpful when we took our problems to her. We called her "Josie" among ourselves, a sign of
affection, for we held her in highest respect.

We were a small class, as is traditional at Pratt — only twenty-four — so she knew us as individuals, was alert to the needs and abilities of each, and addressed herself to their fulfillment or development as the case was. She was a born teacher, and we were fortunate in that she taught many of the courses herself — library history, administration, reference, book evaluation — and presided over a weekly session in current events.

These courses are a blur to me now, but one thing I have kept, because it was instilled continuously through the year: that the essence of librarianship is the bringing together of book and reader in a vital relationship — knowing books and understanding people is primary, all other aspects of our work are secondary to that. Miss Rathbone did not believe in passive librarianship. She urged the study of social trends and movements, and an aggressive alliance with all the constructive forces in our communities, quite in accordance with the thought of today.

It was characteristic of her that she did not confine her guidance of us to the classroom. In her eagerness to make us socially minded, and to broaden our horizons she impressed upon us the importance of making the most of our opportunities while we were in New York, and she saw to it that we did — by inviting us to attend lectures with her at the Rand School of Social Studies, giving us tickets to symphony concerts at the Academy, suggesting that we attend a certain political meeting where La Guardia would speak, informing us of exhibitions and book auctions, arranging expeditions to the East Side, Brownsville, and elsewhere, with dinner afterwards in foreign and inexpensive restaurants (for she was ever mindful of our slim purses), tea at her club, the Cosmopolitan of New York. If there were "provincials" left at the end of the year it was not Miss Rathbone's fault. We were her "flock" and she watched over us, guided us, molded us — directly, in the classroom, and in other ways of which we were not aware at the time.

No one could be associated with Miss Rathbone for any length of time without being broadened and stimulated by her. I have heard a well known New York editor say of her that she had the finest brain of any woman she knew. Combined with breadth of mind were force, progressiveness, enthusiasm, and human understanding. This was Josephine Adams Rathbone as I knew her.

She was seventy-four when she retired from Pratt and went to live in Augusta, Georgia, at her mother's old home. And when I tell you that she bought an automobile and learned to drive it you may see that she was a woman of still youthful eagerness for new experiences, and of mental vigor to effect them.

This paper I am about to read takes me back to our spring field trip visiting libraries in Pennsylvania. We knew her very well by then and, away from the school, we were on a more informal basis — in fact, she acted as one of us. Nights, after dinner, we gathered in her hotel room, spilling over the bed and the floor, and talked, or listened to Miss Rathbone read poetry, which she did very well. And sometimes she used to tell her recollections of library personages very much as she has set them down here for the class of 1939 [in her lecture "Pioneers of the Library Profession", the next paper in this volume].

PIONEERS OF THE LIBRARY PROFESSION

Josephine Adams Rathbone

> Josephine Adams Rathbone (1864-1941) gave the essay here
> reprinted as a lecture in October, 1938, to the Class of
> 1939, Pratt Institute Library School, Brooklyn, New York.
> In 1949 Nordica Fenneman shared her "Recollections of
> Josephine Adams Rathbone" with the American Library
> History Round Table, and closed her talk by reading Miss
> Rathbone's lecture.

The term is a relative one. When I first entered the profession, the pioneers were the founders of the A.L.A., who were
for the most part those who had been active librarians in the
decades of the '60's and '70's. Gradually the date was pushed
forward to include the leaders of the formative period, say from
1876 to 1906. I was first aware of this change of point of view
when I beheld myself referred to in print as a pioneer librarian,
and doubtless the time will come when the class of 1939 will be
so classified by its successors.

But for the purpose of this talk I shall consider only a few
of those who came on the scene before the turn of the century.
As a member of the Albany class of 1893, I arrived early enough
to know many of the real pioneers, Winsor, Poole, Dewey, Cutter, Bowker, etc., some only by sight or with a bowing acquaintance, others well, over a long period of years, while the later
comers, like John Cotton Dana and Herbert Putnam, were my
contemporaries in library service if not in years. The order in
which I shall consider them is arbitrary — that of my own thoughts
as I look back over the years, and note those that stand out most
vividly. So I shall begin with Melvil Dewey (1851-1931), who was
the youngest of the big four who started the A.L.A.

Mr. Dewey was primarily an organizer, secondarily an educator, rather than a book-man. I won't say he never read, but
I never remember hearing him speak of a book. He went into librarianship because he saw in it a chance to organize a new pro-

Reprinted from <u>Wilson Library Bulletin</u>, 23:775-779, June, 1949, by
permission of the publisher.

fession, one that had great educational potentialities, and presented an expanding field both within and without for the exercise of his organizing genius: within, for with the enormous expansion of book production that followed the development of popular education in this country from 1820 to 1870, the older rigid systems of classification and library economy were breaking down, unequal to coping with the rising tide of books, and the library extension of the twentieth century was made possible by the technical improvements of the last quarter of the nineteenth century, in flexible classification schemes, card catalogs, and standard cataloging rules in the development of which Melvil Dewey bore an important part; without, he was also preeminently a starter. In addition to and more important than his contribution to the efficient internal organization of libraries, Mr. Dewey did more for the extension of library facilities than any man of his generation. His was the primary impulse that started the A.L.A.; he founded the first library school; the New York Library Club; the first state library association — these last while still librarian of Columbia University. As librarian of the New York State Library, he developed what is now called the Library Extension Division, i. e., the commission, with its powers of inspection, and of setting and maintaining library standards throughout the state; he developed traveling libraries as means of stimulating the establishment of new libraries and of serving communities too small to maintain libraries.

Among his other interests were spelling reform and the metric system, and the work to which he devoted the last years of his life, the Lake Placid Clubs in the Adirondacks and in Florida. He was the initiating and organizing genius of the profession; once an idea was conceived and launched, Mr. Dewey was off on a new scheme. He did not work out the details of the D.C.; that was done by the quiet scholar, Walter T. Biscoe, his classmate, who lived all his life in Mr. Dewey's shadow, content to do the careful plodding detailed work necessary to bring Mr. Dewey's plans to fruition. Mr. Biscoe taught classification when I was at Albany and I have cheered generations of Pratt students by a remark of his, "The harder a book is to classify the less important it is where you put it."

As a personality Mr. Dewey was dynamic and to some people magnetic. People either liked him enough to be willing to be led by him, or they disliked him with a profound and abiding aversion.

He was dominating, ruthless when opposed, a fighter always, yet capable of generosity and great kindness. His faults were on the same scale as his effective qualities, and unfortunately they grew on him. He went on the theory that he meant to do right, he did what he meant to do, and therefore, what he did was right. But not all his contemporaries accepted his premises, and their conclusions were often very different from his. So his influence waned, his enemies increased, and about 1910 he dropped out of library work to devote himself to the Lake Placid Club.

Mr. Dewey had not a wide range of ideas, his library philosophy was formed early and through repetition it crystalized into a formula. When I was a junior in the library school I used to hear the seniors complain that his lectures, which the whole school had to attend, and which the juniors found inspiring, were just the same as those they had heard the year before. In 1926 he was the speaker at the opening of the Columbia Library School. Our school was invited and on the way over the students asked what he was to talk about. "I don't know what his announced subject is, but I think I can tell you some of the things he will say," I said, and sure enough he did.

In contrast to Mr. Dewey, Charles Ammi Cutter (1837-1903) was a scholar, a bibliographer, and a bookman. He also devised a classification, working it out carefully and painstakingly. It was never finished, and knowing Mr. Cutter, I doubt that it ever could have been had he lived to be a hundred years old, for his was a flexible mind and he never objected to doing work over again if it could be improved thereby. He would have discovered ways to improve the E.C. as long as he lived. The catalog he made of the Boston Athenaeum Library, of which he was librarian for many years (1868-1894), was one of the two or three great bibliographical tools produced in this country in the nineteenth century, the Peabody and the Surgeon General's medical library catalogs being the other two, while Cutter's RULES FOR A DICTIONARY CATALOG has been the basis for cataloging and alphabeting codes from 1876 to date. The author table for the assigning of "Cutter numbers" has made his name generally known.

But Mr. Cutter as a man was greater than his works. A gentle but humorous spirit with a deep love of the outdoors, a redoubtable mountain climber, and a tireless dancer, he never took himself seriously but was always ready to join in any fun

that was going. I remember dancing with him several times at
A.L.A. meetings, a pleasure that was somewhat tempered, however, by his oversprightliness — he hopped, in fact.

Mr. Cutter was slender, wiry, with keen but nearsighted
twinkling eyes, and a long pointed nose. There were those who
declared that the hole in the catalog card was made for the point
of it, so close to his eyes did he hold his work. He was the most
indefatigable of workers, nothing was too much trouble for him.
Years ago, when I was getting up a course in the Cutter classification for the school, I had much correspondence with him, and
used to get long letters written in his own spidery hand, eluci-
dating points I had found obscure or doubtful.

William F. Poole (1821-1894) was librarian of the Boston
Athenaeum, 1856-1869; of the Cincinnati Public Library, 1871-
1873; of the Chicago Public Library, 1874-1887; of the Newberry
Library, 1887-1894. Just as Mr. Cutter is known to the present
generation of librarians by his rules and numbers, and Mr. Dewey by the D.C., so is the name of Poole synonymous with Index,
though Poole's Index was very far from the measure of Mr.
Poole's achievements or his personality. Indeed it was an undergraduate activity while a student at Yale, resulting from his effort to supply the demands for debating material, that came to
him as librarian of a literary society. He kept up a periodical
index started by his predecessor, John Edmands, himself later
librarian of the Mercantile Library of Philadelphia, and a founder of the A.L.A. Mr. Poole found the material so useful that he
finally printed a small edition in 1848; this soon exhausted, a
second edition followed, 1853, which again went out of print;
and there the matter rested until the organization of the A.L.A.
in 1876, when Poole's Index was made a cooperative activity.

Mr. Poole went into library work on graduating from college
and had become one of the two or three leading librarians of the
country by 1876. He was a scholar, a true bookman, who looked
with distrust on such short-cuts to librarianship as library
schools, and who was so strongly opposed to discarding outworn
books or to that "weeding out" process that after one A.L.A.
meeting at which he had been especially vehement in his expressions, a group of twenty-five or so of the younger members sent
him a copy of the old Farmer's Almanac. The records do not
show what became of them!

Mr. Poole was a good deal of a lady's man, and at a time

when women, like children, were seen but not heard. Mr. Bowker used to tell us of seeing some of the older women pluck him
by the sleeve and ask him to express their sentiments for them.
For the library world was in the beginning distinctly a man's
world. There were women in the A.L.A. from the first, and they
were allowed to serve on committees and gradually they appeared on the programs of the meetings, but there was no woman
president for over thirty years, and indeed there have been only
six in the sixty-two years of the association's life.

Justin Winsor (1831-1897), librarian of the Boston Public Library (1868-1877), and of Harvard University (1877-1897), was
the shining light of the profession in 1876, though I fancy today
he is less well known than any other of the big four. Students of
American history and cartography have seen references to his
NARRATIVE AND CRITICAL HISTORY without perhaps realizing
that he was a librarian at all. But so important was he in the beginning that he was president of the A.L.A. for ten consecutive
terms, and his name and prestige did much to establish the professional standing of librarianship. Mr. Winsor was a large,
fine-looking, dignified man — today he might be called pompous —
with whom no one (not even, I am sure, his wife and daughter)
ever took liberties. Of him as a human being, I have no knowledge. I never danced or went hiking with him; never, indeed,
ventured to address him (and one would address rather than talk
with him), though I had known his daughter and we had a very
intimate mutual friend.

John Cotton Dana (1856-1929) was both a great creative force
and a severe, almost a debunking, critic — a very unusual combination — and the most stimulating and interesting personality
of his time. As librarian of the Denver, Springfield, and Newark
libraries, he left the stamp of that personality imperishable on
those three communities. It is said that when fishermen want to
keep a barrel of herring alive they put in it a catfish, which by
its pugnacity and energy keeps the whole barrelful stirred up,
alive and active. John Cotton Dana always reminded me of that
catfish.

Nothing or nobody ever stagnated while he was around. New
ideas flowed from him in inexhaustible abundance. His staffs
were kept on their toes every minute of the time and in consequence they adored him. Nor was he one who wanted to do it all
himself; he bred ideas in others. If any of his staff had sugges-

tions, he encouraged them to go ahead and try them out, even if he himself doubted the results. Pretense or complacency withered in his presence. I never forgot his saying to me soon after I was appointed instructor in the school, "Do you ever find it hard to keep the class from discovering how much you don't know?" My answer, "No, for I don't try", seemed to satisfy him for his only reply was a grin. If you want to experience his quality for yourselves, read his books.

In nothing has our profession been more fortunate than in the fact that the Librarian of Congress for the past forty years was Herbert Putnam (born 1861). He is a man of a very large world, so large that the fact that he is a scholar (I have heard him preside over an international meeting and introduce French, German, and Italian delegates each in his own language), a diplomat, a statesman, and a gentleman, are merely component parts of his many-sided personality. He established the Library of Congress, which before his term of office was an unorganized, heterogeneous mass of books and pamphlets, used chiefly — and with difficulty — by members of Congress, into one of the greatest national libraries in the world, and the most effective.

Mr. Dewey fought to get his way. Mr. Putnam gained his by courtesy, modesty, charm, and persuasiveness. Now that he has retired, it is to be hoped he will write his memoirs. They would be of the utmost value to librarians as a concrete example of how to get things done without friction.

But, as I said before, there were women in the library profession, and the public library movement owes much to their devoted but too often unmarked, self-sacrificing labors. One of the first to gain recognition was our own Mary Wright Plummer (1851-1916). A graduate of the first class of the first library school, she was appointed librarian of Pratt Institute in 1891, and director of the school in 1895. Miss Plummer was a poet (VERSES, 1896) and an author (CONTEMPORARY SPAIN AS SHOWN BY HER NOVELISTS, 1899, and the "Roy and Ray" books of travel for children); she wrote the first elementary treatise on library procedure, HINTS TO SMALL LIBRARIES, which went through four editions and was translated into Russian. She was a fine linguist, and a discriminating reader, whose SEVEN JOYS OF READING has proved stimulating to many. As a woman she had great charm, and a host of friends, though her Quaker upbringing resulted in a reserve that made casual contact difficult for her. She was the second woman A.L.A. president, 1915-1916.

Theresa West Elmendorf (1855-1932) became a librarian in 1877, was made deputy librarian of the Milwaukee Public Library in 1880, and in 1892 was elected librarian, the first woman librarian of a large public library. In 1896 she married H. L. Elmendorf, librarian of the Buffalo Public Library, and after his death in 1906, she was made assistant librarian. She was elected president of the A.L.A. in 1911, the first woman so honored.

Children's work owes much to two women of the earlier generation. Long before children's rooms were heard of, Caroline Hewins, librarian of the Hartford, Connecticut, Public Library, bought books for the younger children and encouraged their use of the library at a time when most libraries had an age limit of twelve to fourteen years. She also compiled and annotated many lists of children's books on which the libraries depended for book selection for many years. Mrs. Hewins had the rare gift of writing just as she talked, and when I read anything of hers, even her condensed book notes, I can hear her voice distinctly.

Milwaukee, under Miss West (Mrs. Elmendorf), was one of the first libraries to abolish the age limit and a report on children and libraries, made by Miss Stearns at the 1894 A.L.A. Conference, made so deep an impression that age limits were abolished all over the country and children's rooms began to open like corn in a popper. Our own, opened in 1896, was, as you may have been told, the first room to be part of the original plan of a building.

So, there were giants in those days — and I believe that impression is not merely a delusion of perspective. I am sure that when the time is ripe for the development of a new movement in government, in religion, in science, or in education, indeed in any of the important fields of human activity, great men will be found to do the creative work necessary. After that is done, lesser men will carry on, while the great creative spirits of the succeeding age will be, as O'Shaughnessy says, "Afar with the dawning and the suns that are not yet high". So librarianship may never again see such a group of truly great men as in its first decades, but they have left us a splendid inheritance it is up to us to develop and further.

JOSEPHINE ADAMS RATHBONE

Wayne Shirley

Wayne Shirley is Librarian of Finch College in New York
City. The essay here reprinted is a paper read before the
American Library History Round Table during the 1959 conference of the American Library Association in Washington, D.C.

Josephine Adams Rathbone was born in Jamestown, New
York, September 10, 1864 and she died in Augusta, Georgia,
May 17, 1941. She studied at the University of Michigan from
1887 to 1891, but she never received a degree from that institution. She graduated from the New York State Library School
in 1893 with the degree of B.L.S. In that same year she was appointed to the staff of the Pratt Institute Free Library as assistant cataloger. According to the account in White's CONSPEC-
TUS she was appointed "chief instructor" in the Pratt Institute
Library School under Mary Wright Plummer. When Miss Plummer went to the New York Public Library to establish its Training Class, Miss Rathbone was appointed vice-director of the library school, a position she held until she retired on June 30,
1938. I shall deal with Miss Rathbone as vice-director, as a
teacher, and as a person.

The account in White's CONSPECTUS was furnished by Miss
Rathbone herself. Generations of library school students had
tried to find out how old she was, but without result. Finally an
assistant in the reference department of the Pratt Institute Free
Library stumbled onto the account in White's CONSPECTUS
about 1932-1933. Miss Rathbone was president of ALA in 1931-
1932. This account is interesting because in it Miss Rathbone
stressed her Colonial and New England forebears, while she
more commonly spoke of her "southern heritage".

The simplest method of presenting Miss Rathbone in this
capacity is to follow her procedures with a given class from application to the award of certificate, but some explanation must

Reprinted from Wilson Library Bulletin, 34:199-204, November,
1959, by permission of the author and the publisher.

first be given of the setting in which Miss Rathbone operated.

Pratt Institute was founded by Charles Pratt, one of the original partners of John D. Rockefeller, and hence a man of very great wealth indeed. Mr. Pratt made many studies of education, and in 1887 he established Pratt Institute to carry his ideas into practice. One sidelight of his studies may be given. His grandson told me that Charles Pratt went to Russia to make a further study of education in that country, and to help him make his point he presented the Czar of Russia with a Catalog of Pratt Institute. This catalog reported that the institute was founded as "a school where young men and women could receive the training that he [Charles Pratt] had been unable to find in his youth; and because he realized what was needed, he planned with rare understanding and foresight". This was shortened in ordinary conversation with the remark that Pratt was founded to help boys and girls to earn a better living. Charles Pratt was referred to always as "the Founder" and many Pratt people remember the short pause after speaking those words, which was characteristic of the long-timers at Pratt.

Charles Pratt appointed his oldest son, Charles M. Pratt as president, another son, Frederic B. Pratt as secretary — executive officer, that is — and his four other sons as trustees. Mr. Pratt died soon after the opening of the institute, but his ideas were carried out, as his sons met shortly after his death to set down what their father had in mind about the institute. Charles M. Pratt was soon stricken with a grave illness, so Frederic B. Pratt succeeded as president, a position he held, enjoyed, and graced for some fifty years. There are many today who recall with pleasure that man of infinite courtesy and charm who resembled President Eliot of Harvard in appearance. In due course Charles Pratt followed his father as president, and he followed his father also in the affections of all Pratt people. His sister is Mrs. Christian Herter, wife of the Secretary of State.

So, the president and trustees were all Pratts, except for Dr. Frank Babbott who is the son of Charles Pratt's only daughter. Mr. Pratt once remarked that all trustees had names ending in two T's. Thus all of Miss Rathbone's time at Pratt Institute was spent under the administration of this benign family. Some called it feudalism, but it was delightful while it lasted. Frederic B. Pratt and his son would take a Mediterranean cruise, or some other long trip during the year, thus leaving the direct-

JOSEPHINE ADAMS RATHBONE

ors of the institute's four schools very much to themselves. If
there was a deficit the trustees would say, "We'll take care of
it." The schools got together to graduate on the same day, but
otherwise they operated more as four separate entities. There
was no central direction, and hence no administrative overhead.
Certainly the library students got through their courses with only a dim idea of the schools "across the street".

The director of the library school was Edward F. Stevens,
and this was a continuing irritant, for the trustees recognized
Mr. Stevens as the head of the school, while the students and
the graduates thought of Miss Rathbone as the head. This situation was not at all unusual as the following anecdote makes clear:

The state librarian, James I. Wyer, was at Pratt one day to
give his annual lecture. He met Mr. Stevens in the hall, and remarked in his genial manner, "Are you as much of a fifth wheel
here as I am at Albany?" Mr. Stevens received the geniality
with doubtful pleasure. But it is a fact that most of the old-time
library schools were run by women.

To put the matter plainly, Mr. Stevens and Miss Rathbone had
nothing in common save the jobs they held. These two Victorians
would now and again address each other in strained voices, but
they never showed their feeling otherwise. Miss Rathbone would
say of her difficulties in this relationship, "It's good discipline",
but I was to learn later that Mr. Stevens was indeed a long-suffer-
ing man. I once heard him say he had allowed Miss Rathbone to
have the title of "vice-director" and since "vice" means "in place
of", he had to put up with the consequences.

And now for Miss Rathbone on the job as vice-director. She
would "make up the class" each June a few days before graduation. After the graduation ceremonies were over she would go
directly to her apartment not to return to her office until a week
or so before the opening of school in September.

May I now ask a rhetorical question of any library school officers? Would you like to run a library school in the city of New
York, with a limit of twenty-five students — all full time — and
all taking the same courses, with the nearest library schools
in Albany or in Philadelphia? Also, many of your students would
not have a degree, but they would have had considerable experience, and they would be admitted only on passing a stiff examination. And since there were no Canadian library schools at the
time, you would have from four to six Canadian students in the

class. No wonder Pratt turned out class after class of first-rate librarians who could do anything in a library, for Miss Rathbone could choose one from four applications. What library school can do that today?

Something should be said about the Pratt examination, for it was famous in the profession. I remember once Keyes Metcalf told me he had taken it, and was proud that he had passed it. The examination was of the essay type, and here are some typical questions.

What American and English writers have been greatly influenced by Flaubert, Dostoyevsky, Chekhov, and Ibsen. Cite specific titles in illustration.

What is the significance of the following and if possible the derivation:

A Roland for an Oliver
Pyrrhic victory
Hobson's choice
Jacobites
Chinese Gordon
Yahoo

Plus ten similar questions covering all fields of literature, history and current events.

Miss Rathbone's duties included the introduction of the visiting lecturers, all of whom were persons prominent in the field. After the introduction, Miss Rathbone would go to the back of the classroom, sit down, and at once begin removing imaginary pieces of lint from her skirt while the lecture continued. But when Miss Mudge came to speak things were different. Miss Mudge would say, "You have heard this before, so you need not stay." Miss Rathbone would march out happily. "March" is the proper word, for that is the way she walked. I can see her to this day advancing with that steady step, and stopping to look a person up and down before beginning to speak.

Pratt was then on the three-term system. Examinations came along and everyone passed. And the big event of the year was the spring trip.

This expedition was compulsory, and many are the tales surrounding it, as class after class went to New England, the Philadelphia area, or up and around Albany. Here also Miss Rathbone was the star of the act. The object was to get her back to Brooklyn without losing her fur piece, her umbrella, or her rubbers, and the whole class took a hand in this. Once the fur piece did seem to be lost but Miss Rathbone calmly told the class that it was of little consequence because her good fur piece was in storage and the lost one of little value.

During the spring placement came to the fore. True, during the year Miss Rathbone had been reading to the class letters describing positions, and it was notable that in those days many of the positions were opportunities to start new libraries. But placement was made official by an interview with Miss Rathbone which all of the class must undergo. The only exceptions were those who had jobs, and since I was among this number, I escaped the ordeal. For "ordeal" it was for some, for Miss Rathbone called attention to each student's weak as well as strong points.

So the year ended, all received their certificates, and Miss Rathbone made out their official records. These were on folio sheets, on the verso of which she wrote her opinion of the student in question. These opinions were fantastically accurate, and they often contained judgments with a strong feminine overtone. Thus of one graduate she wrote, "has taste, but no style". Her letters placing students also were models, and they were filled with such good library phrases as "is a strong person", and they contained wise saws as "has the defects of her virtues".

No account of Miss Rathbone would be complete without mention of her secretary for many years, Justine E. Day. Miss Day's desk faced Miss Rathbone's. Both desks were of the rolltop vintage so that the light in Miss Day's corner must have been very bad. But there Miss Day, who was lame, sat and graced the room by her presence. She knew us all and she loved us all. Her warm and lovely smile is still a dearly-held memory by all Pratt students who knew her.

A digression seems necessary here to give some account of "practice work", which was basic in the curriculum of Pratt for many years. "Practice work" meant assignment to duties in the Pratt Institute Free Library, where such redoubtable department heads as Miss Husted, Miss MacKenzie, Miss Woodruff, and Mr. Hendry took us in charge. Also, we had order work with Miss Roy (delightful memory), and mending and marking with Mrs. Carlin. Thus Pratt students shared in all operations of a public library of some 150,000 volumes.

Like all students we used to say the great advantage of working at Pratt was knowing how a thing should <u>not</u> be done. We said also that we were "exploited", and we were, but to only a slight degree, for all the staff of the library were interested in us, and they all made us welcome. The experience was excellent, for we worked in a library where things were done thoroughly, no corners cut, and record-making so complete that work could be passed from one person to another without a break.

Instruction was given by Mr. Stevens in the graphic arts, in which field he was a recognized expert. He had a fine collection of books from private presses, he had the best of taste in such matters, and he kept up to date with the field. Mr. Stevens even published a book — Trollope's THE WARDEN. He tried to get the backing of ALA but was not successful, so he persuaded F. B. Pratt to underwrite the enterprise. And so THE WARDEN, printed for libraries, came out as an example of a well-made and well-bound book. There must be many copies of this book where Pratt people have been, and it is a fact that Mr. Stevens paid Mr. Pratt in full, and I understand he even made a small profit for his library in the transaction.

Edith P. Bucknam taught cataloging and she taught it well. True many cards had to be made, and it was our ambition to get cards back with no red ink on them, rarely realized in my own case. But when Miss Bucknam was through, a Pratt student could sit down in front of a pile of books, and go to work on them. Can present-day students do this? Miss Bucknam was a personality in her own right, even though she labored in Miss Rathbone's shadow, and she never stinted any effort in our behalf. She was a Christian Scientist, and she followed the beliefs of her faith with such strictness, she would not wear glasses although it meant bending low to read many a page. In later years she was ravaged by disease, but she never quailed and worked until she could no longer make it. Bless her memory. She was a fine teacher, and a sound person. She was on the conservative side, so we had to learn to write "library hand" lest some future typewriter break down, I assume! I cannot write it now, but for a while my handwriting actually was legible.

And now for Miss Rathbone. She gave <u>all</u> the instruction in book selection, fiction seminar, reference work, bibliography, questions of the day — which we called current events — survey of the field, classification, and she gave part of the instruction in library administration.

These course titles are self-explanatory, save survey of the field. This was oral reporting by each student on some of her reading in the library literature. Miss Rathbone used to say that if one did not enjoy reading her professional literature, she was in the wrong profession, but in those days there was something of a literary flavor in professional writing, rather than the management, public relations, and government appeals which we have with us today. Also, it did us good to have to stand on our feet and speak on what we had read.

Miss Rathbone certainly spared the people who made up the mimeographed assignment sheets, for they were so worn, and so festooned with added titles and notes they were legible only by close inspection, but when it came to the verbal part of her teaching, she was a master. She knew how to use humor, and since all classes were one year only, she learned which jokes had mileage in them. Thus in classification she would put a book in one classification, and the next time the class met she would put the same book in a different classification. We would call her attention to the change triumphantly, and Miss Rathbone would say, "But that was the last time. Today I feel differently." Thus she made the point that classification is an art, and not a science.

Her discipline was good, although strict, one of her potent weapons being to look the offender up and down. One incident I do remember. A student was giving a book talk, and the girl in front of Miss Rathbone's desk chose that unpropitious moment to write a note to pass to the classmate in back of her. Miss Rathbone knew what was going on, and so did we, as we looked on in frozen horror of the catastrophe that would soon take place. When the proper moment came to lower the boom, Miss Rathbone said, "You may pass the note back, now." All of us were uncomfortable save the lucky student who was reciting and so had been mindful of only her own difficulties!

All teachers have their personal traits, and here also Miss Rathbone excelled, for hers were spectacular. The most common habit was dropping her glasses when sitting at her desk. She always wore pince-nez glasses on a black ribbon. She was extremely nearsighted, so when she wished to read a page she

would wiggle her nose, and down banged the glasses on the desk.
They never broke. Then, when she wanted to look at the class
again, she would put her glasses on very firmly with both hands.

Miss Rathbone's greatest interests were literature, political
affairs, and the theater. Her knowledge of literature was ency-
clopedic, and it included the literature of the day. The richness
of this background, plus her never-failing interest in libraries
and the people who worked in them certainly entitle her to rank
as one of the greatest of library school teachers. She seemed
remote to the students, who never called her anything but Miss
Rathbone, but when these students became graduates, they knew
always that Miss Rathbone followed their careers with the greatest interest.

Miss Rathbone was a great reader. She read all her life, and
in all places. She was a great traveler and wrote a book about
travel, VIEWPOINTS OF TRAVEL, which ALA published in its
"Viewpoints" series. She was a liberal in politics, and she once
told me that now and again she would drop The Nation or the New
Republic but she would find that she had to have them both again.

Her liberalism extended to people in the mass only. I remember her indignation, which she expressed to the class, when
some coal miners were arrested for singing hymns in their union hall, but her liberalism never extended to voting anything
but the Democratic ticket. She was not one to conceal her dislike
of a person, nor did she fail to hold pretty rigid standards in
regard to conduct. Once Mrs. Shirley and I took her on a trip to
Canada, where we found a fellow-American just over the border
who was trying to drown his loneliness in one too many — Maine
at that time being a prohibition state. This individual approached
us, only to have Miss Rathbone really freeze his advances with
a look. Also, in racial matters, she reflected strongly her southern heritage.

Miss Rathbone dressed well, tailored suits being her specialty. Her only odd article of dress was her white canvas shoes,
which Charles Pratt told me of seeing her wearing when she
came to work on Monday mornings.

Miss Rathbone had a group of intimates among the graduates
whom she called "her public". There were not many, and these
few were invited to come to New Russia in up-state New York,
where Miss Rathbone had owned a run-down farm for some years.
The soil was poor, she said, because farmers had planted rye

there for some years, so it was her pleasure to plant small pine trees on these abandoned fields to bring back the forest which once was there. I understand this "public" lived in tents, but I know nothing about the housing and cooking arrangements in general.

There were, and there are, some of her students to whom Miss Rathbone was less than kind or even fair, but I shall sum up by giving three examples of the place she held and still holds in the minds and hearts of the great majority of her students.

The first example is the fund that the library school alumni gathered for her use while she was president of the American Library Association. It was collected to help her with the expenses of travel that would be hers, but she used it instead to add a few frills to her traveling and labeled it her "joy fund".

The second example is that when I asked Miss Rathbone to appeal to the graduates of the library school for the first Pratt Institute Alumni Fund in 1936, I said I should like to have her ask them to give "for my sake". She put her hands to her face and said, "that is hard", but she added she would do it if Charles Pratt asked her. I asked him to ask her, he did, and she began her appeal like this:

> To the Graduates of the Pratt Institute
> Library School
> or, as I think of you,
> My dear Children:

I have seen many alumni appeals, but I never saw one which brought a greater response from more of the group appealed to than did this letter.

The third example is that when Miss Rathbone retired, the graduates of the library school were asked to contribute to have a portrait of her painted for the school. Over one thousand dollars was raised, and the portrait, by Olinsky, which now hangs in the library school library is generally considered to be the finest portrait at Pratt.

Until 1920 Pratt Institute had its own pension plan. People were retired on half pay, usually on reaching the age of seventy.

When Charles Pratt realized that Miss Rathbone must be around that age, he called her over to his office and said with the kindness and warmth he used always in dealing with Pratt people, "I see you were born in 1869." Miss Rathbone replied, "Oh, but I was born in 1864." So Mr. Pratt looked at the hand-written little black book which comprised the official faculty record in those days, and said, "I guess it does look like a 4 at that."

I was the last one to see her go out of the door of the Pratt Institute Library in 1938 and this is what she said: "I've had a ripping time."

RECOLLECTIONS OF ARTHUR E. BOSTWICK

Margery Doud

Margery Doud — after thirty-five years as Chief, Readers'
Advisory Service, St. Louis Public Library, St. Louis, Mis-
souri — retired on July 1, 1960. The essay here reprinted
is a paper read before the American Library History Round
Table during the 1953 Midwinter meeting of the American
Library Association in Chicago.

Water spilled from the goldfish bowl as we carried it along
the slippery streets, and froze in icicles dripping from our
gloved fingers. It was bitterly cold in the dusk of that early evening as we made our way through banks of snow piled high on
either side of the pavement. We were carrying the last of our
possessions to the "new building" opened that day and would
soon be guiding visitors from one beautiful room to another at
a great public reception.

We were young assistants, classified, but still "low on the
organization chart", as Harry Bauer would say,[1] unimportant
but interested and gay: Clara and Gladys Chew, of the well known
family, Helen Ferguson, and Ruth Overman, who later became
supervisor of children's work, and later still the librarian's
daughter-in-law. Gladys and Ruth were special keepers of the
goldfish and would not trust their charges to a moving van. I can
hear them now laughing, rather desperately, as we relieved
each other of the dripping, freezing bowl.

Once inside the new building, however, the world was warm
and miraculously beautiful. The main hall with arched windows,
walls of Tennessee marble and a ceiling of gold-leaf medallions
inspired by one in the Vatican, was lighted with alabaster lamps
on Italian marble standards. Chandeliers were of bronze and
furniture of hand-carved oak, while exquisite brass grilled door-
ways at either end led into the open shelf and reference departments. It was the city's first central library building, handsome,
spacious, symbolic in itself of progress.

Reprinted from Wilson Library Bulletin, 27:818-825, June, 1953, by
permission of the author and the publisher.

Dr. Bostwick had been appointed librarian in October 1909, succeeding the equally distinguished Frederick M. Crunden, librarian for thirty-two years. But it was with the opening of this new building in January 1912 that a new epoch identified with Dr. Bostwick's administration began. At the time of his appointment the president of the board of directors was Frederick W. Lehmann, then at the head of the St. Louis bar and later solicitor-general of the United States. In 1911 Mr. Lehmann was succeeded as president by George O. Carpenter, who served until 1935. Judge O'Neill Ryan followed Mr. Carpenter, holding office until 1938, when Robert C. Day, the current president, took over. The successive presidencies of these men of high caliber and staunch devotion to the library, coupled with the long administration of Mr. Crunden, developed an atmosphere and a body of tradition that became an ingrained part of the institution and produced a fertile field for such advertising as Dr. Bostwick enjoyed — progressive and imaginative, often experimental, but at the same time conservative and sound.

It was an ideal time for a new librarian to take office. The building itself invited expansion of services, and stimulated the staff to unwonted endeavor. St. Louis seemed a charming city to the New Englander, "One of the few in our country with a decided local flavor", he said. He even defended it from the outrageous slurs of those who claimed that the chief point about the city was its unbearable summer heat!

St. Louis had much to offer a person of Dr. Bostwick's background and experience. Here was a man who had started out to teach with a Ph.D. in physical science from Yale. But after two years of teaching in Montclair, New Jersey, he was recommended for an editorial position on APPLETON'S CYCLOPEDIA OF AMERICAN BIOGRAPHY, and later continued editorial work on the Forum, the STANDARD DICTIONARY, and finally The Literary Digest, where he remained as scientific editor for nearly forty years, while holding other posts. It was after his work on the STANDARD DICTIONARY that he was appointed librarian of the Free Circulating Library in New York City.

In his autobiography, A LIFE WITH MEN AND BOOKS,[2] Dr. Bostwick writes in characteristic fashion of entering this new profession, "in complete ignorance of library administration and library methods". He tells exactly how he taught himself, learning as he went along, and of finally being invited to write

a textbook, THE AMERICAN PUBLIC LIBRARY, which was widely used in Library Schools, and went into several editions.

Born and reared in Litchfield, Connecticut, one of the love-
liest of all New England villages, he had inherited his father's
delight in reading, his mother's love of music, and other fine
qualities — an invincible curiosity, an interest in people, a sense
of humor, a liberal, open mind, a continuous zest for living.

In St. Louis there were numerous organizations and clubs engaged in civic and intellectual pursuits. The new librarian was
called upon to address many of these groups and in time joined
a number of them, making outstanding contributions from his
store of knowledge and the clarity of his ideas.

He joined the Round Table, a dinner club of noteworthy membership; the New England Society, of course; Town and Gown,
the Contemporary Club, the Society of St. Louis Authors, and
certain scientific and sociological associations. He took part in
forums such as the Institute on International Relations held at
Washington University, in company with such men as Dr. Roland
Usher of the university; Rabbi Isserman of Temple Israel; Per-
cival Chubb, leader of the Ethical Society; Wiley B. Rutledge,
then dean of the School of Law; and Clark McAdams, brilliant
editor of the editorial page of the St. Louis Post-Dispatch.

Dr. Bostwick was active in both the Civic League and City
Club, developed largely by Roger Baldwin, later to become nationally known in connection with the Civil Liberties Union of New
York. He contrasted the City Club with those of New York and
Boston and commented on the fact that it was prevented from
taking sides on any public question, being intended merely as
a public forum for discussion. And he expressed surprise at
those persons unwilling even to listen to an opinion with which
they did not themselves agree. Tolerance with him was so natural that one did not think of it as a discipline, yet his was precisely the quality described by David Muzzey in ESSAYS IN
INTELLECTUAL HISTORY:

> Toleration is too often thought of as an amenity. In
> reality it is an arduous and exacting discipline. It is
> the chief element of progress in all cultural advance,
> as distinguished from the inventions and discoveries
> that have steadily augmented our material civilization.
> Even the latter, too, have depended for their success-

ful exploitation far more often than is commonly realized upon the growth of political and religious toleration. . . .

Toleration is a function not of forming, but of realizing our opinions. It is a counsel of patience. Its method is persuasion, not force; education, not regimentation. Its attribute is humility. Its quest, "more light".

In his reminiscences Dr. Bostwick tells delightful stories concerned with members and guests of the organizations he joined, stories which are often miniature portraits of celebrities but which also reflect the personality of the teller.

There were many facets in Dr. Bostwick's personality. Tall and reserved, he was always considered a man of authority and many came to him for counsel and guidance. Sudden animation lighted his face in conversation or when he talked to a group. His eyes twinkled and his laugh came quickly at a joke or good story and his own stories were told with drama, atmosphere and color.

He was a clear and logical thinker. He worked quickly with intense concentration. He wrote a firm, legible hand putting on paper what he wanted to say with almost no alteration or correction. His editing was done in the same manner and our Monthly Bulletin was a model of its kind. He was a great booklover, sharing his enthusiasms with others, but declaring roundly that he would not read any book that did not catch his interest in the first thirty pages. He was considerate in times of stress and compassionate in times of grief, but never paternalistic.

He wrote and spoke widely on many subjects but he talked no nonsense to the American people about good fiction or books read for recreation. He declared them good! He had great faith in "constant exchange and comparison of views and experiences" . . . and he rated higher "the informal conversations on porch or boat deck than the formal papers at library meetings". He considered John Cotton Dana an incomparable porch talker. He was fair in all things and the juxtaposition of two sentences he wrote about Mr. Dana is typical of his manner of thought. In discussing his own administration as president of the ALA and his failure to satisfy some of his more radical associates, he wrote:

This was the beginning of a gradual breach between

Dana and myself which lasted through his life. Dana was altogether the most noteworthy man in the association and perhaps in the profession during my lifetime.

He loved to travel and wanted to know everything about unfamiliar places. Having found out, he appreciated them on their own account and not by comparison with Litchfield or St. Louis! After visiting Mobile, where he was asked to advise the board on their new library building, he wrote:

> Mobile is a fascinating place and the people are delightful, but no one "hustles" very much. They all want to do so, and cheerfully look forward to industrial preeminence, but the prospects seem unfavorable. I am not sorry, for they are more charming as they are.

He enjoyed a joke on himself and loved to tell about a visit to Cleveland when Cleveland's main library building was new. He and another VIP were booming along a corridor, admiring the wall exhibit cases when a young assistant came by and shushed them. "You mustn't talk so loud", she whispered, and he mimicked her to perfection. He also enjoyed jokes on others and one of his best stories was an amusing account of the annual dinner of the New England Society when he was its president. He had selected representatives who were to extol their states in turn, with state songs, printed on the program, to be sung before each address. For Rhode Island there seemed to be no song, so the president sat down and wrote one, to the tune of "Auld Lang Syne", and called it "Narragansett Bay". "It was sung proudly by the Rhode Islanders present, in blissful ignorance that it had been composed by a Connecticut neighbor the day before."

He especially relished the story of the lady who called the reference department and insisted on having "Rock of Ages" sung over the telephone. Georgia Gambrill, now secretary and president-elect of SORT was the victim, and she fled to the telephone in the farthest corner of the stack to do the singing.

Claiming that he had never excelled in sports, Dr. Bostwick emphasized his pleasure as a spectator. "I am able to appreciate fine points of play", he said, "and enjoy seeing experts doing anything well, playing a symphony or making home runs." But he was more than a spectator in many arts and recreations. He read, wrote, played the piano, took long walks in the country, enjoyed good conversation, and loved going to the movies.

Dr. Bostwick's philosophy of librarianship was based on love of books and service to readers and he believed in the public library as an instrument of popular education in its widest sense, including what is usually termed recreation. He quoted Bliss Perry:

> To be aristocratic in taste, and democratic in service is the privilege and glory of the public library.

He always supervised book selection and the shelves today are rich with evidence of his wide knowledge and scholarly interests.

He read in several languages; he read mathematics and music scores for pleasure; he read detective stories before going to sleep and always set himself to discover the murderer by a certain page. He was one of the first of the Perry Mason fans.

Allan Angoff, in a discerning study made at Columbia University in 1951, wrote:

> My reading of Bostwick's life and his many papers, books, articles, interviews, convinces me that he set up the love of books as one of the most important requirements for librarianship at a time when it was much more fashionable to emphasize new techniques — and that is an immense contribution whose importance today is even greater than when Bostwick lived.

Dr. Bostwick liked mechanical devices and manipulated them himself when showing visiting librarians through the building. He told them about the little electric pump in the subcellar, a safety device to curb an old spring that refused to be choked with concrete. "When the subsurface waters rise in the spring", he would say, "the pump starts going chug-chug", and he illustrated so graphically with his hands and his voice, that the little pump sprang into action before the eyes of his guests.

Recalling his enthusiasm for things mechanical, Ann Jaeger, our present auditor, reminded us of the toys he used to buy from sidewalk vendors for his small grandsons. Returning to his office after lunch, he would take them direct to the auditing department next door, where Lula Wescoat, now retired but auditor for many years, would watch, with her admiring staff, as he wound the toys and let them speed the length of the long office tables. "You can find better things on the street than you can in toyshops", he would tell them as he examined each toy's exact construction.

Among many things inaugurated by Dr. Bostwick were weekly staff meetings of department heads and branch librarians, "for the discussion of matters of administration and for the free interchange of opinion". Staff meetings grew lively at times, and occasionally everyone talked at once. When that happened Dr. Bostwick, who often had initiated the subject, would listen for a while with an amused, detached air, then suddenly would tap on the table with a small gold pencil attached to his watch chain.

"Well, we've talked enough about that", he would say, "now let's talk about something else." Once, after an especially hectic session, someone asked him how he could stand all the argument.

"Why, that's how I get to know my department heads", he replied with a laugh.

Bertha Doane and the late Josephine Gratiaa, branch librarians, were two of the persons he enjoyed at staff meetings. Miss Doane, herself a New Englander, a graduate of Wellesley, and the possessor of a great swirl of red gold hair above a cameo face, was and is one of the most pungent members of our staff. Miss Gratiaa, from French and Irish ancestors inherited an unusual blend of admirable qualities, touched off by wit that made any story she told memorable. They were both booklovers, constant readers, and delightful conversationalists. When either felt impelled to relate some experience in staff meeting, Dr. Bostwick's eyes would begin to twinkle and he would settle back with a "now this is going to be good" expression. Responding to such top-level appreciation, they would enhance and develop their stories on the spot, with Dr. Bostwick contributing occasional comments to keep the stories going. And that was one way in which the staff learned to know the chief librarian!

May Lyons Balz, another branch librarian, sent us some notes the other day that represent, I believe, a consensus of opinion.

In my memory, Dr. Bostwick's outstanding characteristic was his broad tolerance of other peoples' opinions — even those he could neither understand nor share. Then there was his eager curiosity about everything that was happening. Do you recall the time he said he could never take his own life because he would be too anxious to know what was around the next corner?

As librarian he appointed his department heads — trusted them and expected them to "cope" as our friends the English say. Somehow that built us up in our own esteem and we were able to handle situations that should have floored us.

He was an encyclopedia of information and a constant source of pride and interest to his staff.

His loyalty to that staff was unswerving and instilled in them a responding loyalty — not only to himself but to the St. Louis Public Library as an institution. With all his university training, the lack of academic degrees meant little to him in comparison with a staff member's personality and ability to "cope".

In giving great freedom to his department heads, with accompanying responsibility, he often achieved results of lasting value. For instance, in the old quarters in the Board of Education Building, Mary Powell had started to work in the reference room without any special preparation. She found there a few cases for art reference books and asked Miss Moody if she could have her desk in that area. Miss Moody, just as did Dr. Bostwick, always encouraged an assistant's initiative, and granted the request. From this beginning Miss Powell built up the art collection which, on completion of the new building, was moved to a beautiful large room on the main floor and became the art department with Mary Powell appointed its chief. After a number of years the City Art Museum decided to establish an educational department, after the manner of Boston and Cleveland. Looking over possible directors, the museum found one person in the city best qualified to undertake the work. That person was Mary Powell.

Leonard Balz, who has worked in the library since boyhood, as page, circulation department assistant, head of the registration department and later of the stations (now Extension) department, was, upon the death of Sula Wagner, placed in charge of the catalog and order department. Mr. Balz is practically self-educated through reading, is a book collector of note, has aristocratic taste in literature, and is considered by many as knowing more about books and publishers than any other man in St. Louis. Immeasurable is the library's gain from giving this bookman the chance to use his knowledge in the important work of the catalog and order department.

One definite piece of advice Dr. Bostwick used to give to staff members who were sounded out on positions elsewhere and invited to submit applications: "Tell them you will consider it if the position is definitely offered you." He explained that head librarians liked to scout around and find several persons equipped for a position, ask them all to apply, and then choose the one that seemed the best, leaving the others in the position of rejected candidates!

"It's all very fine for the head librarians", he said, "but it is not fair to the candidates."

Dr. Bostwick was specific when wording instructions. Frequently we come across green-penciled notes stashed away in our desks. Elizabeth Summersby, chief of the circulation department, came across one the other day signed with the clear initials A.E.B. A.E.B. had evidently been asked to settle some question on classical names and had written, "Where there is a familiar English form, it should be used on the back of the book if the book is in the English language."

He had the quickest way of putting his finger on the vital spot of any problem. Calling me in one day from the small branch library in a school building where we were reveling in everything new — furniture, books, pictures, flowers, southern exposure with streams of sunshine — he offered me the librarianship of a larger older branch, in a library-owned building. The only flaw in the small branch was the constant effort needed to win cooperation from the school custodian, paid by the Board of Education. The older branch was a promotion, but I sat silent thinking of the smaller bright and shining room, the responsive public to whom it was still a novelty, the black-eyed Susans growing in a near-by field in the newly established community.

He spoke again with a smile, "You know if you go to Carondelet you can be lord of all you survey including the janitor." Just that quickly was it settled, not by the mere word "janitor" but by Dr. Bostwick's characteristically courteous and persuasive way of getting you to do what he considered best. For the record it should be noted that the janitor at Carondelet was the incomparable John Smith, originally from the deep South, rich in wisdom and experience, expert in diplomacy, steeped in knowledge of the old neighborhood and its jealously guarded traditions — in fact, the branch's most valuable assistant!

In 1925 Dr. Bostwick was chosen by the ALA to serve as its delegate to survey Chinese libraries and recommend measures for their extension and improvement. The mission was in response to an invitation from the Chinese Association for the Advancement of Education, and elaborate plans were made in advance for his program in China where he was received and honored as a distinguished scholar by civil and military authorities. The chapter in his autobiography devoted to this trip is still fascinating reading and its observations on the country and the people are valuable as the unconscious reflection of the observer's own character.

Before he left for China, the staff gave him a party (he loved parties, and so did we) and presented him with a check with which he was to bring back gifts for Mrs. Bostwick and himself. For Mrs. Bostwick, beautiful and vivacious, he chose a handsome mandarin coat to wear as an evening wrap; for himself, small rugs; and for his staff, twigs from the grave of Confucius. They were believed to bring good luck, were tied in bundles, and on his return were cut in short lengths, so that every person in the institution could share in the luck. So unusual were his opportunities in China that he was called upon to tell of his experiences on numberless occasions. He took to China a wealth of information and understanding. He brought back a love of country and a high opinion of its people and its civilization.

In 1929 Dr. Bostwick went to Italy as one of fourteen ALA delegates to the first World's Library and Bibliographical Congress held in Rome and Venice. Throughout his life in St. Louis he was invited to talk, at one time or another, in practically every state in the Union. His library, his staff, and his city profited greatly from the variety of his experiences and interests.

So sound were his education and training that he could doubtless have been successful in a number of other professions. Margery Quigley, formerly of our staff, wrote of Dr. Bostwick:

He had many of the qualities of a great management

engineer, thinking in large terms, even internationally, when most librarians . . . were placing all their emphasis on techniques and routines. . . . If he had had huge university classes to whom to transfer his ideas of literature and life he would have ranked with "Copey" of Harvard as a legendary teacher.

Another of his staff wrote of him:

Without prejudice, and with an instinctive and unerring sense of right he saw through every situation so clearly and swiftly that, had he chosen the law as his profession, he would most certainly have been one of the eminent jurists of the American bar.

From evidence at hand, had he remained in the field of science, he might well have become one of the great nuclear physicists. But speaking modestly for himself he said: "I was always fond of acting and would have enjoyed going on the stage."

His writings, both in books and scattered articles and essays, show a wide diversity of interests. Many are on libraries, books, and phases of education but others are not, and one of the most important of the others is in A LIBRARIAN'S OPEN SHELF. It was written more than fifty years ago and is called "Atomic Theories of Energy". It suggested atomic structure at a time when many physicists regarded energy as a mere mathematical abstraction, and it bears out Woodrow Wilson's statement in his recently published LEADERS OF MEN:

Our slow world spends its time catching up with the ideas of its best minds. It would seem that in almost every generation men are born who embody the projected consciousness of their time and people. Their thought runs forward apace into regions whither the race is advancing, but where it will not for many a weary day arrive.

January 6, 1937 was one of the great days in our history. The library kept open house from 9 A.M. until 9 P.M. in celebration of the twenty-fifth anniversary of the dedication of the main building. The outstanding event of the day took place in the afternoon

when staff, board members, and a limited number of guests
gathered in the art department to honor the chief librarian. Under Leonard Balz, general chairman for the day's activities,
this occasion was planned as a surprise for Dr. Bostwick by a
special committee: the late Katharine T. Moody, chief of the
reference department; Lula M. Wescoat, auditor; and Bertha
Doane, librarian of Cabanne Branch. Miss Doane presided and
feelingly expressed the sentiments of the staff in her opening
remarks:

> We have gathered here today in honor of Dr. Bost-
> wick. It is by no means a new or unfamiliar experience
> for him. . . . At this ceremony, however, the gesture
> does not come from high places. It comes from mem-
> bers of his staff who feel that on this day it is appro-
> priate that their affection and devotion should become
> articulate. It is a tribute from those who know him
> best, not to his eminence in the world of affairs but to
> his real greatness in the workaday world, to those quali-
> ties which make him deeply loved — his unfailing patience
> and kindness and understanding.

Miss Moody, for years one of the most noted and admired
women in St. Louis, speaking for the staff disclosed the surprise,
after paying tribute to Dr. Bostwick's accomplishments:

> One year ago . . . many of us were assembled here
> when a portrait of Mr. Crunden was given to the library,
> the gift of Mrs. Crunden. Today the staff of the public
> library is presenting to the board of directors a portrait
> of Dr. Bostwick.

Scott MacNutt, who painted the portrait in 1926, was present
and told of asking Dr. Bostwick to sit for him because he felt that
so fine and genial a personality should be recorded upon canvas.
Responses from the board and characteristic words of appreciation from Dr. Bostwick concluded the felicitous occasion.
    Dr. Bostwick was devoted to his home and family and he and
Mrs. Bostwick were at their sparkling best together. She came
down frequently to have lunch with him and when he joined her
they went off gaily, conversing with evident enjoyment. He liked

to tell about a party soon after their arrival in St. Louis. Ex-Governor David R. Francis, afterward ambassador to Russia, was also a guest and asked someone who Mrs. Bostwick was. On being told he remarked, "What is a librarian doing with a wife like that?"

Another abiding influence in Dr. Bostwick's life was Litchfield. On moving to St. Louis, he bought a summer home there, and went back frequently. He thought it the most beautiful village he had ever seen and to read his own account of his childhood is to realize the depth of his affection for his birthplace, and the great American heritage that was his because of it. During his last summer in the East, Ruth Overman Bostwick, widow of his elder son, was taking him on a long drive through the country he had known so well as a boy, when suddenly he said, "Oh, whenever I come back to Litchfield I have such a lift of the heart!"

What does the life of this librarian mean to us today, especially on a program devoted also to intellectual freedom? It leaves us with a double challenge, I believe; first, to protect the rights of our readers to wide open channels of information, declaring with Judge Learned Hand that "we must not yield a foot upon demanding a fair field, and an honest race, to all ideas";[3] secondly, since we assume as an obligation the selection of material on both sides of controversial questions, to increase our own tolerance and understanding through whatever "arduous and exacting discipline" we are able to devise.

Librarians are no more broadminded than other cross sections of the populace, but they need to be and should be, and in Dr. Bostwick we have an outstanding example of one who was! Judge Hand reminds us:

> How tentative and provisional are our attainments, intellectual and moral; how often the deepest convictions of one generation are the rejects of the next . . . and that wisdom is to be gained only as we stand upon the shoulders of those who have gone before.[3]

I should like to mention three things that I believe should be read and studied by students in all library schools, and also by every practicing librarian in the country. The first is Dr. Bostwick's autobiography, A LIFE WITH MEN AND BOOKS, because it reflects the very essence of intellectual freedom.

The second is "The Belligerent Profession", by Frances Clarke Sayers, an address delivered in 1948 as the second in the William Warner Bishop Lectureship Series at the University of Michigan. Here is a magnificent example of a librarian claiming for herself the right of free thought and free speech, while declaring a philosophy of librarianship that might well attract the recruits we are constantly seeking were it widely heralded and applied.

The third suggestion is THE SPIRIT OF LIBERTY, papers and addresses of Learned Hand, collected, and with an introduction and notes, by Irving Dilliard, editor of the editorial page of the St. Louis Post-Dispatch. Mr. Dilliard deserves a special award for making available to the general public these papers filled with wisdom, grace, and beauty, heretofore hidden away in legal journals. There is no library so small that it should not include this volume on its shelves.

If you have not already done so I urge you to read the address, "Sources of Tolerance", which reminded me frequently of Dr. Bostwick. He and Judge Hand had similar backgrounds. After all, didn't Judge Hand's grandfather study law in the pioneer law school founded by Tapping Reeve in Litchfield?

NOTES:

1   "Low Man on an Organization Chart", Harry C. Bauer, ALA Bulletin, January 1953. Wise and humorous reflections, with the St. Louis Public Library in the twenties as background.

2   Bostwick, Arthur E. A LIFE WITH MEN AND BOOKS, H. W. Wilson, 1939.

3   "The Future of Wisdom in America", by Learned Hand, in Saturday Review of Literature, November 22, 1952.

MITCHELL OF CALIFORNIA

Lawrence Clark Powell

> Lawrence Clark Powell — author, lecturer, teacher, librar-
> ian, bookman — is Dean of the School of Library Service at
> the University of California in Los Angeles. The essay here
> reprinted is a paper read before the February, 1954, meet-
> ing of the American Library History Round Table at the
> Midwinter Meeting of the American Library Association in
> Chicago.

Whenever I am depressed about humanity, which is really
not as often as I should be, considering the mess it's in, I con-
sole myself by thinking of the occasional brilliant success it
achieves in producing from out of a million nonentities a personality of such individuality and influence as to make history and
to achieve the immortality of remembrance. Such a man was
Sydney Bancroft Mitchell, university librarian, library educator,
horticulturist, writer, talker, legendary character even in his
lifetime, which came to an end two years ago last September in
his 74th year.

Born in Montreal of Yorkshire and Irish parents, educated
at McGill University and the Albany Library School, Sydney
Mitchell spent nearly half a century in California, a few years
at Stanford, and the balance on the University of California's
mother campus at Berkeley. He taught a year in the Michigan
Library School and traveled roundabout the country and abroad,
thus avoiding provincialism. He was a bilingual North American,
liberal and tolerant, possessed of a tough mind and a tender
heart.

The chronology and details of his life are to be found in his
unfinished memoirs to which this paper is intended to be a preface, and I shall not particularize on them here. I prefer instead
to seek the elements in his character and personality which made

Reprinted from A PASSION FOR BOOKS by Lawrence Clark Powell
(World Publishing Company, 1958, © 1958 by Lawrence Clark Powell, pp. 134-143) by permission of the author and the World Publishing Company.

him such a rare and influential person. It is as a teacher of librarians, rather than as a librarian, that Mitchell is remembered. He could have been a chief librarian either in the university or public library field, but in the mid-1920's he left the associate librarianship of the University of California to found the university's first and only library school, and during the next two decades he built it into one of the country's few first-rate institutions.

I have not counted or classified its graduates. They include some of the country's leading librarians, and they are virtually unanimous in their devoted remembrance of Mitchell. Exceptional is the graduate who portrayed the ... an as a wicked character in her novel — and I have an idea that he might have been secretly as pleased with such literary recognition as he was with the honorary doctorate conferred upon him by Occidental College in 1946. Mitchell was showman enough to know that unfavorable recognition is better than none at all.

What makes a great teacher? Three necessary elements occur to me.

Wide experience and knowledge. A teacher — especially a teacher of librarianship — must be able to draw upon the total library experience of the race, and the more firsthand knowledge of libraries he has, the better is he able to relate and evaluate this experience.

Deep insight into human nature. He must know why people act as they do — from a desire for security, power, recognition, or a wish to help others, or a mixture of all.

The desire to communicate. A great teacher will not only be able to speak or write memorably, he will want more than anything else to communicate with others, to tell and to share.

I want now to examine these three elements of experience, insight, and communication, and see how they combined in Sydney Mitchell to make a great teacher.

The breadth of Mitchell's education, training, and experience kept him from being another frontier character. Although he became a Californian, with perception and appreciation of the state better than that of most native sons, Mitchell never

lost a North of England shrewdness and a Canadian plainness
which saved him from the boosterism and exoticism which make
so many Californians suspect by their more sober colleagues
from east of the Sierra Nevada.

When he was at Stanford from 1908 to 1911 as head of the
order department, the Palo Alto school was really a country college where life was simple and unostentatious, and although the
University of California at Berkeley, where he spent the next
thirty-five years was already large and getting larger, the building of the university library and its staff was slow, hard work.
Everything that he achieved came from his own efforts. He never
inherited a soft set-up. He was truly a pioneer in western library
education, and he ended his career in a pinched wartime economy
that reduced students and faculty.

By the time Mitchell came to teach young people the elements
of librarianship, he had a practical background of three dissimi-
lar university libraries — McGill, Stanford, and California —
plus training and teaching in the dynamic centers of Albany and
Ann Arbor. He knew books from reading them, libraries from
working in them — and people? He knew people from affectionate
firsthand knowledge. He was a student of human nature, a politician in the good sense of the word, a Yankee horse trader, a
patient player of chess, with a loving touch in his moves.

Mitchell was not a scholar. He preferred teaching to research,
and his instinct in this was right. Librarianship will not be advanced as a profession by the accumulation of a corpus of learned writing as much as it will by the challenge and inspiration to
would-be librarians of such leaders and spokesmen as Mitchell
and his too few peers.

If he was not a scholar in librarianship — and this was by
deliberate choice — Mitchell did prove himself a creative researcher in an entirely different line. He was one of the leading
horticulturists of his time, entirely self taught, and for the love
of it alone. . . .

He became internationally known as a breeder of iris and
other flowers, he founded and edited for ten years the quarterly
journal of the California Horticultural Society, and he wrote
four popular books on gardening which had a wide sale and influence. He actually led two separate lives, as a librarian and
as a gardener. A few of his friends were like him and could
speak both languages. My wife is a true gardener, while I am

327

merely a weeder and a waterer, a kind of garden drudge, and our conversation when we were with Mitchell was out of both sides of his mouth, as he modulated easily from shelf-list to sow-bugs. The Mitchell garden in the hills north of the Berkeley campus was one of the most beautiful in all the West, a fairyland in spring when the flowering fruit trees, the daffodils, and the irises caught one's breath with their loveliness.

Mitchell's insight into human nature was deep and luminous. He began by knowing himself and ended by knowing thousands of other human beings. His memoirs[1] are peopled with characters. He had knowledge of some of the great ones of his time, including three extraordinary university presidents, David Starr Jordan of Stanford, and Benjamin Ide Wheeler and Robert Gordon Sproul of California. He knew Stephen Leacock at McGill, Melvil Dewey at Albany, and Thorstein Veblen at Stanford. Mitchell tells a good story about Leacock's way of working up his humorous material. A colleague was returning to campus after Christmas vacation and saw Leacock alone tramping through the snow on the deserted station platform, talking to himself, whereupon he crept up quietly behind Leacock in time to hear him say, "So the chemist said to his assistant, 'I can dispense without your services.'"

Another neat vignette in the memoirs is of Cook, the old porter of the medical building at McGill, who had probably a wider acquaintance with the medical students of his day than any teacher. Though his manner was austere he became a sort of foster father to them, and by the early nineties he had a unique place. It became traditional that there should be an annual parade and a ceremonial crowning of King Cook, with some chosen student delivering a laudatory address full of hits on the medical school, the performance ending up with the presentation of tribute, a conclusion very pleasing to the tough and thrifty old Scot. But said tribute was always in unique form, one year fifty dollars in pennies scattered through a barrel of sawdust. Next year, when the students realized how easily he recovered the money by dumping the whole contents into a tub of water, they substituted a barrel of molasses to hold the money.

I have said that Mitchell's insight into human nature commenced with a pretty thorough knowledge of himself. He was not a likely prospect for the success he eventually achieved. Most library schools today would probably reject a candidate such as

MITCHELL OF CALIFORNIA

Mitchell. He was badly crippled. Congenital dislocation of the hips made his legs too short and gave him a gait more rolling than that of most mariners. He was extremely homely, with thin blonde hair, red face, and icy blue eyes.

Although he did not ignore his handicap and was always ready to refer objectively to it, his conduct was largely based on the assumption that being physically crippled was not as much of a burden as the mental handicaps of most people. After the first shock of meeting him, you found yourself as unconscious of Mitchell's crippling as he himself was of it. Certainly it never slowed him up. He played street games and football as a boy; he was a page in the McGill stacks; he drove a car and gardened.

And he married the one love of his life, Rose Michael of Montreal, who went with him by his side in all that he did, up to the day of his death. She also was a librarian and a gardener; she was a good cook, and best of all, she was a magnificent listener. Mitchell's emotional normality, which made him such a good counselor, was due to Rose. She truly made a man of him. They formed one of the best married teams this earth has ever seen.

In the notebook in which he outlined his memoirs, Mitchell listed his own personal characteristics, crediting himself, for example, with tenacity, patience, and tolerance, with self-confidence, a capacity for argument and long talking. He listed a dislike of self-pity and an incapacity for abstract thought. Don't seek a fight, he noted, and don't avoid one if it becomes necessary; divert an opponent rather than stop him, and never humiliate one you have beaten. On a campus noted for its politicians, Mitchell was one of the best. He was fast and rough and clean. He was honest and loyal. More than once the president of the university sought his advice, and on more than library matters.

Because of his wide experience and his deep knowledge of men and women, Mitchell became the most influential personal adviser Western librarianship has ever known. No other librarian held such a respected position. Former students came back to him from far and near for advice both professional and personal. Nothing astonished or shocked him. Knowing the worst there is to know about people, he still liked them. He made few errors in judging people, and the one or two he did make were so colossal as to become classics. He knew more about libraries and librarians in the West than anyone else. Hardly a move was made, even in the smallest libraries, without Mitchell's hand somewhere apparent. People came to him and told of their hopes and fears, their successes and failures, because they liked him and trusted him.

Typical was my own experience, in the last months of his life, when I was faced with a choice in my own career, a forking of the ways which meant a radical change if I took the divergent one. I could not seem to make the choice, so torn way I by the possibilities which beckoned in both directions. Then I did what many another had done before me: made my was to the hillside house of the Mitchells and put my problem in his hands. Expertly and lovingly he revolved it so that every facet was revealed; asking, telling, listening, talking; until finally it was crystal clear what I should do. He walked to the door with me and as we said good night, I saw his eyes cloudy with pain. He was old and ill and I had stayed too long. In another month he was dead.

It was the desire to communicate with others that completes the triumvirate of his qualities as a great teacher. He was egocentric and superbly self-confident, a natural showman and a born actor; and at the same time he was essentially humble. He was a master in unwinding the tangled skein of human behavior. His stories went on for days, his parentheses within parentheses were fabulous. As he grew older and his graduates more numerous and wider spread on the map and in various kinds of libraries, his epic narratives ranged higher, wider, and handsomer; and all of them became connected and interconnected, with the old dean at the center of the web, a most wide-eyed, far-seeing, and benevolent old spinner.

His tales took off from the most unlikely points of departure, as for example once when we were eating in a San Francisco restaurant, a radio was broadcasting news which included a final item from a town in the Central Valley. Mitchell was talking steadily through the broadcast, but when the name of the town penetrated his consciousness, he shifted stories without a pause and took off on a lively account of library life in the valley, from town to town, county to county, all the way from Red Bluff in the north to Bakersfield in the south.

I am one of the few students who never actually sat in a class of his. Mitchell was on sabbatical the year I was at Berkeley, and I came to know him only toward the end of the second semester, and then at his home. There and in restaurants and libraries and gardens roundabout the state our friendship ripened in the years that followed. I owe him more than I can say.

His classroom courses had names and numbers, but actually they were all classes in Sydney Mitchell. He was salty and humorous, the deadly enemy of the stuffed shirt and the phoney. He hewed the truth as he saw it and the chips came down all over California. People are still picking them up.

The figure of Socrates comes to mind when I think of Sydney Mitchell. He was homely, even ugly, and he was wise; he dressed truth in anecdote; he was a tireless talker. Breakfast time beside a fire of bittersweet eucalyptus was a favorite time for talk — Mitchell talk, while his listeners swallowed vast amounts of tea. His favorite comment about me, and which he never tired of repeating, was, "That man's piped for tea!"

And even as Socrates, he walked with his students in the garden. Yes, he was a great gardener, this man Mitchell whose wife was truly a rose; he made flowers more beautiful, he made people more fruitful. His students are his immortality, and from them to their students will be handed on the truths he taught, and this is what makes a profession great and lasting. Mitchell of California! I speak his name with affection, and pride, and renewed faith in the humanity of which he was such a magnificent example.

NOTE:

1   It is hoped that these memoirs of Dean Mitchell will be published
    by the alumni of the University of California's School of Librarianship.

"MR. WILSON" — AN INFORMAL REMINISCENCE

Howard Haycraft

> Howard Haycraft is President of The H. W. Wilson Company. The essay here reprinted is a talk given at the American Library History Round Table during the 1954 conference of the American Library Association in Minneapolis. Chairman Wayne Shirley introduced the speaker with these words: "All of us have read the many tributes which have appeared in the library press to Mr. Wilson, but it seemed to me that he should be spoken of at an ALA conference, for he loved our conferences, and who attended more of them? If Mr. Wilson should be spoken of at a conference, it should be at a Minneapolis conference, for here is where he got his start. It is equally clear that the person to speak of him should be the president of the Company he founded . . ."

To say that Halsey W. Wilson was one of the great and best loved leaders of the library profession in our time is a simple statement of fact that requires neither amplification nor defense before this audience. Indeed it is singularly comforting to recall that as nearly as any man could, he received in his own lifetime the recognition he so richly deserved, from this Association and from others.

Your chairman, with his customary sense of fitness, therefore proposed that today I should attempt neither a strictly biographical memorial — because so much has been written and published about Mr. Wilson — nor yet a definitive evaluation, which would be premature at this time as well as presumptuous coming from an associate. Rather, he suggested that it would be appropriate at this Minneapolis conference to go behind the public facade and tell you, somewhat informally, the manner of man who dwelt there, as his coworkers saw him. If in these remarks I can succeed in adding in some small way to your understanding of the essentially simple yet sometimes surprisingly complex man who was the benefactor of us all, I shall be content.

Reprinted from Wilson Library Bulletin, 29:52-57, September, 1954, by permission of the author and the publisher.

"MR. WILSON" — AN INFORMAL REMINISCENCE

An alternative title for this paper might well have been "Living With a Legend". For of Mr. Wilson it was more literally true than most of whom it is said, that he became a legend in his own lifetime: a courtly, benevolent symbol to generations of librarians. What, then, was it like to live and work with such a man?

Since it was my privilege to know and work with Mr. Wilson for a mere twenty-five years (the last) of his exceptionally long life and career, I turned first in preparing this paper to some of those who knew him in the earlier days. To Edith Phelps, who joined The Wilson Company in Minneapolis in 1907. To Erling Erickson (the "Eric" of our Old Magazine Department) who came in 1911. To Florence Arnold, one of the first new Eastern employees after the move to White Plains in 1913.

The composite picture that emerges is not strikingly different from the Mr. Wilson you and I have known, except in degree. The moustache and fringe of hair around the bald dome were dark, not white, but the eyes twinkled behind the same rimless eyeglasses. There was perhaps a closer personal relationship in those days between "the boss" and all the employees — we hear of picnics at Lake Minnetonka and, later, of rides from White Plains to Rye Beach on scorching summer afternoons. The Company then was only a fraction of its present size, Mr. and Mrs. Wilson were younger, and the pace and tempo of life, one cannot help believing, were simpler.

The anecdote of the Minneapolis days I like best — and find most typical — is told by Erling Erickson, whose duty it was during the bitter winter of 1912 to see that just enough heat was kept in the old Company building at the corner of the University campus to prevent the pipes from freezing over the weekend; for every economy was essential. Coming into the building for this purpose late one subzero Sunday night, "Eric" spied a light behind Mr. Wilson's famous rolltop desk at the rear of the first floor. Suspecting burglars (there had been a rash of robberies in the vicinity), he armed himself with a furnace poker and cautiously crept around the corner — only to find Mr. Wilson hard at work at his desk, hat on head, overcoated, fur collar turned up around his ears against the piercing cold.

(By the way, we are making plans at The Wilson Company to preserve that same rolltop desk — which he used to the end — as a permanent memento.)

The streak of indomitability illustrated by this story might well, I think, be called Mr. Wilson's outstanding characteristic both in public and private life — next, of course, to his innate kindliness. (The combination in itself is rare.) Recently, that elder library-statesman Asa Don Dickinson wrote, "How fortunate for the world that Halsey W. Wilson had a single-track mind." Perceptive as the remark is, I somehow feel that it does not do its subject entire justice. I would add that never was a man so impervious to opposition, so heedless of possible ridicule, once he felt that he was on the right course. Never was anyone more fearlessly ready to say, "They're all out of step but me." And the amazing thing is how often he was right!

Early in 1946, when I returned from the Army, Mr. Wilson called me to his office. Before resuming my regular Company duties, he asked me to undertake a special job, extracurricular so to speak. You will recall that the basic <u>Library of Congress Catalog of Printed Cards</u> had recently been published, with a terminal date of July 31, 1942, and perhaps you will also remember that up to 1946 no definite plans had been announced to continue it. This latter circumstance seriously disturbed Mr. Wilson. It seemed to him wrong — and to a descendant of Roger Williams, Anne Hutchinson, and the martyr Mary Dyer, wrongs exist to be corrected. Therefore he had decided (and this was my assignment) to send a questionnaire at Wilson Company expense to all libraries likely to be interested, to determine their need and support for a continuing, cumulative publication. There was never any thought of monetary gain for The Wilson Company, nor indeed that the Company would be in any way associated with the publication; Mr. Wilson simply regarded the expense of the questionnaire as a professional contribution.

Along with several other members of the Company directorate, I must confess that I was a little apprehensive about the project. Not about the expenditure, which we all agreed was justified, but lest in some quarters the questionnaire might be misunderstood and considered meddlesome interference. We need not have worried. I think you all know the outcome: the results of the questionnaire magnificently vindicated Mr. Wilson's belief; they were transmitted to Washington; and the publication of the continuing, cumulative catalog we all know today followed as a matter of course. And two years later, at the time of the Company's golden anniversary, Dr. Luther Evans, then Librarian of Congress, paid handsome tribute to Mr. Wilson's persistence in these words:

> . . . I am certain that without your planning and your urging and your compilation of important information as to the wishes of American libraries, we would not have acted as soon as we did. I am also certain that had we seen the light as soon as we should have seen it, we should have acted more promptly than we did. All librarians owe you a large debt of gratitude for your role in this important development.

It was in the same year that Paul North Rice, at that time president of the American Library Association, wrote:

> . . . It is not exaggeration to say that you have done more for libraries than any living man.

If I have strayed a little here from my announced purpose of picturing the private rather than the public man, it is because the two — with a stubbornness which would do credit to Mr. Wilson himself — sometimes refuse to stay in separate compartments. I shall try to keep them in better control as I pass to other aspects.

Oddly enough, he was not (at least in his later years) a great reader in the usual sense of the term, this man who so increased the usefulness of the printed word the globe over. It was somehow as if knowing that he had the keys to published knowledge at his fingertips was sufficient. Or perhaps the very effort of conceiving and making those keys left him with time and energy for only a little reading, and that usually along professional lines. But that did not keep him from having opinions on all manner of current affairs — and usually pronounced opinions at that.

Politically and philosophically, he underwent the changes of many of his generation. A Wilsonian Democrat and early advocate of the League of Nations, he was outraged by the New Deal to the point that he became almost an isolationist. Rightly or wrongly, like so many of his years, he felt that the New Deal philosophy represented a denial and denigration of everything he stood for: if it has not been implicit heretofore, let me say that for all his benignity he was above all else an individualist. There was, for example, the weekend trip he took in the early 1930's to Montreal with the serious thought of moving the Company across the Canadian border to escape the NRA, which to his last day he persisted in considering as dangerous a dictatorship as any totalitarian European police state.

Yet — and let me say this quickly — this was the same man who instituted a pension system for older employees as early as 1920, when pensions in American private industry were almost unknown and Social Security was unheard of. It was no accident (as John Lawler pointed out in his history of the Company) that Mr. Wilson held an abiding admiration for the elder Henry Ford.

This brings me to the happier harbor of Mr. Wilson's personal kindliness, the quality which I think those of us who worked with him will remember above all others. I think it is a fair statement that no one who came to Mr. Wilson in trouble was ever sent away without help in some form. He was at his best in dealing with such emergencies. In fact, it was the basis of his social philosophy that people should so order their lives as to meet minor or normal difficulties themselves, but that they should be helped in cases of real emergency,

This thinking was illustrated in such early Company benefits as cumulative sick-pay and hospitalization. Closely akin were the numerous occasions when he provided employment opportunities for the physically handicapped. He was also a pioneer advocate of bonus vacations for older workers. Though he never took a vacation himself, it was characteristic that he believed in them for others. And it should surprise no one who knew him to learn that after Mrs. Wilson's lifetime his modest estate will pass, by his direction, to a charitable foundation established by him primarily for the benefit of former employees.

As it was no accident that Mr. Wilson admired that other great paternalist, Henry Ford, so too it was no accident that the only nickname I have ever heard applied to him (except the inevitable "the boss") was a half-humorous but always affectionate "Papa" or "Pop", spoken with warmth by some older employee — though never, needless to say, to his face.

To make Mr. Wilson a plaster saint would be a disservice to him, and the last thing he would want, I am sure. I should perhaps tell you that he had a temper — as no one who survived one of its rare but devastating outbursts ever forgot. And he had the New Englander's capacity for a righteous, satisfying grudge, though never for a mean or petty reason. Nor will I pretend that his famous pertinacity was altogether an unmixed blessing to those who worked with him. No idea, once held, was ever forgotten; and even those rare publications that had failed had the disconcerting habit of popping up — like King Charles's head in DAVID COPPERFIELD — disguised as new proposals.

But enough of such minor considerations. It was perhaps at lunch at the corner table in the Company cafeteria that we enjoyed Mr. Wilson most and learned to know his "other self". Never a smoker or partaker of alcohol, his abiding vice was the sweetest tooth known to man, and our daily pastime was counting the number of desserts on his lunch tray. This often led to legalistic arguments which he enjoyed the most of any of us: whether, for example, the chocolate cookies that he broke into his soup in preference to soda crackers should count as a dessert or not.

Another perennial lunch table topic was spectatorship versus participation in sports, with Mr. Wilson supporting the latter — or, rather, opposing the former. I should perhaps explain that with the Company situated in sight of both the Yankee Stadium and the Polo Grounds, baseball, to Mr. Wilson's considerable annoyance, sometimes crowded bibliography out of the conversational running. Unable to understand the vast appeal of the national pastime to nonplaying fans, he would inquire plaintively why — if baseball was so popular — the Company shouldn't publish a baseball index?

This recalls inevitably the famous day some twenty years ago when the late Frederick Keppel, president of the Carnegie Corporation, came unexpectedly to call on Mr. Wilson, who at once delightedly began to plan for his guest a tour of the Company, with all the trimmings. No one who saw it will ever forget the expression of incredulity on Mr. Wilson's face when the distinguished visitor explained that he had only dropped in for a few minutes on his way to the World Series opener at the Polo Grounds across the river.

Getting back to those lunch hour seminars, we learned, too, to watch for the warning twinkle that meant a particularly horrendous pun was on the way. (I wish I could recall some of them for you — but perhaps it is just as well!) Sometimes, when he alone took the unpopular side of a more serious argument, we thought he was pulling our legs. Then we would remember that

he was the man who had started the Reference Shelf in the belief
that every question has two sides, and that both should be heard.

His own willingness to listen to the opinions of others was no
less true within the Company than in his famous questionnaires
to libraries. This in turn brings to mind a compensating aspect
of his character which it seems to me is too often overlooked,
and which I should therefore like to mention for the record. Mr.
Wilson became the benefactor of libraries that he was, and escaped the heartbreaking failure so common among bibliographical ventures, not only by knowing what projects to undertake,
but equally by knowing what projects not to undertake. Even in
selfless service to others, a sense of proportion and the knowledge when to say no are just as essential as the will to cooper-
ate. Mr. Wilson had these leavening virtues, along with his capacity for listening to many points of view.

I hope that I have been able to suggest here and there in these
remarks something of the unique family relationship that existed
between Mr. Wilson and the Company he founded. Ever since he
and Mrs. Wilson lost their only child in infancy near the turn
of the century, it had been understood that they looked upon the
growing Wilson staff as their children. In the beginning, as is
always the case, the emphasis was on the parental side of the
relationship. Then, as the years — so many of them — rolled
slowly by, the dependency gradually shifted, at first in little
things, then in those of larger moment. And we were proud that
it could be that way.

Mr. Wilson was never a demonstrative man, and I remember
the sense almost of shock when I went to say good-by to him before leaving on a trip abroad in April 1953. He seemed to have
something on his mind, and looking rather away into space he
told me of a visit he had paid to R. R. Bowker in his last years
in the Berkshires, and how Mr. Bowker had complained of an
ailment which he called "tired-out-itis". The parable was plain.
Then, when we shook hands, for the first time in my remembrance I saw moisture in his eyes.

Almost certainly he felt some premonition, for by early summer he was a sick man, so ill that he had to miss A.L.A. for
the first time in almost half a century. Autumn brought a brief
Indian summer of recovery, and we rejoiced that he could attend
the annual stockholders' meeting and come to his beloved office

a day or two a week. In December, confident of his regained
health, he and Mrs. Wilson and their companion set out for Ari-
zona by automobile, and we happily pictured them enjoying a
well earned season in the sun, Mr. Wilson's first real vacation
in a lifetime. But it was not to be.

Early in January Mr. and Mrs. Wilson returned suddenly to
New York by airplane. While we were arranging to reopen their
Westchester home, they stayed for several days in a hotel only
a few minutes away from the Wilson Company. When Mr. Wilson
did not even suggest coming to his office, we feared in our hearts
what we refused to admit in our minds.

To anyone who has watched a beloved parent fade slowly away,
I need not dwell in detail on the heavy-hearted weeks that followed. We stored up items of office news to tell him on our visits.
We brought him messages from old friends at A.L.A. Midwinter,
and that pleased him. Even on the days he was too weak to talk,
he managed a welcoming smile. One such day, the last week in
February, he roused as we were leaving and asked how business
was at the office. When we gave the expected reply, he whispered, "That's good", and closed his eyes. That was the last time
we saw him.

The end came peacefully early on the morning of March 1,
1954. I wonder how many others have noticed the coincidence —
poetic, fitting — that Mr. Wilson left this life exactly sixty years
to the day after his great predecessor in library indexing, William Frederick Poole, who died on March 1, 1894?

It has been said that Mr. Wilson must have been a happy man.
Certainly, if the knowledge of tremendous and worth-while accomplishment is any criterion, he was a satisfied man. If he departed this life with any serious wish ungranted, I believe that
it must have been the desire to attend this Minneapolis conference, which (as a distinguished librarian has said) would have
brought the wheel to full circle.

In conclusion, it seems to me that I can do no better than to
quote from Marie Loizeaux's Wilson Bulletin editorial, written
within a few days of Mr. Wilson's passing, and expressing so
well what his fellow workers felt and still feel:

> Our "Boss" is gone. . . . But we'll be more on our
> mettle than ever to carry on the high standards Mr. Wil-
> son set, knowing he chose us for our jobs with confidence

we could do them. We have a triple responsibility now, knowing Mr. Wilson believed in us, to justify his belief to the Company, to ourselves, and to the library profession.

"The Boss" is gone. . . . And yet, in the libraries of the world, thousands of issues of Wilson publications are used day after day, year after year, a constant practical reminder of the man who envisioned them and brought them into being. No memorial could please him more.

I like, too, John Lawler's simple summing up, which could well serve as an epitaph: "He built for far more than a lifetime."

DR. WILLIAM WARNER BISHOP:
OUR FIRST INTERNATIONAL LIBRARIAN

Foster E. Mohrhardt

Foster E. Mohrhardt is Director of the United States Department of Agriculture Library in Washington, D.C. The
essay here reprinted is a paper read before the American
Library History Round Table during the 1957 conference
of the American Library Association in Kansas City, Missouri.

There is an appropriateness in presenting a sketch of Dr.
William Warner Bishop in Missouri, since he was born in 1871
in the City of Hannibal, the boyhood home of Mark Twain. He
retained a fond affection for this state although he lived here
only a few years. When his father died in 1878, and left his
mother with three children, they moved to Detroit to live with
his grandmother. Mr. Bishop's mother taught in the Detroit
Central High School.

As Dr. Bishop pointed out many times later, his early education in Detroit was obtained not only in the public schools but
also at the Detroit Public Library. Coming from a family with
literary and scholarly interests, it was natural for him to evidence a proclivity in this direction. His mother was in the first
graduating class at Vassar and two of her sisters were alumnae
of that school.

Dr. Bishop began his long and distinguished association with
the University of Michigan when he came to Ann Arbor to enroll
in July of 1889. He had just graduated from Central High School
in Detroit, where he had been an outstanding student. His interests were varied, but he had early decided that his field of specialization would be the classics and, from the beginning of his
enrollment, he specialized in the classical languages and literature. Supplementing his regular class work, he also audited
classes in international law, medicine, philology, philosophy,
and engineering. In addition to this, he carried extra work so

Reprinted from Wilson Library Bulletin, 32:207-215, November, 1957,
by permission of the author and the publisher.

341

that he received his AB in 1892 after only three years of college studies. He stayed on for a fourth year and earned his AM degree in 1893.

As he pointed out later, he was not rugged enough to participate in sports but he was an avid spectator and retained his enthusiasm for the Michigan teams for the rest of his life.

It was evidently at this time that his deep interest in the field of librarianship developed and, as he pointed out later, "During my last two years, I practically lived in the library and came to know the staff very well."[1] The librarian "gave me access to the stacks of the library, and, though I at first took up teaching, I have always felt that this opportunity to get acquainted with a large collection of books made me a librarian".[2]

It was also during this college period that he began his association with booksellers which ultimately resulted in his intimate knowledge of the methods and techniques of this field. He formed a close acquaintanceship with George Wahr, the noted Ann Arbor book dealer. As his career unfolded, he came to know the book stores of New York thoroughly, and later, in his trips to Europe, became acquainted with most of the leading booksellers in England and on the Continent. All this formed part of the background that enabled him later to carry out the purchase of large and expensive collections with the same competency that he showed in individual purchases. The development of the University of Michigan book collection under his guidance came in part from this skill in evaluating books. The great American book collectors, as well as book dealers and librarians, turned to him for guidance in evaluating important book collections.

Upon his graduation from the University of Michigan with an AM in classical studies, Mr. Bishop accepted a teaching position in the classics at Missouri Wesleyan College. He remained for one year and then moved to a position with greater responsibilities at Garrett Biblical Institute.

While connected with the institute in Evanston from 1895 to 1898, Bishop had the joint responsibilities of instructor in Greek and assistant librarian. Thus his library career dates from this appointment in 1895. During the first year his primary responsibilities were in teaching, but as a result of his own competency and interests, his work shifted so that by 1898 he was predominantly a librarian. He still thought of himself as an educator and planned his career in that field. However, he found himself

drawn toward librarians and librarianship. He was active in the
Chicago Library Club and joined the American Library Association in 1896, attending his first meeting in Cleveland. He became acquainted with such well known library figures as Edwin
H. Anderson, George Watson Cole, Melvil Dewey, James Hanson, Anderson Hopkins, Josephus Larned, Charles Martel, Carl
Rodin, Reuben Thwaites and George Wire. It was from George
Wire, a graduate of the library school in Albany, that he received his formal training in library techniques and methods.

During the summers from 1895 to 1898 Bishop became active
in the famous adult education program at Chautauqua, New York,
and was on the staff teaching Greek. In addition, he conducted
a Chautauqua correspondence course in Greek for three years
under the direction of Dr. Harper, who later became president
of the University of Chicago. Chautauqua, in addition, always
had a romantic interest for him since it was there in the summer
of 1897 that he met the future Mrs. Bishop.

His scholarly abilities were formally recognized in 1898 when
he was offered one of three fellowships at the American School
of Classical Studies in Rome. Much of his time was spent in the
Vatican Library, since he was working on a project involving
early Greek and Latin manuscripts. Here, as in his student days
and in his earlier positions, he found himself closely drawn to
a study of the library. During this period Bishop not only carried on his research work and began his acquaintanceship with
the important Vatican Library but, in addition, visited many
other libraries, met important European librarians, and cata-
loged the book collection of the American School library. Many
of his later activities derive directly from this period. Notable
are his work in reorganizing the Vatican Library, his leadership in the International Federation of Librarians, his contributions to the League of Nations Library, and his development of
a special interest in cataloging.

Although he had hoped to renew his scholarship for a second
year, he found that it was not possible to extend it. Hence, it
was necessary to find a position back in the United States. He
became Latin instructor and librarian at the Preparatory School
of the Polytechnic Institute of Brooklyn, where he remained
from 1899 to 1902. He accepted this position since there was no
market for New Testament or archeology scholars at that time.
He found the library part of his responsibilities far more stimu-

lating than teaching and was greatly interested in the book selection and cataloging activities. As he said later, "The experience in gathering, organizing, and developing service to a secondary-school library was an excellent bit of training," adding that teaching was "a disheartening job".[3]

Mary Wright Plummer at that time was head of the Pratt Institute Library School and was greatly impressed with Bishop's ability as a librarian and his scholarly attainments. She did much to interest him in librarianship as a career. In 1902, Dr. E. C. Richardson, librarian at Princeton, asked her for suggestions for the head of his cataloging department. Miss Plummer strongly recommended Dr. Bishop and he was invited by Dr. Richardson to join his staff. This, Dr. Bishop then realized, was to be the important decision concerning his future career. Although the profession of librarianship had appealed to him earlier, he still felt that his niche might be in the field of classics. He had started his doctorate study at Columbia in 1900 but was forced to drop the work in 1901, due to a serious illness. It was, therefore, with a breadth of experience in two fields that he decided to accept Dr. Richardson's offer at Princeton and embark upon his career in librarianship. The three years' experience in Brooklyn was, as he pointed out later, a very rewarding one which gave him many opportunities to develop in his new profession. He met many people important in the library field, studied the book trade in New York, met publishers and dealers, visited the important libraries, and, through an acquaintanceship with Helen Haines, began to write articles for the Library Journal. His career of teaching librarianship began in 1902 with a lecture series at Pratt Institute on "The History of Learning".

Bishop's influence on library cataloging and classification is not as well recognized today as it was twenty-five years ago. However, students of cataloging are well aware of the basic contributions which he made toward the analysis, simplification, and formalization of cataloging and classification. Bishop had had cataloging experience in most of his previous assignments. However, it was at Princeton that he received guidance and stimulation from Dr. Richardson and developed his own concept of the subject. Richardson's book, CLASSIFICATION, THEORETICAL AND PRACTICAL, had been published just prior to Bishop's arrival at Princeton. As head of the cataloging department, Bishop was able to scrutinize carefully both the theoretical and practical aspects of Richardson's work and it was the practical part that had the most interest for Bishop. He insisted later that this was one of the most valuable experiences which he had in library training, and he always counseled young librarians to obtain as extensive experience in cataloging and classification as possible, since he considered this a basic in library training. Bishop's own summary of the Princeton experience is most revealing. He says:

> Professionally, I regard the same period in charge of the catalog department as equally formative and influential. It was the time of rapid crystallization of what had been more or less in the air for years — the printing of cards by several libraries (the Carnegie Library of Pittsburgh, the New York Public, the John Crerar, Harvard University, and the Library of Congress), the distribution and sale of the cards from the Library of Congress, thus creating a central cataloging office for the country, the formation and adoption of the Anglo-American Code of cataloging rules, and the inauguration of cooperative bibliographical projects. I was privileged to have a hand in this movement — a minor part, to be sure, but one which permitted and developed knowledge of the whole field and its relations to library administration. Among other things, I became convinced that there was great need for improvement in subject cataloging. At Princeton we filed the author and subject cards in two alphabets, and I was greatly struck by the fact that faculty men consulted the subject catalog very little, while their use of the author catalog was constant. I began to work at some problems of subject cataloging and finally read a paper on that topic at the Narragansett Pier Conference of the ALA in 1906, a paper which was published in full in its Proceedings and which I afterward expanded to make the last chapter of my HANDBOOK. I was gratified by Richardson's comment on the paper: "You've given us all something to think about."[4]

The year earlier an article by him, summarizing the problems of the cost of cataloging in his characteristic thorough man-

345

ner, appeared in the January 1905 <u>Library Journal</u> and developed guide lines that served as a basis for future studies in this field.

Although Bishop was a great admirer of Richardson, he pointed out later that Richardson's forte was theory rather than practice. Bishop, on the other hand, was in most ways a completely practical librarian and, although he was interested in and sympathetic with theory, he was much more concerned with the practical aspects of the field. In addition to his interest in the cost studies, his 1906 article included many indications of his practical point of view. Typical are his comments on subject headings, for he indicates that it would be wise for librarians to study the encyclopedias as guides. Referring to this he says:

> Since the seventeenth century the makers of encyclopedias have been working on this problem. Scores of excellent encyclopedias have been in constant use in our reference rooms — and even in our cataloging rooms — but have they been studied diligently as models for headings?[5]

His PRACTICAL HANDBOOK OF MODERN LIBRARY CATALOGING, which first appeared in 1914 and was revised in 1924, had a continuing influence not only in the United States and the other English speaking countries, but was also translated into Chinese and Russian. Even today the book is a useful training and reference tool for catalogers.

Bishop was successful in his work in the cataloging department and highly regarded on the campus. Two years after his arrival at Princeton he was invited to join the Greek Department as a preceptor, and about the same time was offered the position of reference librarian. Knowing then that librarianship was to be his field, he accepted the latter position and began his new work in the reference field.

In June 1905 Bishop married Fini Murfree Burton of Louisville, Kentucky. Miss Burton was a charming southern belle whom he had met at Chautauqua some years earlier and who had many interests similar to his. They were inseparable companions during their entire married life, and it was with great reluctance that Dr. Bishop would ever make even a short trip without taking her. Much of his personal and professional development was due to her constant interest and devotion.

Through his active membership in the New Jersey Library Association, as well as in the American Library Association, he formed a close acquaintanceship with and admiration for John Cotton Dana. Dana had a strong influence on Dr. Bishop's approach toward librarianship.

Richardson at this time was at the peak of his proficiency and was one of the outstanding American librarians. He was greatly interested in Bishop's development and through him Bishop met many important American and foreign librarians. In addition, Bishop himself was active in library association affairs and was contributing regularly to library publications. Hence, it was no surprise to the library profession that Dr. Putnam invited him in 1907 to come to the Library of Congress as superintendent of the reading room.

Bishop, therefore, left Princeton after five years of service and growth to assume one of the important positions in government library work. Here again there was a constant challenge to him to keep pace with new and complex demands upon his professional abilities. Not only was he responsible for the reading room at the Library of Congress, he also was the liaison with Congressional users, was responsible for an area of book selection, and had under his supervision the work for the blind, interlibrary loan, and tours for distinguished visitors.

To the job itself Bishop brought organization and systematization, both of which he developed to a high degree. He indeed felt himself fortunate to be working under the direction of Dr. Putnam whom he regarded as the model for librarians. Evaluating his years at the Library of Congress, Bishop said:

As I look back on my service in the Library of Congress, I am convinced that it did much for me. I learned to work with and through other people and to do my work in accordance with federal law. I was extremely fortunate in working under Putnam, who held one up to the best that was in him. The Library was huge, by far the largest in the country, and one of the largest in the world; consequently, I became accustomed to dealing with masses of books and with problems imposed by size and complicated conditions. The methods used were in most cases modern, and the contrast with older ways was marked. I

became acquainted with libraries and librarians throughout the land, a knowledge which was to prove invaluable.
I came to realize to the full the value — and the weakness —
of specialists. And I developed a sense of kinship with
people who are doing the daily work of the world. It was
good training, and I think Brett was right when he said
to me that I brought to my major post at Michigan an
equipment which could only have been gained through service in Washington.[6]

Among the visitors whom he conducted through the Library
of Congress in 1915 was William L. Clements, a regent of the
University of Michigan. Clements was one of the great collectors
of Americana and one of the real experts in this field. During
his trip through the library he evidenced great interest in the
Americana collection and found Bishop to be amazingly well-informed in this specialized field. He evidently was greatly impressed by this librarian, who was not only an administrator but
a bookman. Two months later, in June 1915, Clements returned
to the library and personally requested Bishop to assume the librarianship of his alma mater. Both Putnam and Bishop felt that
Michigan offered an unusual opportunity for a librarian with
Bishop's background and abilities. In September 1915 Bishop assumed the directorship of the University of Michigan Library,
where he exhibited the qualities that finally brought him distinction as one of the world's great librarians.

Bishop's span of service as librarian at Michigan covered
the years from 1915-1941 and most of his significant accomplishments are tied directly to activities during his tenure in Ann
Arbor.

For the remainder of this paper, therefore, I shall depart
from a chronological report and try to summarize some of Bishop's achievements. Included in this categorization are his accomplishments as bookman, building expert, international librarian, and library administrator.

Regent Clements, who had offered Bishop the Michigan position, had been collecting for many years one of the finest collections ever assembled of early material on America. The collection had been housed in Clements' home but he wanted to set
up a permanent library to house this important material. This
in 1923 eventuated in the building of the William L. Clements

Library on the campus at Ann Arbor. Clements relied heavily upon Bishop for guidance in acquiring materials and for the formulation of plans for the building to house them. After its completion, Clements wrote to Bishop as follows:

> I have tried to establish at Michigan a research laboratory. . . . And to you, Sir, much of that ambition is due.[7]

This is pointed out as only one of the many unusual and rare collections which were added to the university as the result of Bishop's knowledge of books and manuscripts, bookdealers and book collectors. Other valuable additions were made in history, political science, medicine, and mathematics. In the collection of printed materials alone, Bishop left a heritage at Michigan unsurpassed in American librarianship.

Bishop was elected in 1918 to the presidency of the American Library Association and his term in office covered one of the most difficult periods in the history of the organization. Many problems had developed as a result of the war service and Bishop was to be the arbiter in a bitter personal quarrel between F. P. Hill of the Brooklyn Public Library and Dr. Putnam of the Library of Congress. There were also many other problems which resulted from the war service of the association. Bishop, with his diplomacy and tact, handled them in such a manner as would cause least disturbance to the association and its members.

Bishop had been a member of the ALA since 1896, when he had joined upon the urging of James I. Wyer of the New York State Library. He had worked very closely with the association and had devoted himself to its problems. It was with a real feeling of disappointment that he found the members unsympathetic to the new and improved constitution for ALA which came up during his presidency. The Constitution was voted down and for a short time after that Bishop retired from active ALA work. He soon found himself, however, called upon by various elements in the organization and he continued as one of the strong advisers and supporters even after his retirement.

The next category is a more complex one since it covers his relationship to the Carnegie Corporation, his international activities, and his shaping of the course of American academic librarianship through his work on various advisory committees.

Probably the initiation of this complex of activities may be traced to the year 1919 when Dr. Bishop was president of the American Library Association. As he reported it in one of his articles:

> Another reason for remembering the Asbury Park conference is that there I first met Fred Keppel, who was then Third Assistant Secretary of War, in charge of all the work that we were privileged to do for the Army. We were to be thrown together a great deal later, when he was president of the Carnegie Corporation, but this first meeting showed him to be a very human sort of man. He came to Ann Arbor as the commencement speaker, and I succeeded in adjusting his schedule to permit him to address the ALA and yet keep his Ann Arbor appointment.[8]

He had also met Keppel again in 1924 in Paris when he was on a European tour. Dr. Keppel was impressed with Dr. Bishop's unusual combination of scholarliness, administrative ability, and skill in finance. Dr. Keppel, as president of the Carnegie Corporation, and his assistant, Dr. Robert Lester, worked out in 1929 with the trustees of the corporation a plan for stimulating college librarians.

Bishop reporting on this says:

> For a number of years, Dr. Keppel, president of the Carnegie Corporation, had been familiar with my work. In 1929 he asked me to come to New York to confer with him on a new project of the corporation. He had been increasingly concerned with college libraries, and he had brought his trustees to see that they offered a considerable field for development.[9]

At this meeting they discussed the general objectives of the program for the college libraries, methods which could be used in developing it and people who might serve in an advisory capacity. As a result of these discussions, the Carnegie Corporation set up an "Advisory Group on College Libraries" composed of college presidents, deans, officials of academic associations, and librarians. Fortunately for the development of college libraries, Dr. Bishop was selected as chairman of the group. The Carnegie Corporation trustees selected for their first study the

special group of privately controlled liberal arts colleges. At
its first meeting the Advisory Group:

> . . . definitely determined that its purpose would be
> the stimulation of careful thinking about the problem of
> college libraries on the part of the executive officers,
> governing boards and the faculties of American colleges.[10]

They decided that extensive strengthening of the book collections in a select group of colleges would focus attention on and
stimulate interest in the development of the college library as
"an integral factor in the educational work of the college itself".[11]
Dr. Bishop, as chairman of the group, was himself active in developing the standards for selection of the colleges, outlining
the specialized books on college librarianship which were needed in this field, and generally directing the studies of individual
colleges which were made prior to the allocation of funds. Eighty-
four colleges were selected for grants and $1,011,000 was allo-
cated to these colleges for the purchase of books. The first advisory group terminated in 1932.

Following this, Dr. Bishop served on an advisory group which
made grants to libraries in Canadian colleges. In 1934 he chaired a new group concerned with libraries in junior colleges. This
group continued until 1937 and made 92 grants totaling $300,000.
Later groups which Dr. Bishop chaired provided similar services to teachers colleges, land grant institutions, and Negro colleges. He also assisted the Carnegie Endowment for International Peace in making grants for colleges in the Near East.

On many occasions when Dr. Bishop was asked to evaluate
the significance of the programs which contributed about
$2,000,000 in purchases for books for academic libraries over
a period of ten years, he was greatly impatient of any attempts
to apply purely quantitative evaluations. He stated:

> After all, the value of books, or of any particular
> book, to a student is not a matter which can be deter-
> mined by counting. The reading of a single work, nay,
> even of a single chapter of a work, may influence a
> student's entire subsequent career. We all know this is
> true in our own experience. I am convinced that two or
> three books which I read quite casually in college did

more to shape my own development than the sum of instruction which I received. I am, therefore, profoundly
distrustful of any statistical approach to an evaluation
of this whole enterprise. It is to me a matter of great
gratification to have been able to share in providing in
fairly large quantities books which would not have otherwise been added to the libraries of over 200 colleges in
the United States and Canada.[12]

To those, however, who were intimately familiar with the
program and who had association with college libraries, it is
evident that this series of advisory groups and the resultant
grants may have given academic libraries in this country as
great an impetus as any other single event in their development.
If this is true, it constitutes a tribute to the quality of advice
that was given by the members of the various advisory groups,
and is in particular tribute to the guiding hand of Dr. Bishop.

Although educators had been pressing for some time for the
expansion of library facilities and educational programs began
to use assigned and supplemental reading in the library, these
were academic suggestions unless the books were available in
the library to carry out the proposals. It is to the credit of the
Carnegie Corporation and the advisory groups that they did provide the tools for this educational development.

Special emphasis should be given to the superb direction
which Dr. Bishop gave as chairman of these groups. Not only
were they handled efficiently but, because of his prestige, his
scholarship, his knowledge of educational methods, as well as
his leadership in librarianship, he was able to weld together
these groups of university presidents and librarians into effective operating units.

Dr. Bishop's contributions to the Carnegie Corporation work
were varied and were valuable to both participants. On his side,
Dr. Bishop had a high regard for Dr. E. P. Keppel and for Dr.
Robert M. Lester and, on their side, they recognized in Dr.
Bishop the type of administrator with scholarly background,
wide acquaintanceship with libraries throughout the world, and
an uncanny ability at relating costs to objectives. The partnership was one which has left a lasting impression upon American
college libraries and librarianship.

President Keppel of the Carnegie Corporation wrote of him:

DR. WILLIAM WARNER BISHOP

Native intelligence and an instinct for cooperation may be taken for granted; as to his librarianship, you will read elsewhere in this volume. A word may be said, however, as to three other qualifications: the first is the thoroughness and range of his scholarship, including his competence as a linguist; the second is the place he has earned as an outstanding university figure. There have been instances, as we all know, when presidents or deans or professors have failed to remove the academic high hat in the presence of a librarian. I assert with confidence that this has never occurred when the librarian in question happened to be William Warner Bishop. Thirdly, there is his incredible industry and his power to cause industry in others. Let me, in passing, lay a wreath on the desk of the, to me, unknown soldier who types his letters and memoranda, and sees that the right copies go to the right people.

I would miss my purpose if I left the impression that Dr. Bishop has no faults. That is not the case. He can be very inconsiderate. For instance, he is capable of writing you, in revolting detail of fishing triumphs in Canada when he well knows you are chained to your office desk. He can also be overconsiderate, which is quite as bad. In all the cases where the events have proved him to be right and me to be wrong, he has never once said, or looked, "I told you so!" The perfect colleague would at least occasionally have done so. Then he has another imperfection; he answers letters too soon. When you hope you have secured a brief respite from some bothersome duty by seeking counsel, it isn't fair to have such excellent advice shot back at you by return mail that further exertion upon your part becomes a prompt necessity. Some day I am going to tell him my mother-in-law's story of the lady who wouldn't stay visited, but I doubt if it will do any good.

But balancing his good qualities against these unfortunate attributes, it is my considered judgment that William Warner Bishop has exerted a deeper and a more salutary influence on what may be called the Carnegie Library tradition than any other single individual, and I am confident that with this judgment the many other members of his profession who singly and in groups have themselves done so much for that tradition will be found in generous and sincere accord.[13]

In the 1920's Dr. Bishop's influence was also felt in the design of library buildings. The University of Michigan had constructed a new building which opened in 1919. With his usual thoroughness, Bishop had worked closely with the architect, Albert Kahn, in attempting to develop a completely functional building. Funds were limited and the architectural design was prescribed and, in addition, it was necessary to use the old library as a core for the building. However, they surmounted these problems and worked out what was then a new development in university libraries at a low per-cubic-foot cost. They were insistent that the bookstacks be "designed primarily as research workrooms rather than as storehouses". This foreshadowed most modern academic libraries. Bishop also insisted on the importance of natural light and quickly appreciated the advantages of reinforced concrete construction. The library was one of the first to be built in such a manner that its internal design could be easily changed to meet new or unanticipated demands. It should be recognized that as early as 1919 Bishop stressed the importance of designing buildings for reader use; flexibility in design, so that the building could be adapted to unforeseen needs; and emphasis upon adequate lighting. These criteria are still important in the design of library structures. He was consulted by librarians and architects on the design of many important libraries here and abroad.

Recognition of his great contribution to international librarianship was shown by the ALA Executive Board in 1945 when it elected him representative emeritus for life to the International Federation of Library Associations. This was a fitting culmination to his unique service to international affairs. It began as early as 1898 when Dr. Bishop first went to Europe as a student. Although at that time he was a Greek and Latin scholar, he later became proficient in Italian, French, German, Spanish, and Dutch. The university sent him to Europe on book-buying trips in 1921 and 1922 during which time he came to know many foreign librarians. Then in 1924 on sabbatical leave he took his family on a European tour.

His first important contribution to international library co-

operation was made in 1927 when the Carnegie Endowment for
International Peace selected him to head the project for the recataloging and reorganization of the Vatican Library in Rome.
This assignment continued from 1927 to 1935, and Dr. Bishop's
early familiarity as a user of the library enabled him to provide
unusual guidance to the entire project. Cardinal Tisserant became an admirer of William Warner Bishop and once wrote:

> The progress of the Vatican Library index is slow,
> but it is continuous, and among the many undertakings
> to which Dr. Bishop gave beginning and impulse, none
> perhaps will have a wider repercussion than this one,
> in which the trustees of the Carnegie Endowment for
> International Peace manifested their "wish to cooperate
> with the Church in its great task of promoting education,
> and, through education, international understanding and
> international peace".[14]

In 1933 he made arrangements for a group of foreign librarians to visit this country and attend the ALA meeting. The American Library Association had recognized his international interests by continuing him on the ALA International Relations
Committee for the period from 1926-1936, and he was internationally recognized in 1928 with an invitation to become one
of the first members of the International Federation of Library
Associations. The federation elected him vice-president in that
year and made him its president in 1931. He presided at the
conference in Madrid in 1935.

His opinion was as eagerly sought abroad as in this country
and among his foreign assignments were: adviser to the League
of Nations and Special Consultant on plans for the library building, member of Bodleian Library Commission, and adviser to
many individual librarians from other countries. His varied experiences abroad, as well as his knowledge of American librarians and librarianship, enabled him to serve as a truly international librarian. His comparison of American and European
librarians is interesting:

> Thus I have known and admired the leading European
> librarians of my day. They have much to teach us in the
> way of scholarship, but none of them has a problem at

all like that confronting the Librarian of Congress, or the director of the New York Public Library or the director of the Harvard University Libraries. Here we demand executive ability plus scholarship in our heads of libraries and render a service not to be compared with that in Europe. To be a successful American librarian demands qualities different from the scholarship required of our European colleagues but based on such scholarly attainments. To have had a part in bringing these extremes together is a privilege.[15]

In addition to these accomplishments, Dr. Bishop is also responsible for other developments which must be mentioned. In 1926 he opened the library school at the University of Michigan with a faculty that attracted scholars from all parts of the world. Through his personal interest and understanding the extension work of the department was unusual in its breadth and scope. As indicated earlier his development of the book collection was unusual. He surveyed the Huntington Library in 1930.

And what of his accomplishments as a library administrator? He had a rigid standard for quality of workers to be employed in the library; he was firm in insisting that proper salaries be paid to professional workers; and he was conscious of problems which were to develop and cause great concern to librarians of the present time. In 1931 he published an article on university libraries, in which he acknowledged the growing cost of library services.

What is to be the university's attitude toward this huge equipment in books? What sort of library policy may we expect of governing bodies, presidents, deans, faculties? The cost of a great library building absorbs millions which might perhaps go toward the endowment of teaching and research. The cost of conserving and rendering available for use the books in a university library grown to these huge modern proportions is greater by far than was ever dreamed of even thirty years since. The cost of adequate annual supplies of old and new books is a heavy drain on the university's income — a sum in many cases representing a capital of two or three million dollars. Even the rental cost of land for

356

libraries covering these large areas is a serious charge
on university funds. When wood-pulp paper begins to
break down freely, there will come a further charge
for either expensive photographic reproduction or for
chemical preservation against decay and disintegration.
University presidents and trustees must, it would seem,
have grave reasons to count the cost of huge libraries —
and they will find it portentous. These libraries have
reached their present and their prospective size in
strict response to academic demand, aided, it must be
confessed, by an ever-growing acquisitiveness of their
librarians, but still a demand originated and urged on
by the faculties themselves. This cost is certain to be
greater, rather than less, in the future. It obviously
costs more to administer a library of two millions
than one of a million volumes. Library processes grow
more complex with greater numbers. Is the expense
justified?[16]

The alternative to neglect or to a drifting policy
is a frank recognition of the size and importance of the
problem. It is perfectly patent that we must have books
and that it costs money to buy, house, arrange, record,
and serve them. Try to cut down these costs as every
good librarian must; they will remain large and they
will probably grow larger. The task will never be
finished. I recall a senator impatiently asking the Superintendent of the Coast and Geodetic Survey when he
would get through mapping the shores and rivers of the
country. "Never!" was the emphatic reply, "until tides
and currents cease and rivers stop their flow." Even
so the librarian's work will never be done; and while
he may — and will — reduce the cost of individual operations, he can never greatly cut the flow of books and
the demand for service. The presidents and governing
bodies of universities are going to be troubled with this
financial problem so long as books are printed.[17]

It could never be said that Dr. Bishop's work went without
recognition here and abroad. He received honorary doctorates
from Miami University, New York University, Columbia University, Catholic University of America, Oberlin College, West-

ern Ontario University, National University of Ireland and Ohio
Wesleyan. In addition he was made an honorary member of the
Library Association of China, the Argentine Association of Li-
brarians and an honorary fellow of the Library Association of
Great Britain. He was elected honorary president of the Inter-
national Federation of Librarians in 1936.

Personally, Dr. William Warner Bishop was a distinguished
figure — tall and erect with a striking white goatee. He looked
like what he was, a scholarly librarian. Those who did not know
him intimately often thought that he was somewhat stiff and a
little forbidding. He once confided that in his adult life only two
people ever called him "Bill".

The exterior, as is often the case, hardly presented a true
or complete picture. He was genuinely interested in the librarians who worked for him; in the students who attended the library
school; and in those with whom he had worked. His characteriza-
tion of Herbert Putnam could be directly applied to him.

> He was not an easy man to know, and had few inti-
> mates either in the library or out of it. He held his
> staff at arm's length, never encouraging familiarity,
> and yet showing himself always kind, considerate, and
> friendly.[18]

Dr. Bishop was genuinely kind in many ways and when the
bank holiday was declared in the 1930's he personally offered
loans to those who had financial difficulties. He was some times
brutally frank in his appraisal of the librarians whom he had
known, but he was tolerant and always willing to give credit no
matter what his personal relationship with the individual might
have been.

In Ann Arbor in May 1935 Dr. Bishop was preparing to leave
to officiate as president of a second International Congress of
Libraries and Bibliography at Madrid and Barcelona. The newspaper correspondents were familiar with his accomplishments
and honors, and felt that it would be proper to ask him what important books and journals he planned to read on his trip abroad.
Dr. Bishop somewhat shocked them by stating that his reading
would be primarily of detective stories and that he was greatly
addicted to this kind of reading. He owned a practically complete
set of Edgar Wallace, and there were few mysteries that he had

not read. He then said, "Any professional man has to keep up with a certain amount of professional reading, but you can't tell what a man's real reading interest is until you see what he takes along on vacation trips."

The picture of Dr. Bishop, the scholar, the gentleman, librarian, is not complete unless we also see him as a detective story fan and an avid fisherman.

One of our great librarians, Harry Lydenberg, epitomized his accomplishments and character as follows:

Few fellow laborers in this country have equalled him in contacts with scholars and librarians abroad, none have surpassed him as interpreter to those at home of what their friends are doing overseas, or as a representative over there of the best expressions of the strivings, hopes, ideals of the tillers of library fields on this side of the water.

A unique record of activity, achievement, accomplishment, recognition. A prophet not without honor tendered quite as sincerely in his own country as in more distant lands, a tribute to sound scholarship, spontaneous sympathy for new or different points of view, to thoroughly laid foundations, to fittingly planned and built superstructures, to an outlook wide of scope, all in all a constant source of stimulation and admiration, of healthy envy and rivalry for the ever-widening circle of friends throughout the world.[19]

In talking about the Philadelphia ALA conference in 1897, Bishop said that he and Josephus Larned played "hooky" from the main session in order to go to a concert, adding,

I would rather hear an orchestra any day than listen to talk about library work.[20]

MOHRHARDT

NOTES:

1 Bishop, William Warner. "College Days — 1889-93". Michigan Alumnus. Quarterly Review. 54:349, Summer 1948.

2 Ibid., p. 349-50.

3 Bishop, William Warner. "Rome and Brooklyn: 1899-1902. Fragments of Autobiography". Library Quarterly. 15:329-30, October 1945.

4 Bishop, William Warner. "Princeton. 1902-7, Fragments of Autobiography". Library Quarterly. 16:219-20, July 1946.

5 Bishop, William Warner. Subject Headings in Dictionary Catalogs. Papers and Proceedings of the 28th General Meeting of the American Library Association. 1906:114.

6 Bishop, William Warner. "The Library of Congress. 1907-15: Fragments of Autobiography". Library Quarterly. 18:23, January 1948.

7 Bishop, William Warner. "Some Recollections of William Lawrence Clements and the Formation of His Library". Library Quarterly, 18:191, July 1948.

8 Bishop, William Warner. "The American Library Association. II. Fragments of Autobiography". Library Quarterly, 21:37, January 1951.

9 Ibid., p. 39.

10 Bishop, William Warner. CARNEGIE CORPORATION AND COLLEGE LIBRARIES: 1929-1938. p. 14.

11 Ibid., p. 15.

12 Ibid., p. 43.

13 Keppel, Frederick Paul. "William Warner Bishop" in Lydenberg, Harry M. and Keogh, Andrew, WILLIAM WARNER BISHOP: A TRIBUTE 1941. (New Haven, Yale University Press, 1941). pp. 3-4.

14 Eugene, Cardinal Tisserant. "The Preparation of a Main Index

for the Vatican Library Manuscripts", in Lydenberg, Harry M. and Keogh, Andrew, WILLIAM WARNER BISHOP: A TRIBUTE 1941. (New Haven, Yale University Press, 1941), p. 185.

15 Bishop, William Warner. "International Relations: Fragments of Autobiography". Library Quarterly. 19:284, October 1949.

16 Bishop, William Warner. University Libraries: Some Reflections on the Dedication of the Sterling Memorial Library of Yale University. Library Quarterly. 1:249. 1931.

17 Ibid., p. 251.

18 Bishop, William Warner. "The Library of Congress, 1907-15: Fragments of Autobiography". Library Quarterly. 18:16, January 1948.

19 Lydenberg, Harry M. "William Warner Bishop", in Lydenberg, Harry M. and Keogh, Andrew, WILLIAM WARNER BISHOP: A TRIBUTE 1941 (New Haven, Yale University Press, 1941), pp. 11, 17.

20 Bishop, William Warner "The American Library Association: Fragments of Autobiography". Library Quarterly. 19:39. January 1949.

HERBERT PUTNAM: LIBRARIAN OF THE UNITED STATES

David C. Mearns

David C. Mearns is Chief of the Manuscript Division of the Library of Congress, Washington, D.C. The Minneapolis section of the essay here reprinted is a paper read before the American Library History Round Table during the Minneapolis conference of the American Library Association in 1954.

When Thomas Jefferson, embarking upon his services as American minister to France, was asked whether he was "replacing" Benjamin Franklin in that office, he instantly responded: "No one can replace him, sir; I am only his successor." I can but echo these words — and I am sure that my two immediate predecessors as Librarian of Congress would do the same — in speaking of Herbert Putnam. The 40 years of his administration of the Library's affairs were truly anni mirabiles. They were years in which, under his vigorous guidance, the Library was transformed from a mere reservoir of books, having a narrow public, into one of the world's great cultural institutions, serving the entire Nation.

I am happy to introduce to the readers of D.C. Libraries this paper on Dr. Putnam. The Library of Congress as it now exists bears his mark more than that of any other individual, and those of us who follow the path he laid out for us are ever mindful that "he who hath builded the house shall have more honor than the house".

L. Quincy Mumford
Librarian of Congress

Reprinted from D.C. Libraries, 26:1-24, January, 1955, by permission of the author and the publisher. The Minneapolis section of this paper was first published in Wilson Library Bulletin, 29:59-63, September, 1954, and is reprinted by permission.

HERBERT PUTNAM

[PROEM]

This has been for me a chastening exercise. A greater intellect, possessed of keener powers of analysis, and governing a less discursive pen, could, with eloquence and discernment, present an appreciation or assessment of that continuing career without bursting the merciful constrictions of allotted time. But as I have struggled with, and succumbed to, the problem, brevity and comprehensibility have become irreconcilable.

There are simply too many essentials to understanding: there is the personality, the milieu, the adventitious introduction to librarianship, the prodigious and instant capacities for it, the abandonment of the profession, the return to it, the eminence gained, the narrowly averted forfeiture of the post at Washington, the singleness of purpose, the relations with people and associates and boards and Congress, the patience and the long years, the achievement and its measure . . . Subtract any of these considerations, slight any of them, there can be only confusion and misapprehension. There are already enough fables and myths and legends and false ascriptions.

Instead, I have tried to summarize the story as I have found it, allowing the characters sometimes to speak for themselves.

MINNEAPOLIS

The Speaker of the House was disturbed. An office was to be filled. Candidates were plentiful. Politicians gave them eloquent encouragement, pleading their causes in high places. Precedents being what they were, it was not inconceivable that an injudicious appointment would be made. The Speaker communicated his anxieties to William McKinley:

Mr. President [he wrote]: It seems to me that I ought to call your attention to the situation of the Congressional Library. It is a great library now, and ought to be the greatest. In order that it may be such it needs a suitable person at the head of it. A librarian needs training, capacity, and special faculty, as much as the chief of the Army, or the Attorney General, or the Chief Justice. I have no suggestion to make as to who ought to fill the office, for I have not the requisite knowledge of men, but in my opinion an effort should be made to get somebody

363

worthy of the position and capable of carrying on the
work in a satisfactory way. If the salary is inadequate
it would seem as if application ought to be made to
Congress representing the facts in preference to the
reduction of the office to the grade of an inadequate
salary.

I write this letter both as a member of Congress
and because of the very deep interest which I take in
the subject, and the very great hope I have that the
Library of Congress will sometime take a high, if not
the highest place among the libraries of great nations
In order that it should do this the very best man possible should be had now.

Very respectfully
T. B. Reed[1]

The Speaker was an old and important friend to the Library
of Congress. He believed in its national character and its importance to the people of the United States. He had repeatedly
demonstrated his interest.[2] But was there, in January 1899, a
man of distinctions so outstanding that he possessed the qualifications called for by the Honorable Thomas Brackett Reed?

There was: in the person of a great-great nephew of old Israel Putnam[3] of whom it is said that he violated every principle
of military etiquette by leaving his plow and dashing into the
skirmish at Lexington without taking time to dress for the occasion. His young relative was less impetuous, but much more enduring. Still in his thirties, he had already established himself
as a successful administrator. Uninfluenced by the precepts of
his elders in the guild, he had nevertheless won their admiration, enthusiasm, and respect. He had never occupied a subordinate post, his apprenticeship (if that it could properly be called)
had been served exclusively as top-dog. He had deserted librarianship for the law, then law for librarianship, but it was silly
to think of him as a rolling stone. He would make a virtue of
tenacity. Now, he stood at the head of his profession. A fledgling organization, a group known as the A.L.A., looked upon
him as a comer. He would, its members believed, make a place
for himself. But could he sustain the promise of his precocity?
And who was he anyway?

Herbert Putnam was born with a book in his mouth. The site

was a home on New York's East Seventeenth Street. The date was September 20th, 1861. His father, George Palmer Putnam, was founder of a great publishing house, whose sons (Herbert would be an exception) were one day admitted to the imprint. His mother, Victorine Haven Putnam, it is said, "had herself never had anything that could be called an education", but, in journeys through Europe, "she secured enough knowledge of French, German, and Italian to keep herself interested in the literature of the three countries", and managed to make "herself very much a part of the life of her children".[4] Abraham Lincoln had been in the White House a few months, and was experiencing some difficulty in quelling a disturbance below the Potomac. A few weeks before Herbert Putnam's advent, Putnam pere had been witness to the precipitous departure of Union warriors from Bull Run; later organizing the Loyal Publications Society with some functions comparable to the A.L.A.'s War Service, directed by Herbert Putnam more than fifty years later.

When Herbert Putnam was eleven years old his father died; Mrs. Putnam managed the younger children; George Haven Putnam (Herbert's elder brother) managed the firm. Summers were spent on Long Island Sound, near Darien, Connecticut.[5] In town during the winter months, Herbert attended a private English and Classical School, on upper Broadway, conducted by James H. Morse, a product of the Leicester Academy, Brookline High School, and that college at Cambridge, Massachusetts. A sound scholar, author of graceful verses, essays, and reviews, world traveler,[6] Mr. Morse appears to have been an excellent teacher. His erstwhile pupil entered Harvard in the fall of 1879.

For the future overseer, the four years at college must have been altogether satisfactory. He played lacrosse, "heeled" the Crimson, joined the Harvard Union and the O.K. Society, received a detur as a freshman; as a sophomore, walked away with the Lee Prize for reading; thereafter excelled in Latin, Political Economy, and English Composition; reached the highest honors group; presented a dissertation at commencement; and made Phi Beta Kappa. An engrossed parchment, dated in 1883, proclaimed him a bachelor of arts.[7]

The next year he "spent in New York, attending the lectures at the Columbia Law School".[8] Somewhere along the way he attracted the attention of Samuel Hill.

By birth and by Harvard, four years Mr. Putnam's senior,

Mr. Hill would have a gratifying career. A native of North Carolina and long-time resident of Minneapolis, Mr. Hill is, perhaps, best remembered for having organized and presided over the Minneapolis Trust Company;[9] for having (in 1903) "brought Professor Yamashita to the United States, and introduced the art of Judo (the Japanese art of defense without weapons) in this country generally";[10] and for having promoted the "Peace Portal" between the United States and Canada for which he received the special thanks of Congress and the Canadian Government.[11] His lineage in directories of directors would be almost excessive. His fortunes were not adversely affected by his marriage, on Thursday, September 6th, 1888, to Mary, daughter of James Jerome Hill. The bride was spared the nuisance of changing her name; the ceremony was one of the events of the season. "The invitations specially requested that no presents be sent, but nevertheless the bride and groom received many beautiful tributes. . . . Among the presents was a check from J. J. Hill for $200,000."[12]

At Harvard, Mr. Hill had been counted among the "literary fellers",[13] which may explain his later devotion to the Fortnightly Club, and the Minneapolis Athenaeum. In 1884, when he made his outstanding contribution to the cultural history of the United States, Mr. Hill was a rising and prosperous attorney, with a passion for his alma mater and for the success of all her sons. Having learned that Mr. Putnam aspired to the bar, Mr. Hill proposed to him that he remove to Minneapolis, assume the librarianship of the Athenaeum, and work his way through the law by communing in off moments with Blackstone.[14] The invitation was accepted; before very long 800 Nicollet Avenue had a new tenant.[15]

That, as I say, was in the autumn of 1884. The Minneapolis Athenaeum, founded, nearly a quarter of a century before, upon proceeds from a popular lecture by Bayard Taylor, was a subscription library, supported, primarily, by annual assessments upon its members, but recently the beneficiary of impressive private endowment.[16] Untutored as he was in the craft, lacking technical experience of any kind, Mr. Putnam seems instinctively to have responded to the requirements of "the shabby old library". Indeed, one highly competent witness has related how —

He began at the start to modernize its antiquated meth-

ods; he installed a charging system with a borrower's
card instead of the old way of charging in a big book.
He began a new system of cataloguing and classification, and opened up the alcoves to readers so that they
could find titles for themselves. Not only were his
methods new and thoroughgoing, but his courteous,
genial manner created a new atmosphere.[17]

More recently it has been stated that "he displayed from the beginning the vision and leadership which have so conspicuously
marked his subsequent career".[18] It was characteristic of Herbert Putnam to understand his problems before looking for so-
lutions.

He had not been in Minneapolis for two months before the
Athenaeum's directors had abandoned their earlier plan for a
new building in favor of an "alliance with a municipal library if
one were established".[19] The idea of a public library had been
promoted as early as 1876, but nothing had come of it. The
State Legislature took the position that before an enabling act
could be introduced, the City Council should be convinced that
a tax-supported library would be advantageous to the community
and publicly approved. Now the city authorities declined assent
unless and until fifty thousand dollars was raised by gifts. The
sentiment of the citizenry was demonstrated by over-subscribing
the fund by ten thousand dollars. The enabling act was passed
in March, 1885.[20] Mr. Putnam was credited with being "the
leading spirit". He had told the press: "There are two great
problems of library management, one to get the books for the
readers, the other to get the readers to the books."[21]

In the spring of the following year, he wrote to his class
secretary: "I have not indulged an appetite for exploration 'in
this or foreign countries'; what journeys have fallen to my lot
have been between Minneapolis and New England, with some
deviations to other cities whose libraries deserved investigation."[22] There are two implications to be drawn from this guarded statement: first, that librarianship engaged his serious attention; second, that an unspecified object attracted him to New
England. As to the latter, a satisfactory explanation was given
a few months later when Herbert Putnam, of Minneapolis, Minnesota, was joined in marriage by Dr. Alexander McKenzie[23]
to Charlotte Elizabeth, daughter of the Reverend Charles and

Susan Hall Munroe, of Cambridge, Massachusetts. Mrs. Putnam's brother, Kirk Munroe, author of many books, world traveler, first editor of Harper's Round Table, was friend to Kit Carson and Buffalo Bill. Perhaps Mr. Putnam thus acquired by marriage his constant interest in western novels.

During the summer of 1888, he visited the cities and provincial towns of England and Scotland on a book-buying expedition, and returned with "some eight thousand volumes". In September, the Unitarian Review published his article on the ethical teachings of Tolstoi, which he entitled "Simplicity as a Test of Truth".[24] Two months later he was named librarian of the public library, then in course of construction: this was an office he would hold simultaneously with the librarianship of the conjoined Athenaeum.

In fulfillment of his dual responsibilities, Mr. Putnam undertook a survey of the Athenaeum collections, and discarded, as inappropriate, nearly a quarter of them. But with the remainder, and the accessions from the United Kingdom and the Continent, he was able to transfer to the shelves of the new building a formidable array of 30,000 volumes. More than this, he determined the policy, consistently followed throughout the years, that the Athenaeum's income should be applied to the purchase of the more expensive reference books.[25]

The Public Library was formally opened on Monday, December 16th, 1889. The newspapers recounted the proceedings with spirit and obvious delight; one reported:

> Of the many public events that have occurred in Minneapolis since the city came to be recognized as a factor in the development of the great Northwest, the one that stands pre-eminent as a mark of the intellectual growth of the community is the opening of the public library. . . .
>
> The citizens of Minneapolis, without reference to social position, or business standing simply turned out en masse to look over and admire their beautiful building. . . .
>
> As people arrived they were met at the doors by colored men in full dress, who directed them into the building. Those who wished to lay aside their wraps proceeded to the basement, the ladies using the room

in the northwest corner for a toilet room, the gentlemen being accomocated [sic] in the newspaper reading
room. . . . The scene in the staircase hall was an attractive one. On the second and third floor landings,
next to the iron railings, were grouped potted palms,
hollies, rhododendrons, Japanese chrysanthemums
and other choice plants.

The large glass swing doors revealed within other
elegant floral decorations, potted plants stationed here
and there among the statuary and tasty wreaths of smi-
lax hanging from the chandeliers. These decorations
were furnished gratuitously by Mendenhall. Danz' orchestra was stationed on the second floor landing, and
discoursed appropriate music during the evening. The
niches in the outer wall were occupied by some of the
choicest of the Exposition casts.[26]

The psalm was illustrated with a line-drawing portrait of the
stern-visaged young librarian, drooping moustache dependent
from the upper lip, throat encased in a wing collar, it surround-
ed by a cravat knotted according to the strictest principles of
Ascot, and the coat was evidently frock, tailored to conform
with a fashion set by Victoria's Prince Consort.

The Minneapolis Public Library was off to a good start. Herbert Putnam had given it momentum, torque, and acceleration.
Within an astonishingly brief time, it would establish itself in
a high place among comparable institutions in the United States.
A year later the President of the Board would proudly remark
with satisfaction: "Probably a freer access to books has been
permitted here than in any similar library, and yet the percentage of loss has been much less than that almost invariably exper-
ienced under the most stringent regulations,"[27]

Those who came in contact with Herbert Putnam at that time
never forgot him. There exists, for example, a letter written
almost sixty years later; it reads:

Your personal service to me when I was a student
at the University of Minnesota has always been outstanding in my memory.

You had just recently opened the Minneapolis Public
Library in a store running through a block between Hen-

nepin and Nicollet Avenues. I had heard about the new
library and the librarian and when I had a real need for
a book I ventured to ask for it at the new Public Library.
You gave me the most cooperative service, found the
right book for me and gave me my card. This service
was much appreciated by me and never forgotten but it
was the friendly cooperative spirit that made the permanent impression on my mind. I am sure that it is that
same cooperative spirit that has made your life so successful.

The letter continues with a few lines of felicitation; then
comes the complimentary close: "Sincerely and respectfully
yours, H. W. Wilson."[28]
Herbert Putnam had identified himself with the city; he was
heading a thriving enterprise; his residence might have been
indefinitely prolonged, had not the serious illness of Mrs. Putnam's mother obliged them to return to Massachusetts.[29] His
resignation was effective at the close of the calendar year, 1891.
He could look back upon the experience with satisfaction. His
successor, Dr. James Kendall Hosmer, recorded the general
and personal opinion of Herbert Putnam's administration: "His
management of the trust had been faithful and able: a fine foundation had been laid by him for a great library: he left all departments in excellent condition; the service he had organized
was efficient."[30]
But to measure Mr. Putnam's achievement it is necessary
to project the history of the Minneapolis Public Library into
future decades. His former colleague and later herself city librarian, Gratia A. Countryman, wrote of him in 1929:

Looking back over the development of the past forty
years, it is hard to find any undertakings of later years
which were not foreshadowed by the things he started or
planned to start. Indeed, in the light of these years, he
must be counted as one of the leaders who shaped the intellectual mold of Minneapolis. . . . The mantle of his
spirit is still over the Minneapolis Public Library.[31]

And from the perspective of half a century, the Library made
this acknowledgment to his enduring influence:

370

HERBERT PUTNAM

The organization of the activities of the Library was worked out by Dr. Putnam before he resigned . . . The pattern for the development of the Library's services which he laid out has been in a large measure followed by his successors. The continuity in the development of library service in Minneapolis has resulted from the close cooperation of the Board, the well-defined program which Mr. Putnam had set up, and the fact that a nucleus of the staff received its training under the first Librarian and remained with the Library for many years in positions of leadership.[32]

Now the gift which Herbert Putnam brought to Minneapolis and the nation was the gift of continuity and steady growth; the gift of the well-set course and strength for its running. There is power in it. Sometimes nowadays a nonogenarian of irrefragable experience, agile and alert, looks with impersonal, penetrating brown eyes hard at a short, shivering, red-headed man, still in his twenties. The youngster is wearing an overcoat and a fur cap. He sits beside a stove. He places a log on the fire. He is in the Athenaeum. He is compiling the Great Itinerary.

Then the ancient turns impatiently away; "Yesterdays don't interest me", he says, "Only tomorrow."[33]

BOSTON

Having been admitted to the Minnesota Bar, in about 1885, Herbert Putnam was from there certified to the Bar of Suffolk County at Boston. There he was admitted to the bar and entered the office of Nichols and Cobb, the lawyer thus displacing the librarian. He was not a member of the firm; his practice was "relatively unimportant".[34] He followed his "second" profession for three years. Then, one day, he was visited by Josiah Henry Benton.

A native of Vermont, a veteran of the Civil War, Mr. Benton was one of Boston's leading citizens. "His whole life", it is said, "was marked by a sturdy Americanism, and by an outspoken loyalty to American institutions." He possessed notable collections of the products of John Baskerville's press, of liturgies, and of prayer books. It was, therefore, natural that "of all his civic interests the Public Library stood easily first".

371

Mr. Benton had recently become a trustee.[35]

Mr. Benton proposed to Mr. Putnam, on whose part there had been "no solicitation nor appearance of candidacy",[36] that he become librarian. On February 11th, 1893, Herbert Putnam, aged thirty-three, assumed his duties. The magnificent building on Copley Square had opened only a few days before. His "chief work", as he put it, would be "in adapting the library to the new building and in popularizing its facilities".[37] From the start, he met with remarkable success "in increasing the interest of the public in its privileges and resources; in enlarging its scope and patronage; and, especially, in conducting its work in close cooperation with the public schools".[38] Rooms for children and for readers of newspapers were established. A Special Libraries Department was initiated. The branch library system was developed and rapidly expanded. Women were assigned to responsible positions. Impetus was given to bibliographical studies. The Boston Public Library quickly became the nation's most satisfactorily operated institution of the kind,[39] and within four years it would be said that "with the Boston Public Library, now the most thoroughly organized and the foremost free public library in the world, the great modern movement had its beginning".[40] Herbert Putnam had launched it.

One who met him at that time has set down this reminiscence:

Herbert Putnam began to teach me lessons nearly sixty years ago, all of lasting importance and of value fitting to their source. . . .

Befell that in that season on a day, bright and sunny in the merry month of May (or, it might have been April or June) a Harvard sophomore heard from home that the assistant librarian of the Dayton Public Library would be in Boston in the spring of 1895 on a trip to the east studying library methods. Electra Collins Doren had given to this youngster a glimpse of the satisfactions of library work while he was "the" page and errand boy of the library after school hours all through his high school years. When he heard she would be in Boston at this time he took for granted that she would turn to the Library of course, would be welcomed by the Librarian so new in his post, this much if not greeted by him at the railway station.

And so did he — ingenuous, ignorant, brash, callous youth — scamper over to Boston and to the office of the Librarian to ask for the news about Miss Doren. Just like that!

To this day does he recall the quiet, courteous attention he got as he put his question, recall too the reply that the Librarian had not yet heard of the honor of this visit but felt the visitor would probably be in the reference reading room if in the building, and asked if the boy had looked in Bates Hall.

The words were few. The interview was short. Just a moment or two. Brusque? A rebuff? Be off with ye and don't bother a busy man? Not one bit! It served its purpose, finished its task, did its work. Nothing more was needed. The boy did find his friend in Bates Hall, did see his good luck, did come to see how neatly he had been handled.

As he grew in years, if not in wisdom, he came to grasp how sensible was the greeting from the older man. He came to see how a wise man with kindly instincts would be patient with the brashness of the uninvited, unexpected, unnecessary demand on his time, patient with the interruption of his daily task, would see that the intruder was as earnest as he was ingenuous, inexperienced, ignorant, unaware of how such things are done; would settle the trifling immediate problem with least waste of time and effort and with neither intention nor suspicion of discourtesy; would set the inquirer on his way in most effective fashion.

It took some time to learn the lesson, but the whole affair did sink way down deep into the youngster's mind, did let him see the kind, instinctive understanding by the elder man of the object of the intrusion, did let him see the spirit behind the greeting, did help him thus early in his self education to benefit by that spirit moving Herbert Putnam.

Herbert Putnam and that Harvard sophomore came in touch with one another in various ways in later years, came to have different contacts, all letting the younger man glimpse some of the facets of that soul, but never in all the years that followed did he fail to be the better and the stronger for what he saw of that forceful, gentle, kindly, understanding spirit. Never did he fail to remember that interview on that spring morning of 1895.

For him Herbert Putnam ranks with John Shaw Billings high in the group of men that taught him lessons of lasting value and importance.[41]

The memorialist can be identified with Harry Miller Lydenberg! But even his trustees reposed perfect confidence in Herbert Putnam; they recorded their gratulations in his selection at the end of his first year, writing:

> He has proved to be most competent and faithful in the discharge of his duties, which have been unusually difficult and trying by reason of the change of the Central Library to the new building, fitting up the West Church Branch, and other matters incident to the general administration of the affairs of the Library . . . The Trustees desire to express their appreciation of his services and to say that to him and to heads of departments and other employees of the Library, who have earnestly cooperated with him, any success which the Library may have had in meeting the just requirements of the public during the past year is largely due.[42]

Nor was the Librarian himself niggardly in praise; insisting, with his faculty of oblique emphasis:

> In a document intended for the public my inclination is always to abstain from commendation of associates who may, equally with the chief executive, be presumed to have the interest of the service at heart. But I have often occasion to regret that I cannot share with the public the knowledge which I gain (as no one else can) of the earnestness, conscience, good faith and high endeavor which enter into the work of employees of this library who get general credit for no more than the routine performance of routine duties.[43]

Mr. Putnam's professional standing, already high, was considerably enhanced by the Boston experience. If, as has been stated, he did not follow in the footsteps of his elders among the library administrators of the nation, it was for the simple reason that he led the way. Those elders held his talents in highest honor and respect. It was only natural, therefore, that he should be one of those summoned to Washington, in the fall of 1896, to consult with the Joint Committee on a new charter for the Library of Congress. For him it was a first encounter:

The chairman asked him: "Is there such a thing as library science?" and he replied: "I believe there is." Being pressed to explain its content, he described it as consisting "of a certain knowledge of bibliography, of the process of book making, of the historical production of books, of the essentials which govern the cataloguing of a book — making the book useful after you have received it — of the questions of administration that enter into the mediation between the book and the readers — the reference use of the library". He confessed to knowing "something" about library schools, but knew little of the proficiency of their graduates.[44]

He was asked what work "the Library of Congress could wisely engage in other than that of furnishing the public a reading room and some books to read". He replied that "the Library should properly stand nationally for what the State libraries are to the State, with regard to all documentary material, because the National Library is the final depository of national archives, and it could so serve in helping to place the State libraries with respect to their archives, on a similar plan, strengthen and render uniform their methods by its influence as a national institution". He considered "uniformity in system" an objective of great importance.[45]

To the question: "Do you think that eight cataloguers could do the work of cataloguing the Library of Congress?" he answered: "It is incredible to me that they should." In his opinion, fifty might be adequate.[46]

He urged independence for the Librarian:

> I believe [he said] in centering responsibility. I should say that if the Librarian of Congress is absolutely free from political control in the selection of his men, if he will not have to recommend persons who are forced upon him, then it is safe to leave it to him. I believe that librarians in general, if they have the respon-

sibility vested in them, that, as a class — I speak, of course, of the Librarian of Congress as belonging to that class — they will not misuse their authority.[47]

He was told to comment on "the qualities that the chief administrative officer of this new Congressional Library ought to possess". Then came this extraordinary affirmation:

This should be a library, the foremost library in the United States — a national library — that is to say the largest library in the United States and a library which stands foremost as a model and example of assisting forward the work of scholarship in the United States. . . .

I should suppose that the man who is to have the final administration of that library must have above all things else administrative ability — the same kind of a man who is to manage the property or interest of any large corporation, is to handle large funds, is to manage a large force of employees; such a one should have administrative capacity. It is as much required in a library as anywhere else. When you have a department that has so many people there is need of any administrative officer who shall have superior executive ability and efficiency. I do not believe that your chief administrative officer, attending properly to the business problems of the library, need be a profound bibliographer or need to know the most of all the persons in the library, as to what the library contains. I should regard him as bearing a relation to the library something similar to that corresponding to, or borne by the president of a university to the several departments of that university.

I take it that President Eliot would say that he does not know as much Greek as the chief of that department, or of Latin, as the chief of that department, or about chemistry, as the chief of that department. . . . I don't say that a knowledge of specialties, in addition to these capacities, would be inconsistent with them, but it seems to me that those capacities are undoubtedly necessary, and that the chief executive must have them preeminently.[48]

There it was, but as he thought it over, back in Boston, he ruefully concluded that he had "probably slighted the other requisite, equally indispensable, that he [the Librarian of Congress] should know enough of the literary side of the Library, of bibliography, etc., to appreciate intelligently the needs of the several departments of specialized work".[49]

A few months later, Herbert Putnam was off to Europe where he attended the International Congress of Librarians.[50] While he was gone, William McKinley appointed a Scot, John Russell Young, to the post of Librarian of Congress. Mr. Young's tenure was distressingly brief; he died January 17th, 1899.

WASHINGTON

The completion of the magnificent building, eastward from the Capitol, an expanded staff with consequently increased appropriations, and new dignities vested in the office, had conspicuously enhanced the Librarianship of Congress. A provision inserted in H.R. 9643, of the Fifty-fourth Congress, had transferred to the Librarian authority formerly exercised by the Joint Committee, and the members of the Committee had openly acknowledged that their powers had been "repealed".[51] Not only was the Library Washington's most glittering show-place, but Mr. Young had been the recipient of many evidences of Presidential favor. This had markedly added to the prestige of the position.

Popularly regarded as a sinecure, possible of distinguished fulfillment by any affable gentleman of polished manner, the aspirants to succeed to Mr. Young's emoluments constituted a small but clamorous army. Among them were journalists like Murat Halstead, George Alfred Townsend and Henry Watterson; military leaders such as M. Fred Bell, Adjutant General of Missouri, General J. C. S. Clarkson, and General H. V. Boynton; also prominently mentioned were William W. Rockhill, a former Assistant Secretary of State, Orville J. Victor, Beadle dime novelist, James H. Canfield, President of Ohio State University, and Ainsworth Rand Spofford, the Chief Assistant Librarian who, for thirty-three years, had administered the Library.[52] Two years before, George S. Boutwell had interceded for him, writing:

377

The rumor comes to me that Spofford is to be superseded in his office of Librarian. I hope that the rumor
is false. He ought to be allowed to remain until he is
in the new building and in a good degree identified with it.

To discharge him now would be a repetition of the
treatment that was meted out to the Ancient Moses, and
with less reason, for he had slain a man, and his manner of fleeing from Egypt is not free from reproach.

That he was kept out of the Promised Land may have
been a just punishment for his violation of his own com-
mandments . . . Let Spofford enter the Promised Land.[53]

Mr. Spofford had been permitted to pass over, but not at the
head of the procession. It is no disparagement of him to note
that though he was a superb collector he was deficient in those
exalted executive capacities which Herbert Putnam regarded as
the first requisite. But Mr. Spofford who, aside from sentimental considerations, was not seriously a candidate, held a different view of qualifications. In a confidential letter to the President, he wrote: "He who stands at the head of America's foremost
Library must mingle with the foremost men of science and literature, native & foreign, who resort to it, or correspond with it,
on terms of something like equality."[54]

Actually, the principals in the contest of 1899, were New
England men; specifically they were men of Massachusetts. Outstanding was an agreeable divine, the Reverend Samuel June
Barrows. Possessed of scholarly tastes and a philanthropist's
passion for prison reform, with experience as journalist and
editor, Mr. Barrows was, at that moment, a lame-duck Congressman from the Boston neighborhood.

Among those who dismissed as "fiddle-faddle" the supposition
"that the head of a department must train himself in its every
detail, — that no man can be a commander of cavalry unless he
can stuff a saddle or shoe a horse", Mr. Barrows seemed emi-
nently eligible.

Mr. Barrows [they said] knows the world. He knows
America as few Americans do. He is easily at home in
half a dozen languages. He is ready of access. He is at
ease with all sorts and conditions of men; and he believes
in the institutions of his own country, while he has had

singularly good opportunities for studying the literature
and institutions of the rest of the world.[55]

With astonishing energy, and without awaiting the lapse of
the "decent interval" which propriety might prescribe, Mr. Barrows set out straightway to secure the nomination as Librarian
of Congress. On the very day of Mr. Young's death, Mr. Barrows's good friend and fellow-citizen of Massachusetts, the
Secretary of the Navy, the Honorable John Davis Long, presented Mr. Barrows's name to the President.

Twenty-four hours later, Mr. Barrows wrote to William
Coolidge Lane, Librarian of Harvard College, and the then
President of the American Library Association, appealing for
the Association's support of his candidacy.[56] This, Mr. Lane
withheld, in a letter dated January 19th:

> I have received your letter of yesterday [he wrote]
> and have given the subject very careful consideration,
> and regret that I cannot oblige you. It seems to me of
> the first importance, both for the sake of the Congres-
> sional Library and for the general interests of the coun-
> try that the Librarian of Congress should be a man of
> the widest possible previous library experience, whose
> ability to manage the largest and most important library
> in the country should be assured by his previous success
> in administering one of the other large libraries.
>
> Such experienced and able librarians exist and the
> Congressional Library has a right to their services.
>
> You will believe me then, I am sure, when I say
> that it is no personal unfriendliness or want of consider-
> ation for yourself that prevents me from acceding to
> your request.[57]

That was a Thursday, on the following Monday Mr. Lane addressed the President:

> The appointment of a Librarian of Congress being now
> before you, I beg to be allowed, as President of the Amer-
> ican Library Association, to present for your considera-
> tion certain points which in the judgment of librarians
> should have special weight in making the selection. . . .

The director of a library so large and with such
varied activities must have more than mere intelligence,
general education or literary culture. He must have to
an unusual degree the capacity for administration on a
large scale, involving the wise adjustment of many departments; he must have tact and firmness and breadth
of view; and the position also calls for a familiarity
with library affairs and successful experience in the
actual management of a large library.

There are not, in my opinion, many men who com-
bine all these qualifications, but there are a few librarians who have won conspicuous success and a national
reputation in the conduct of large libraries. May I not
respectfully urge that you will not make the appointment
to the Library of Congress without giving careful consideration to the possibility of obtaining a man who has
already proved his ability in this work. The appointment
of an untried man is at best a hazardous experiment, not
to be resorted to in the case of the foremost library in
the country unless it is found that a man cannot be got
whose capacity to grapple with the difficult problems
of library administration has already been demonstrated
by previous experience.

The position of Librarian of Congress and the opportunities it should offer ought to command the services of
the best men in the country.[58]

But despite these counsels and strictures, the "untried man",
Mr. Barrows, held the inside track. On January 26th, it was
announced that "the Massachusetts delegation in Congress" had
"proposed Mr. Barrows",[59] and, on the same day, William E.
Chandler, powerful Senator from New Hampshire, had strongly
recommended Mr. Barrows to the President.[60] His political
advantage was redoubtable, but so also redoubtable was professional opposition. On January 30th, the unanimous Council of
the A.L.A. memorialized the President, respectfully representing "the importance of appointing as Librarian of Congress, a
man whose ability to deal with the problems of a large library
has already been demonstrated by successful library administration".[61]

But Mr. Barrows persisted. He wrote to each member of
the Senate:

380

I have been informed by Secretary Long, whom I
have known for more than twenty years, that, without
consulting me, but simply from his knowledge of my
history, experience and predilection, he has cordially
recommended me to the President to succeed my friend,
John Russell Young, as Librarian of Congress. I have
already been indorsed by the Massachusetts Senators
and the entire Massachusetts delegation in the House;
also by ten Senators and some forty Representatives,
and more have promised their support. As members
of both houses are brought into personal relation with
the Librarian, I should like to know whether my appointment would be acceptable to you, providing you have no
candidate from your own State. If you would like to talk
with me on the matter I will gladly see you and lay before you indorsements I have received.[62]

The circular probably did more harm to his cause than good.
One newspaper observed: "Mr. Barrows has been regarded as
a likely choice for the desirable post of Librarian of Congress,
but his latest epistolary effort has made many people wonder
whether the President can afford to choose an applicant whose
canvass for so dignified a place can be conducted with so re-
sounding a bass drum."[63] Simultaneously it was said the President "wavers about appointing Mr. Barrows".[64] Perhaps the
President wavered because the A.L.A. had come up with a formidable contender. In any event, Mr. Lane wrote to the President from Washington's St. James Hotel, on Saturday, February 4, 1899:

I saw Speaker Reed this afternoon as you advised,
and he immediately consulted with the members of the
Senate Committee and promises that the increase in
salary of the Librarian of Congress shall be made. I
shall see Mr. Putnam Monday morning, & understand
that I am authorized by you to say that you will appoint
him Librarian of Congress if you are assured that he
will accept the appointment.
I will telegraph you his decision as soon as possible.[65]

Lane wired the President, from Cambridge, on Monday
morning:

Putnam will probably accept appointment. He wishes to delay formal decision till Wednesday not already having considered the matter. Is this satisfactory to you. [?][68]

On the same day the Speaker of the House, from his suite at the Shoreham, reported progress to Mr. McKinley:

Mr. Lane told me Saturday that you desired to appoint Putnam of the Boston Library and that Putnam would accept on the same salary ($6,000). [Actually the salary remained for the time being at $5,000 a year.] I then saw Senators Allison & Cockerill and they assured me that they would attend to that on the Legislative Bill. This I told Mr. Lane who has I presume informed you. On the chance that he may not have communicated with you I write this.[67]

Herbert Putnam kept his promise to report a decision. On Wednesday, February 8th, this message reached the White House at 2:55 p.m.:

Have notified Mr. Lane that I am prepared to place myself at your disposal with exceeding appreciation.

Herbert Putnam.[68]

Everything appeared to be in order, but at 3:21 p.m. came another wire:

Putnam asks me to say that since telegraphing you he learns that Barrows' attitude toward his appointment is such that he is obliged to decline unless Barrows withdraws his candidacy. Regret exceedingly that Barrows has taken this course.

W. C. Lane.[69]

Whatever the course Mr. Barrows had taken it must have been a change, for on that Saturday when Mr. Lane had visited the President, Mr. Richard Rogers Bowker, who accompanied him, had come upon Mr. Barrows, and Senator Henry Cabot Lodge in a White House anteroom. Mr. Bowker had told Mr.

Barrows "that the members of the Association favored a trained librarian for the post if one could be had, but that in default of such his candidacy seemed preferable to that of others; and Mr. Barrows [had] replied as frankly that if such a librarian were in the running he would not himself be a candidate".[70] Mr. Bowker stated that "Mr. Barrows' ambition had meantime been stiffened and, in place of fulfilling his word to me, he insisted on right of way to the position."[71] Mr. Lane reported simply that "certain complications intervened".[72]

A likely explanation is the explanation that Mr. Barrows refused to release his sponsors from their commitments to him. The situation must have embarrassed George Frisbie Hoar and Henry Cabot Lodge, the Massachusetts Senators. They were bound to Barrows by the sometimes abrasive hemp of local politics. They had pledged themselves to his candidacy. At the same time both were good Harvard men; Mr. Lane was a good Harvard man; Mr. Putnam was a good Harvard man; Mr. Barrows was a good Harvard man. The Senators had a reputation for scholarship to sustain around the Capitol. They could not champion Mr. Barrows without opposing two other constituents: Lane and Putnam. But what made their position particularly awkward and distressing was the knowledge that Mr. McKinley's preference was for Putnam. It was their misfortune to be obliged to counter the Executive intention. And there was one other circumstance, Mr. Barrows's conduct had seemed to many to be in bad taste, whereas Mr. Putnam's deportment had been exemplary.

The contretemps had been resolved for them when Mr. Putnam, ascribing as his reason Mr. Barrows's obduracy, had declined the nomination. On February 14th, Mr. McKinley's Private Secretary, John Addison Porter, telegraphed Mr. Lane:

> The President cannot undertake to decide for Mr. Putnam. The President received with deep regret Mr. Putnam's message that he did not feel at liberty to accept the tender to him of the office of Librarian of Congress. The President felt that his appointment would be most fitting and was anxious that the Library should have the benefit of his ripe experience. After Mr. Putnam declined the President notified Mr. Barrows who had been strongly recommended by literary men and librarians as well as by public men, that he

would nominate him for the place.[73]

The next day Mr. McKinley sent this document to the Senate of the United States: "I nominate Samuel J. Barrows, of Massachusetts, to be Librarian of Congress, vice John Russell Young, deceased."[74] It is interesting to speculate on the motives underlying this action. There is every reason to suppose that it was made in good faith; but it is possible to suppose that its purpose was actually little more than legislative face-saving. This is not to suggest that it involved skulduggery; at worst it was a carefully planned discharge of a debt of honor.

The exuberant Mr. Barrows was delighted in the prospect of his new station. He even went so far as to interview himself under the pseudonym of "A Floor Correspondent", the result of which was published in The Independent, in which he bestowed praises upon the Chief Magistrate's amazing acumen in making so splendid a choice. He wrote:

> Before he left yesterday . . . the President sent a few nominations to the Senate, and among them was the name of the Hon. Samuel J. Barrows, Representative of Congress from Massachusetts, as Librarian of Congress . . . On the threshold of a new era in the history of the Library the position is one of commanding opportunity, and it is not surprising that the President did not have to advertise for candidates. It must be said that he has given ample time to the consideration of the question, and has looked at it from every aspect and with a preeminent desire to sacrifice every other consideration to the supreme interests of the Library.
>
> I do not find myself in a position to treat this subject with the freedom I should like. I should like to say something about the condition and needs of the Library, and what must be done for its development. But there are reasons why such a statement might be premature. I should like to discuss various points in regard to the organization and administration of that institution, but I fear that my remarks might command too much attention. I might also, as your Washington correspondent, be expected to comment upon the appointment of Mr. Barrows. But I am embarrassed by the mere suggestion.

This is not because I do not know the new Librarian,
and not because I am not friendly to him. It is because
I know him too well. I have watched his growth and the
changing features of his career from childhood to man-
hood with a rare interest, not wholly relieved at times
from anxiety. I have been with him in scenes of danger
and have enjoyed with him many scenes of calm repose.
I was with him one day at R. Hoe and Co.'s works on
Sheriff Street, New York, when a block of wood fell
on his head as he passed under the hoistway, and he
was taken bleeding to the apothecary. I was with him
when he was prostrated by a fall of the big stable door
at Hoe's stables on Broome Street. I was with him in
the Indian battles on the Yellowstone when a Springfield
rifle ball penetrated a tree two inches above his head.
These and many other experiences seemed to threaten
his candidacy as a librarian, and I do not think any one
of them can be said to constitute an argument for his
fitness. But when you have bunked and eaten and traveled and studied and rested and toiled and suffered
and enjoyed as much as I have with Barrows it is not
surprising that you cannot somehow get yourself into
focus with the subject.[75]

At this point Mr. Barrows proceeded to interview Mr. Barrows. It is doubtful if the article added to the popularity of the
Librarian designate. The Washington Post (which was on to the
secret) commented derisively:

It seems to us that the Independent's Washington
correspondent has obtained a pretty serviceable focus
on the Hon. Samuel June Barrows. A gentleman who
can see a wooden block fall upon the head of another
gentleman and not enter into his most intimate feelings,
then and there, must be a block himself. A gentleman
who is present when a stable door falls upon and crushes
another gentleman — and on Broome Street at that —
writes himself down a graven image if he does not,
instanter, thrill to every emotion of the other gentleman with several extra thrills thrown in.[76]

But common fairness insists that there should be put down some of the things which Mr. Barrows told Mr. Barrows about the Library. On that subject Mr. Barrows quoted himself in these terms:

> I like to look out at night and see the lantern burning in the dome of the Congressional Library. It seems to symbolize a function of the Library itself. It ought to become a great national beacon light. . . .
> Let me say that there is a vast deal of work in every direction to be done at the Congressional Library, and it will take time to do it. The Library needs to be built up systematically, and it must be cataloged. . . .
> The Library was primarily established for Senators and Representatives, and those who properly insist that it shall now become a great national library must not overlook this function. . . .
> I am confident . . . that my experience as a member of Congress, as well as a journalist and maker of books, will be of much value to me in my new office.
> But while the Library should not lose its Congressional function, it ought to become in time, through liberal appropriations and wise development, a great national institution of far-reaching educational influence. It is very encouraging to me that so many educators of prominence all over the land have wished me to take the post, and have assured me of their cooperation.[77]

Mr. Barrows's installation was taken for granted. Said the Library Journal:

> The President's appointment of Samuel J. Barrows . . . to be Librarian of Congress is neither the appointment that was hoped for nor the appointment that was feared. Credit should be given to the President for his wish to appoint a librarian of first rank. It has become an open secret that he had caused to be indicated to Mr. Herbert Putnam two years ago his desire that it would be possible for his services to be at the disposal of the national library. It is to be regretted that circumstances made it impracticable for Mr. Putnam to accept. Mr. Barrows

was the most satisfactory of candidates outside the library profession or the field of trained and tried executives.[78]

But the greatest deliberative body in the world, the United States Senate, did not act impetuously to inaugurate the new librarian. Instead, on Tuesday, February 28th, the Honorable Henry Clay Hansbrough, "from the Committee on the Library, to which was referred the 15th instant, the nomination of Samuel J. Barrows, reported adversely thereon".[79] This was serious. The Fifth-fifth Congress would adjourn in three days. Presumably there was a rallying of the forces, but at 3:16 on the afternoon of the last day of the session, George F. Hoar, H. C. Lodge, Eugene Hale, W. E. Chandler, and J. H. Gallinger wired the President:

We find that Mr. Barrows cannot be confirmed because he is not a skilled librarian, and therefore we advise that his name be withdrawn from the Senate.[80]

Fifteen minutes later Senator Hoar sent another and individual telegram to Mr. McKinley:

I am satisfied Mr. Barrows will be almost unanimously rejected, if a vote [is] taken now. If, on full inquiry, you can find a competent skilled librarian I hope one may be appointed; otherwise that Mr. Barrows may be considered again hereafter.[81]

At 4:11 p.m. Mr. Lane, in his capacity as President of the American Library Association, wired the President:

If Senate opposes present nominee for Librarian I earnestly and respectfully request in behalf of library interests of the country that Putnam be nominated immediately; that confirmation may be had promptly. I see no other chance of a strong and generally acceptable appointment.[82]

The President did nothing of the sort; on the contrary he offered a recess appointment to Mr. Barrows. On March 8th,

Secretary Long, Mr. Barrows's great patron asked Mr. McKinley: "Please give Mr. Barrows a moment to give you his letter declining the appt."[82]

Written the day before, the text of the letter read:

> Permit me to express my sincere thanks to you for again tendering me the appointment of Librarian of Congress and thus renewing your expression of confidence in my ability to fill the office. I feel, however, that it would be impossible for me to meet your expectations, or to do justice to your wise and enlightened policy concerning the library without the hearty support which the Senate, by its failure to act on my previous nomination has not given.
>
> Thanking you for this evidence of your very kind consideration, I feel constrained to decline the honor, and remain, with the most cordial regard,
>
> Your obedient servant,
> S. J. Barrows.[83]

In a letter to Senator Chandler, Mr. Barrows gave his own version of the episode:

> I wish to drop you a line wherever you may be [he wrote] to thank you for your kind defence of me in the Senate. That burden ought not to have fallen upon you but it was very generous of you to take it up. I may frankly admit I made some mistakes, but they were simply episodes in the matter and did not determine the result. I was endorsed by my Senators without reservation to start with. They allowed the President to appoint me and indeed had asked him to do so. Then when my name came before the court of which they were members they defended my character without defending my capacity. Hansbrough had assured me before my name was brought in that he would vote for my confirmation, and then did what he could to defeat it. I suspect he was the tool of others. That distorted lampoon in the Post was not a fair description of the Independent Letter most of which was devoted to tributes to various librarians. There was no self glorification in

it as would have been seen had the Post dared to publish it in full. But the funny man of that paper was committed to another candidate as was Senator Hansbrough. As for Senator Cockrell I have much respect for his industry and sincerity. He did not assume to be friendly at any time to my face and therefore cannot be accused of stabbing me in the back.

Several Senators sent word to me that they hoped I would accept a recess appointment. In a pleasant interview with the President he told me it was for me to decide, but I felt that under the circumstances something was due to my self respect and that it was best for me to decline.[84]

On the day that Mr. Barrows had waited upon the President to inform him that, with an assist from the Senate, he had decided to reject a recess appointment, Mr. Barrows, garbed in black Prince Albert, closely buttoned, a string tie of the same color, and neat linen, received a caller in the plainly but comfortably furnished parlor of his residence at 424 East Capitol Street. "I am packing up", he said, "to start at once for Boston."[85] He would live "long enough to be thankful", said his wife, that the Librarianship had not "taken him from his older interest in prison reform".[86]

President McKinley was about to leave Washington for a short vacation. Bluff Senator Platt, of New York, hoped that he would not consider it necessary to announce his choice for Librarian until after his return. The Senator felt that "the interests of the Library of Congress will not suffer by a brief postponement".[87]

But on March 7th, Mr. Lane had sent a long letter to the President, in the course of which he had stated:

It is . . . unnecessary for me even to mention the name of the man who in my opinion is the best qualified of any in the country to take this responsible position, for it was a satisfaction when I was in Washington to learn that you had already in your own mind fixed upon the same man as the one to whom you desired to offer the appointment. . . .

I can only assure you once more of the great satis-

faction it will be to the whole library profession, in behalf of whom I feel I have a right to speak, if the way is
now open for the appointment which you desired to make
before, an appointment which will place the Library of
Congress, the National Library, in the position of leadership to which it is entitled, and will give it an administration sound and liberal, free from political entangle-
ment and commanding the hearty support and co-operation
of the library world.[88]

Just before leaving for the South, on the afternoon of Monday, March 13th, 1899, Mr. McKinley appointed Herbert Putnam
to be Librarian of Congress.[89] According to the press it was
"understood that Mr. Putnam intends to come to Washington and
assume his new duties as soon as he can arrange his business
and personal affair".[90] On March 18th, George B. Cortelyou,
Assistant Secretary to the President, wired from Thomasville,
Georgia, to John Addison Porter, Secretary to the President:
"The President directs me to say that the official notification
to Mr. Putnam will be his commission, and if commission is
sent here at once it will be promptly signed and returned."[91]
On the same day Mr. Putnam wrote to a New York newspaper
man, George F. Bowerman, later Washington's first Public
Librarian:

It was not until this afternoon that I received direct
information of the appointment and reached a decision;
so that not until now have I been able suitably to acknowledge your telegram of the 14th. My acceptance of the
appointment will be forwarded to the President upon receipt of the formal notification.[92]

The announcement of the appointment was cordially received.
The Library Journal rejoiced: "The President . . . has . . .
put the right man in the right place."[93] The Washington Post reported that "the selection of Mr. Putnam is regarded as a most
excellent one, and the circumstances surrounding his appointment indicate that the choice was made without any consideration to political favor, but solely upon merit and ability".[94]
Even The Independent, which lamented the defeat of Mr. Barrows, conceded the fact that Mr. Putnam was "one of the best

where for the flashes that lighted the long way. From the outset
of his coming to Washington, for example, Herbert Putnam's
purpose was, as he told his friends, "the nationalization of the
Library of Congress by developing its resources for service to
scholarship and by extending the benefits of its collections and
of its technical processes to the country at large".[103] Within
thirty months of his advent he was expatiating on this theme, in
a long letter to Theodore Roosevelt:

A national library for the United States should [he
wrote] mean in some respects much more than a national library in any other country has hitherto meant.
The public library in its modern form began in the United States fifty years ago. It is receiving a development
here not paralleled elsewhere, in the activity of its
service for the general public and also for the scholar.
There are over 5,000 public libraries in the United
States to-day. . . .

In the aggregate they represent a great educational
interest distinct from the schools; and the movement
which has resulted in their creation, development, and
enrichment is the most characteristic movement in
education during the past half century.

Now as a whole, these libraries in the United States
are organizing their work with reference to uniformity
in methods, to cooperation in processes, to interchange
of service, and in general, to the promotion of efficiency
in service.

They look to the National Library for standards, for
example, for leadership, in all these enterprises. It
is now in position to "standardize" library methods, to
promote coöperation, to aid in the elimination of wasteful duplication, to promote interchange of bibliographic
service. And not merely by the accumulation and liberal
administration of a great collection at Washington, but
by the distribution of the results of the bibliographic
work which it is putting upon that collection it will be
able to perform a service of the greatest utility to the
library interests of the United States and to American
scholarship.

The past two and a half years have been in part a

preparation for such a service. Equipment, apparatus, and experts are being acquired. . . .

The Library is now to initiate some of those projects of service for which the past four years have prepared. In these it will make return to the country for the recent great expenditure upon it.[104]

It is a remarkable document. Herbert Putnam had fixed upon the dimensions. His Library of Congress, his national library, would be a library's library and a scholar's destination. Implicit in it were the evolution of techniques capable of national application; the distribution of printed catalog cards (which he had found so effective and economical back in Boston) to other libraries throughout the land; the accumulation of great specialized collections. And he had secured the means; he had "obtained from Congress all the important requests" which he had "formulated . . . the working force in all departments having been largely increased, and the appropriation for books doubled".[105] In discussing "What May Be Done For Libraries By The Nation", he had hinted at a system of interlibrary loans. Listen to this Waukesha soliloquy:

A university professor at Madison or Berkeley or San Antonio, in connection with research important to scholarship, requires some volume in an unusual set. The set is not in the university library. It is too costly for that library to acquire for the infrequent need. The volume is in the National Library. It is not at the moment in use at Washington. The university library requests the loan of it. If the National Library is to be the National Library — ?

There might result some inconvenience. There would be also the peril of transit. Some volumes might be lost to posterity. But after all we are ourselves a posterity. Some respect is due to the ancestors who saved for our use.

That was in the summer of 1901. A few months later, books which might advance the boundaries of knowledge were being borrowed by other libraries from the national stores on Capitol Hill. Herbert Putnam was sending the Library of Congress to the nation. Those first thousand days were the days when he formed his concept; his remaining fourteen thousand days at the head of the Library would be the days of fulfillment.

During the tenure of Herbert Putnam, the Librarian of Congress was the most completely independent public officer in the Federal Government. As a consequence of the Act of 1897, the Joint Committee on the Library ceased to give directions or to function as a board of trustees, and devoted its attention largely to the art and decoration of the Capitol. Mr. Putnam's relations to its members were almost exclusively social, ceremonial, or honorific, rather than official and obligatory. When he appeared before the appropriations committees, as he did once a year, he came not as a suppliant, but as instructor, patient and aloof, and he once complained that although his "aims encountered no opposition in Congress, they did require incessant explanation and effort".[107] He told the House Committee in 1902: "I am not here as petitioner. . . . I have always considered myself rather the adviser to the board." But his requests were notoriously modest; he was treated with unusual civility; his faith in the fund-purveyors was ordinarily returned. Indeed, in the early months of his translation to Columbia's District, he composed a creed:

> I believe in Congress. I believe in the men who in Congress are controlling these [Library] matters. I believe in their fairness. I believe in their common sense. My experience during the past eight months has confirmed my general belief and has given me a particular confidence. I have already had occasion to submit recommendations and I have been delighted with the courtesy, consideration and fairness with which they have been received. Congress is not to blame for the existing conditions in the Library. So far as I know, Congress has never had before it a fair statement of what was necessary. That statement is now possible and with that statement in its hands I fully believe that Congress will do whatever is necessary for this Library.[108]

Half a century later Mr. Putnam had not altered this charitable view. In December, 1950, he said to an audience gathered at Washington's Mayflower Hotel:

There were, and are, certain elements within . . .
[the Library of Congress] peculiarly favorable that few
other institutions could boast.

For one thing, it has no constitution. It does not,
like even the A.L.A., have to suspend its business from
time to time to amend its constitution, as a relief to its
growing pains. Its authority, its enabling authority, depends on the appropriation bills, that is to say, on grants
from Congress in aid of what it proposes to <u>do</u>. But it's
always a proposal to <u>do</u> something. The grant isn't a
definition of function, nor any evidence that Congress
meant to define the function of the Library, or put a
limit such as would be put in the case of a Constitution
for the Library. Congress itself proceeds under a Constitution, and except so far as the Library is an implement for its own family service, domestic service, what
it enables the Library to do is authorized by the Constitution under the clause of "General Welfare".[109]

Following an aside, he continued:

In another respect the Library has had peculiar good
fortune. It was in the <u>idealism</u> to be counted upon in
Congress. Now I'm not using the term "idealism" loosely. I mean it. During the period of my ministrations
there were several instances in which this was tested.
In a smaller way it was tested when I reported to an
Appropriation Committee — confessed to an Appropriation
Committee — that I had spent a half year's appropriation
for the purchase of 80,000 Russian books, and I was asking for an increase of the appropriation for the following
year. Some of my colleagues were apprehensive. They
said they won't give you any increase, they'll cut down
the present one when they learn that you've wasted all
that money — on 80,000 books that nobody can read and
that Congress does not need in its deliberations. Well,
I told them the story of that purchase. They listened
absorbedly. They gave the additional appropriation.

It was tested, this idealism, in a majestic way, when
a Representative from Mississippi . . . introduced his
Bill for the purchase of the Vollbehr Collection, 3,000

Fifteenth Century books, plus the vellum Gutenberg, at
the expenditure of a million and a half dollars, from the
public treasury. Now that Bill of Mr. Ross Collins' went
through the House unanimously, went through the Senate
unanimously, and on the last day of the session, was approved by the President. What carried it through both
Houses of Congress, unanimously? After the passage
of it in the House, I had a word with a Representative
who had the reputation in money matters involving the
United States Treasury of being — to use an F Street
term — rather "hard boiled" or "close-fisted". I asked
him why he'd voted for that Bill.

"Well", he said, "Mr. Putnam, you know we are a
young country. We have no monuments. If we know
where they are and can get them, we ought to get them."
That was that.[110]

This constant cordiality which existed between the Congress
and its Librarian was the condition precedent to the progress
of the institution itself. Occasionally it took tangible form, as
when, on January 26th, 1928, the Honorable Robert Luce, Chairman of the Committee on the Library, reported to the House:

The present incumbent of the position of Librarian,
Mr. Herbert Putnam, has occupied the place since April,
1899, to the complete satisfaction of Congress. The work
under his care has gone on with remarkable absence of
friction and with great efficiency. Due to his zeal and
ability, the activities of the Library have been broadened to a remarkable degree. He has aroused the admiration and enlisted the sympathetic interest of men whose
aid in still furthering the usefulness of the Library bids
fair to be of far-spreading benefit. Surely his long,
faithful, and efficient service may justly be recognized.

In view of these things the American Library Association has passed resolutions declaring the position of
Librarian of Congress to be "the most distinguished and
responsible library position in the United States" and expressing the belief that its salary ought to be fixed at
not less than $10,000. Agreeing with this your Committee
on the Library recommends the passage of H.R. 9036,

making the salary of the Librarian of Congress $10,000 a year.[111]

That Bill became a law, and in 1939, that same Robert Luce, who had played chess with him at Harvard, paid him another tribute. The occasion was Mr. Putnam's fortieth anniversary. Within a few moments Mr. Putnam would become Librarian of Congress Emeritus. A successor would become the Library's Governor. But on April 5th, Mr. Luce said:

In this period, of three score years he [i.e. Herbert Putnam] and I have seen the work of a librarian become a profession . . . Putnam is responsible more than any other living man for this profession. It has increased in size, usefulness and popularity. He is the Librarian of Congress, and I have always deemed it one of the fortunate things in my life that I could come in contact with him in that capacity. It implies oversight by the Committee, direction, and yet I cannot recall any occasion in these years for the exercise of such powers. Somebody has said, you remember, "Fortunate the country without a history." And fortunate the librarian without a history in Congress. He has accomplished this through enviable possession of one of the rarest of characteristics in public life — tact. You may praise him for his gifts of scholarship, for his contributions to the cultural life of the country. We in Congress who have watched him commend him most for his skill in displaying this quality of tact. He has shown phenomenal capacity in handling that most unruly body. It is supposed to be one of the chief ambitions of a Member of Congress to get jobs for his constituents. Ambition is not the right word. Necessity. And now Putnam has withstood the attacks of several thousand Congressmen without failing at all in his integrity, in his duty to his office, and has kept it a non-political organization. And pray God it may continue to be.[112]

This allusion may well have been especially gratifying to Mr. Putnam. Upon first assuming the Librarianship, he had resolved "to take the National Library out of the contentions of politics",[113] and throughout the years his conduct of the institution had been so incorruptible, so unimpeachable that when, not so long before, the panting plunderers of patronage had attempted a collective raid upon the Library, they had been disdainfully repulsed and put to shame and rout.

During Mr. Putnam's tenure the staff of the Library was scrupulously selected (as prescribed by law) solely upon the basis of fitness. He made no compromise with that injunction. And he was usually fortunate in his immediate associates; among his Chief Assistant Librarians were the incomparable bookman, Ainsworth Spofford, the elegant Appleton P. C. Griffin, and the resourceful and learned executive, Frederick W. Ashley. And his chiefs of division were, by and large, an outstanding group: in music, men like Oscar Sonneck and Carl Engel; in the Reading Rooms, a William Warner Bishop and a Martin A. Roberts; in maps, a P. Lee Phillips and a Lawrence Martin; in manuscripts, a Worthington Chauncey Ford and a J. Franklin Jameson; for the technical processes, a James Christian Hanson, a Charles Martel, a Charles Harris Hastings, and a Theodore W. Koch. Because he trusted their capacity, he allowed them extraordinary latitude and encouraged their initiative.

But the subordinate personnel was never numerically adequate nor adequately remunerated. The first fault was corrected by long hours of overtime joyfully given, the second was compensated by a sense of dedication to a great cause, the cause espoused by and revealed to the Librarian himself.

Him they held not so much in affection, as in awe. They rarely saw him. It was his habit to reach the Library early in the mornings, hours before the staff arrived. Except for receiving visitors, he shunned his ostentatious office, with its high-backed chair, and those gauzy ladies peering down from the ceiling. Instead, he would go to a smaller room down the corridor, place his feet high on a hassock, light his pipe, and dispose of his mail. Between nine and twelve twenty-five he would admit, individually, his chiefs of division, who came seeking a decision. It would be promptly given. Sometimes it would be given so very promptly as to confuse the applicant as to just what it had been. One of them came to interpret a raised eyebrow as assent, impassivity as refusal.

At twelve-thirty he would be in his private dining room, in the upper story of the building, presiding over the Round Table.

399

Present would be a few colleagues and a larger company of distinguished scholars. The talk was good. It was never "shop". Early in the afternoon, he might be glimpsed going out the west door, clad in brown tweeds, brown reefer, and brown fedora, a Harvard bag swinging gaily from his fingers. He would be off for the tennis court, or for the golf links, or, perhaps, for a game of pool.

Twice a week, he would visit the office of the Superintendent of the Reading Rooms, select three or four books from a shelf of new fiction and withdraw. Once a year, specifically on Christmas Eve, he would make a grand tour of the work-rooms and wish well the members of his force. They knew that they were in the presence of a great man. It was a little like receiving a Papal blessing. Ordinarily he took long summer vacations, sailing his "little boat" around Penobscot Bay or the waters off Cape Porpoise. But wherever he was, he was never off duty. The sweltering man, who acted for him back in Washington, kept him fully informed of proceedings and awaited his direction when unusual cases arose. In those years, the perspicuity of the head, the perspicacity of his deputies, and the perspiration of their henchmen propelled the Library.

His detractors have charged that Herbert Putnam's administration was paternalistic or despotic. Perhaps it was; but it was also benevolent and equitable. Possessing the appointive power, as he did, his authority was absolute — absolute but unabused. To be sure discipline was vigorously enforced; mediocrity was intolerable. It was likewise true that Mr. Putnam would, with flashing eye, reprimand a transgressor, rebuke a fool, or reject a preposterous suggestion with an arctic elegance that would keep the victim in the lower temperatures for weeks. But he was justified by reason and by fairness. He once wrote Theodore Roosevelt:

> I shall always thank you for an intimation that there
> is reported to be, in the service under me, an injustice
> which I can remedy, or a failure of just opportunity
> which I can make good.[114]

He meant just that.

Perhaps it was the aura of primacy, which clung so firmly to him, that made him seem remote, a being from another world, with whom one communicated through garbling interpreters. Perhaps it was due to his reticence, to his impenetrable self-communion and self-assurance. He was not the most approachable of men nor the most disarming. He was given more to command than to commend. But those who were sensitive to forces separating them from the Librarian had no understanding of his personality. Those forces, actually, were false, completely illusory, and outrageously absurd. For certainly Mr. Putnam himself was unaware of his solitude and isolation. Evidences of his conscious claim to kinship with his cohorts are not hard to find. He once assured "My Immediate Family — All Six Hundred of You":

> In sharing with you the commendations of these days, and the new zests which they inspire, let me ask you to give still freer exercise to those qualities in you without which, in spite of building, books, and apparatus, the Library will never express or fulfill its proper nature.
>
> And I ask it of you, not as subordinates, serving under me, but as associates, serving abreast of me.[115]

But the greatest mark of Mr. Putnam's confidence in his staff was his generous appreciation, manifest in his steady promotion of young people to positions of responsibility. It is not unusual for heads of institutions to surround themselves with their contemporaries. Mr. Putnam resisted that temptation. Instead, he offered a future and a good life to his juniors. They remember and they are grateful.

What a builder he was! The two eastward courtyards were filled with bookstacks to hold swelling collections. A westward courtyard gave way to an auditorium and a pavilion. The building was extended to provide suitable accommodations for rare books and a union catalog. An unattractive gallery was transformed into a handsome Hispanic Room. And on his fortieth anniversary the bronze doors to the splendid, functional, modern Annex were opened in celebration.

Asked what he considered his greatest single satisfaction, Mr. Putnam declined, not so long ago, an answer, but he once let slip the conviction that the creation, by Congress, in 1925, of the Library of Congress Trust Fund Board was "the most significant phase of the evolution of the institution" because it permitted the "addition of the human expert — in liaison relation between the collections and the public".[116] From that enactment have come great endowments and gifts of money for immediate disbursement.

It was Herbert Putnam who brought a grandeur to the Library. It was he who fostered and secured the magnificent array of books and newspapers, he who brought to being the unparalleled special collections of Slavica, Semitica, Orientalia, Hispanica, music, maps, rariora, fine arts, and manuscripts. And it was he who fulfilled the glowing aspiration of Speaker Reed. Using almost the same words, another Harvard man, Franklin Roosevelt would make the announcement: "Under your direction", he wrote, "our national library has become one of the great libraries of the world."[117]

Fifteen years ago Mr. Putnam acceded to the unique position of Librarian of Congress Emeritus. Later in describing his sensations at the time, he remarked:

> It wasn't the commander laying aside the baton; it was merely a departing guest who was concluding a visit with you — a visit that had been in some ways precious — and was now going out with only friendship and contented memories behind him.[118]

He had made, as he had wished to make, an "exemplary exit".[119] In his new post, he has found a new career. He comes daily to his office. He appears to be in his usual excellent health. He is active and alert and very wise. He feels himself to be, as he puts it, "contemporary with my own posterity: a privilege granted to few executives indeed". He is happy, when occasions center about him, that they can, in his words, "take the form of eulogy rather than elegy".[119] He is not legend but life. He is author and master of a Golden Age. May his works endure forever

HERBERT PUTNAM

NOTES:

1 Thomas Brackett Reed to William McKinley, January 25, 1899. William McKinley Papers. Library of Congress. Vol. 24, f. 4720.

2 See, for example, his speech on the floor of the House, December 12, 1882. Congressional Record, Vol. 14, Pt. 1, 221-222.

3 The New York Times, Saturday, December 21, 1872, p. 6, col. [7].

4 George Haven Putnam: MEMORIES OF MY YOUTH, 1844-1865; New York, G. P. Putnam's Sons, 1914, p. 47.

5 Herbert Putnam in interview with David Mearns, April, 1954.

6 Harvard College: Report of the Secretary of the Class of 1863. June, 1863 to June, 1888; Cambridge, John Wilson and Son, 1888, p. 154.

7 Harvard College Class of 1883: Secretary's Report No. 1; Cambridge, 1883, v. p.

8 Harvard College Class of 1883: Triennial, June, 1886, Secretary's Report No. 2; Cambridge, 1886, p. 65.

9 Harvard College Class of 1879: Secretary's Report No. IV, 1890; Cambridge, 1890, p. 47.

10 Harvard College Class of 1879: Report of the Secretary . . . 1900-1905; Boston, T. W. Ripley, 1905, p. 70.

11 WHO WAS WHO IN AMERICA, VOL. 1, 1897-1942; Chicago, A. N. Marquis Company, 1942.

12 The Minneapolis Tribune, Friday morning, September 7, 1888, p. 4, col. [7]

13 Harvard College Class of 1879: Secretary's Report No. V.; Cambridge, 1895, p. 57.

14 Herbert Putnam in interview with David Mearns, April 1954.

15 Davison's Minneapolis City Directory for 1886-7; Minneapolis, Johnson, Smith & Harrison, 1886, p. 646.

16 Minneapolis Public Library: FIFTY YEARS OF SERVICE, 1889-1939; Minneapolis, 1939, p. 7.

17 Gratia A. Countryman: "Mr. Putnam and the Minneapolis Public Library"; in ESSAYS OFFERED TO HERBERT PUTNAM, edited by William Warner Bishop and Andrew Keogh; New Haven, Yale University Press, 1929, p. 7.

18 Minneapolis Public Library: FIFTY YEARS OF SERVICE, 1889-1939; Minneapolis, 1939, p. 7.

19 Gratia A. Countryman: "Mr. Putnam and the Minneapolis Public Library"; in ESSAYS OFFERED TO HERBERT PUTNAM, edited by William Warner Bishop and Andrew Keogh; New Haven, Yale University Press, 1929, p. 6.

20 Minneapolis Public Library: FIFTY YEARS OF SERVICE, 1889-1939; Minneapolis, 1939, p. 7-8.

21 Gratia A. Countryman: "Mr. Putnam and the Minneapolis Public Library"; in ESSAYS OFFERED TO HERBERT PUTNAM, edited by William Warner Bishop and Andrew Keogh; New Haven, Yale University Press, 1929, p. 7.

22 Harvard College Class of 1883: Triennial, June, 1886, Secretary's Report No. 2; Cambridge, 1886, p. 65.

23 Boston Morning Journal, Thursday, October 7, 1886, p. 3, col. [3].

24 Harvard College Class of 1883: Secretary's Report No. III, July, 1890; Cambridge, 1890, p. 78-79. The date, 1887, for these transactions appears to be in error.

25 Minneapolis Public Library: FIFTY YEARS OF SERVICE, 1889-1939; Minneapolis, 1939, p. 10-11.

26 Minneapolis Tribune, Tuesday, December 17, 1889, p. 1, col. [7].

27 T. B. Walker in Minneapolis Public Library: First Annual Report . . . For the Year Ending December 31, 1900; Minneapolis, Harrison & Smith, 1890, p. [5].

28 H. W. Wilson to Herbert Putnam, March 30, 1949; in the Library of Congress Archive, Dr. Herbert Putnam's Fiftieth Anniversary as Librarian of Congress, April 5, 1949.

HERBERT PUTNAM

29 Herbert Putnam in interview with David Mearns, April, 1954.

30 Minneapolis Public Library: Third Annual Report . . . For the Year Ending December 31, 1892; Minneapolis, Harrison and Smith, 1893.

31 Gratia A. Countryman: "Mr. Putnam and the Minneapolis Public Library"; in ESSAYS OFFERED TO HERBERT PUTNAM, edited by William Warner Bishop and Andrew Keogh; New Haven, Yale University Press, 1929, p. 9.

32 Minneapolis Public Library: FIFTY YEARS OF SERVICE, 1889-1939; Minneapolis, 1939, p. 12.

33 Herbert Putnam, April 1, 1953, upon a presentation of recordings; in "Librarians of Congress", a dossier in the office of the Chief of Manuscripts Division.

34 Herbert Putnam in interview with David Mearns, April, 1954.

35 Boston Public Library Trustees: Sixty-sixth Annual Report, 1917-1918; Boston, 1918, p. 3.

36 Harvard College Class of 1883: Records of the Class, 1883-1908; Cambridge, 1908, p. 116.

37 Harvard College Class of 1883: Thirtieth Anniversary, 1883-1913, Sixth Report; Cambridge, 1913, p. 156.

38 Harvard College Class of 1883: Records of the Class, 1883-1908, Cambridge, 1908, p. 116-118.

39 Charles F. D. Belden: "The Library Service of Herbert Putnam in Boston"; in ESSAYS OFFERED TO HERBERT PUTNAM, edited by William Warner Bishop and Andrew Keogh; New Haven, Yale University Press, 1929, p. [10]-14.

40 The Christian Register, Boston, September 14, 1899, Vol. 78, No. 37, p. 1034.

41 Harry Miller Lydenberg to David Mearns, April 23, 1954.

42 Boston Public Library: Annual Report of the Trustees of the Public Library of the City of Boston, 1895; Boston, Rockwell and Churchill, 1896, p. 7.

43 Boston Public Library: Annual Report of the Trustees of the Public Library of the City of Boston, 1896; Boston, Municipal Printing Office, 1897, p. 47.

44 United States Congress, Senate, 54th Congress, 2d Session, Report No. 1573, Condition of the Library of Congress; Washington, 1897, p. 185-186.

45 Ibid., p. 187-189, passim.

46 Ibid., p. 190.

47 Ibid., p. 202

48 Ibid., p. 220-221.

49 Ibid., p. 225.

50 Boston Public Library: Annual Report of the Trustees of the Public Library of the City of Boston, 1897; Boston, Municipal Printing Office, 1898, p. 49.

51 United States Congress, Senate, 54th Congress, 2d Session, Report No. 1573, Condition of the Library of Congress, Washington, 1897, p. i-ii.

52 The Library Journal, Vol. 24, No. 2, February, 1899, p. 60.

53 George S. Boutwell to Justin S. Morrill; Boston, March 15, 1897; Morrill Papers, Library of Congress, Vol. 47, f. 11745.

54 Ainsworth Rand Spofford to William McKinley, January 28, 1899; McKinley Papers, Library of Congress, Vol. 24, f. 4741.

55 The Christian Register, Boston, Vol. 78, No. 4, January 26, 1899, p. 90-91.

56 William Coolidge Lane: "The Appointment of a Librarian of Congress"; in The Library Journal, Vol. 24, No. 3, March, 1899, p. 99.

57 Ibid.

58 Ibid.

59   The Christian Register, Boston, Vol. 78, No. 4, January 26, 1899, p. 90-91.

60   J. A. Porter to William E. Chandler, January 27, 1899; Chandler Papers, Library of Congress, Vol. 125, f. 14062.

61   The Library Journal, Vol. 24, No. 3, March 1899, p. 100.

62   New-York Tribune, Thursday, February 2, 1899. p. 3, col. [1].

63   Ibid.

64   George Alfred Townsend to William E. Chandler, February 1, 1899; Chandler Papers, Library of Congress, Vol. 125, f. 14081.

65   William C. Lane to William McKinley, February 4, 1899; McKinley Papers, Library of Congress, Vol. 24, f. 4775.

66   William C. Lane to William McKinley, February 6, 1899; McKinley Papers, Library of Congress, Vol. 24, f. 4809.

67   Thomas Brackett Reed to William McKinley, February 6, 1899; McKinley Papers, Library of Congress, Vol. 24, f. 4812.

68   Herbert Putnam to William McKinley, February 8, 1899; McKinley Papers, Library of Congress, Vol. 25, f. 4850.

69   William C. Lane to William McKinley, February 8, 1899; McKinley Papers, Library of Congress, Vol. 25, f. 4847.

70   Richard R. Bowker: "The Appointment of Herbert Putnam as Librarian of Congress"; in ESSAYS OFFERED TO HERBERT PUTNAM, edited by William Warner Bishop and Andrew Keogh; New Haven, Yale University Press, 1929, p. 17.

71   Ibid., p. 20.

72   The Library Journal, Vol. 24, No. 3, March, 1899, p. 100-101.

73   John Addison Porter to William Coolidge Lane, February 14, 1899; McKinley Papers, Library of Congress, Letter Book 43.

74   United States Congress, Senate: Journal of the Executive Proceedings, Vol. XXXI, Pt. II; Washington, Government Printing Office, 1909, p. 1315.

75 A Floor Correspondent: "Our Washington Letter"; in The Independent, February 23, 1899, p. 555.

76 The Washington Post, Wednesday, March 1, 1899, p. 6, col. [2].

77 A Floor Correspondent: "Our Washington Letter"; in The Independent, February 23, 1899, p. 556-557, passim.

78 The Library Journal, Vol. 24, No. 2, February, 1899, p. [51].

79 United States Congress, Senate: Journal of the Executive Proceedings, Vol. XXXI, Pt. II; Washington, Government Printing Office, 1909, p. 1344.

80 George F. Hoar, H. C. Lodge, Eugene Hale, W. E. Chandler, and J. H. Gallinger to William McKinley; recipient's copy in McKinley Papers, Library of Congress, Vol. 26, f. 5195; original in Chandler Papers, Library of Congress, Vol. 125, f. 14179.

81 George Frisbie Hoar to William McKinley, March 3, 1899; McKinley Papers, Library of Congress, Vol. 26, f. 5194.

82 John Davis Long to William McKinley, March 8, 1899; McKinley Papers, Library of Congress, Vol. 26, f. 5230.

83 Samuel June Barrows to William McKinley, March 7, 1899; McKinley Papers, Library of Congress, Vol. 26, f. 5224.

84 Samuel June Barrows to William E. Chandler, March 17, 1899; Chandler Papers, Library of Congress, Vol. 126, ff. 14223-14225.

85 The Washington Post, Thursday, March 9, 1899, p. 4, col. [5].

86 Isabel C. Barrows: A SUNNY LIFE, THE BIOGRAPHY OF SAMUEL JUNE BARROWS; Boston, Little, Brown and Company, 1913.

87 Thomas Collier Platt to William McKinley, March 8, 1899; McKinley Papers, Library of Congress, Vol. 26, f. 5233.

88 The Library Journal, Vol. 24, No. 3, March, 1899, p. 101.

89 The Washington Post, Tuesday, March 14, 1899, p. 2, col [2].

90 Ibid.

91 George B. Cortelyou to John Addison Porter, March 18, 1899; William McKinley Papers, Library of Congress, Vol. 27, f. 5364.

92 Herbert Putnam to George F. Bowerman, March 18, 1899; Library of Congress Archive, Bowerman-Putnam, AC9495.

93 The Library Journal, Vol. 24, No. 3, March, 1899, p. [97].

94 The Washington Post, Tuesday, March 14, 1899, p. 2, col. [2].

95 The Independent, March 23, 1899, p. 846.

96 Herbert Putnam to John Addison Porter, Lakewood, N. J., March 29, 1899; George B. Cortelyou Papers, Library of Congress.

97 The Washington Post, Thursday, April 6, 1899, p. 2, col. [3].

98 David C. Mearns: THE STORY UP TO NOW; Washington, 1947, p. 169.

99 Herbert Putnam to "My Immediate Family", April 7th, 1929; Alexis V. Babine Papers, Library of Congress.

100 Harvard College Class of 1883: Fiftieth Anniversary [7th Report]; Cambridge, Printed for the Class, 1933, p. 276.

101 Ibid.; p. 178.

102 Told to David Mearns by Henry F. Pringle, June 10, 1954.

103 Harvard College Class of 1883: Thirtieth Anniversary, 1883-1913, Sixth Report; Cambridge, 1913, p. 156.

104 Herbert Putnam to Theodore Roosevelt; October 15, 1901. Theodore Roosevelt Papers, Library of Congress.

105 Harvard College Class of 1883: Fourth Report, 1890-1900; Cambridge, 1900, p. 95-96.

106 Herbert Putnam: "What May Be Done For Libraries By The Nation"; in American Library Association: Papers and Proceedings of the Twenty-Third General Meeting . . . Held at Waukesha, Wisconsin, July 4-10, 1901; 1901, p. 15.

107 Harvard College Class of 1883: Fiftieth Anniversary, [7th Report];

Cambridge, Printed for the Class, 1933, p. 276-278.

108 Herbert Putnam to George F. Bowerman, January 26, 1900; Library of Congress Archive, Bowerman-Putnam, AC9495.

109 Herbert Putnam: "Remarks at the Conclusion of the Banquet Tendered in Behalf of the American Library Association and Associates to the Library of Congress, Mayflower Hotel, Washington, December 12, 1950", typescript, p. 2.

110 Ibid., p. 3-4.

111 Quoted from David C. Mearns: THE STORY UP TO NOW; Washington, 1947, p. 205.

112 HERBERT PUTNAM, LIBRARIAN OF CONGRESS, FORTIETH ANNIVERSARY, 1899-1939; [Washington, 1939], p. 15.

113 Harvard College Class of 1883: Fourth Report, 1890-1900; Cambridge, 1890, p. 95-96.

114 Herbert Putnam to Theodore Roosevelt, August 10, 1904; Roosevelt Papers, Library of Congress.

115 Herbert Putnam "To My Immediate Family — All Six Hundred of You"; April 7, 1929; Alexis V. Babine Papers, Library of Congress.

116 Harvard College Class of 1883: Fiftieth Anniversary, [7th Report]; Cambridge, Printed for the Class, 1933, p. 276-278.

117 HERBERT PUTNAM, LIBRARIAN OF CONGRESS, FORTIETH ANNIVERSARY, 1899-1939; [Washington, 1939], p. 11.

118 Herbert Putnam: "Remarks on Receiving a Gift of Recordings, April 1, 1953"; typescript, Librarians of Congress, a dossier in the office of the Chief of the Manuscripts Division, Library of Congress.

119 Herbert Putnam: "Remarks at the Conclusion of the Banquet Tendered in Behalf of the American Library Association and Associates to the Library of Congress, Mayflower Hotel, Washington, December 12, 1950"; typescript, p. 5.

THE CONTRIBUTIONS OF LOUIS ROUND WILSON
TO LIBRARIANSHIP

Maurice F. Tauber

Maurice F. Tauber — editor of College and Research Libraries and co-author (with Louis R. Wilson) of THE UNIVER-
SITY LIBRARY (2d ed., 1956) — is Melvil Dewey Professor
of Library Service, Columbia University. The essay here
reprinted is a paper read before the American Library History Round Table at the Miami Beach conference of the American Library Association, June, 1956.

Louis Round Wilson was trained in philology. His doctoral
dissertation was entitled CHAUCER'S RELATIVE CONSTRUC-
TIONS, the first number of studies in philology issued by the
University of North Carolina. Wilson was also a member of the
faculty of the German department of the university. He had not
really thought of librarianship as a career when he started his
work in the university at Chapel Hill in the autumn of 1901. But
Wilson had early been taught to do things thoroughly. So, before
he took over the post in the university library, he prepared for
his responsibilities. His work as a student assistant in the library at Haverford College had given him some background in
the problems of lending books, checking periodicals, posting
debate references, and handling books on reserve. The other
operations of the library were a mystery to him.

So in the summer of 1901 he set to work. He obtained copies
of the Dewey abridged classification scheme, a book of rules
and forms for cataloging, and examples of accession records
and other forms used in library work. He read carefully Dana's
LIBRARY PRIMER and Spofford's A BOOK FOR ALL READERS,
the two nearest approximations of manuals on library practice.
With these aids in hand, he set about accessioning, classifying,
and cataloging the books in the Wilson home. Scrupulously and
painfully, he developed the stereotyped library hand, and fa-
miliarized himself with library terminology. The names of

Reprinted from Wilson Library Bulletin, 31:315-323, December,
1956, by permission of the author and the publisher.

411

other library leaders such as Melvil Dewey, C. A. Cutter, Arthur E. Bostwick, W. C. Lane, J. I. Wyer, C. C. Soule, N. C. D. Hodges, Ernest C. Richardson, W. D. Johnston, and Mary W. Plummer, became familiar to him. Even though he had not thought seriously that the position at Chapel Hill would mean that he would be a librarian, he had immersed himself in the literature of the field. This has always been a characteristic of Wilson: be sure of your ground before starting an undertaking, and if there is a literature involved, master it. In many ways, this is a philosophy of librarianship in its purest sense.

In December 1901 Wilson prepared his first annual report on the library for President Francis P. Venable. The report was an important event in his career for, although he had been a librarian for only four months, he included as a major recommendation a statement that the development of an adequate policy for the growth and support of the library was a matter of primary significance to the university if teaching and research were to be based on a sound foundation.

He urged the various departments to keep careful watch over new and standard publications in their respective fields and to assist the librarian in building up the collections; he pointed out the difficulty of operating the library without permanent assistants; he emphasized the need for carefully handling rare items and North Caroliniana. He saw the position of librarian being handed around rather loosely. In the thirty months preceding his assumption of the position, four librarians had occupied the post before they took assignments on the faculty or went on other jobs. Wilson was certain that temporary librarians could do nothing in developing the library systematically. Fifty-five years ago he therefore recommended:

> That the university make the position of librarian such that he, from a financial point of view, can remain in it for several years at least. Within the past thirty months four men have filled the position and although they have performed their duties carefully and faithfully still the university has not been served to that degree of efficiency and skill which should be characteristic of the service of an experienced library officer. If the present system of low salary and frequent change continues, I am unable to see how a policy can be devised

and carried out which will result in the steady upbuilding
of the departmental divisions of the library in the most
wise, and for that reason the most economic, administration of library affairs. As the university grows and
becomes more efficient in its work it can ill afford to
allow a part of its machinery so essential to its usefulness as the library to suffer from a lack of most careful
and continued oversight.

Wilson's concept of the function of the university library was
developed from his careful analysis of the methods of faculty
members, students, scholars, and research workers. He was
early convinced that a college or university was only as good
as its library, and the top-level institutions of the country had
extensive and carefully selected collections. He knew also that
although many academic persons spoke of "the library as the
heart of the university", there were many more who did not
care too much about the "heart trouble" which usually existed.
Certain in his own mind that it was impossible to provide high-
level teaching or learning without a good library, he was just
as sure that it was not possible to attract progressive and promising faculty members unless there were adequate library collections and library support. He also considered the library as
a vital educational instrument in its own right, not just a depository for old books and periodicals. Although he admits that he
has had little time to read extensively of the literary production
of the world's authors, he was conscious of their values in relation to the work of the professorial staff and the student body.
To Wilson, books were to be used, and although his interest in
and appreciation of finely bound volumes and their conservation
was high, he considered them primarily in their relation to the
dynamic function of the university library: instruction and research.

In the summer of 1904 Wilson offered a course in library
science. It was the first course in library administration presented in any southern institution and antedated by one year the
establishment of the School of Library Science by the Carnegie
Library of Atlanta. He used as an outline a carefully prepared
series of lectures fully illustrated with library forms relating
to the organization and administration of small libraries, including the selection and ordering of books, their accessioning,

classification and cataloging, circulation, and various other procedures essential in making them available to the public. At the
time, Wilson thought of developing the outline into a textbook,
since it dealt with the handling of library operations in a much
more specific way than did the Dana LIBRARY PRIMER, but it
was never prepared for publication.

In his report for 1904-1905, Wilson envisaged the need for
physical expansion of the library. He called attention to the con-
gestion in the library, the lack of space for readers and books,
and the hazardous, non-fireproof nature of the structure then
used for library purposes. Wilson had seen other libraries which
were planned for library service, and he was determined to
arouse the president to the great need for a new building. The
general principles of library planning projected by C. C. Soule
had made a deep impression upon him.

Although he was thoroughly devoted to the development of
the university library at this time, Wilson saw the need for push-
ing library progress through state association work and legislative action. Thus, he took a leading part in the founding of the
North Carolina Library Association, which held its first meeting in Charlotte in the autumn of 1904. Three years later, he
assisted in drafting the first proposed law for the establishment
of the North Carolina Library Commission. He worked hard for
its enactment by the Legislature, and although the effort failed
in 1907, the law was passed in 1909.

Wilson had completed his doctoral work in 1905. He had the
opportunity of continuing as an assistant professor in the German
department, but he saw more in the potentialities of the librarianship. In 1907 he was appointed associate professor of library administration, and a department of library science was established
at the university. The summer course was formalized, and Wilson found it a useful device for training a number of competent
assistants for the university library as well as for other libraries in the state. Moreover, the faculty status enabled him to
associate with other faculty members of the university in committee work and other activities. Later, additional courses were
added, both for the summer sessions and for the regular academic period.

During this period Wilson was also extending his influence
into other areas of librarianship. In 1906 he attended the meeting of the American Library Association at Narragansett Pier,

THE CONTRIBUTIONS OF LOUIS ROUND WILSON

Rhode Island, where he joined forces with representatives of the North Carolina Library Association, the Chamber of Commerce of Asheville, and the Southern Railway in inviting the American Library Association to hold its annual meeting in Asheville. The invitation was accepted and in May 1907 the meeting was held in Asheville, with a postconference excursion to Lake Toxaway. The preceding month he had written to Robert C. Ogden, president of the Conference for Education in the South, telling him about the development of libraries in the South, and asking for cooperation with the librarians meeting at Asheville. Wilson very early saw the essential relationships between library service and educational movements of all kinds.

Fifty years ago Dr. Wilson wrote his first item for a professional journal. This was a brief statement on "The North Carolina Library Association" which appeared in the Library Journal. The following year he had published in the World's Work an article entitled "The Growth of Libraries", his first contribution to a national publication for which he proudly received a check. The issue of the journal dealt with the South and Wilson had written the article to show how libraries were developing in the region.

Wilson had certain problems as a librarian. Despite his plea for adequate support of the library, funds for acquisitions and operations were hardly adequate. From 1901 to 1906 the annual funds for books and periodicals remained relatively stationary at about $1,200. In 1906 he had distributed a circular soliciting an endowment for the library. He was able to secure clear title to 12,000 of the 32,000 volumes which belonged to the Dialectic and Philanthropic Societies. An endowment of $55,000 had been raised to match a Carnegie gift for a new library building. Before the new library was opened in the fall of 1907, Wilson was able to see an increasing sum for books and periodicals through the Armfield Fund (for English) and the May Fund (for French and German). The Groome Fund, which was available for a short period, was established for American poetry. Thus, the departmental funds of the early 1900's were increased from $30 to as much as $300 or more for certain departments, and Wilson was able to place subscriptions for important journals in all fields. Valuable sets of the works of American and foreign authors were acquired. He also developed programs for acquiring North Caroliniana and other Southern collections.

Although President Venable was impressed with Wilson's work in developing the library, he was concerned about the young librarian's increasing demands for funds. An important point of policy arose in September 1907.

Nan Strudwick, a young woman just graduated from the library school at Atlanta, had become assistant librarian at this time, and President Venable informed Wilson that he was going to pay Miss Strudwick's and Wilson's salaries out of the income from the $55,000 endowment. The librarian went to see the president.

"You just can't do this", said Wilson firmly.

The president was equally firm. "Oh, yes, I can; and I intend to do it", he said. "Why do you take this attitude?"

"You seem to forget, President Venable, that the instrument providing for the transfer of the title of the books from the Di and Phi societies to the university included a statement that all income derived from endowment and student library fees would be used for the purchase of books, and that all charges for administration would be borne by the university as charges for other university departments were borne. You and I signed that statement as representatives of the university and the library."

There was a silence, and the president appeared stumped for a moment. He was unhappy by this disclosure.

"Why did you bind me with such a limitation?" he asked.

"Because of what I saw going on at Virginia", answered Wilson. "President Alderman applied income from library endowments to administrative purposes. This is the easy way out. It is more important to build up the book collections than to relieve the administration of the responsibility of securing money from the Legislature for administrative purposes."

Although he was not entirely convinced, President Venable accepted Wilson's frank point of view. As the young librarian was about to leave, Venable said: "Wilson, I believe you lie awake at night thinking of ways in which you can ask me for additional funds for the library."

Wilson smiled at this left-handed compliment, but he was pleased that the president had seen his point.

This incident may appear to be a simple one which might occur in any institution. The point of view of Wilson, however, is the important issue. He was steadfast in his pursuit of a properly supported library. He realized the need for a constant supply of funds if the library were to continue to develop as a research center. He knew that if you did not acquire materials when they were available, they were either impossible to get later or they would be obtained at a premium. He knew that a library had to have its own funds for an acquisition program that could be developed by a qualified personnel. There could be no fortuitous procedure in obtaining adequate support for books, personnel, and quarters. His point of view was later put into his writings, and has become a standard recommendation in surveys and textbooks on library management.

There is not time for recounting here the many anecdotes which one may cite in developing a profile of Louis Round Wilson. His activities as librarian at the University of North Carolina include many incidents involving staff members and clientele, students and faculty members, which demonstrate Wilson's application of administrative principles to library operations.

In her tribute[1] to Dr. Wilson in The Southeastern Librarian in 1951, Tommie Dora Barker remarked that

> his identification with a single position, whether at the University of North Carolina or at the University of Chicago, seems . . . irrelevant, since his interests and activities have always extended far beyond the bounds of the position with which he happened to be immediately associated.[2]

Although one may find among his writings a large number of items which deal with North Carolina and the South, he has been concerned with all types of libraries and library services in all parts of the country. Indeed, he has seen librarianship as an international service.

A further contribution for North Carolina was his part in the development of the extension division of the university. Together, with such men as Edward K. Graham, Nathan W. Walker, Edwin Mims, and others on the university faculty, Dr. Wilson pushed the idea of library extension to the point where it was formally established as an important aid to the citizens of the state. In his annual report for 1906-1907, Dr. Wilson stated his proposal for increased extension work of the university, with the library as a pivotal agency in the plan. All librarians, and Southern librarians in particular, know of the role that books and other library materials, distributed through the extension division, have played in supporting the work of the people in their various activities.

In the autumn of 1909 Wilson was guest speaker before the Georgia Library Association. It was the beginning of many talks before library and other groups. On December 28, 1909, he became a member and officer of the library department of the Southern Educational Association, before which he read a paper on "The Public Library as an Educator".[3] In reference to this paper, in which he set forth a carefully prepared statement of the library in all of its forms as an educational institution, Wilson has observed:

> I do not know where I acquired that philosophy, but I voiced it in the paper and I have held it throughout my life.

In these days when librarians are searching for a philosophy of their profession and sometimes require sociological jargon or mathematical formulae to explain their goals, it is worth suggesting that they read this paper if they have never done so. The functions of the library are clearly expressed in terms of services which it might provide the child, the adult, the general scholar, and the specialist. The paper is remarkable in that a reading of it today will reveal its soundness in terms of a national plan of libraries. Wrote Miss Barker:

> His is a fighting faith in the power of knowledge and ideas, with the library as a medium for their diffusion for the upbuilding of a region. His has been an articulate, authoritative voice. And he has been listened to with attention and respect in all councils where the library has had a stake.[4]

Librarians in the South — Southeast and Southwest — are familiar with Dr. Wilson's efforts in behalf of libraries for the region. He envisaged libraries as part of the total program of educational and social progress, along with schools, transportation, health, agriculture, and other attributes of man's well-being. Unless the idea of libraries was instilled firmly in the minds of men from every walk of life, he saw little chance that progress would be accelerated. Libraries were to be known as vital agencies of education and research, not as mausoleums and museums. For the South, Wilson viewed the library as an active resource which would help materially in raising the educational level of the people, so that they could attain for themselves and their communities a prominent place in the main current of American life.

It would not be possible to include in this summary a lengthy statement of the work of the Library Extension Service at North Carolina. As Agatha Boyd Adams has stated:

> The early growth of this type of library extension service was due largely to Dr. Wilson, who understood what such a service could mean to a state meagerly supplied with libraries, and who encouraged its progress in every possible way, both as librarian and later as director of the Extension Bureau.[5]

Although he had been writing about educational and library problems in the South generally, it was through his relations with the Southeastern Library Association that Dr. Wilson gave impetus to his concern for cooperative efforts for regional library development. Among the founders of the Southeastern Library Association, Dr. Wilson, who served as president of the group during 1924-1926, presented his ideas on regional development in his paper on "The Library in the Advancing South",[6] presented at Signal Mountain, discussing some of the elements — rural areas, racial problems, low income, illiteracy, attitudes, and other characteristics — which were relevant to library development in the South. Specific suggestions for improving the situation included:

> establishment of a professorship in the use of books and bibliography at each state university,
> establishment of library schools and summer courses in library science,
> development of libraries in high schools,
> development of library commissions concerned with extension of library service in each state,
> provision of library service on a county or multi-county basis rather than by smaller units,

utilization of "field representatives and standing
committees" to secure financial assistance and advice
following the pattern established in education, agriculture, and other fields.

Anyone examining this paper must conclude that Dr. Wilson
had outlined a stimulating program. The various representatives
from libraries in the South, as well as from the American Library Association and other groups, were impressed with both
the seriousness and the enthusiasm that were evident at the
meeting. Tommie Dora Barker and Mary Edna Anders,[7] who
have written about Dr. Wilson's part in this program have pointed to the specific influence that his ideas have had on the development of librarianship in the South. Later papers by Dr. Wilson —
at Biloxi, in 1928, at which he spoke of the "Southern Library
Achievements and Objectives", and at the joint meeting of the
Southeastern and Southwestern Library Associations at Memphis
in 1934, at which he spoke of "New Objectives for Southern Libraries"— suggest steps for the development of academic, public, county, special, and school libraries, and relate these to
redefinitions of library service in terms of the South, studies
of Southern library conditions, expanded library training, adequate library service to elementary schools, organization and
expansion of library resources for research, development of
library standards, and new legislation to implement the library
program.

Working for North Carolina, the Southeast, or the entire
South would be enough for most people. But not for Louis Round
Wilson. His influence on American librarianship had begun to be
felt before he went to the University of Chicago in 1932 to take
over the deanship of the Graduate Library School. Actually, he
had been called to Chicago in 1926 to consult on the program
being planned at the university. In a "Memorandum Concerning
the Advanced Graduate Library School" dated May 1926, Wilson
envisaged a school that would help in the development of the profession of librarianship as schools for medicine, law, and engineering had been doing successfully in those fields. The proposed school would be an advanced graduate school conducted
in accord with the best standards of American university graduate instruction and would be open to students who held bachelor
degrees which included, or were supplemented by, one year of

technical training in library science.

In his estimation of the curriculum outlined by the committee that had been called to Chicago to discuss the Graduate Library School, Wilson found that the areas of statistics and research methods had been omitted. He recommended that these areas be included. He also suggested that specialization be emphasized, especially for students preparing for the Ph.D. degree. From the point of view of various groups of library workers, the school should provide training for administrators and executives in public libraries, which were distinctive institutions with a wide variety of administrative problems; college and university libraries, which were well behind public libraries in efficient administration; school and children's libraries, which required high-level personnel with knowledge of curriculums and educational methods, as well as educational and child psychology and a wide range of children's literature; special libraries, including those of industrial, technical, scientific, and business organizations; library commissions, which were charged with the formation of libraries and specialized library service for the entire state, including library legislation, certification, and the conduct of library institutes; and library schools and departments, which were charged with the responsibility of providing instruction in library science. He also saw the need for the school to prepare teachers for positions in library schools, normal schools, and summer schools giving instruction in school library methods, training classes in public libraries, and librarian-teachers in colleges and universities, who would orient freshmen and other undergraduates in the best utilization of books and other library materials and also offer courses in bibliography to graduate students working on projects and dissertations. The school would further prepare bibliographical experts to administer special collections outside of large libraries, special collections in large public, university, and private scholarly libraries, libraries of research institutes in special subjects, and legislative reference libraries. In 1926, Wilson foresaw the need of having trained investigators and conductors of surveys in the library field. He was concerned with the future need of examining closely the functions, practices, and effectiveness of both public and academic libraries. He envisaged the need for textbooks in librarianship, and the development of personnel classifications by libraries.

To attempt to appraise the impact of an institution upon a great university or upon any base of American culture is at best hazardous. Such an attempt calls for dissociation, objectivity, and long perspective. There appears to be general agreement, however, that the Graduate Library School, particularly during the period of Wilson's direction of its affairs, influenced American librarianship in a number of ways.

The school, as directed by Wilson, became an integral part of the University of Chicago, accepted by it and by the library profession of the United States as the nation's leading center for graduate training and research in librarianship. Through its deliberate program, which may have been disconcerting to some librarians who held no brief for research into library problems, the concept of librarianship was expanded to include the social aspects of the library. By developing librarianship as a field for scientific study and research, it subjected the field to the same methods of study and procedures of investigation that were applicable to other social institutions.

Particularly important was the emphasis by the school on the critical, objective point of view. It challenged the accepted assumptions upon which library practice rested and trained students to question and criticize library problems scientifically as students in other fields were trained to question and criticize. Librarianship was related to other disciplines from which it could derive breadth and enrichment. Previous study had been primarily technical, bibliographical, historical, and literary. By drawing upon the humanities, the social sciences, the physical and biological sciences, it gave librarianship a depth that greatly enhanced it. Education for librarianship was significantly affected by the development of curricula and method. The University of Chicago, distinguished among American universities for the sound use of its advanced study and research, received the school as a valuable addition to its professional and graduate schools. Wilhelm Munthe, writing in his AMERICAN LIBRARIANSHIP FROM A EUROPEAN ANGLE, in 1939, observed:

In the space of seven or eight years the limited staff of the school and a few of the graduates have managed to translate into action the program which the 100 esteemed members of the exalted American Library Institute had brooded over for about a generation: To direct the efforts toward the more scholarly aspects of librarianship hitherto neglected, and toward a careful and scientific study and discussion of the more important problems of library service.

Through its publication program, which Wilson pushed constantly, the school contributed to a further development of a philosophy of librarianship. Concerned with the social values of library service, it dealt with theory and practice and pressed toward standards. Finally, it furnished leaders in the field of librarianship through the students it trained. Its graduates assumed major administrative posts in university and public libraries in the country, as well as directorships and professorships in a number of the nation's leading library schools. Graduates have likewise risen to important posts in professional associations and have contributed significantly to publication in the library and related fields.

It would take a whole morning to tell you of Wilson's activities as a library surveyor. In 1928, Dr. Wilson accepted his first invitation to be a consultant on library problems at the Union Theological Seminary, in Richmond. This started a whole new line of activity. In the years that followed he surveyed, either by himself or with colleagues, the libraries of Davidson College, Guilford College, Columbia Seminary in Decatur, Georgia, the Vanderbilt-Peabody-Scarrit Group, Alabama Polytechnic Institute, Tuskegee Institute, Grosvenor and Buffalo Public libraries, New York State Library, Louisiana State University, and the Universities of Georgia, Florida, South Carolina, Stanford, Denver, Atlanta, Cornell, and Notre Dame. He worked closely with the Southeastern States Cooperative Library Survey, and was a collaborator in the preparation of the final report.

During his first survey — that of the Union Theological Seminary, in Richmond — Wilson found a library which contained a number of incunabula, an extensive body of theological works, and complete sets of the journals and proceedings of the presbyteries, synods, and the general assemblies of the Presbyterian Church of the United States (Southern Presbyterian Church). Entirely unorganized, the library was under the supervision of a professor of church history who gave it such attention at odd moments as he could spare. Wilson particularly noted the lack of books on social aspects of religion, and asked the supervisor how he accounted for it. Wilson was somewhat astonished by his reply.

"Well", answered the professor, "so far as I am concerned, I depend on my notes. I know what they contain, and if the students follow them they will not be likely to stray after false gods."

The first thing that came to Wilson's mind after an observation of that kind was a comment made by Rufus King in answer to a question he raised with Wilson during his early days as librarian at North Carolina. King, an itinerant Quaker layman, had asked Wilson if the library at Chapel Hill contained the works of "those infidels, Robert Ingersoll and Thomas Paine". Wilson replied that he thought it did.

"Do you think it advisable to expose the plastic minds of youth to such works?" asked King.

"I think it generally a good idea to allow people to look at all phases of questions when they are seeking the truth", answered Wilson.

King's condemnatory comment was: "Oh, well, my boy, thee may pride thyself on thy liberality of thought, but I will remind thee that if thee wrestles with the devil he may throw thee!"

Wilson strongly recommended to the president of the seminary that the library might well be more effective in the instructional program of the institution if it contained the important works dealing with social problems.

In many ways, Wilson's surveys have had effects beyond the institutions studied. In an observation on his work as a surveyor of libraries for almost thirty years, Wilson said:

> These special investigations gave me an insight into the administrative procedures of American universities that I could never have acquired otherwise and an acquaintance with some of the leading college and university administrators, faculty members, and librarians of the nation from which I have derived continued and unusual satisfaction. I have also had the satisfaction of seeing the analyses and discussions of problems considered in the surveys and the recommendations made by me embodied in the permanent literature of college and university administration in particular and of librarianship in general.

THE CONTRIBUTIONS OF LOUIS ROUND WILSON

As important as these personal gains were the significant by-products of the surveys. On all the campuses where he appeared for the purpose of making a survey, he left an impression with faculty members and administrators that librarianship was an important calling, and that libraries were indispensable for successful instruction and research. Moreover, he has had the great satisfaction of training young librarians to carry on the work of analyzing library programs. One could not work with Wilson on a survey and fail to observe his unbending search for principles and high standards. In many ways, this search was the same as that his students in classes have observed and appreciated.

Although Wilson has said that writing was laborious for him, he has been an astonishing contributor to library literature to say nothing of the other publications he has either written or edited. His publications, and particularly his articles, have covered practically every aspect of librarianship. The fourteen-page bibliography developed by Mary L. Thornton in the Library Quarterly for July 1942, at the time of Dr. Wilson's retirement from the Graduate Library School, could be lengthened considerably by his publications from 1942 to the present time. His work since 1942 would be considered sufficient for most librarians' lifetime production.

In his review of "Library Literature" in the 1953 volume, CHALLENGES TO LIBRARIANSHIP, edited by Louis Shores, Dr. Wilson calls attention to the rapid growth of publication in the field since 1923. His substantial papers, the volumes he has edited, the books that he has published either by himself or with colleagues — such as COUNTY LIBRARY SERVICE IN THE SOUTH, THE GEOGRAPHY OF READING, THE UNIVERSITY LIBRARY, THE LIBRARY IN COLLEGE INSTRUCTION, and LIBRARIES OF THE SOUTHEAST, among others — and the surveys on which he has reported represent important additions to the literature of the profession. But his greatest influence in this area has been his encouragement of others to produce useful works.

Wilson's early efforts for the establishment of the North Carolina Library Association and the Southeastern Library Association reflected his genuine concern for the usefulness of organizations in the development of a professional sense. His activities with the American Library Association and its various committees and boards represented substantial contributions to associational progress. His work with other library groups and related educational and research agencies, as well as philanthropic foundations, was directed at the betterment of libraries in America. He was one of the early and active workers for the Library Services Bill, just passed by Congress and enacted into law.

Frederick Keppel, president of the Carnegie Corporation of New York, has referred to Dr. Wilson's qualities of modesty and confidence in his work as dean of the Graduate Library School.[8] He wrote further:

> These same qualities of modesty and confidence have assured him a permanent place in the steady, but disappointingly slow, recognition of the professional status of the librarian. Forty years of modest but distinguished service as a professional librarian have made a demonstration and set an example; and he has taken confident advantage of his many opportunities for speaking and writing to contribute to the building-up of a much needed body of doctrine on the subject.

Forty years have grown to fifty-five years, and as Dr. Wilson approaches his eightieth birthday in December, he may well have satisfaction in work well done — as a university librarian, as a scholar and researcher in his chosen field, as a teacher, as a dean, as a consultant to librarians and administrative officials, as an editor, and as a friend to libraries and librarians. The story is not yet finished. But what feelings does one have at this point in regard to Dr. Wilson's contributions? Certainly there is gratitude to a librarian who can write so feelingly of the usefulness of libraries in American democratic life, a usefulness which he has seen so constantly and clearly. There is admiration for his keenness of mind, for his ability to energize others to make contributions to the profession, for his studied patience, and for his tenacity of purpose. And finally, there is respect for a man, who despite many trials and tribulations in his private and personal life, has made lasting contributions to our profession. We have gone a long way since Dana's LIBRARY PRIMER and Spofford's A BOOK FOR ALL READERS, and Dr. Wilson's indelible impression upon American librarianship is a tangible guide for the present and the future.

THE CONTRIBUTIONS OF LOUIS ROUND WILSON

NOTES:

1   Tommie Dora Barker, "Louis Round Wilson: A Tribute", The Southeastern Librarian, 1:74-89, Fall 1951.

2   Ibid., p. 74

3   "The Public Library as an Educator", Library Journal, XXXV (1910), 550-51.

4   Ibid., pp. 78-79.

5   "Library Extension Service", in Russell M. Grumman, UNIVERSITY EXTENSION IN ACTION. Chapel Hill: University of North Carolina Press, 1946, pp. 52-53.

6   Southeastern Library Association. Proceedings, Fourth Annual Conference, 1926, pp. 3-11.

7   "The Southeastern Library Association, 1920-1950", (unpublished manuscript.)

8   "Louis Round Wilson", Library Quarterly, 12:583-84, July 1942.

MR. ALA — CARL HASTINGS MILAM

Emily Miller Danton

Emily Miller Danton — editor of THE LIBRARY OF TOMOR-
ROW (1939) — lives in Birmingham, Alabama. The essay
here reprinted is a paper read before the American Library
History Round Table during the Washington, D.C., conference of the American Library Association in 1959; the
author's interpretation of Mr. Milam's career is based on
a number of years of work with him in Birmingham (1914-
1919) and in Chicago (1924-1935).

The parents of a little boy, born on a sandy farm in south
central Kansas in 1884, would have been amazed and incredulous
had a soothsayer told them that their son would become known
to thousands of people in this country, in Europe, in South and
Central America; that the work he would do would broaden the
lives of other thousands who would not know his name; that he
would be received by one king and decorated by another; welcomed at the Vatican by pope and cardinal; fly the Atlantic to
sit in various important councils; receive honorary degrees and
honorary memberships in associations at home and abroad; help
to create a vital international organization; inspire great gifts
to that association to which he was destined to devote so great
a part of his life and effort; serve the then undreamt-of United
Nations and Unesco; be lauded as planner, promoter, integrator,
administrator, catalyzer, pacifier, internationalist. These and
other things has Carl Milam been and done in his career, but
he remains what he was when he left his native heath, simple
and natural, as American as peanut butter.

The farm was a poor one for the sand blew and destroyed the
crops, and only the rattlesnakes and prairie dogs flourished.
The boy walked with his sister a mile or two to a one-room
school and had early memories of Indian alarms. But when he
was still small the family moved back to Missouri, where the
parents had come from, and then, when the Cherokee Strip was

Reprinted from ALA Bulletin, 53:753-762, October, 1959, by permission of the author and the publisher.

about to open, his father sold out his business and made the run. He acquired a farm, drove off some would-be jumpers with his Colt 45, and took his family to it in a covered wagon. Somewhat later, he moved the family to Newkirk, Oklahoma, the nearest town, and there the parents spent the rest of their lives.

The boy, Carl, grew tall and broad and strong, and in 1903 entered the University of Oklahoma, where he became a student assistant in the library under Milton J. Ferguson, thus acquiring his vocation. Here, too, he majored under Professor Vernon L. Parrington, whom he greatly admired, and, more important, here he met the girl whom he later married. Such good grounding did he receive from Mr. Ferguson that the course at Albany, where he entered library school in 1907, was almost too easy for him and he would have taken the two years in one had he been allowed. His first real job was at Purdue University, where he spent a year, and where job scarcity made a cataloger of him — a reluctant one, we can imagine.

Milam thought of himself at this time as a promising young university librarian, but when in 1909 he was offered the secretaryship of the Indiana Public Library Commission the salary of $125 a month was too good to decline, as it would enable him to get married. Thus was the curve of his career deflected to another branch of library work, and in this job he remained for four years.

As chief of Indiana's library extension agency, Milam clearly exhibited traits that characterized the man in his prime: broad vision, a singular capacity for promotion, and boundless energy. The record amply proves this. Thirty-six new public libraries were established; the Indiana Library Trustees Association was organized; significant library legislation was secured. One enactment was the initial move that came to fruition twenty years later in the beautiful Indiana Library and Historical Building. Other legislation contributed substantially to public library development in the state, mostly the provision for larger units of service by combining townships, antecedent to county library service. As early as 1910 Milam was proclaiming that country dwellers must have as good library service as those in town.

Milam was not yet out of his twenties when he was called from his Indiana post to be the director of the Birmingham Public Library. "Director" was a rather grandiose term for the head of that library in 1913, for it was small and poor, housed in the top floor of the dingy old one-elevator City Hall, and with only three or four trained persons on its staff. The setup would have appeared grim to many a young librarian, but to Carl Milam it was a challenge, and he met it brilliantly. He worked furiously; went out and begged for money to buy books; convinced big industrialists that a good public library would have value to them; brought about a constant flow of excellent newspaper publicity; conceived bold plans and carried them out; stirred the staff to enthusiastic support.

The five branches had come into being in five small suburban towns, which later were absorbed by the growing city; they brought book collections but no money and their buildings were mostly inadequate. But under the new director they began to grow and to become more useful and more used. Milam believed that a public library should be open 365 days in the year, and this was the rule as long as he remained in Birmingham. It is a tribute to his tact that he worked side by side with his predecessor — now become vice director — in perfect harmony and with mutual respect, until his departure six years later.

The library's income in 1913 was $10,000; its book collection numbered 40,000. By 1915 the circulation was up 100 per cent, though a business slump that year brought a cut in the library's budget and everyone earning more than fifty dollars a month received salary cuts. Two years later the budget was up to $25,000 and a sixth branch had been opened. Library rules had been liberalized; exhibits appeared in business windows, cards in streetcars, signs in stores. Eight mammoth billboards were given free to the library during a book-fund campaign. Additions were made to the staff as fast as finances would allow. Birmingham was low in the scale of Southern cities, with only 16.6 books per hundred of the population.

A Birmingham reporter described the library director glowingly:

> He is young, practical, energetic, and enthusiastic. He has to an extraordinary degree the combination of the everyday business man and the vision — the ideals — of the poet and the dreamer. Too, this young library expert has the faculty of making friends as he works along — friends to keep. He is considerate, tactful, sincere, thoroughly well equipped for his task and gifted with a

happy faculty of expression and the ability to do team
work.

This was high praise, but no one on the Birmingham staff
would dispute it, for they found it exciting to be members of his
team, despite long hours and low pay. He made them stretch
themselves, mentally, and do things they had thought they could
not do. And they learned to accompany every important proposal
with a budget — else it would come straight back. Staff meetings
were lively because everyone felt free to speak, and because all
felt a sense of responsibility toward their jobs and the library,
a sense of pride, and each had a feeling of importance. Milam's
enthusiasm was unfailing and infectious; he never appeared down-
hearted, even after a real disappointment. He seemed to brush
aside the ruins of an old plan and get to work at once on a new
one, his zest undiminished.

During this period in Birmingham, the influential head of a
large corporation asked a popular minister to do him a service.
"I have been watching that young man at the public library", he
said. "He has a great deal of ability and I want him in my organization. I have no idea what his salary is but I am ready to double it. Will you sound him out and see whether he would accept?"
When the clergyman explained his errand to the librarian, the
latter smiled. "Why, Sir, I am a librarian. I chose this field
because it was what I wanted to do. I would work in a library
for a tenth of what I might get in business." The matter was
dropped.

When the first World War came, Milam put all the resources
of the public library at the service of city and state; he began
the collection of books for the soldiers encamped in Alabama,
and fostered the establishment and growth of camp libraries.
Here was a chance, not only to relieve the boredom of those
young men, not just to help them advance themselves, but to
make lifelong readers and library users of many who never before had been exposed to books and library service. He thought
up new ways to help people save, and substitute, and "make do".
The old entrance hall of the library became the War Service
Department, and in addition to books, pamphlets, book lists,
and posters, there were displayed weekly attractive dishes, in
which substitute ingredients had been used, with recipes posted
beside the inverted glass covers. The exhibits were made by a

local housewife; the staff ate them when they were removed. The poorly paid staff bought Liberty Bonds as a matter of course and of pride. Was not their director setting them an example, from a salary little better than their own?

When men were mustered out, or invalided out of the service, if they lived in Birmingham, or paused there, they were very likely to become aware of the fact that the public library had their interests at heart. A great banner was stretched across a busy downtown intersection:

BACK TO THE JOB
WHAT JOB?
CONSULT THE PUBLIC LIBRARY

Every book on occupations, on adult study, on job classification that could possibly be acquired was put to use. Useful clipping files were built up; an index of helpful community consultants was compiled; large corporations were called on for advice and help; government documents were combed for ideas; pamphlets were sought from every likely source. The vibrant director was never more active, more resourceful, more fruitful of ideas. The library began a series of classified ads in the newspapers in January 1919. Here is a sample: "HELP. What job do you want? Books will help you get it. Use the Public Library. Books on your job. Free." Specific advertisements were pointed toward the various trades and skills. Posters broke out everywhere. The War Service Department, by a simple adjustment, became the Vocational Department!

During these years, Milam was deep in the war effort and directed the library with his left hand. He had become state director of the book drive, under the War Service Committee of the ALA. The goal for the country was a million dollars and a million books. Then Milam assisted in installing a library at Camp McClellan. There followed an indefinite leave in Washington, and during 1918 he was mostly at the Library of Congress, working under Dr. Putnam, who was national chairman of Library War Service. He also made inspection trips to training camps and cantonments, coming occasionally to Birmingham to fire the staff with new enthusiasm, fill them with new ideas, and, once, to assist at the opening of the first Negro branch.

Finally, late in 1919, he returned to offer his resignation: the ALA had called him to be its secretary. He was well prepared for the post. He had been on ALA Council, on the Publications Board, and on the Executive Board, and was very familiar with the structure and operations of the Association.

Thus began, in 1920, a career which continued for twenty-eight years, during which the Association expanded enormously, went through another war, moved its headquarters from the Chicago Public Library to the John Crerar, to 520 North Michigan Avenue, and finally to its own East Huron Street building. Its membership grew from 4,500 to 17,000, and its budget from $33,000 to $540,000. Was it at the Swampscott Conference of 1921 that signs reading "Welcome ALA!" were read by the uninitiated, "Welcome, American Laundry Association"? I doubt that that ever happened again, for those initials became a widely known symbol for the reader, the book, and the person who brought them together.

An ALA staff member of the twenties expressed, long after, her recollection of CHM: "Vigor, energy and cheerfulness — a general male quality in a sea of femininity. Definitely a leader with progressive ideas, bucking conservatism." He was ever ready to break with tradition. Nothing so irritated him as to be told "We've always done it this way." Another of his colleagues of that period has written perceptively of the Milam she remembers:

> Looking back upon the years of my assignments at ALA under Carl Milam, I find a certain dualism in the remembered atmosphere. It was a time of tremendous drive, push and promotion. I used to resent that atmosphere. It seemed to me . . . that emphasis was put on the wrong things; on the spectacular program, the Big Design, at the cost of neglecting the small people who made up the membership of the ALA. I often disagreed with the method, and with Carl Milam. But I never lost my affection for the man.
>
> I think the reason for this was that it was perfectly obvious that the push and the drive were never for his own aggrandizement. He was peculiarly selfless, and one was not aware of personal ambition. He drove us all toward goals he felt proper for the profession. In the light of library history, he was right. Certainly, due to him, libraries and the Library Idea were given

new directions, nationally and internationally, and new dimensions, never previously attained. They have held, too, for all time.

He is a kind man. I hold warm remembrances of jokes, and laughter, and the right word said at a time of personal difficulty. I still hear the enthusiasm in his voice when he reported on some subject that interested him: the studies of Thorndike on the ability of adults to learn, for instance. I sometimes judged him as being blind to certain sensibilities in people. But he was never conceited, never small, and the man simply does not know the meaning of snobbery.

Carl Milam conducted an unceasing audit of experience, on himself, his associates, on organizations, programs and movements — an audit by which he endeavored to extract the best from the past as a guide to future action. In this he was adept and relentless, and always without rancor. He has the gift, beyond most men, of synthesizing the thoughts of others. Many an ALA President has commented on this — on the fact that, after hours of rambling, diffuse discussion in some board meeting, Carl could pull out of it all that was significant, and with a casual, "I wonder if this isn't what you mean?" present the meat in phrase succinct, vigorous, direct.

One of his aphorisms of those days is well remembered: Never let what is merely urgent crowd out what is important. It seems to me as characteristic as anything I know. Once a colleague looked in at the door of his office. Mr. Milam was busily writing, but he looked up. "May I come in?" "Of course. I can always be interrupted when I am writing. But if I'm gazing out of the window, please be careful: I'm probably very busy." Everyone who has been associated with him has heard him say — and most of us have borrowed the line without giving credit: Librarians do not tell people what to think, but they put before them the materials that will help them to think and to form opinions. The ALA had of course long been a publisher, but its output was largely composed of pamphlets and reading lists, with an occasional annotated catalog. It was in 1924 that the first large sums began to come from the Carnegie Corporation of New York, and an immediate result was a greatly expanded publishing program. For the first time, the ALA brought out items to be put into the hands of the public. More than a million Reading with a Purpose courses were distributed over a few years and made the ALA better known than any of its other activities. Its sights were aimed high: the very top men in their fields were invited to prepare these booklets, and for a mere honorarium, and nearly every one accepted the assignment. In 1920, sales of publications amounted to $14,000; in 1947 they reached $137,000.

If the headquarters staff worked hard, at least they were never bored — and they knew that their chief worked harder. Work was parceled out with definite lines of authority drawn, and no overlapping. They worked as a team, each knowing what was expected of him and when his activity affected the field of another. At meetings of department heads information was cleared and all were made aware of what the ALA was doing. The secretary delegated definite responsibility and was always generous in giving credit for performance to others. Milam has never considered himself an originator of ideas, but he has pushed those of others for all they were worth. Examples that will be remembered are the one-dollar-per-capita support slogan, and microfilming of documents.

In the middle twenties important boards and committees came into being; frontiers were pushed back; the atmosphere was exhilarating. Library Extension took on new meaning, and Adult Education, and Education for Librarianship, and International Relations. There were many visitors at headquarters, librarians from everywhere, consultants from Northwestern and the University of Chicago, literary lights like Christopher Morley. When time allowed they were invited to address the staff.

Before the United States had entered the first World War, the proposal had come for an American library in Paris, after the war, as a result of correspondence with French and Belgian groups on reconstruction plans. That was looking forward! When we did get into the war, many thousands of books were sent to Europe for the use of the American servicemen based there. It was these books, and the funds left over from Library War Service, that made possible the establishment of the library in Paris, with Burton Stevenson as its first director. It is the largest English-language library on the continent of Europe.

For nearly half a century there had been a trickle of Europeans coming to American library schools, but now it was pro-

posed that a library school be set up in the American Library
in Paris, to meet the demand for American-type training among
Europeans. The American Committee for Devastated France
gave $50,000 as a starter, and contributions from various or-
ganizations made possible some scholarships. Mary P. Parsons
was the resident director of the school, with Sarah Bogle (who
had become assistant secretary of the ALA) its over-all director.
Miss Bogle shuttled back and forth across the Atlantic with something of the regularity of Mr. Dulles in later days. The school
lasted for five years, then closed for lack of funds. Carl Milam
had a large part in all these things, but I must here pay tribute
to Miss Bogle, whose work so beautifully complemented his.
They were a great team during the twenties. Her vision and her
personal connections, antedating her service at headquarters,
must never be forgotten or discounted. She knew her way around
in international relationships and she did much to help her younger chief gain background in these aspects of his work. They supplemented each other in many ways, and both were highly stimulating to their associates.

During this period China came into the international picture,
when the ALA was asked to send over a library authority to survey Chinese libraries and advise on means for their development.
Dr. Arthur Bostwick of St. Louis was the happy choice, and perhaps you have seen at headquarters the miniature replica of an
ancient bullock cart — itself more than a thousand years old —
which was sent in appreciation of Dr. Bostwick's successful
mission there.

Thanks to these and many other ventures, the intangible
growth of the ALA in the twenties and thirties was as spectacular
as its physical growth, for it became known all over the civilized
world. In 1926, when the ALA met in Atlantic City to celebrate
its fiftieth anniversary, there were 63 delegates from 15 foreign
countries. That was of course no spontaneous happening. Milam's
attendance at an international meeting in Prague had acquainted
European librarians with plans for the conference and stirred
their interest, and thanks to Dr. Frederick P. Keppel, its president, the Carnegie Corporation of New York gave generously toward the expense involved. From this time on the ALA and its
secretary were more and more involved in library progress on
an international scale, and the prestige of the Association grew
accordingly. The Charter of the ALA originally read thus:

MR. ALA — CARL HASTINGS MILAM

"Whereas Soandso and Soandso have associated themselves . . .
for the purpose of promoting the library interests of the country. . . ." In 1942 this was amended to read ". . . for the purpose of promoting library interests throughout the world. . . ."
That is Carl Milam speaking.

Milam became well known in the offices of many national organizations and many philanthropic foundations. A representative
of another association asked a librarian at an adult education
conference, "I wonder if you librarians realize how fortunate
you are to have a man like Milam to represent you?" And he
won and held the interest, friendship, and trust of foundation
executives like Keppel and Fosdick and Stevens and Embree,
all of whom believed that any project which Carl backed, whether they aided it or not, made sense in relation to the advancement and diffusion of knowledge. Robert Lester has said that in
his more than thirty years of foundation experience, he has
never known any other person to whom foundation doors were
open so wide in welcome.

In 1927 in Edinburgh, Milam, with about seventy other librarians, assisted in forming what was to become the International Federation of Library Associations. In 1929 the new organization met in Rome, in 1933 in Chicago, and in 1935 in
Madrid. The ALA secretary was always active in these gather-
ings and his views were listened to with respect. Flora B.
Ludington, who was chairman of the International Relations Committee, wrote of Milam in this connection: "His interest in international library relations and knowledge of the Association
helped us through many long hours of deliberations and in securing funds to carry out some of the special projects which
were recommended." In addition to the library conferences,
Mr. Milam sat in at the UN organization meetings as educational adviser, served on State Department cultural committees, and
took part in conferences which prepared recommendations for
what became Unesco.

Later on, while Hitler was in power and propagandizing
against the democracies, Milam went to the Rockefeller Foundation with his idea for the Books for Europe project. Too wise
to say the purpose would be to combat Nazism, he made a more
positive approach by saying that the intent would be to interpret
democratic ideals and to show what comes out of democratic
societies. The first grant was for $60,000, and more came later.

Milam was elated and very optimistic. Thousands of books found their way to the popular libraries of Western Europe, and more friends were made for the United States and the ALA — if there were no more significant results. Milam himself, with his genius for friendship, made warm friends over the years among European librarians, such men as Esdaile, Colijn, Munthe, Cain, Godet, Sevensma, Cardinal Tisserant, and dozens more; and among Asiatics Ranganathan should be mentioned. These friendships he treasures as among the greatest satisfactions of his life, and out of them he gained understanding of what is involved in true international relations.

After his earlier trips to Europe, Milam was prepared for introduction to Latin American cooperation, largely through John Vance, who had been a consular officer in a Caribbean country and was then law librarian of Congress. He aroused and stimulated Milam's interest in Latin America, and accompanied him to Mexico when Milam secured a special grant from the Carnegie Corporation for the trip and to invite some Mexican librarians to visit the United States. During a second visit plans were made for the establishment of the Benjamin Franklin Library, the second American library in a foreign country. It was set up by contract with the United States Government through the State Department; it was Milam who convinced the State Department that libraries could be strong agencies of international understanding.

In January of 1947 Carl Milam went abroad, on invitation of the State Department, to serve as consultant on libraries to the United States delegation to Unesco. This meant about three weeks in Paris, with a short stop in Geneva for a meeting of the International Library Committee, where Milam played a key role. After some vague and wandering discussion, he induced the chairman to present his twelve to fourteen proposals as the basis of a report, and then got them adopted. In his later report to the ALA, he stated his opinion that Unesco could become "the most important of all agencies for the preservation of peace, because it is concerned with what happens in the minds of men, or it could be just another bureaucratic agency for boondoggling on an international scale." Which could depend on the ability of the permanent staff, on participation without interference of the member governments, and on the extent to which the peoples of the world — and especially of the United States — participate

creatively and critically in Unesco's program through libraries,
schools, universities, and national and international organizations. Librarians, he felt, had unusual opportunities in this area.
How entirely fitting it was that Carl Milam, who had figured
with such conspicuous success on the international scene, should
be invited in 1948 to come to Lake Success as director of the
United Nations Library for the two final years of his professional
career. Besides attending the organization meeting, he had already surveyed the UN Library, with Luther Evans and Ralph
Beals, and had recommended that the UN not go in for large collections, but rely much on the libraries of New York City — still
a guiding principle. There were heartaches. The Personnel Department wanted to fill every vacancy from an underrepresented
country; Milam wanted to fill it with the best qualified person
he could find. He usually had fair success. He considers his
greatest achievement there the fact that he persuaded the UN to
rate and pay librarians on the same scale as other professionals,
even though the prevailing salaries in many libraries were lower.

Before he had been many months at the UN there came the
disruptive episode of his nomination as president-elect of the
ALA. He had left the secretaryship only recently; his successor
had been installed; it was too soon to bring Milam back as head
of the Association. But a well-disposed nominating committee,
animated more by zeal than by judgment, and in spite of contrary
advice, put it through and persuaded a reluctant Milam to accept.
The Fourth Activities Committee Report was still a burning issue; reorganization of headquarters was under way; a new spirit
was stirring and Milam represented the old.

Certainly the nomination was badly timed; perhaps there
would have been no revolt after the lapse of a year or two. At
any rate, there was objection to it; another nomination was made
by petition, and Milam was defeated in the election which followed. A former president of the ALA wrote:

> I don't think the young revolutionaries were out after
> Carl Milam, the individual, they were after the power
> group that was putting him forward. And when he was
> their age, I have no doubt he would have been on their
> side — against the Hills and the Bishops and the Danas
> and the Bostwicks. ALA didn't repudiate Carl Milam
> and his great accomplishments; the members who voted

were taking sides between the "ins" and the "outs" and
in such cases the outs nearly always win.

A lawyer, member of a big city library board, a stranger to
Milam and new in library circles, was told of the explosive Chicago meeting and said:

He will not be elected. No executive secretary of any
organization, if he has accomplished anything, can ever
be elected president of that organization. In the course
of years of accomplishment, he will have offended one
small group, later another, and this is their chance to
get even. You will find this is true of practically every
national organization in the country.

So, in his defeat, we can read a tribute to his stature. And,
though the episode was embarrassing to Milam and painful to
his friends, it left no bitterness in his heart, no lessening of
his dedication to the profession he loved.

To return to Milam, director of the UN Library, Mr. Andrew
Cordier, executive assistant to the secretary-general, wrote in
a letter:

Mr. Milam . . . established firmly the foundation of the
United Nations Library. He had a very clear conception,
which he executed with exceptional ability, of the role
of the United Nations Library as a library highly specialized in international affairs. The very broad scope of
the activities of the United Nations in the political,
economic and social fields was used by him as a gauge
providing the basis for the acquisition of materials which
could be used, not only by members of Delegations and
of the Secretariat, but also by distinguished representatives of non-governmental organizations, the press and
outstanding scholars. Mr. Milam had exceptional contacts with leading librarians in this and in other countries and formulated library standards which correspond
with the highest concepts of library development.

Andrew Osborn was an important consultant of Milam's at
the UN. Before he left last year for Australia, he prepared a

statement which seems so valuable that I wish to quote the greater part of it:

> The United Nations Library was barely three years old when Carl Milam was invited to take charge. But into those three years the Organization had managed to crowd enough errors to give the Library a particularly difficult start. There was no clear conception of the kind of library activities the United Nations should develop, no understanding of the way in which the complex and rapidly growing research needs of the international Secretariat should be practically evaluated and translated into an appropriate library program. In the face of the Administration's groping and indecision, chaos was bound to develop. Various departments started acquiring and setting up their own collections; they hired their own staffs to serve them and the management of the central Library was steadily losing ground and reputation.
>
> The situation called for strong and resourceful direction which Carl was eminently able to provide. His first achievement was to give the Library an articulate policy, clearly defining its aims and its means. For this purpose an International Committee of Library Experts was convened at Lake Success. It resulted in the writing of a sort of library charter, the official document on Library policy and organization, which later received the blessing of the General Assembly. . . . Much needed central control was established over all departmental libraries. . . . The valuable Reference Service of the Department of Public Information was transferred to the main library, with its staff and collections, thus providing the backbone for the reorganized reference service of the Library as a whole.
>
> The Organization responded to Carl's efforts by increasing the budget to allow for more staff and more books. . . . In a short space of time the Library had tidied itself up, straightened out its procedures, and was hard at work . . . clearing up the arrearages. . . . Everywhere there was drive and good organization.
>
> Transfer of the Library to the Secretary-General's

office — it had been a part of Conference and General Services, then of the Department of Public Information — gave the Library independent status. This wise change of affiliation carried with it recognition of the fact that the Library was now in capable hands and was ripe to administer its own affairs. There was no need for Andrew Cordier, Lie's right-hand man, to defend the Library's budget before the powerful Fifth Committee; instead, Carl could and did perform that function with great credit.

Osborn goes on to describe other achievements, like the acquisition of the Woodrow Wilson Foundation Library for the UN, for which Carl carried through the negotiations; his putting the international system of exchanges in order, his support and direction of the bibliography of UN publications, and inception of the United Nations Documents Index, then continues:

There was a poignancy to Carl's leaving the United Nations. When his two-year contract was about to expire, he was invited to stay on. This invitation gave him real pleasure because he was eager to see the Library installed in its new home in New York City. But this was not to be. When the doctors told him of Mrs. Milam's illness, he sacrificed his ambitions and desires, and decided to return to his Illinois farm where he could personally tend her.

His lieutenants in the Library saw in this decision still another mark of respect, the intensely human man they had come to love and admire, a beloved personality. For a little over two years they had enjoyed the daily contacts with him, in the office and away from it — even at the polo games on Long Island where they accompanied him as he took Mrs. Milam for recreation. They had known his accolade as he slipped an arm on their shoulder, giving words of counsel or support, or giving praise for a job well done. It was with deep regret that they had to concur in Carl's decision; but at the same time they were grateful for having been able to share the warmth of his personality and the excellence of his administration. It must surely fall to few men to end

442

their professional careers on such a note of genuine
affection, high regret, and poignancy.

So Carl and Nell, his companion of forty-six years, returned
to the farm near Barrington which they had bought some years
before. There they grew irises and apples and Christmas trees,
and there he nursed his wife tenderly through the slow encroach-
ments of a progressive disease, until her death in 1956. They
were good comrades, and Nell Milam, while never a showy
person, had been an active, valued citizen during the years when
they had lived in Evanston. She was the right wife for him, the
easy hostess, sympathetic friend, warm companion.

Carl now lives alone in his small house. He loves to dig in
the earth and he does as much as a painful back and a tricky
heart will allow. He cherishes his solitude, but welcomes bird
friends and human ones, and the occasional visits of his daughters, who come to mother him and sew on his buttons. Sometimes he visits Mary and her family in Iowa, or sees a polo
match nearby, or goes in to Chicago to meet old friends at a
Midwinter Meeting.

After Nell's death Carl sought some occupation on which he
could fix his attention, something to fill the hours when garden
work had been forbidden. He began to develop an idea that had
been in his mind, of compiling and editing a book on librarianship, one that would show library work as the thrilling, soul-
satisfying adventure he had always found it. He secured an able
collaborator in Helen Wessells. The book grows slowly. Nineteen chapters are in hand and more promised. It should be a
fine book to put into the hands of young people casting about for
a profession. Naturally, it will carry the ALA imprint.

Honors have come to Carl. He was very pleased — and who
wouldn't be, at 28? — when first invited to furnish his biography
for inclusion in WHO'S WHO IN AMERICA. He has honorary
degrees from Southwestern and from Lawrence College, was
president (in his twenties) of the League of Library Commissions, was given the Royal Order of Vasa, first class, by the
King of Sweden. During the twenties the Carnegie Corporation
gave him a bronze medal especially designed for him, in recognition of his work for libraries. The ALA headquarters staff
gave him a life membership in the Association on his fiftieth
birthday, and in 1954 Council voted to make him an honorary

life member. The citation, and the speeches made at the time of his resignation, pleased him greatly. He has been a member of various national boards, councils, committees, and he has enjoyed his clubs — the Cliff Dwellers in Chicago and the Cosmos in Washington.

His pipe is almost a physical part of him and was once the constant companion of his rod and reel. He has liked to camp and fish, to enjoy good food and drink with friends, to spin yarns and talk freely with them about books, ideas, events, and in general to create an atmosphere of good comradeship.

I believe his stature grows in retrospect, but it would be presumptuous in me to attempt to appraise his worth or to try to fix his place among the greats of the library profession. He is often compared to Melvil Dewey, for though they were very unlike in many respects, they were alike in dreams and projects of growth, expansion, progress, and in aggressive leadership. Each has been a leader in his time, and we are glad that we have known Carl Milam in our time.

PART FOUR — A LIBRARY HALL OF FAME

A LIBRARY HALL OF FAME
COMPILED FOR THE 75TH ANNIVERSARY OF THE
AMERICAN LIBRARY ASSOCIATION, 1876-1951

The Library Journal, in this issue, is taking a backward
look over the past 75 years of library history as a prelude
to joining in the American Library Association's Anniversary emphasis on "The Heritage of the U.S.A. in Times of
Crisis".

Seventy-five years is not a long span. At the great 50th
Anniversary Convention in Philadelphia, two of A.L.A.'s
founders, Mr. Dewey and Mr. Bowker, were the speakers.
As with all chronicles, whether of nations or of groups,
the values are best appreciated by recalling the individuals
who gave direction and color to the record.

To bring the names of the leaders forward as pleasant
memories to many, and as inspiration to the leaders of the
next quarter century, Library Journal has ventured to
make a list of the names of outstanding librarians of the
past with a brief paragraph placing these men and women
in the library world while suggesting the character of their
special contributions.

That this list of names should be as nearly acceptable
to all as possible, the Journal, after canvassing past library records, made a tentative list. This tentative list
was sent to 20 librarians known to be familiar with and
interested in library history. These 20 were asked to cross
off and add to the list. These replies, with their very helpful comments, provided a vote by which to decide on the
inclusions.

As further aid to the right listings, the A.L.A., at Midwinter meetings, asked its History Round Table to represent them, and [Chairman] Wayne Shirley, [then] dean of
the library school at Pratt Institute [and now Librarian of
Finch College in New York City], accepted the responsibility.

It had been agreed that this present list should not include

Reprinted from Library Journal, 76:466-472, March 15, 1951, by permission of the publisher.

the living, however obvious and significant had been their
contribution. The list, with such additions, would promptly
be doubled.

It was further understood that only librarians should be
included, though the publishers of Library Journal have not
failed to be pleased that there have been so many suggestions
that the name of R. R. Bowker belonged on any such list.

40 LEADERS OF THE LIBRARY MOVEMENT

Mary Eileen Ahern, 1865?-1938

Founder of Public Libraries (later Libraries) 1895-1931,
edited especially to meet the needs of library workers in the
Middle-West. Effective friend of new libraries and young librarians.

Indiana State Library, 1893-95; organizer and secretary,
Indiana Library Association, 1889-96; Library Bureau as
editor.

Edwin H. Anderson, 1861-1947

Developed the personnel of The New York Public Library
to notable level. Directed growth of the Reference and Circulation Divisions of the library and introduced new services;
readers advisory, theater, photostat, municipal reference
library, traveling book wagons.

Organizer-director, Carnegie Library, Pittsburgh, 1895-
1904; established a school for children's librarians. Director,
The New York State Library and Library School in succession
to Melvil Dewey, 1906-08; assistant director and director,
The New York Public Library, 1909-34. President, A.L.A.,
1913-14.

Sarah B. Askew, 1863-1942

Organized the New Jersey Public Library Commission,
established libraries in small communities. Pioneered for
county libraries. Developed interlibrary loans. Her personality made deep impression on public audiences everywhere.

Assistant, Cleveland Public Library, 1903; organizer,
librarian, secretary, New Jersey Public Library Commis-

sion, 1905-42. Library war service under A.L.A., 1917-19.

John Shaw Billings, 1839-1913

Army surgeon who turned to librarianship; the first director of the consolidated New York Public Library. Obtained Carnegie interest to establish its great system of branch libraries. Planned the central building with its reference collections.

Librarian, Surgeon-General's Office. Editor, Index Medicus. First director, The New York Public Library, 1895-1913. Author of numerous books and articles on medicine. President, A.L.A., 1901-02.

Sarah C. N. Bogle, -1932

Developed library work with children at Pittsburgh. Fine efforts to raise the professional standards and guide library schools made her nationally influential. Showed in Paris what an international library school could mean to the profession.

Carnegie Library, Pittsburgh, 1911-17; principal, Carnegie Library School, 1911-20; secretary, A.L.A. Board of Education for Librarianship, 1924-32; director, Paris Library School under A.L.A., 1924-29.

Arthur E. Bostwick, 1860-1942

As chief of circulation in New York, made the foreign population feel at home in the library. Introduced children's libraries and cooperation with schools. At the invitation of the Chinese National Association for the Advancement of Education surveyed Chinese libraries. Superb public-relations officer for the library profession.

Editor, 1886-94; librarian, Brooklyn Public Library, 1899-1901; chief, Circulation, New York Public Library, 1901-09; librarian, St. Louis Public Library, 1909-38. Author, THE AMERICAN PUBLIC LIBRARY (1910). President, A.L.A., 1907-08.

William Howard Brett, 1846-1918

His Cumulative Index (1896) later became the Reader's Guide to Periodical Literature, indispensable in reference work today. Elevated Cleveland to a leadership among city libraries. Established the open shelf and a department for the young, with a story-telling hour in 1903. Did conspicuous work at Newport News, Va., under the A.L.A., in World War I.

Bookstore clerk, 1874-84; librarian, Cleveland Public Library, 1884-1918; organizer and dean, Western Reserve University Library School, 1903-18. President, A.L.A., 1896-97.

Frederick M. Crunden, 1847-1911

Advanced libraries as a leading educational agency. Secured passage of Missouri library law, in 1893, divorcing the library from school administration. Particularly interested in the relations of school and libraries and contributed to a closer understanding between the N.E.A. and the A.L.A.

St. Louis Public School and Public Library, 1877-1903. President, A.L.A., 1899-90.

Charles A. Cutter, 1837-1903

A founding member of A.L.A. His pioneering RULES FOR A PRINTED DICTIONARY CATALOGUE (1876) is still in use in American and foreign libraries.

Assistant, Harvard College Library, 1860-68; librarian, Boston Athenaeum, 1869-93; bibliographical editor, Library Journal, 1876-81; general editor, 1882-93. President, A.L.A., 1887-89.

John Cotton Dana, 1856-1929

At the Denver Public Library introduced open shelves and department for children. Museum work begun at Springfield expanded in Newark as a Museum of Art, Science and Industry in 1909. Newark business library, housed in a special building in 1927, became the largest library collection on business in the country. Excelled as interpreter of the library movement to the world.

Denver Public Library, 1889-97; Springfield (Mass.) City Library, 1898-1902; Newark, 1902-29; director, Newark Museum, 1909-29. Author. President, A.L.A., 1895-96.

A LIBRARY HALL OF FAME

Melvil Dewey, 1851-1931

Signed as secretary the call for the 1876 library meeting at Philadelphia and served as secretary for 15 years. First editor of Library Journal (1876); founded the Decimal Classification (1876) and the first library school in the country, at Columbia University (1887); a prime mover in the organization of the New York Library Club (1885), the New York State Library Association (1890) and the American Library Institute (1905). He established the Library Bureau (1882) of which he was president for twenty-five years.

Acting librarian, Amherst College, 1874-76; editor, Library Journal, 1876-81; librarian, Columbia University, 1883-88; director, New York State Library, 1889-1906 and the State library school until 1906; president, A.L.A., 1890-July 1891, 1892-93.

Wilberforce Eames, 1855-1937

Noted bibliographer who specialized in American history and general ethnology. Edited volumes 15-20 of Sabin's DICTIONARY OF BOOKS RELATING TO AMERICA (1885-92), continued in 1927-29, and contributed to the Indian bibliographies of the late James C. Pilling.

Lenox librarian, 1892, until its consolidation into The New York Public Library, 1895; librarian, Bibliographical Society of America from its inception to 1909.

Theresa Elmendorf, 1855-1932

Stressed the benefits of public school and public library cooperation. An exceptional knowledge of books and confidence in the value of library service popularized her name and work in the professional world.

Young Men's Association, Milwaukee, assistant librarian and city librarian, 1892-96; vice-librarian, Buffalo Public Library, 1906-26. Editor for selection of A.L.A.'s CATALOGUE OF BOOKS FOR SMALL LIBRARIES (1904). First woman president, A.L.A., 1911-12.

Charles Evans, 1850-1935

Author of AMERICAN BIBLIOGRAPHY, a chronological

dictionary of all books, pamphlets and periodical publications printed in United States of America from 1639 to 1820, of which twelve quarto volumes, bringing the record down to 1799, were issued before his death.

Organizer, Indianapolis Public Library, 1872-80, 1899-92; Enoch Pratt Free Library, 1884-87, and other libraries. Classified Newberry Library, Chicago, 1892-95. Associate editor, Library Journal in early years. Founding member of A.L.A.

Salome C. Fairchild, 1855-1921

An authority on book selection and evaluation, an inspiring lecturer and a pioneer in work for the blind.

Cataloger, Columbia University, 1884; vice-director, instructor, New York State Library School, 1889-1905; organizer, New York State Library for the Blind, 1899. Author. Vice-president, A.L.A., 1894-95, 1900-01.

William I. Fletcher, 1844-1917

Renowned as indexer, collaborated with William Poole in the enlarged edition of the Index to Periodical Literature (1882) and edited Cooperative Index to Periodicals (1883), A.L.A. Index to General Literature (1893).

Amherst College, 1883-1911; teacher, library economy, Amherst Summer School, 1891-1905. Author, PUBLIC LIBRARIES IN AMERICA (1894). President, A.L.A., 1891-92.

Jennie Flexner, 1882-1944

With rare ability to bring books and people together, did pioneer work as readers' advisor of The New York Public Library. Her studies for the A.L.A. led to her CIRCULATION WORK IN PUBLIC LIBRARIES (1927).

Head, Circulation Department and instructor in the training class, Louisville, Free Public Library. Readers' advisor, the New York Public Library, 1928-44; chairman, Library Committee, Council on Books in Wartime. Author, MAKING BOOKS WORK (1943).

William E. Foster, 1851-1930

Influential in moulding course of A.L.A. One of first to

develop contacts with schools, establish an art, industrial
and foreign department, and a business branch. Originator
of modern form of subject departments and compiler of
valuable reference lists. Built his library to notable stature
during his more than half century administration.

Hyde Park (Mass.) Public Library, 1873-76; Providence
Public Library, 1878-1930. A founding member of A.L.A.
and its vice-president, 1904-05.

James L. Gillis, 1857-1917

As state librarian of California directed the development
of model county library system, 1909. He extended the usefulness of the state library, previously of value only to the
legislators, to all parts of the state. The California State
Library School was established in 1913 at his suggestion.

Railway and government service; state librarian, 1899-
1917.

Samuel Swett Green, 1837-1918

His was the first large New England library to open on
Sunday. Encouraged factory workers to visit the library. In
1890 was appointed to new State Library Commission, the
first of its kind in America, and served for nineteen years.

Worcester Free Public Library, 1871-1909. Author,
THE PUBLIC LIBRARY MOVEMENT IN THE UNITED
STATES, 1853-1893, (1913). President, A.L.A., July-Nov.
1891.

J. C. M. Hanson, 1864-1943

Established the L. C. card and was chief compiler of
A.L.A. CATALOGING RULES (1908).

Cataloger, Newberry Library, Chicago, under apprenticeship of Dr. Poole, 1890-93; chief cataloger, University of
Wisconsin Library, 1893-97; chief, Catalog Division of Library of Congress, 1897-1910; associate director, University of Chicago Libraries, 1910-27; Graduate School, University of Chicago, 1928-34; lecturer, School of Library
Service, Columbia, 1930-34. Participated in reorganization
of the Vatican Library.

A LIBRARY HALL OF FAME

Mary E. Hazeltine, 1868-1949

Long head of the Wisconsin Library School, she was noted for the independence of thinking and for the competency of her students who have filled important library posts.
Bibliographer-librarian, Prendergast Free Library, Jamestown, N.Y., 1893-1906; organizer-principal, Wisconsin Library School, 1906-38; associate professor of bibliography, 1924-38. Author, ANNIVERSARIES AND HOLIDAYS (1928) and other writings.

Caroline M. Hewins, 1846-1926

Crusader for library service to children. Hartford established a children's department in 1904. Pioneer figure in the developing interest in children's work.
Library training at Boston Athenaeum under Dr. Poole; Hartford Library Association, 1875-92; Hartford Public Library, 1892-1926. Author, BOOKS FOR THE YOUNG (1882) and others. Vice-president, A.L.A., 1891.

Judson T. Jennings, 1872-1948

In the Pacific Northwest in the early 20th century, he promoted adult education by employing a skilled staff which had had its training in all parts of the country. Liberal state aid largely due to his efforts. At the New York State Library gave young men the feeling that librarianship was not exclusively a woman's job.
New York State Library, 1889-1903, 1906-07; Carnegie Free Library, Duquesne, Pa., 1903-06; Seattle Public Library, 1907-42. Organizer, camp library service at home and in Germany, World War I. President, A.L.A., 1923-24.

Charles C. Jewett, 1816-1868

Presided at the 1853 conference of librarians in New York. His NOTICES OF PUBLIC LIBRARIES IN THE UNITED STATES OF AMERICA (1851) was the first extended collection of statistics and facts on American libraries. Inaugurated in Boston easy access to the library's books, then unusual. Catalogs prepared under his direction at Brown, Smithsonian and Boston Public met with praise at home and abroad.

A LIBRARY HALL OF FAME

Brown University, 1841-43; professor of Modern Languages and Literature at Brown, 1843-48; Smithsonian Institution, 1848-58; first librarian, Boston Public Library, 1858-68.

Alice B. Kroeger, -1909

Administrator who exerted wide influence to give the library profession greater distinction. Author of GUIDE TO THE STUDY AND USE OF REFERENCE BOOKS (1902) and AIDS IN BOOK SELECTION (1908).

Librarian, Drexel Institute, and director of its library school from its establishment, 1892.

William C. Lane, 1859-1931

While president of the A.L.A., 1898-99, instrumental in securing President McKinley's approval of the appointment of Herbert Putnam as Librarian of Congress. First chairman of A.L.A. Publishing Board where he organized its publishing activities and developed Portrait Index.

Assistant librarian, Harvard College, 1887-93, librarian, in succession to Justin Winsor, 1898-1928; Boston Athenaeum, 1893-98.

Josephus N. Larned, 1836-1913

His was the first library to be completely classified under the Dewey Decimal system. Planned and established one of the first children's rooms in the country, started a school room in the library and an open-shelf room.

Editorial staff, Buffalo Express, 1859-72; superintendent, Buffalo Young Men's Association, reorganized by him into the Buffalo Library. Historian, also editor, HISTORY FOR READY REFERENCE (7 vols., 1895-1910). President, A.L.A., 1893-94.

George H. Locke, 1870-1937

Leader in Canadian public library developments. Personified a coordinated relationship between the libraries of Canada and the United States. Participated in the development of the A.L.A.

Teacher of history, education, philosophy, universities of Chicago, Harvard, McGill, 1893-1908; chief librarian, City of Toronto, Canada, 1908-37. Author. President, A.L.A., 1926-27.

Charles Martel, 1860-1945

His L.C. classification schedules and cataloging records have been adopted by the nation's libraries.

Newberry Library, Chicago, under apprenticeship of Dr. Poole, 1892-97; chief classifier, Library of Congress, 1897-1912; chief, Cataloging Division, 1912-30; consultant in cataloging, classification and bibliography, Library of Congress, 1930-45; member of commission that planned the modern Vatican Library catalog, 1926.

Mary W. Plummer, 1856-1916

Fostered special training for work for children. As delegate to the International Congress of Libraries at Paris, 1900, aroused much interest in libraries in field of education. Included a children's room, the first of its kind in the planning of Pratt's new building, 1896, and art-reference collection for general use. Her warm personality was an inspiration to her students. Graduate of the first class of the library school, at Columbia, 1888.

Cataloger, St. Louis Public Library, 1888-90; assistant director, Pratt Institute Free Library, 1890-94; director, 1896-1904; Library School, 1896-1911; organizer, Library School, The New York Public Library, 1911. Author. President, A.L.A., 1915-16.

William F. Poole, 1821-1894

As librarian of Brothers in Unity at Yale, he maintained on slips an index to material in books and magazines useful to students, the forerunner of his indispensable Index to Periodical Literature. Contributions to the theory and principles of library administration still an important part of modern practice. Trained in the front rank of librarianship.

Boston Athenaeum, 1856-69; Cincinnati Public Library, 1869-73; Chicago Public Library, 1873-87; Newberry Li-

brary, 1887-94. Associate editor, Library Journal. Author.
President, A.L.A., 1885-87.

Josephine Rathbone, 1864-1941

Outstanding teacher who developed her school along the
lines of current social and intellectual requirements and
taught her students professional integrity and practical vision.
Chief instructor, Pratt Institute School of Library Science,
1895-1911; vice-director, 1911-38. Author. President, A.L.A.,
1931-32.

Ernest C. Richardson, 1860-1939

Bibliographer who wrote ably on many library subjects.
First assistant librarian, Amherst College, 1879-80,
Hartford Theological Seminary, 1884-90; Princeton University, 1890-1920; director, 1920-23; research professor of
bibliography, 1923-25; consultant in bibliography and research, Library of Congress, 1925-39. President, A.L.A.,
1904-05.

Ainsworth Spofford, 1825-1908

Industry, an extraordinary memory and a great success
in his book purchases on a very limited appropriation of not
more than $10,000 a year enabled him to increase the collec-
tions he administered at the Library of Congress from 60,000
items in 1861 to more than a million in 1897 and to lay the
foundations for the great national library he insisted the L.C.
should be. The new building, completed in 1897, was the
result of twenty years of his striving for this recognition by
Congress.
Associate editor, Cincinnati Commercial, 1861; chief
assistant to Dr. John Stephenson, Librarian of Congress;
Librarian of Congress, 1864-97. Founded European agency
for collection of government documents for L.C. Author.

Lutie E. Stearns, 1866-1943

A field worker for libraries of extraordinary devotion and
effectiveness. Responsible for establishing traveling libraries
in Wisconsin and for advancing library work with children.

Head, Circulation Department, Milwaukee Public Library, 1890-97; Wisconsin Free Library Commission, 1897-1914; lecturer on libraries in library schools throughout the country. Author, ESSENTIALS IN LIBRARY ADMINISTRATION (1922).

Reuben G. Thwaites, 1853-1913

As secretary of the Wisconsin Historical Society, he expanded its serviceability by building up its manuscript collection and making it available to the scholars of the University of Wisconsin. His JESUIT RELATIONS AND ALLIED DOCUMENTS (73 vols., 1896-1901) with its fine annotations and translations established his re utation as one of the best historical editors of his day.

Managing editor, Wisconsin State Journal, 1876-86; superintendent-secretary, State Historical Society of Wisconsin, 1887-1913. President, A.L.A., 1899-1900.

Alice S. Tyler, 1859-1944

Pioneered in state library expansion as secretary of the Iowa State Library Commission. Library school director of exceptional influence.

Catalog librarian, Cleveland Public Library, 1895-1900; secretary, Iowa State Library Commission, 1900-13; dean, School of Library Science, Western Reserve University, 1913-29. President, A.L.A., 1920-21.

George B. Utley, 1876-1946

Laid the foundations for centralizing library organization by setting up an A.L.A. central headquarters, in Chicago. Did noteworthy work in supplying reading material to the military and naval forces during World War I.

Assistant librarian, Watkinson Library, Hartford, Conn., 1899-1901; librarian, Jacksonville, Fla., 1905-11; secretary, A.L.A., 1911-20; executive secretary, A.L.A. Library War Service, 1917-19; librarian, Newberry Library, 1920-42. President, A.L.A., 1922-23.

A LIBRARY HALL OF FAME

Justin Winsor, 1831-1897

While remembered chiefly as a historian, his bibliographic output on literary and historical subjects was prolific, and his annual reports and notes in the bulletins and catalogs of the Boston Public Library led the way to a new era in library practice. By keeping pace with the new methods of instruction then being introduced at Harvard, increased the usefulness of the university library.

Boston Public Library, 1868-77; Harvard University, 1877-97; associate editor, Library Journal, in early years. President, A.L.A., 1876-85; July-October, 1897.

AUTHOR-TITLE INDEX

[When an individual is the subject of an essay, his or her name (last name first) appears in this index followed by the name of the author of the sketch with the number of the first page of the essay.]

461

AUTHOR-TITLE INDEX

AUTHOR-TITLE INDEX